Royal Armouries Research Series

Volume I

The Medieval Tournament as Spectacle

Royal Armouries Research Series

About the series

The Royal Armouries Research Series is published in partnership with Boydell & Brewer. The series is a forum for the study of arms and armour and cognate subjects from antiquity to the present day.

We welcome proposals for future volumes – either edited collections or monographs – from the broad world of arms and armour study, unlimited by geography, discipline or time period. Volumes that focus on objects within the Royal Armouries collection, or that support the organisation's research strategy (available at www.royalarmouries.org), are particularly encouraged. Critical editions and translations of arms and armour texts (such as fencing manuals and fight books) will also be considered.

Proposals and queries should be sent in the first instance to the Publishing Manager at the address below:

Dr Martyn Lawrence
Royal Armouries Publishing
Armouries Drive
Leeds LS10 1LT
Email: martyn.lawrence@armouries.org.uk

About the Royal Armouries

The Royal Armouries is the UK's national museum of arms and armour, and one of the most important museums of its type in the world. Its origins lie in the Middle Ages, and at its core is the celebrated collection originating in the nation's working arsenal, assembled over many centuries at the Tower of London. In the reign of Elizabeth I, selected items began to be arranged for display to visitors, making the Royal Armouries heir to one of the oldest deliberately-created visitor attractions in the country. The collection is now housed and displayed at three sites: the White Tower at the Tower of London, a purpose-built museum in Leeds, and Fort Nelson near Portsmouth.

The Medieval Tournament as Spectacle

Tourneys, Jousts and *Pas d'Armes* 1100–1600

Edited by Alan V. Murray and Karen Watts

THE BOYDELL PRESS

© Contributors 2020

All Rights Reserved. Except as permitted under current legislation
no part of this work may be photocopied, stored in a retrieval system,
published, performed in public, adapted, broadcast,
transmitted, recorded or reproduced in any form or by any means,
without the prior permission of the copyright owner

First published 2020
The Boydell Press, Woodbridge
Paperback edition 2023

ISBN 978-1-78327-542-7 (hardback)
ISBN 978-1-83765-108-5 (paperback)

The Boydell Press is an imprint of Boydell & Brewer Ltd
PO Box 9, Woodbridge, Suffolk IP12 3DF, UK
and of Boydell & Brewer Inc.
668 Mt Hope Avenue, Rochester, NY 14620–2731, USA
website: www.boydellandbrewer.com

The publisher has no responsibility for the continued existence or accuracy of
URLs for external or third-party internet websites referred to in this book, and
does not guarantee that any content on such websites is, or will remain, accurate
or appropriate

A catalogue record of this publication is available
from the British Library

Contents

List of Illustrations	vii
List of Contributors	xi
Preface and Acknowledgements *Martyn Lawrence*	xiii
Introduction: From Mass Combat to Field of Cloth of Gold *Alan V. Murray*	1
Research on the Medieval Tournament (1100–1600): A Select Bibliography *Compiled by Alan V. Murray*	7

1. Now Form Up Close Together! Tactics and Ethos of the Tourney in Early German Sources (Twelfth to Thirteenth Centuries)   21
Alan V. Murray

2. *Por pris et por enor*: Ideas of Honour as Reflected in the Medieval Tournament   44
James Titterton

3. Richard II of England and the Smithfield Tournament of October 1390: An Instrument to Establish Royal Authority   62
James Beswick

4. *Alle myn harneys for the justes*: Documents as a Source for Medieval Jousting Armour   77
Ralph Moffat

5. The Tournament Saddle   99
Marina Viallon

6. Between Sport and Theatre: How Spectacular was the *Pas d'armes*?   120
Catherine Blunk

7. Art Imitating Life Imitating Art? Representations of the *Pas d'armes* in Burgundian Prose Romance: The Case of *Jehan d'Avennes*   139
Rosalind Brown-Grant

8. The Foot Combat as Tournament Event: Equipment, Space and Forms   155
Iason-Eleftherios Tzouriadis

Contents

9. Power and Pageantry: The Tournament at the Court of Maximilian I   185
   Natalie Anderson

10. The Field of Cloth of Gold: Arms, Armour and the Sporting Prowess of King Henry VIII and King Francis I   208
    Karen Watts

Index of Objects   238
Index of Manuscripts   240
General Index   242

Illustrations

Now Form Up Close Together! Tactics and Ethos of the Tourney in Early German Sources (Twelfth to Thirteenth Centuries), *Alan V. Murray*

Table 1   Numbers of Knights at the Friesach Tourney.   37

Alle myn harneys for the justes: Documents as a Source for Medieval Jousting Armour, *Ralph Moffat*

Fig. 1   Illustration of a miniature from the Codex Balduini Trevirensis, German, c. 1300, from R. Freiherr von Mansberg, *Wäfen ... des Deutschen Ritter des Mittelalters* (Dresden, 1890). Glasgow Museums, RL Scott Library, E.1939.65.1862. © CSG CIC Glasgow Museums Collection.   79

Fig. 2   Ivory mirror case, French, early fourteenth century (21.10), detail. © CSG CIC Glasgow Museums Collection.   79

Fig. 3   Miniature from the Sherborne Missal, English, illustrated by John Siferwas between 1396 and 1407. London, British Library, Add. MS 74326, fol. 216v. © British Library Board.   81

Fig. 4   Vamplate, German, mid sixteenth century (2.131.b). © CSG CIC Glasgow Museums Collection.   81

Fig. 5   Manifer, German, c. 1490 (E.1939.65.q.[5]). © CSG CIC Glasgow Museums Collection.   84

Fig. 6   Polder-mitton, probably Flemish, mid-fifteenth century (E.1939.65.q.[6]). © CSG CIC Glasgow Museums Collection.   87

Fig. 7   Miniature, French, c. 1470. London, British Library, Cotton MS Nero D. IX, fol. 40r. © British Library Board.   88

Fig. 8   Illustration from the *Libro di Giusto*, Tuscan, c. 1435, detail. Rome, Istituto Nazionale per la Grafica. © Ministerio per i Beni e la Attività Culturali.   88

Fig. 9   Stained glass panel, German, c. 1380–1400 (45.486.1.b). © CSG CIC Glasgow Museums Collection.   89

Fig. 10 Engraving of an early fourteenth-century helm and reinforce from D. Ure, *The History of Rutherglen and East-Kilbride* (Glasgow, 1793), fig. 1 opposite p. 60. Reproduced with the kind permission of the Mitchell Library, Glasgow.   91

All images reproduced with the generous assistance of the Friends of Glasgow Museums.

The Tournament Saddle, *Marina Viallon*

Fig. 1 Main styles of war saddle used in western Europe between the eleventh and fifteenth centuries (author's illustration). A = eleventh century; B = twelfth century; C = thirteenth century; D = fourteenth century; E = fourteenth century (high); F = fifteenth century.   98

Fig. 2 Albrecht Marschall von Rapperswil winning a joust, Manesse Codex (Cod. Pal. Germ. 848), fol. 192v. Zürich, c. 1310–40. © Universitätsbibliothek Heidelberg.   102

Fig. 3 Funerary statue of Cangrande della Scala, lord of Verona, c. 1335. © Verona, Museo di Castelvecchio, Archivio fotografico.   104

Fig. 4 Tourneyers on high saddles, after a drawing in a boxwood sketchbook attributed to the circle of Jacquemart de Hesdin, France, third quarter fourteenth century, Morgan Library, New York (author's illustration).   105

Fig. 5 Funerary statue of Mastino II della Scala, lord of Verona, c. 1351–60. © Verona, Museo di Castelvecchio, Archivio fotografico.   106

Fig. 6 Tournament high saddle, first quarter fifteenth century, German. Leeds, Royal Armouries, VI.94. © Royal Armouries.   110

Fig. 7 Hinged tournament high saddles. A = detail of a mid-fifteenth-century Flemish tapestry showing Greeks and Amazons fighting a *Kolbenturnier* (tourney with maces). After *Hercules Initiating the Olympic Games*. Glasgow, The Burrell Collection. B = High saddle for the tourney, second half fifteenth century. Nuremberg, Germanisches Nationalmuseum (author's illustrations).   112

Fig. 8 Saddle, possibly Hungarian, 1410–40. Leeds, Royal Armouries, VI.95. © Royal Armouries.   114

Fig. 9 Schenk Konrad von Limpurg receiving the prize of a tournament, Tross'sche Fragment, 1430–40. Berlin, Staatsbibliothek (destroyed 1945). Image from A. von Oechelhäuser, *Die Miniaturen der Universitäts-Bibliothek zu Heidelberg*, vol. II, 1895 (plate 16). © Universitätsbibliothek Heidelberg.   116

Fig. 10 Low saddle for the *Rennen* used in the tournaments of Maximilian I. South German, late fifteenth century, Vienna, Kunsthistorisches Museum, B.64. © KHM-Museumsverband.   117

Fig. 11 Ernst von Braunschweig in a *Rennen* (detail), from 'Tournament Book of the Electors of Saxony'. Image from the facsimile edition: *Der Sächsischen Kurfürsten Turnierbücher*, ed. Erich Haenel (Frankfurt, 1910), p. 31.   118

Between Sport and Theatre: How Spectacular was the *Pas d'armes?*, Catherine Blunk

Fig. 1   The textual layout of the *pas d'armes* account in *Jehan de Saintré*. Brussels, KBR, MS 9547, fols. 110v–111.   128

Fig. 2   Construction of the venue for Saintré's *pas d'armes*. Brussels, KBR, MS 9547, fols. 109v–110.   129

Fig. 3   The image of the Virgin Mary, the Lady of Tears fountain, and the herald Charolais at the *Pas de la Fontaine des Pleurs*. Paris, Bibliothèque nationale de France, MS fr. 16830, fol. 124.   134

Art Imitating Life Imitating Art? Representations of the *Pas d'armes* in Burgundian Prose Romance: The Case of *Jehan d'Avennes*, Rosalind Brown-Grant

Fig. 1   Jehan d'Avennes fights the Duke of York. *Jehan d'Avennes*, Paris, Bibliothèque nationale de France, MS fr. 12572, fol. 34.   150

Fig. 2   Jehan d'Avennes fights the Seigneur de Duras. *Jehan d'Avennes*, Paris, Bibliothèque nationale de France, MS fr. 12572, fol. 37v.   150

Fig. 3   Jehan d'Avennes fights the Seigneur de Beaumont. *Jehan d'Avennes*, Paris, Bibliothèque nationale de France, MS fr. 12572, fol. 42v.   151

The Foot Combat as Tournament Event: Equipment, Space and Forms, Iason-Eleftherios Tzouriadis

Fig. 1   Portions of an armour, German, 1560. Leeds, Royal Armouries, II.173 © Royal Armouries.   164

Fig. 2   Foot combat armour composed of pieces of different armours from a set of twelve of Christian I, Elector of Saxony, German, 1591, by Anton Peffenhauser. Leeds, Royal Armouries, II.186 © Royal Armouries.   167

Fig. 3   Pollaxe, English, 1475–1510. Leeds, Royal Armouries, VII.1509 © Royal Armouries.   170

Fig. 4   *Bec-de-corbin*, English, first half sixteenth century. Leeds, Royal Armouries, VII.1510 © Royal Armouries.   170

Fig. 5   Painting, *Portrait of Robert Radcliffe*, English-Flemish, about 1593, by Marcus Gheeraerts the Younger. Leeds, Royal Armouries, I.36 © Royal Armouries.   173

Fig. 6   Tournament sword, German, mid-seventeenth century. Leeds, Royal Armouries, IX.1217 © Royal Armouries.   174

The Field of Cloth of Gold: Arms, Armour and the Sporting Prowess of King Henry VIII and King Francis I, *Karen Watts*

Fig. 1   Engraving of *The Field of Cloth of Gold* (c. 1545), British, 1771–99. Leeds, Royal Armouries, I.224 © Royal Armouries.   225

Fig. 2   Armour for the foot combat of Henry VIII, made in the royal workshop by the master armourer Martin van Royne. English, Southwark, 1520. Leeds, Royal Armouries, II.6 © Royal Armouries.   226

Fig. 3   Armour for the foot combat of Henry VIII, assembled in the royal workshop at Southwark by the master armourer Martin van Royne. English with Italian and Flemish components, 1520. Leeds, Royal Armouries, II.7 © Royal Armouries.   227

Fig. 4   Armour of Robert III de La Marck, lord of Fleuranges, duke of Bouillon and lord of Sedan, by master armourer Martin van Royne. English, Southwark, 1525 (Paris, Musée de l'Armée, G.46, H.57). The missing armet (H.47) was later identified and reunited with the armour, but it is not the one shown here © Royal Armouries.   228

Contributors

Natalie Anderson received a Ph.D. in Medieval Studies from the University of Leeds in 2017 with a thesis entitled 'Tournaments in the Reign of Emperor Maximilian I (1459–1519)'.

James Beswick received an MA in Medieval History from the University of Leeds in 2019, which included a dissertation entitled 'Boucicaut, Deeds of Arms, and Reputation Management', investigating how the performance of martial activities affected a knight's reputation and career.

Catherine Blunk is an Associate Professor of French at Drury University (Springfield, Missouri). Her research interests lie in the poetics of the tournament in late medieval French narrative. She is currently working on the pas d'armes in fifteenth-century chronicles.

Rosalind Brown-Grant is Professor of Late Medieval Literature at the University of Leeds. She has published on medieval French romance, Christine de Pizan, and Burgundian historiographical writing. Her latest monograph is *Visualizing Justice in Burgundian Prose Romance: Text and Image in Manuscripts of the Wavrin Master (1450s–1460s)* (2020).

Ralph Moffat is Curator of European Arms and Armour at Glasgow Museums. He is currently working on a sourcebook for the study of medieval arms and armour and is also developing exhibits on this theme for the redisplay of Glasgow's Burrell Collection.

Alan V. Murray is Senior Lecturer in Medieval Studies at the University of Leeds. He has published extensively on warfare, the crusades and chivalry and on medieval German language and literature. He is currently researching tournaments in the Holy Roman Empire, particularly their depiction in the works of Wolfram von Eschenbach and Ulrich von Liechtenstein.

James Titterton received his PhD in Medieval Studies from the University of Leeds in 2019. He is currently working on a monograph entitled *Deception in Medieval Warfare* and a translation of the *History of Gilles de Chin* by Gautier de Tournai, which contains many detailed descriptions of early thirteenth-century tournament practice.

Iason-Eleftherios Tzouriadis is Assistant Archivist and Assistant Curator of the Worshipful Company of Gold and Silver Wyre Drawers (London). He is co-author (with Roberto Gotti and Daniel Jaquet) of *European Martial Arts: From Vulcan's Forge to the Arts of Mars* (2019), and is currently preparing a monograph on the production and forms of European staff weapons up to the eighteenth century.

Marina Viallon is currently working for a Ph.D. at the École Pratique des Hautes Etudes, Paris, focusing on tournaments at the court of France during the sixteenth and seventeenth centuries. She has published several essays and articles on equestrian equipment, tournaments, and chivalric culture.

Karen Watts is former Senior Curator of Armour and Art at the Royal Armouries, Leeds.

Preface and Acknowledgements

It is a privilege to introduce this first volume in the new Royal Armouries Research Series. As the UK's national museum of arms and armour, the Royal Armouries is heir to one of the oldest visitor attractions in the country. With our roots in the Middle Ages and our original home at the Tower of London, we are ideally placed to bring this unique perspective to a wider research community.

The Medieval Tournament as Spectacle marks the beginning of a new venture for the museum. We are very pleased to work in partnership with Boydell & Brewer to bring together curators, conservators and academics to develop a greater understanding of arms and armour. Given the different traditions that underpin these areas, an emphasis on cross-functional research is particularly important. Too often, museums and universities travel on parallel tracks without realising how close their interests lie. Yet as curators seek to interpret their work for the public and academics pursue broader impact, the need for closer collaboration has never been more evident. As this volume makes clear, research on arms and armour is far wider than an isolated knowledge of particular objects: instead, these objects act as keys to unlock the stories of the people who inhabited worlds teeming with noise and colour.

I am extremely grateful to the team in Woodbridge for their efforts to bring this first volume into the light: Caroline Palmer, Michael Richards, Elizabeth McDonald and Sean Andersson are but four of a team whose unbounded patience has been greatly appreciated.

Martyn Lawrence

Introduction: From Mass Combat to Field of Cloth of Gold

Alan V. Murray

Five hundred years ago, from 7 to 24 June 1520, the kings of England and France held a series of meetings on the frontiers of their respective domains, between the settlements of Guînes, situated in the English-held territory of Calais, and Ardres, in the kingdom of France, an event that has come to be known from its sumptuousness and magnificence as the Field of Cloth of Gold. Both monarchs were young men. Henry VIII of England (born 28 June 1491) was only weeks short of his twenty-ninth birthday; Francis I of France (born 12 September 1494) was three years younger. At what was in effect a political summit between the rulers of two of Europe's most powerful kingdoms, each man wished not only to display the splendour of his own realm and court, but to demonstrate his personal vigour and virility, and so alongside diplomatic negotiations, feasting and entertainments, much time was devoted to jousts, tourneys and foot combats, in which both kings and members of their respective nobilities took part. The Field of Cloth of Gold thus demonstrates the importance of tournaments not only as a noble pastime, but as a fundamental expression of courtly culture.

Henry VIII and Francis I were monarchs at the beginning of the early modern age, but in their enthusiasm for tournaments they were following a long medieval tradition. The earliest form of tournament originated in the late eleventh century as a military exercise in which knightly retinues could practise riding and fighting in formation. The tourney (sometimes described as a mêlée) was a form of training for mounted combat which encouraged cohesion and group discipline, while also offering the opportunity for participants for financial gain through ransoms or by capturing the horses of opponents. In some cases tourneyers might achieve renown for their prowess, although the physical circumstances of the earliest tourneys, often fought over long distances, did not favour the presence of spectators. This is one reason why in the twelfth century, tourneys often came to be preceded by jousting, which functioned on a more or less informal basis. In contrast to the mass combat of the tourney, a joust at this time featured a pair of knights, each of whom would try to strike (and ideally unhorse) his opponent with his lance. This form of individual combat offered a greater opportunity for knights to display their prowess to their peers and to other spectators, and thus to gain the fame and honour that were so important to aristocratic society.

From the early thirteenth century onwards, in a process which is still only partially understood, jousting acquired a far greater prominence by being featured in new and increasingly elaborate forms of tournament. These new forms, known as *table ronde* (round table), *pas d'armes* (passage of arms) and *foreis*, featured jousting, but usually within a literary or allegorical framework, which was often reflected in costumes and staging. Tourneys continued to be held, in many cases in city squares or other central locations rather than the open country favoured in the twelfth century, but by the fifteenth century they were proving to be far less popular than these new jousting competitions, which were often combined with other forms of entertainment or ceremony. The introduction of safer weapons (such as lances with coronels and rebated swords), the imposition of often precise rules (rather than rough and ready conventions), and the development of better-quality armour made these new forms less dangerous than the original tourney and joust, while the concentration on individual combat and the emphasis on theatrical spectacle increased their value as entertainment. The increasing use of plate armour in particular was undoubtedly a significant factor in the introduction of foot combat as a distinct tournament form, featuring the use of two-handed weapons, namely the sword and pollaxe.

In modern popular perceptions, tournaments are probably one of the cultural phenomena most readily associated with the Middle Ages, but, by contrast, the academic study of tournaments is a relatively young field. Some important studies and collections of materials appeared in the late nineteenth and earlier twentieth centuries, but these tended to be relatively diverse and specialised in scope. The most important single breakthrough in the study of tournaments occurred on the occasion of a conference in 1982 organised by Josef Fleckenstein, then Director of the Max-Planck-Institut für Geschichte in Göttingen, which brought together experts based at universities and research institutes in Germany, France, the United Kingdom, Switzerland, Czechoslovakia and Hungary. They explored not only the sources and forms of tournaments in most of the countries of Western Christendom, but also much of the literary and material culture associated with them. The publication of the twenty papers from this conference, giving a truly international and comparative perspective, opened up the subject as never before.[1]

---

[1] *Das ritterliche Turnier im Mittelalter: Beiträge zu einer vergleichenden Formen- und Verhaltensgeschichte des Rittertums*, ed. Josef Fleckenstein (Göttingen, 1985).

Introduction: From Mass Combat to Field of Cloth of Gold

A number of publications have offered general studies of tournaments, or at least have investigated thematic issues on an international basis (for example, the origins of tournaments, their variant forms and terminology, regulations and prohibitions by the church). The vast majority of approaches, however, have tended to be far more specific, dealing with particular regions or events or individuals within them. As we might expect of the regions where the tourney originated, France and the Low Countries have received the greatest attention, with a particular concentration on the great feasts and festivals of the Valois duchy of Burgundy. An especially important subject is René d'Anjou (1409–80), titular king of Naples and Jerusalem, although in wider scholarship his writings on tournaments have tended to be eclipsed by interest in his political ambitions and artistic patronage.

The study of tournaments in England owes much to the pioneering studies of Sydney Anglo, Richard Barber and Juliet Barker. A complicating factor here is that tournaments were either prohibited or tightly controlled by government edict in England for much of the twelfth and thirteenth centuries, and so research on English practice has been mostly directed towards the later Middle Ages and into the reign of Henry VIII.

While important materials were brought together by Alwin Schultz at the end of the nineteenth century, the study of tournament culture in German-speaking countries did not develop significant momentum until well after the Second World War, although in recent decades it has ranged over many territories and towns between the twelfth and fifteenth centuries.[2] Most attention has been given to tournament culture in the time of Maximilian I, king of the Romans and Holy Roman Emperor (1459–1519), for whom there is a particularly rich array of surviving documentary, literary and material sources relating to his sponsorship of and participation in tournaments. It is likely that major exhibitions held in Austria, Germany and the U.S.A. in the anniversary year 2019 and publications resulting from them will provide further stimulus to research on Maximilian.

Surprisingly, given Italy's thriving civic culture and rich archival holdings, the study of tournaments in its principalities and city-states lags a long way behind that of the countries north of the Alps.

One final theme must be mentioned: the depiction of tournaments in medieval literature. Tournaments played a major role in the romances of Chrétien de Troyes, Hartmann von Aue, Wolfram von Eschenbach and Sir Thomas Malory, and a host of others who were inspired by them, many of which have

---

[2] Alwin Schultz, *Das höfische Leben zur Zeit der Minnesinger*, 2nd edn, 2 vols (Leipzig, 1889), 2: 106–50.

been little studied. Indeed, it is quite possible that there are more accounts of entirely fictitious tournaments in imaginative literature than there are of actual historical events. A knowledge of medieval literature is vital for understanding later tournament forms, such as the round table and *pas d'armes*, most of which were directly inspired by literary themes. So while it is safe to say that the study of tournaments is flourishing as never before, there is still much to be done, especially on the publication of sources, such as illustrated tournament books and accounts of *pas d'armes*.

Among its entertainments the Field of Cloth of Gold featured several different forms of tournament, exemplifying how a form of mass combat originating as training for warfare had in the course of four centuries diversified into more specific formats combining features of sport and spectacle. The five hundredth anniversary of this event presented an apposite opportunity to examine this complex process and in particular to present new research on little studied themes or texts. The International Medieval Congress held at the University of Leeds in 2018 offered a suitable venue for papers and discussions involving medievalists based in Leeds and elsewhere in the United Kingdom, the U.S.A., France, Italy and the Netherlands. Several of the essays presented here are revised versions of papers originally presented there, while others were subsequently commissioned for this publication. The study of tournaments should ideally be an interdisciplinary activity, and the University of Leeds has been fortunate in having several specialists in the Institute for Medieval Studies, working in the disciplines of history, medieval literatures and arms and armour, who between them have supervised several doctoral students either working on tournaments or aspects of material culture directly related to them.[3] They also have good links with the Royal Armouries, whose collections include important examples of tournament armour, as well as with specialists overseas.

The essays are arranged in roughly chronological order, with the aim of giving a sense of the diversification of tournament forms and the development of specialised equipment. We now know a great deal about the origins and workings of the twelfth-century tourney in the Francophone countries, in no small part thanks to the existence of a unique text, the *Histoire de Guillaume*

---

[3] Notably an edition and translation of a previously unpublished codex containing fifteen different texts relating to tournaments. See: Ralph D. Moffat, 'The Medieval Tournament: Chivalry, Heraldry and Reality. An Edition and Analysis of Three Fifteenth-Century Tournament Manuscripts' (unpublished Ph.D. thesis, University of Leeds, 2010) [http://etheses.whiterose.ac.uk/1430/]. See also references to the theses by Natalie Anderson and Iason-Eleftherios Tzouriadis under Further Reading below.

Introduction: From Mass Combat to Field of Cloth of Gold

le Maréchal, which narrates the life of the Anglo-Norman nobleman William Marshal, earl of Pembroke (1146/1147–1219), who spent much of his life as a professional tourneyer.[4] For the period up to the mid-thirteenth century there is no comparable source for the German-speaking lands, and so the first essay, by Alan V. Murray, attempts to provide a picture of how tourneys were organised and practised by drawing on the evidence of key literary texts written in Middle High German. In particular it stresses the tension between the tourney and its requirements for discipline, and the desire for fame which encouraged the practice of jousting in connection with tourneys.

While tourneyers originally fought using the same weapons and armour that they employed in war, the development of more specialised tournament formats also led to the invention of dedicated equipment. Ralph Moffat discusses how documentary sources can be used to reveal the existence of arms and armour designed to be used in tournaments rather than warfare. Since a large amount of this material comes from unpublished archives, his approach shows an important way forward for future research. Marina Viallon examines the development of saddles designed for tournament combat, making use of important iconographical evidence as well as rare surviving material culture.

James Titterton draws on both historical and literary texts to show the ways in which tournaments could be used by participants to secure and gain that most important (yet elusive) aristocratic value, honour. While the acquisition of honour undoubtedly contributed to the popularity of tournaments among the noble and knightly classes, it is striking how it took a considerable time before European kings began to involve themselves in tournaments as patrons. Certainly the theatrical possibilities associated with the new forms of joust made them more attractive for royal involvement than the mass tourneys had been. James Beswick shows how the young King Richard II of England (1367–1400) staged an elaborate tournament held at Smithfield in 1390 as a means of projecting his royal authority after a long period in which he had languished under the tutelage of powerful aristocrats. Two complementary essays, by Catherine Blunk and Rosalind Brown-Grant, investigate the *pas d'armes*, a new form of the fourteenth and fifteenth centuries in which jousting was showcased within a literary framework. One of the main forms of tournament to feature at the Field of Cloth of Gold was foot combat, which seems to have gained in popularity during the fifteenth century in parallel with such fighting methods in actual warfare. Nevertheless, it has been much less

---

[4] *History of William Marshal*, ed. Anthony J. Holden, trans. Stewart Gregory, notes by David Crouch, 3 vols (London, 2002–2006). On William's life and career as a tourneyer, see David Crouch, *William Marshal: Court, Career and Chivalry in the Angevin Empire, 1147–1219* (London, 1990), pp. 26–52.

intensively researched than events, and Iason-Eleftherios Tzouriadis investigates the different formats which foot combat took, as well as the armour and weapons employed in them.

Like Richard II of England, many medieval monarchs were keen patrons of tournaments, but some of most powerful rulers of the fifteenth and sixteenth centuries were also keen participants as well as patrons. Natalie Anderson examines the career of Maximilian I, showing how he not only fostered diverse and often innovative tournament forms (particularly variants of the joust), but was himself an enthusiastic jouster well into his middle age. An impecunious ruler with an itinerant court, Maximilian exploited the possibilities of tournaments as a key means of forging and maintaining bonds with princes and nobles of his own domains and the wider empire. Henry VIII of England and Francis I were also keen to demonstrate their prowess in jousting and foot combat, and the volume fittingly concludes with a detailed investigation by Karen Watts of the place of the different tournament forms in the context of the Field of Cloth of Gold. By 1520, the tournament was a truly royal entertainment.

This collection was conceived as a way of fostering discussion and cooperation between specialists in history, literature and material culture. The editors and contributors hope that it will help provide impetus to the study of tournaments in all their diversity.

Alan V. Murray
Leeds 2020

Research on the Medieval Tournament (1100–1600): A Select Bibliography[1]

Compiled by Alan V. Murray

General Works

Anglo, Sydney, 'Jousting: The Earliest Treatises', *Livrustkammaren: Journal of the Royal Armoury* 19 (1991–92), 3–23.

Barber, Richard, 'Chivalry in the Tournament and *pas d'armes*', in *A Companion to Chivalry*, ed. Robert W. Jones and Peter Coss (Woodbridge, 2019), pp. 119–37.

Barber, Richard, and Juliet Barker, *Tournaments: Jousts, Chivalry and Pageants in the Middle Ages* (Woodbridge, 1989).

Barber, Richard, Juliet Barker and Georges Duby, *Les tournois* (Paris, 1989).

Barthélemy, Dominique, 'Les origines du tournoi chevaleresque', in *Agôn: La Compétition, Ve–XIIe siècle*, ed. François Bougard, Régine Le Jan and Thomas Lienhard (Turnhout, 2012), pp. 112–29.

Clephan, Robert Coltman, *The Tournament: Its Periods and Phases* (London, 1919).

Cripps-Day, Francis Henry, *The History of the Tournament in England and France* (London, 1918)

Hardy, Stephen H., 'The Medieval Tournament: A Functional Sport of the Upper Class', *Journal of Sport History* 1 (1974), 91–105.

Keupp, Jan, 'Verschwendung – Luxus – Kapital. Das Turnier des Hochmittelalters als Beispiel adeliger Ökonomie', in *Recht und Verhalten in vormodernen Gesellschaften. Festschrift für Neithard Bulst*, ed. Andre Bendlage, Andreas Priever and Peter Schuster (Bielefeld, 2008), pp. 35–49.

Krause, Stefan, 'Turnierbücher des späten Mittelalters und der Renaissance', in *Turnier: 1000 Jahre Ritterspiele*, ed. Stefan Krause and Matthias Pfaffenbichler (Munich, 2017), pp. 181–202.

---

[1] The bibliography listed is intended to give an overview of the main trends in research on tournaments from the late nineteenth century to the present. It is indicative rather than exhaustive, and the final two sections in particular are confined to a few key works. Considerations of space make it impossible to list relevant primary sources, although most of the secondary works given here will provide good starting points to find these.

Krüger, Sabine, 'Das kirchliche Turnierverbot im Mittelalter', in *Das ritterliche Turnier im Mittelalter: Beiträge zu einer vergleichenden Formen- und Verhaltensgeschichte des Rittertums*, ed. Josef Fleckenstein (Göttingen, 1985), pp. 401–22.

McGlynn, Sean, 'Pueri sunt pueri: Machismo, Chivalry, and the Aggressive Pastimes of the Medieval Male Youth', *Historical Reflections / Réflexions historiques* 42 (2016), 88–100.

McLean, Will, 'Outrance and Plaisance', *Journal of Medieval Military History* 8 (2010), 155–70.

Mölk, Ulrich, 'Philologische Aspekte des Turniers', in *Das ritterliche Turnier im Mittelalter: Beiträge zu einer vergleichenden Formen- und Verhaltensgeschichte des Rittertums*, ed. Josef Fleckenstein (Göttingen, 1985), pp. 163–74.

Mölk, Ulrich, 'Remarques philologiques sur tornoi(ement) dans la littérature française des XIIè et XIIIè siècles', in *Symposium in Honorem Prof. Martí de Riquer. Departament de Filologia Romànica de la Facultat de Filologia de la Universitat de Barcelona* (Barcelona, 1986), pp. 277–87.

Nickel, Helmut, 'The Tournament: An Historical Sketch', in *The Study of Chivalry: Resources and Approaches*, ed. Howell Chickering and Thomas H. Seiler (Kalamazoo, Mich., 1988), pp. 213–62.

Pfaffenbichler, Matthias, 'Die Anfänge des Turniers im 12. und 13. Jahrhundert', in *Turnier: 1000 Jahre Ritterspiele*, ed. Stefan Krause and Matthias Pfaffenbichler (Munich, 2017), pp. 15–22.

Riddarlek och Tornerspel / Tournaments and the Dream of Chivalry, ed. Lena Rangstrøm (Stockholm, 1992).

Ritterturnier: Geschichte einer Festkultur, ed. Peter Jezler, Peter Niederhäuser and Elke Jezler (Lucerne, 2014).

Rösener, Werner, 'Ritterliche Wirtschaftsverhältnisse und Turnier im sozialen Wandel des Hochmittelalters', in *Das ritterliche Turnier im Mittelalter: Beiträge zu einer vergleichenden Formen- und Verhaltensgeschichte des Rittertums*, ed. Josef Fleckenstein (Göttingen, 1985), pp. 296–338.

Rühl, Joachim, 'Regulations for the Joust in Fifteenth-Century Europe: Francesco Sforza Visconti (1465) and John Tiptoft (1466)', *International Journal of the History of Sport* 18 (2001), 193–208.

Le Tournoi au Moyen Âge: Actes du colloque des 25 et 26 janvier 2002, ed. Nicole Gonthier (Lyon, 2003).

Vale, Juliet, 'Violence and the Tournament', in *Violence in Medieval Society*, ed. Richard W. Kaeuper (Woodbridge, 2000), pp. 143–58.

Vaucelle, Serge, 'Le cheval, le chevalier, le cavalier. La mutation des jeux équestres de la noblesse (XIIe-XVIIe siècle)', *Ludica: Annali di storia e civiltà del gioco* 9 for 2003 (2004), 152–65.

France, the Low Countries and Burgundy

Anglo, Sydney, 'L'Arbre de chevalerie et le Perron dans les tournois', in *Les Fêtes de la Renaissance*, ed. J. Jacquot (Paris, 1975), pp. 283–98.

Annunziata, Anthony, 'Teaching the *pas d'armes*', in *The Study of Chivalry: Resources and Approaches*, ed. Howell Chickering and Thomas H. Seiler (Kalamazoo, Mich., 1988), pp. 556–82.

Barthélemy, Dominique, 'The Chivalric Transformation and the Origins of Tournament as Seen through Norman Chroniclers', *Haskins Society Journal* 20 (2009), 141–60.

Blunk, Catherine, '*Faux pas* in the Chronicles: What Is a *Pas d'armes*?', *The Medieval Chronicle* 11 (2017), 87–107.

Bousmar, Eric, 'Jousting at the Court of Burgundy. The *Pas d'armes*: Shifts in Scenario, Location and Recruitment', in *Staging the Court of Burgundy*, ed. Wim Blockmans et al. (Turnhout, 2013), pp. 75–84.

Bousmar, Eric, 'Pasos de armas, justas y torneos en la corte de Borgoña (siglo XV y principios del XVI)', in *El Legado de Borgoña: Fiesta y ceremonia cortesana en la Europa de los Austrias (1454–1648)*, ed. Krisa de Jonge, Bernardo José García García, and Alicia Esteban Estríngana (Madrid, 2010), pp. 561–606.

Brassart, Felix, *Le Pas du Perron Fée* (Douai, 1874).

Brown, Andrew, 'Urban Jousts in the Later Middle Ages: The White Bear of Bruges', *Revue belge de philologie et d'histoire* 78 (2000), 315–30.

Carolus-Barré, Louis, 'Les grands tournois de Compiègne et de Senlis en l'honneur de Charles, prince de Salerne (mai 1279)', *Bulletin de la Société nationale des antiquaires de France* (1978–79), 87–100.

Cassard, Jean-Christophe, 'Les tournois dans le duché de Bretagne', *Cahiers du Centre d'histoire médiévale* 2 (2003), 165–82.

Chevalier-De Glottal, Anne, 'Les joutes à la cour de Brabant aux 14ème et 15ème siècles', *Cahiers du Centre d'histoire médiévale* 2 (2003), 105–12.

Contamine, Philippe, 'Les tournois en France à la fin du Moyen Age', in *Das ritterliche Turnier im Mittelalter: Beiträge zu einer vergleichenden Formen- und Verhaltensgeschichte des Rittertums*, ed. Josef Fleckenstein (Göttingen, 1985), pp. 425–99.

Crouch, David, *Tournament* (London, 2005).

Damen, Mario, 'Tournament Culture in the Low Countries and England', in *Contact and Exchange in Later Medieval Europe: Essays in Honour of Malcolm Vale*, ed. Hannah Skoda, Patrick Lantschner and R. L. J. Shaw (Woodbridge, 2012), pp. 247–65.

Damen, Mario, 'The Town as a Stage? Urban Space and Tournaments in Late Medieval Brussels', *Urban History* (2015), 1–25.

Damen, Mario, 'The Town, the Duke, his Courtiers, and their Tournament. A Spectacle in Brussels, 4–7 May 1439', in *Staging the Court of Burgundy*, ed. Wim Blockmans et al. (Turnhout, 2013), pp. 85–95.

Elliot, Loïs, 'Le pas d'armes au XVe siècle', *Annales de l'Est* 2 (1993), 83–120.

Ferré, Rose-Marie, 'Les ecclésiastiques et les fêtes profanes à la cour de René d'Anjou: L'exemple du *Pas de Saumur*', in *L'artiste et le clerc: Commandes artistiques des grands ecclésiastiques à la fin du Moyen Âge (XIVe–XVIe siècles)*, ed. Fabienne Joubert (Paris, 2006), pp. 351–70.

Freigang, Christian, 'Le tournoi idéal: La Création du bon chevalier et la politique courtoise de René d'Anjou', in *René d'Anjou, écrivain et mécène (1409–1480)*, ed. Florence Bouchet (Turnhout, 2011), pp. 179–96.

Gaier, Claude, 'Technique des combats singuliers d'après les auteurs "bourguignons" du XVe siècle', *Le Moyen Âge* 91 (1985), 415–57.

Goodman, Jennifer R., 'Display, Self-Definition, and the Frontiers of Romance in the 1463 Bruges Pas du Perron Fée', in *Persons in Groups: Social Behavior as Identity Formation in Medieval Europe*, ed. Richard C. Trexler (Binghamton, N.Y., 1985), pp. 47–54.

Jourdain, Jean-Pierre, 'Le thème du pas dans le royaume de France (Bourgogne, Anjou) à la fin du Moyen Âge: L'emergence d'un symbole', *Annales de Bourgogne* 62 (1990), 117–33.

Jourdan, Jean-Pierre, 'Le perron de chevalerie à la fin du Moyen Âge: Aspects d'un symbole', in *Seigneurs et seigneuries au Moyen Âge: Actes du 117e Congrès national des sociétés savantes (Clermont-Ferrand, 1992). Section d'histoire médiévale et de philologie* (Paris, 1993), pp. 581–98.

Jourdan, Jean-Pierre, 'Le thème du pas d'armes dans le royaume de France (Bourgogne, Anjou) à la fin du Moyen Âge: Aspects d'un théâtre de chevalerie', in *Théâtre et spectacle hier et aujourd'hui: Moyen Âge et Renaissance. Actes du 115e Congrès national des sociétés savantes (Avignon, 1990). Section d'histoire médiévale et de philologie* (Paris, 1991), pp. 285–304.

Jourdan, Jean-Pierre, 'Les fêtes de la chevalerie dans les états bourguignons à la fin du Moyen Âge: Aspects sociaux et économiques', in *Jeux, sports et divertissements au Moyen Âge et à l'âge classique: Actes du 116e Congrès national des sociétés savantes (Chambéry, 1991). Section d'histoire médiévale et de philologie* (Paris, 1993), pp. 257–77.

Lindner, Annette, 'L'influence du roman chevaleresque français sur le pas d'armes', *Publications du Centre Européen d'Études Bourguignonnes* 31 (1991), 67–78.

Mérindol, Christian de, 'Le *Livre des tournois* du roi René. Nouvelles lectures', *Bulletin de la Société nationale des antiquaires de France* (1992), 177–90.

Mérindol, Christian de, *Les fêtes de chevalerie à la cour du roi René: Emblématique, art et histoire (Les joutes de Nancy, le Pas de Saumur et le Pas de Tarascon)* (Paris, 1993).

Muhlberger, Steven, *Jousts and Tournaments: Charny and the Rules for Chivalric Sport in Fourteenth Century France* (Union City, Calif., 2002).

Nadot, Sébastien, *Le Spectacle des joutes: Sport et courtoisie à la fin du Moyen Âge* (Rennes, 2012).

Parisse, Michel, 'Le tournoi en France, des origines à la fin du XIIIe siècle', in *Das ritterliche Turnier im Mittelalter: Beiträge zu einer vergleichenden Formen- und Verhaltensgeschichte des Rittertums*, ed. Josef Fleckenstein (Göttingen, 1985), pp. 175–211.

Parisse, Michel, 'Naissance et développement du tournoi chevaleresque', in *Lettres, musique et société en Lorraine médiévale. Autour du 'Tournoi de Chauvency' (Ms. Oxford Bodleian Douce 308)*, ed. Mireille Chazan and Nancy Freeman Regalado (Geneva, 2012), pp. 239–43.

Le Pas du Perron Fée, ed. Chloé Horn, Anne Rochebouet and Michelle Szkilnik (Paris, 2013).

Paterson, Linda, 'Tournaments and Knightly Sports in Twelfth- and Thirteenth-Century Occitania', *Medium Ævum* 55 (1986), 72–84.

Planche, Alice, 'Du tournoi au théâtre en Bourgogne. Le Pas de la Fontaine des Pleurs à Chalon-sur-Saône, 1449–1450', *Le Moyen Âge* 81 (1975), 97–128.

La Ronde: Giostre, esercizi cavallereschi e loisir in Francia e Piemonte fra Medioevo e Ottocento, ed. Franco Varallo (Florence, 2010).

Santucci, Monique, 'Pas et joutes au service de la politique des princes bourguignons', in *Moyen Âge, livres et patrimoines: Liber amicorum Daniel Quéruel*, ed. Maria Colombo Timelli, Miren Lacassagne and Jean-Louis Haquette (Reims, 2012), pp. 153–61.

Stanesco, Michel, *Jeux d'errance du chevalier médiéval: Aspects ludiques de la fonction guerrière dans la littérature du Moyen Âge flamboyant* (New York, 1988).

Strubel, Armand, 'Le *pas d'armes*: Le tournoi entre le romanesque et le théâtral', in *Théâtre et spectacle hier et aujourd'hui: Moyen Âge et Renaissance. Actes du 115e Congrès national des sociétés savantes (Avignon, 1990), Section d'histoire médiévale et de philologie* (Paris, 1991), pp. 273–84.

Sturgeon, Justin, 'Text and Image in René d'Anjou's *Livre des Tournois*, c. 1460' (unpublished Ph.D. thesis, University of York, 2015) [http://etheses.whiterose.ac.uk/11345/].

Taylor, Jane H. M., '"Une gente pastourelle": René d'Anjou, Louis de Beauvau et le *Pas d'armes de la bergère*', in *René d'Anjou, écrivain et mécène (1409–1480)*, ed. Florence Bouchet (Turnhout, 2011), pp. 197–208.

Das Turnierbuch für René d'Anjou (Le Pas de Saumur): Vollständige Faksimile-Ausgabe des Codex Fr. F. XIV Nr. 4 der Russischen Nationalbibliothek in St. Petersburg, ed. N. Elagina, J. Malinin, T. Voronova, and D. Zypkin (Moscow, 1998).

Vale, Malcolm, 'Le tournoi dans la France du Nord, l'Angleterre et les Pays-Bas (1280–1400): Étude comparative', in *Théâtre et spectacle hier et aujourd'hui: Moyen Âge et Renaissance. Actes du 115e Congrès national des sociétés savantes (Avignon, 1990), Section d'histoire médiévale et de philologie* (Paris, 1991), pp. 263–71.

Van den Abeele, Andries, 'De Wapenpas van de Betoverde Burcht, voorbode van de machtsgreep door Karel de Stoute', *Handelingen van het genootschap voor geschiedenis te Brugge* 146 (2009), 93–139.

Van den Neste, Evelyne, *Tournois, joutes, pas d'armes dans les villes de Flandre à la fin du Moyen Âge, 1300–1486* (Paris, 1996).

Williams, Harry F., '*Le pas de la bergère*: A Critical Edition', *Fifteenth Century Studies* 17 (1990), 485–513.

England and Scotland

Anglo, Sydney, 'Anglo-Burgundian Feats of Arms, Smithfield, June 1467', *Guildhall Miscellany* 2/7 (1965), 271–83.

Anglo, Sydney, 'Archives of the English Tournament: Score Cheques and Lists', *Journal of the Society of Archivists* 2 (1961), 153–62.

Anglo, Sydney, 'Financial and Heraldic Records of the English Tournament', *Journal of the Society of Archivists* 2 (1962), 183–95.

Barker, Juliet, and Maurice Keen, 'The Medieval English Kings and the Tournament', in *Das ritterliche Turnier im Mittelalter: Beiträge zu einer vergleichenden Formen- und Verhaltensgeschichte des Rittertums*, ed. Josef Fleckenstein (Göttingen, 1985), pp. 212–28.

Barker, Juliet, *The Tournament in England, 1100–1400* (Woodbridge, 1986).

Daniel, Catherine, 'Tournois et tables rondes d'Edouard Ier à Edouard III. Du jeu militaire à l'Ordre de Chevalerie', in *Armes et jeux militaires dans l'imaginaire, XII–XV siècles*, ed. Catalina Gîrbea (Paris, 2016), pp. 262–92.

Denholm-Young, Noël, 'The Tournament in the Thirteenth Century', in *Studies in Medieval History Presented to F. M. Powicke*, ed. R. W. Hunt et al. (Oxford, 1948), pp. 240–68.

Edington, Carol, 'The Tournament in Medieval Scotland', in *Armies, Chivalry and Warfare in Medieval Britain and France: Proceedings of the 1995 Harlaxton Symposium*, ed. Matthew Strickland (Woodbridge, 1998), pp. 46–62.

Fradenburg, Louise Olga, *City, Marriage, Tournament: Arts of Rule in Late Medieval Scotland* (Madison, Wisc., 1991).

Green, Richard F., 'A Joust in Honour of the Queen of May, 1441', *Notes and Queries* n.s.27 (1980), 386–89.

Lindenbaum, Sheila, 'The Smithfield Tournament of 1390', *Journal of Medieval and Renaissance Studies* 20 (1990), 1–20.

Norman, A. V. B., 'A Scottish Tournament of the Early 16th Century', *Livrustkammaren: Journal of the Royal Armoury* 19 (1991–92), 88–103.

Sherb, Victor, 'The Tournament of Power: Public Combat and Social Inferiority in Late Medieval England', *Studies in Medieval and Renaissance History* n.s. 12 (1991), 105–28.

Simpson, Sue, 'Something for the Weekend: Elizabethan Tournament Texts and an Entertainment for 16-17 November 1577', in *New Perspectives on Tudor Cultures*, ed. Mike Pinocombe and Zsolt Almási (Newcastle upon Tyne, 2012), pp. 158–76.

Stevenson, Katie, *Chivalry and Knighthood in Scotland, 1424–1513* (Woodbridge, 2006).

Tomkinson, A., 'Retinues at the Tournament of Dunstable, 1309', *English Historical Review* 74 (1959), 70–89.

Vale, Malcolm, 'Le tournoi dans la France du Nord, l'Angleterre et les Pays-Bas (1280–1400): Étude comparative', in *Théâtre et spectacle hier et aujourd'hui: Moyen Âge et Renaissance. Actes du 115e Congrès national des sociétés savantes (Avignon, 1990). Section d'histoire médiévale et de philologie* (Paris, 1991), pp. 263–71.

Watts, Karen, 'Henry VIII and the Pageantry of the Tudor Tournament', *Livrustkammaren: Journal of the Royal Armoury* (1993), 131–41.

Whitbread, Rachael, 'Tournaments, Jousts and Duels: Formal Combats in England and France, circa 1380–1440' (unpublished Ph.D. thesis, University of York, 2013) [http://etheses.whiterose.ac.uk/5473/].

Young, Alan, *Tudor and Jacobean Tournaments* (London, 1987).

The Holy Roman Empire[2]

Anderson, Natalie, 'The Tournament and its Role in the Court Culture of Emperor Maximilian I (1459-1519)' (unpublished Ph.D. thesis, University of Leeds, 2017) [http://etheses.whiterose.ac.uk/18205/].

Baumgartner, Flurin, 'Auf die Schranken! Zur sozialen Funktion der ritterlichen Turniere 1436 und 1438 in Schaffhausen', *Schaffhauser Beiträge zur Geschichte* 87 (2013), 65–84.

Bloh, Jutta Charlotte von, 'Rennen, Stechen, Turniere und Mummereien – die sächsischen Kurfürsten Friedrich III. (1463-1525) und Johann (1468-1532) in Interaktion mit Kaiser Maximilian I.', in *Turnier: 1000 Jahre Ritterspiele*, ed. Stefan Krause and Matthias Pfaffenbichler (Munich, 2017), pp. 253–84.

---

[2] Excluding the Low Countries and Bohemia, but including the Slovene-speaking lands.

Fleckenstein, Josef, 'Das Turnier als höfisches Fest im hochmittelalterlichen Deutschland', in *Das ritterliche Turnier im Mittelalter: Beiträge zu einer vergleichenden Formen- und Verhaltensgeschichte des Rittertums*, ed. Josef Fleckenstein (Göttingen, 1985), pp. 229–56.

Jackson, William Henry, 'Lance and Shield in the *buhurt*', in *German Narrative Literature of the Twelfth and Thirteenth Centuries*, ed. Volker Honemann (Tübingen, 1994), pp. 39–51.

Jackson, William Henry, 'The Tournament and Chivalry in German Tournament Books of the Sixteenth Century and in the Literary Works of Emperor Maximilian I', in *The Ideals and Practice of Medieval Knighthood: Papers from the First and Second Strawberry Hill Conferences*, ed. Christopher Harper-Bill and Ruth Harvey (Woodbridge, 1986), pp. 49–73.

Jackson, William Henry, 'Tournaments and the German Chivalric *Renovatio*: Tournament Discipline and the Myth of Origins', in *Chivalry in the Renaissance*, ed. Sydney Anglo (Woodbridge, 1990), pp. 77–91.

Jaser, Christian, 'Turniere auf Reichstagen zwischen Präsenz und Performanz. Einige Vorüberlegungen zu den Politiken des Agonalen', *Zeitsprünge: Forschungen zur Frühen Neuzeit* 18 (2014), 178–203.

Jezler, Peter, 'Turnierhöfe der oberdeutschen Adelsgesellschaften – Gestech und Rennen, Kolbenturnier, Schwertkampf um die Helmzier, Friedensrat, Standesgericht und Heiratsmarkt', in *Turnier: 1000 Jahre Ritterspiele*, ed. Stefan Krause and Matthias Pfaffenbichler (Munich, 2017), pp. 41–60.

Kaiser Maximilian I. Ein großer Habsburger, ed. Katharina Kaska (Salzburg, 2019).

Kaiser Maximilian I: Der letzte Ritter und das höfische Turnier, ed. Sabine Haag, Alfried Wieczorek, Matthias Pfaffenbichler, and Hans-Jürgen Buderer (Regensburg, 2014), pp. 129–39.

Kos, Dušan, 'Das Turnierbuch des Caspar von Lamberg (Karriere eines Turnierhelden von Krain)', *Waffen- und Kostümkunde* 43 (2001), 103–32.

Kos, Dušan, 'Vitezi iz slovenskih dežel na viteških turnirjih in igrah doma in na tujem' [Knights from Slovene Lands in Tournaments and Games at Home and Abroad], in *Vitez, Dama in Zmaj: Dediščina srednjeveških bojevnikov na Slovenskem*, ed. Tomaž Lazar und Tomaž Nabergoj, 2 vols (Ljubljana, 2011), 1: pp. 147–60.

Krause, Stefan, '"They Call It Royal for Good Reason": The Tournaments of the Late Middle Ages and the Renaissance', in *Habsburg Splendour: Masterpieces from Vienna's Imperial Collections at the Kunsthistorisches Museum*, ed. Monica Kurzel-Runtscheiner (New Haven, 2015), pp. 4–55.

The Last Knight: The Art, Armor and Ambition of Maximilian I, ed. Pierre Terjanian (New York, 2019).

Lehmann, Hans-Dieter, 'Der Beginn des Turnierwesens am deutschen Königshof', *Blätter für deutsche Landesgeschichte* 130 (1994), 65–73.

Maximilian I. (1439-1519): Kaiser. Ritter. Bürger zu Augsburg, ed. Christoph Emmendörffer (Regensburg, 2019).
Meyer, Werner, 'Turniergesellschaften. Bemerkungen zur sozialgeschichtlichen Bedeutung der Turniere im Spätmittelalter', in *Das ritterliche Turnier im Mittelalter: Beiträge zu einer vergleichenden Formen- und Verhaltensgeschichte des Rittertums*, ed. Josef Fleckenstein (Göttingen, 1985), pp. 500–12.
Meyer-Hofmann, Werner, 'Turniere im alten Basel', *Basler Stadtbuch* (1970), 22–38.
Militzer, Klaus, 'Turniere in Köln', *Jahrbuch des Kölnischen Geschichtsvereins* 64 (1993), 37–59.
Morsel, Joseph, 'Le tournoi, mode d'éducation politique en Allemagne à la fin du Moyen Âge', in *Education, apprentissages, initiation au Moyen Âge* (Montpellier, 1993), pp. 309–31.
Murray, Alan V., '"Bog vas sprejmi, kraljeva Venus!": Ulrik Liechtensteinski in turnirsko bojevanje na Štajerskem, Koroškem in v Avstriji' [Ulrich von Liechtenstein and the Practice of Tournaments in Styria, Carinthia and Austria], in *Vitez, Dama in Zmaj: Dediščina srednjeveških bojevnikov na Slovenskem*, ed. Tomaž Lazar und Tomaž Nabergoj, 2 vols (Ljubljana, 2011), 1: 135–45.
Murray, Alan V., 'Tourney, Joust, Foreis and Round Table: Tournament Forms in the *Frauendienst* of Ulrich von Liechtenstein', in *Pleasure and Leisure in the Middle Ages and Early Modern Age: Cultural-Historical Perspectives on Toys, Games, and Entertainment*, ed. Albrecht Classen (Berlin, 2019), pp. 365–94.
Niedner, Felix, *Das deutsche Turnier im XII. und XIII. Jahrhundert* (Berlin, 1881).
Pfaffenbichler, Matthias, 'Kaiser Maximilian I. – der letzte Ritter und das höfische Turnier', in *Turnier: 1000 Jahre Ritterspiele*, ed. Stefan Krause and Matthias Pfaffenbichler (Munich, 2017), pp. 93–110.
Pfaffenbichler, Matthias, 'Das Turnier zur Zeit Maximilians I.', in *Der Aufstieg eines Kaisers: Maximilian I. von seiner Geburt bis zur Alleinherrschaft 1459–1493* (Wiener Neustadt, 2000), pp. 81–89.
Pfaffenbichler, Matthias, 'Les tournois des Habsbourg en Europe centrale, de Maximilien Ier à Rodolphe II', in *Les Arts de l'équitation dans l'Europe de la Renaissance*, ed. Patrice Franchet d'Espèrey and Monique Chatenet (Paris, 2009), pp. 370–87.
Pfaffenbichler, Matthias, 'Das Turnier als Instrument der Habsburgischen Politik', *Waffen- und Kostümkunde* 34 (1992), 13–36.
Pfaffenbichler, Matthias, 'Die Turniere an den Höfen der österreichischen Habsburger im 16. Jahrhundert', in *Turnier: 1000 Jahre Ritterspiele*, ed. Stefan Krause and Matthias Pfaffenbichler (Munich, 2017), pp. 155–70.
Ranft, Andreas, *Adelsgesellschaften: Gruppenbildung und Genossenschaft im spätmittelalterlichen Reich* (Sigmaringen, 1994).

Ranft, Andreas, 'Adliges Turnier und gesellschaftlich-höfische Propaganda', in *Adlige Lebenswelten in Sachsen: Kommentierte Bild- und Schriftquellen*, ed. Martina Schattkowsky (Vienna, 2013), pp. 1-6

Ranft, Andreas, 'Die Turniere der vier Lande: Genossenschaftlicher Hof und Selbstbehauptung des niederen Adels', *Zeitschrift für Geschichte des Oberrheins* 142 (1994), 83–102.

Reichert, Hermann, 'Vorbilder für Ulrichs von Liechtenstein Friesacher Turnier', *Carinthia I: Mitteilungen des Geschichtsvereines für Kärnten* 173 (1983), 171–92.

Rohr, Alheydis von, 'Ein Turnierbuch Herzog Heinrichs des Mittleren zu Braunschweig-Lüneburg', *Niedersächsisches Jahrbuch für Landesgeschichte* 55 (1983), 181–200.

Rühl, Joachim, 'German Tournament Regulations of the 15th Century', *Journal of Sport History* 17 (1990), 163–82.

Sandbichler, Veronika, 'Torneos y fiestas de corte de los Habsburgo en los siglos XV y XVI', in *El Legado de Borgoña: Fiesta y ceremonia cortesana en la Europa de los Austrias (1454–1648)*, ed. Krisa de Jonge, Bernardo José García García, and Alicia Esteban Estríngana (Madrid, 2010), pp. 607–24.

Sandbichler, Veronika, 'Ain [...] puech darinnen ir fürstlich durchlaucht allerlei turnier – die Turnierbücher Erzherzog Ferdinands II.', in *Turnier: 1000 Jahre Ritterspiele*, ed. Stefan Krause and Matthias Pfaffenbichler (Munich, 2017), pp. 203–16.

Schultz, Alwin, *Das höfische Leben zur Zeit der Minnesinger*, 2nd edn, 2 vols (Leipzig, 1889), 2: 106–50.

Schwarzmaier, Hansmartin, 'Das ritterliche Turnier in staufischer Zeit', in *Das Nibelungenlied und seine Welt*, ed. Jürgen Krüger (Darmstadt, 2003), pp. 95–97.

Silver, Larry, 'Shining Armor: Emperor Maximilian, Chivalry and War', in *Artful Armies, Beautiful Battles: Art and Warfare in Early Modern Europe*, ed. Pia Cuneo (Leiden, 2001), pp. 61–85.

Vocelka, Karl, 'Das Wiener Turnier von 1571 – Ritterspiele anlässlich der Hochzeit von Erzherzog Karl und Maria von Bayern', in *Turnier: 1000 Jahre Ritterspiele*, ed. Stefan Krause and Matthias Pfaffenbichler (Munich, 2017), pp. 171–80.

Zotz, Thomas, 'Adel, Bürgertum und Turniere in deutschen Städten vom 13. bis 15. Jahrhundert', in *Das ritterliche Turnier im Mittelalter: Beiträge zu einer vergleichenden Formen- und Verhaltensgeschichte des Rittertums*, ed. Josef Fleckenstein (Göttingen, 1985), pp. 450–99.

Italy and Iberia

Cardini, Franco, 'Lorenzo als Turnierreiter', in *Lorenzo der Prächtige und die Kultur im Florenz des 15. Jahrhunderts*, ed. Horst Heintze, Giuliano Staccioli and Babette Hesse (Berlin, 1995), pp. 55–68.

La Civiltà del torneo (sec. XII-XVII): Giostre e tornei tra Medioevo ed Età moderna, ed. Maria Vittoria Baruti Ceccopieri (Narni, 1990).

Delle Donne, Fulvio, *L'esercizio della guerra, i duelli e i giochi cavallereschi: Le premesse della disfida di Barletta e la tradizione militare dei Fieramosca* (Barletta, 2017).

Fallows, Noel, *Jousting in Medieval and Renaissance Iberia* (Woodbridge, 2011).

Fallows, Noel, 'Das kastilische Buch des Orden de la Banda – die früheste schriftliche Quelle zum Turnierwesen (um 1330)', in *Turnier: 1000 Jahre Ritterspiele*, ed. Stefan Krause and Matthias Pfaffenbichler (Munich, 2017), pp. 61–92.

Forcella, Vincenzo, *Tornei e giostre: Ingressi trionfali e feste carnevalesche in Roma sotto Paolo III* (Rome, 1885).

Giochi e giocattoli nel Medioevo piemontese e ligure, ed. Rinaldo Comba and Riccardo Rao (Rocca de' Baldi, 2005).

Hinojosa Montalvo, José, 'Torneos y justas en la Valencia foral', *Medievalismo: Boletín de la Sociedad Española de Estudios Medievales* 23 (2013), 209–40.

Mattaloni, Claudio, 'Tornamenti, tripudi, feste e manifestazioni pubbliche della magnifica comunità di Cividale del Friuli (secoli XIII-XVIII)', *Memorie storiche forogiuliesi* 85 for 2005 (2006), 49–77.

Szabó, Thomas, 'Das Turnier in Italien', in *Das ritterliche Turnier im Mittelalter: Beiträge zu einer vergleichenden Formen- und Verhaltensgeschichte des Rittertums*, ed. Josef Fleckenstein (Göttingen, 1985), pp. 344–70.

Truffi, Riccardo, *Giostre e cantori di giostre: Studi e ricerche di storia e di letteratura* (Rocca S. Casciano, 1911).

Eastern Europe (Poland, Bohemia, Hungary and Byzantium)

Brzustowicz, Bogdan Wojciech, 'Margrabia Jan z Kostrzyna i turnieje rycerskie' [Margrave Johann of Brandenburg-Küstrin and the Tournament], *Nadwarciański Rocznik Historyczno-Archiwalny* 4 (1997), 29–40.

Brzustowicz, Bogdan Wojciech, 'Turnieje rycerskie na dworze książąt zachodniopomorskich w średniowieczu' [The Tournament at the Court of the Dukes of Western Pomerania in the Middle Ages], *Przegląd Zachodniopomorski* 18 (2003), 29–56.

Brzustowicz, Bogdan Wojciech, *Turniej rycerski w Królestwie Polskim w późnym średniowieczu i renesansie na tle europejskim* [Tournaments in the Kingdom of Poland in the Later Middle Ages and Renaissance in European Perspective] (Warszawa, 2003).

Brzustowicz, Bogdan Wojciech, and Katie Stevenson, 'Tournaments, Heraldry and Heralds in the Kingdom of Poland in the Late Middle Ages', in *The Herald in Late Medieval Europe*, ed. Katie Stevenson (Woodbridge, 2009), pp. 145–64.

Fügedi, Erik, 'Turniere im mittelalterlichen Ungarn', in *Das ritterliche Turnier im Mittelalter: Beiträge zu einer vergleichenden Formen- und Verhaltensgeschichte des Rittertums*, ed. Josef Fleckenstein (Göttingen, 1985), pp. 390–400.

Gulyás, Borbála, 'Die Turniere am Hof der ungarischen Könige im 16. Jahrhundert', in *Turnier: 1000 Jahre Ritterspiele*, ed. Stefan Krause and Matthias Pfaffenbichler (Munich, 2017), pp. 131–54.

Iwańczak, Wojciech, 'Le tournoi chevaleresque dans le royaume de Bohême. Essai d'analyse culturelle', *Studi medievali* ser.3, 28 (1987), 751–73.

Jones, Lynn, and Henry McGuire, 'A Description of the Jousts of Manuel I Komnenos', *Byzantine and Modern Greek Studies* 26 (2002), 104–48.

Macek, Josef, 'Das Turnier im mittelalterlichen Böhmen', in *Das ritterliche Turnier im Mittelalter: Beiträge zu einer vergleichenden Formen- und Verhaltensgeschichte des Rittertums*, ed. Josef Fleckenstein (Göttingen, 1985), pp. 371–89.

Schreiner, Peter, 'Ritterspiele in Byzanz', *Jahrbuch der Österreichischen Byzantinistik* 46 for 1996 (1997), 227–41.

Weapons, Armour and Other Equipment

Blair, Claude, *European Armour, circa 1066–circa 1700* (London, 1958).

Breiding, Dirk H., 'Turniere und Turnierausrüstung in Mitteleuropa – von den Anfängen bis zum ausgehenden 15. Jahrhundert', in *Turnier: 1000 Jahre Ritterspiele*, ed. Stefan Krause and Matthias Pfaffenbichler (Munich, 2017), pp. 23–40.

Capwell, Tobias, *Arms and Armour of the Joust* (Leeds, 2018).

Curl, Michael S., 'Late Medieval Lance Use: Mounted Combat and Martial Arts in Western Europe from the 14th to the 16th Century', *Arms & Armour* 16 (2019), 27–55.

Dalewicz-Kitto, Suzanne, and Alex Cantrill, 'Conservation of a Jousting Reinforcement, Belonging to Emperor Maximilian I', *Arms & Armour* 10 (2013), 172–82.

Dillon, Harold, 'Barriers and Foot Combats', *Archaeological Journal* 61 (1904), 276–308.

Eaves, Ian, 'The Tournament Armours of King Henry VIII of England', *Livrustkammaren: Journal of the Royal Armoury* (1993), 2–45.

Gambler, Ortwin, 'Ritterspiele und Turnierrüstung im Spätmittelalter', in *Das ritterliche Turnier im Mittelalter: Beiträge zu einer vergleichenden Formen- und*

Verhaltensgeschichte des Rittertums, ed. Josef Fleckenstein (Göttingen, 1985), pp. 500–12.

Gillmor, Carole, 'Practical Chivalry: The Training of Horses for Tournaments and Warfare', *Studies in Medieval and Renaissance History* n.s. 13 (1992) 5–29.

Gravett, Christopher, 'Early Tournament Armour', *Livrustkammaren: Journal of the Royal Armoury* (1993), 62–88.

Kuster, Thomas, 'Die Plattnerei in Prag und Innsbruck zur Zeit Erzherzog Ferdinands II. (1529–1595)', in *Turnier: 1000 Jahre Ritterspiele*, ed. Stefan Krause and Matthias Pfaffenbichler (Munich, 2017), pp. 217–22.

Moffat, Ralph D., 'Arms and Armour', in *A Companion to Chivalry*, ed. Robert W. Jones and Peter Coss (Woodbridge, 2019), pp. 158–85.

Moffat, Ralph D., 'The Importance of Being Harnest: Armour, Heraldry and Recognition in the Melée', in *Battle and Bloodshed: The Medieval World at War*, ed. Lorna Bleach and Keira Borrill (Newcastle, 2013), pp. 5–24.

Moffat, Ralph D., 'The Manner of Arming Knights for the Tourney: A Re-Interpretation of an Important Early 14th-Century Arming Treatise', *Arms & Armour* 7 (2010), 5–29.

Pfaffenbichler, Matthias, 'Die deutsche Harnischgarnitur im 16. Jahrhundert', in *Turnier: 1000 Jahre Ritterspiele*, ed. Stefan Krause and Matthias Pfaffenbichler (Munich, 2017), pp. 223–40.

Pfaffenbichler, Matthias, 'Die Produktion von Turnierrüstungen – Plattnerzentren in Süddeutschland und Österreich', in *Turnier: 1000 Jahre Ritterspiele*, ed. Stefan Krause and Matthias Pfaffenbichler (Munich, 2017), pp. 111–30.

Southwick, Leslie, 'The Great Helm in England', *Arms & Armour* 3 (2006), 5–77.

Tzouriadis, Iason-Eleftherios, 'The Development, Use and Significance of Staff Weapons in Medieval Europe, c. 1300–1500' (unpublished Ph.D. thesis, University of Leeds, 2017).

Viallon, Marina, 'A German High Tournament Saddle in the Royal Armouries, Leeds', *Arms & Armour* 12 (2015), 103–23.

Williams, Alan et al., 'A Technical Note on the Armour and Equipment for Jousting', *Gladius: Estudios sobre armas antiguas, armamento, arte militar y vida cultural en Oriente y Occidente* 32 (2013), 131–84.

Tournaments in Literature

Benson, Larry D., 'The Tournament in the Romances of Chrétien de Troyes and *L'Histoire de Guillaume Le Marechal*', in *Chivalric Literature: Essays on the Relationship between Literature and Life in the Later Middle Ages*, ed. Larry D. Benson and John Leyerle (Kalamazoo, Mich., 1980), pp. 1–24.

Bergeron, Guillaume, *Les Combats chevaleresques dans l'œuvre de Chrétien de Troyes* (Oxford, 2008).

Cline, Ruth H., 'The Influence of Romances on Tournaments of the Middle Ages', *Speculum* 20 (1945), 204–11.

Gîrbea, Catalina, 'L'imaginaire du tournoi', in *Armes et jeux militaires dans l'imaginaire, XII–XV siècles*, ed. Catalina Gîrbea (Paris, 2016), pp. 7–33.

Hable, Nina, 'Die Tjost. Zeichen der Gewalt – die Macht der Zeichen', in *Aktuelle Tendenzen der Artusforschung*, ed. Brigitte Burrichter et al. (Berlin, 2013), pp. 147–60.

Hellenga, Robert, 'The Tournaments in Malory's *Morte d'Arthur*', *Forum for Modern Language Studies* 10 (1974), 67–78.

Jackson, William Henry, 'Das Turnier in der deutschen Dichtung des Mittelalters', in *Das ritterliche Turnier im Mittelalter: Beiträge zu einer vergleichenden Formen- und Verhaltensgeschichte des Rittertums*, ed. Josef Fleckenstein (Göttingen, 1985), pp. 257–95.

Jackson, William Henry, 'The Tournament in the Works of Hartmann von Aue: Motifs, Style, Functions', in *Hartmann von Aue: Changing Perspectives. London Hartmann Symposium 1985*, ed. Timothy McFarland and Silvia Ranawake (Göppingen, 1988), pp. 233–51.

Jackson, William Henry, 'Tournaments and Battles in *Parzival*', in *A Companion to Wolfram's Parzival*, ed. Will Hasty (Columbia, S.C., 1999), pp. 159–84.

Lindquist, Josefa, 'Medieval Depiction of Spaces: Battle and Tournament Fields in the Tristan and Ysolt Legend', *La Corónica: A Journal of Medieval Hispanic Languages, Literatures & Cultures* 44 (2015), 163–75.

Nadot, Sébastien, 'Tournois et joutes chez les écrivains du Moyen Age', *Essays in French Literature and Culture* 46 (2009), 183–202.

Orgelfinger, Gail, 'Reality and Romance in Fifteenth-Century Burgundian Literature: The Tournaments in Olivier de Castille', in *Literary and Historical Perspectives of the Middle Ages: Proceedings of the 1981 SEMA Meeting*, ed. Patricia W. Cummins, Patrick W. Conner and Charles W. Connell (Morgantown, W.Va., 1982), pp. 104–19.

Peters, Ursula, *Frauendienst: Untersuchungen zu Ulrich von Liechtenstein und zum Wirklichkeitsgehalt der Minnedichtung* (Göppingen, 1971).

Sandoz, Edouard, 'Tourneys in the Arthurian Tradition', *Speculum* 19 (1944), 389–420.

Santina, Mary Arlene, *The Tournament and Literature: Literary Representations of the Medieval Tournament in Old French Works, 1150–1226* (New York, 1999).

Szkilnik, Michelle, 'Que lisaient les chevaliers du XVe siècle? Le témoignage du *Pas du Perron Fée*', *Le Moyen Français* 68 (2010), 103–14.

1

Now Form Up Close Together! Tactics and Ethos of the Tourney in Early German Sources (Twelfth to Thirteenth Centuries)

Alan V. Murray

Writing in the third quarter of the sixteenth century, the Swabian historian and humanist Froben Christoph, count of Zimmern and lord of Meßkirch and Wildenstein (1519–66), claimed to know the exact circumstances of the origin of tournaments in Germany. In his family chronicle he wrote that King Henry I of Germany (r. 919–36) wished to commemorate a great victory over the Hungarians so that it would be remembered forever; as tournaments were unknown in any of the German lands at that time, the king decreed that such honourable knightly games, which had hitherto been practised only in France and Great Britain, should be established and promoted in the German *Reich*, so that the prowess of every knight might be recognised and that the younger members of the nobility might become braver and more skilled in war against their enemies, but that this should not be done 'for the entertainment of ladies and damsels'. And so, in the year 938, the king, his two sons and some 1,500 princes, counts, free lords and knights took part in this first tournament on German soil.[1]

Froben Christoph's chronology was wanting. Apart from the fact that he dates this tournament to two years after King Henry's death, it becomes clear from his own testimony that he was relying on inaccurate accounts from his own time, notably the tournament book by Georg Rüxner (*al.* Rixner) who produced a catalogue of thirty-six tournaments held in Germany between their supposed beginning in 938 and the late fifteenth century. Rüxner was a herald in the service of Habsburgs and Wittelsbachs (with the official title of

---

[1] *Die Chronik der Grafen von Zimmern: Handschriften 580 und 581 der Fürstlich Fürstenbergischen Hofbibliothek Donaueschingen*, ed. Hansmartin Decker-Hauff, Arne Holtorf, Sönke Lorenz and Rudolf Seigel, 7 vols (Constance, 1964–), 1: 56. The king (also known as Henry the Fowler) is incorrectly described as emperor.

'Jerusalem'), a profession associated with tournaments and other events involving coats of arms, but most of the tourneys listed in his book are invented or fanciful.[2] Yet as this example shows, Rüxner's history was highly influential among his contemporaries. As was typical for his day, Froben Christoph believed that nobility had existed since time immemorial and that typical attributes of the noble lifestyle, such as heraldry and tournaments, had been adopted in the distant past. Thus he claims that his putative ancestors the Cimbri, a Germanic tribe that had invaded the Roman empire in the second century BC, had decorated their helmets with wings and heads of animals, which he took as proof that they had a noble class which used crests in the same manner that tourneyers did many centuries later.[3] Froben Christoph's account can thus be dismissed, although he was correct in his belief that tournaments were introduced to Germany from the lands lying to its west. It is now generally accepted that the earliest form, the tourney, originated in the late eleventh and early twelfth centuries in northern France, Normandy and the mostly Francophone parts of the southern Low Countries. It took several decades before the new form of knightly game appeared in the German-speaking countries.[4] The French influence on German tournament practice can be seen in the vocabulary applied to the two main forms found in the period

[2] Georg Rüxner, *Anfang, Ursachen, Ursprung und Herkommen des Turnier ... in Teutscher Nation* (Simmern, 1530); Klaus Graf, 'Herold mit vielen Namen. Neues zu Georg Rüxner alias Rugen alias Jerusalem alias Brandenburg alias ...', in *Ritterwelten im Spätmittelalter: Höfisch-ritterliche Kultur der Reichen Herzöge von Bayern-Landshut*, ed. Franz Niehoff (Landshut, 2009), pp. 115–25.

[3] *Die Chronik der Grafen von Zimmern*, 1: 34–35. On the chronicle and its interpretations of the past, see Beat Rudolf Jenny, *Graf Froben Christoph von Zimmern: Geschichtsschreiber, Erzähler, Landesherr. Ein Beitrag zur Geschichte des Humanismus in Schwaben* (Constance, 1959); Steffen Krieb, 'Erinnerungskultur und adeliges Selbstverständnis im Spätmittelalter', *Zeitschrift für Württembergische Landesgeschichte* 60 (2001), 59–75, and Alan V. Murray, 'Hochmittelalterlicher Kreuzzug als frühneuzeitliche Adelslegitimation: Die schwäbisch-rheinländischen Teilnehmer des Ersten Kreuzzugs in der Chronik des Grafen Froben Christoph von Zimmern', in *Herrschaft und Legitimation: Hochmittelalterlicher Adel in Südwestdeutschland*, ed. Sönke Lorenz and Stephan Molitor (Leinfelden-Echterdingen, 2002), pp. 171–85.

[4] Michel Parisse, 'Le tournoi en France, des origines à la fin du XIIIe siècle', in *Das ritterliche Turnier im Mittelalter: Beiträge zu einer vergleichenden Formen- und Verhaltensgeschichte des Rittertums*, ed. Josef Fleckenstein (Göttingen, 1985), pp. 175–211; Ulrich Mölk, 'Philologische Aspekte des Turniers', in *Das ritterliche Turnier im Mittelalter*, pp. 163–74; Helmut Nickel, 'The Tournament: An Historical Sketch', in *The Study of Chivalry: Resources and Approaches*, ed. Howell Chickering and Thomas H. Seiler (Kalamazoo, Mich., 1988), pp. 213–62; Richard Barber and Juliet Barker,

discussed.[5] These were the tourney (*turnei, turney* < OFr *tornoi*), with its associated verb *turnieren*, denoting a mass combat between two opposing teams, and the joust (*tjoste, ziost* < OFr *jouste*) and its associated verbs *tjostieren* and *stechen*, denoting an individual combat.[6]

For the earliest period of tournaments – roughly up to the mid-thirteenth century – most of our knowledge derives from the few texts that give detailed descriptions of actual events. Foremost among these are *Histoire de Guillaume le Maréchal*, an Old French rhymed history of the life of the Anglo-Norman nobleman William Marshal (d. 1219), earl of Pembroke,[7] and the *Chronicon Hanoniense* by Gislebert of Mons, chancellor of the county of Hainaut.[8] This situation has meant that most research on tournaments has tended to focus on the Francophone countries, which can be taken as including England, where French was the everyday language of the nobility. The rather less expansive research on the tournament in Germany has – understandably – been mostly published in German, but as an apparent consequence it has not received the attention it deserves, either in wider scholarship or in work aimed at students. It has also been biased to the better documented tournament forms of the fifteenth and sixteenth centuries.[9] The aim of this essay is therefore to set out

---

Tournaments: Jousts, Chivalry and Pageants in the Middle Ages (Woodbridge, 1989), pp. 13–27; David Crouch, *Tournament* (London, 2005), pp. 10–16.

[5] In what follows, unless specified as Latin or Old French (OFr), it is assumed that the tournament terminology given in italics is in Middle High German (MHG).

[6] The form of group combat is sometimes referred to by modern authorities as 'mass tournament' or 'mêlée tournament'. I prefer to use the English term 'tourney' on the grounds that this corresponds most closely to OFr *tornoi* and MHG *turnei*. The MHG scribal forms beginning in *tj-* (sometimes *ty-*) and *z-* are attempts to represent the phoneme /ʒ/ (written as <j> in Old French). The ending *-ieren* is typical of verbs formed from French roots. The verb *stechen* ('strike, stab') is of German origin, although used in a more restricted sense in the context of tournaments, normally specifically of jousting.

[7] *History of William Marshal*, ed. Anthony J. Holden, trans. Stewart Gregory, notes by David Crouch, 3 vols (London, 2002–2006). On William's life and career as a tourneyer, see David Crouch, *William Marshal: Court, Career and Chivalry in the Angevin Empire, 1147–1219* (London, 1990), pp. 26–52.

[8] *La Chronique de Gislebert de Mons*, ed. Léon Vanderkindere (Brussels, 1903); translation available as Gilbert of Mons, *Chronicle of Hainaut*, trans. Laura Napran (Woodbridge, 2005).

[9] For the period under discussion here: Josef Fleckenstein, 'Das Turnier als höfisches Fest im hochmittelalterlichen Deutschland', in *Das ritterliche Turnier im Mittelalter*, pp. 229–56; William Henry Jackson, 'Das Turnier in der deutschen Dichtung des Mittelalters', in *Das ritterliche Turnier im Mittelalter*, pp. 257–95; Werner

for an English-speaking readership the characteristics of the tourney as it was practised in Germany in the twelfth and thirteenth centuries and to explain the terminology used to describe it in Middle High German, the variety of the language spoken in central and southern Germany up to around 1350.

The earliest mention of a tournament in a German-speaking country occurs in the *Gesta Friderici* of the chronicler Otto, bishop of Freising (d. 1158), in the context of fighting in Franconia in 1127 during a territorial dispute between Frederick II of Hohenstaufen, duke of Swabia (d. 1147) and his brother Conrad (d. 1152), on the one hand, and Emperor Lothar III (d. 1137) on the other. Lothar had unsuccessfully besieged Nuremberg, which was held by the two Hohenstaufen brothers, and withdrew to Würzburg. Frederick and Conrad pursued him there with their forces, and during the ensuing siege they held a '*tyrocinium*, which is now popularly called a *turnoimentum*'.[10] This terminology is worthy of some consideration. The noun *tyrocinium* was evidently well known to those who knew Latin. It is derived from the word *tiro* (pl. *tirones*), meaning a youth, or more specifically, a young, inexperienced warrior. For this reason several commentators have argued that what was described was not in fact a tournament, but a non-violent form of military exercise known as a *bûhurt* in Middle High German and *béhourd* in Old French (which will be discussed below).[11] I do not find this argument compelling. To fully explain the nature of the event in Latin, Otto uses the neologism *turnoimentum*,

---

Rösener, 'Ritterliche Wirtschaftsverhältnisse und Turnier im sozialen Wandel des Hochmittelalters', in *Das ritterliche Turnier im Mittelalter*, pp. 296–338; Joachim Bumke, *Höfische Kultur: Literatur und Gesellschaft im hohen Mittelalter*, 2 vols (Munich, 1986), 1: 342–79 [translation available as *Courtly Culture: Literature and Society in the High Middle Ages* (Los Angeles, 1991)]; Hansmartin Schwarzmaier, 'Das ritterliche Turnier in staufischer Zeit', in *Das Nibelungenlied und seine Welt*, ed. Jürgen Krüger (Darmstadt, 2003), pp. 95–97. Important collections of relevant primary material are given in Alwin Schultz, *Das höfische Leben zur Zeit der Minnesinger*, 2nd edn, 2 vols (Leipzig, 1889), 2: 106–50, and *Die Ritteridee in der deutschen Literatur des Mittelalters: Eine kommentierte Anthologie*, ed. Jörg Arentzen and Uwe Ruberg (Darmstadt, 1987), pp. 193–226.

[10] Bischof Otto von Freising und Rahewin, *Gesta Frederici seu Cronica / Die Taten Friedrichs oder richtiger Cronica*, ed. Georg Waitz, Bernhard Simson and Franz-Josef Schmale, trans. Adolf Schmidt, Ausgewählte Quellen zur deutschen Geschichte des Mittelalters: Freiherr vom Stein-Gedächtnisausgabe 17 (Darmstadt, 1965), p. 158: *tyrocinium, quod vulgo nunc turnoimentum dicitur, cum militibus eius extra exercendo usque ad muros ipsos progrediuntur*.

[11] Fleckenstein, 'Das Turnier als höfisches Fest', p. 230; Bumke, *Höfische Kultur*, 1: 111, 359; Crouch, *Tournament*, p. 10.

adding a Latin noun ending to OFr *tornoi*, a term which originally could refer to diverse forms of combat, but in the course of the twelfth century came to develop the more restricted meaning of tourney.[12] Otto had studied at the University of Paris and subsequently became a Cistercian monk at the abbey of Morimond in Lorraine; he was certainly well versed in French. He could undoubtedly have found an unambiguous way of indicating a *bûhurt* if this was the type of event he wanted to describe, but he chose to coin a new Latin word derived from a French term associated with violent combat in order to designate the new form of military game which was in the process of being introduced from France. A final argument that Otto's description relates to a tourney is the context of a siege. It is far more likely that knights exercising outside an enemy-held city would be fully armed and armoured than it would be for them to take part in the much less warlike *bûhurt*.

Otto's statement is typical of the way tournaments are described in most contemporary Latin narrative sources from Germany, which tend to provide laconic accounts mentioning only the date, place and organisers. If other details are provided, these tend to be the names of accidental casualties, a sure indication of clerical disapproval of a pastime which had been prohibited by the Church.[13] This situation means that in the absence of any texts comparable with the Old French history of William Marshal, we are obliged to turn to vernacular poetry, and the following discussion will draw on relevant evidence from texts that are literary rather than historical. Tournaments are mentioned in a wide range of Middle High German works, but there are five in particular whose extended descriptions are sufficient to provide detailed evidence about tournament practice in Germany from the later twelfth century up to around the year 1260:

1   The Arthurian romance *Erec*, by the Swabian knight Hartmann von Aue, is an adaptation of *Erec et Enide* by Chrétien de Troyes. Both works contain a description of a tourney held to celebrate the marriage of the

---

[12] Mölk, 'Philologische Aspekte des Turniers', pp. 163–70, 174.

[13] Casualties at tournaments were often regarded by clerical authors as indications of divine disapproval. A case in point is the death of Leopold V, duke of Austria, who died as a result of injuries sustained at a tournament at Vienna in 1194, which was regarded by many as retribution for his imprisonment of the crusader Richard the Lionheart while the latter was returning from the Third Crusade. See Jeffrey Ashcroft, 'Der Minnesänger und die Freude des Hofes. Zu Reinmars Kreuzliedern und Witwenklage', in *Poesie und Gebrauchsliteratur im deutschen Mittelalter: Würzburger Colloquium 1978*, ed. Volker Honemann, Kurt Ruh, Bernhard Schnell and Werner Wegstein (Tübingen, 1979), pp. 219–37. A range of fatalities mentioned in Latin sources is given by Schultz, *Das höfische Leben zur Zeit der Minnesinger*, 2: 114–16.

poem's hero, Erec, son of King Lac and a knight at the court of King Arthur, to an impoverished but high-born lady known as Enide (OFr) or Enîte (MHG). Chrétien's account of this event, which takes up 136 lines, is expanded more than fourfold by Hartmann to 629 lines, a clear indication of the growing interest in tournament culture on the part of his patrons and audiences. *Erec* belongs to Hartmann's earlier oeuvre, being generally dated to the period 1180–90. It thus not only contains the first extended description of a tournament in German, but was also written down only about twenty years after the date of the earliest tourney described in the *Histoire de Guillaume le Maréchal*, and well before the completion of the latter work.[14]

2 The romance *Parzival* by Wolfram von Eschenbach, composed around 1210/1220, is also based on a text by Chrétien, known as *Perceval* or *Le Conte du Graal*. However, it shows a far greater degree of adaptation, as well as describing characters and adventures unknown to the original. Material added at the beginning of the story tells of Gahmuret, son of a king of Anjou and father of the romance's eponymous hero, whose main pleasure is to take part in tournaments and other deeds of knighthood. After winning the love of Belacane, the heathen queen of Zazamanc, he goes off in search of further adventures, which involve a tourney at Kanvoleis in the land of Waleis.[15]

3 The poem *Willehalm von Orlens* by Rudolf von Ems defies precise generic categorisation. It is based on a French original which is now lost. Its hero is Willehalm, son of a count of Hainaut, who loses his parents at an early age, and grows up at the court of Jofrit, duke of Brabant. Most of the text narrates his adventures intended to win the love of Amalie, daughter of the king of England, but it also contains elements of the genre known as

---

[14] *Erec von Hartmann von Aue*, ed. Albert Lietzmann (Halle an der Saale, 1939) [henceforth cited as *Erec*, with references to lines]; William Henry Jackson, 'The Tournament in the Works of Hartmann von Aue: Motifs, Style, Functions', in *Hartmann von Aue: Changing Perspectives. London Hartmann Symposium 1985*, ed. Timothy McFarland and Silvia Ranawake (Göppingen, 1988), pp. 233–51; Jackson, *Chivalry in Twelfth-Century Germany: The Works of Hartmann von Aue* (Cambridge, 1994), pp. 26–27, 103–7. There is a new edition with facing-page English translation: Hartmann von Aue, *Erec*, ed. and trans. Cyril Edwards (Cambridge, 2014).

[15] Wolfram von Eschenbach, *Parzival: Studienausgabe*, 6th edn, ed. Karl Lachmann (Berlin, 1926) [henceforth cited as *Parzival*, with references to strophes]. The most accessible English translation is Wolfram von Eschenbach, *Parzival and Titurel*, trans. Cyril Edwards (Oxford, 2006).

advice for princes. It was composed before 1243 for the patron Konrad von Winterstetten, a Swabian *ministerialis* who held the aulic office of imperial butler and successively acted as counsellor to two of the sons of Emperor Frederick II, Henry (VII) and Conrad IV. The plot seems to be set in a distant past, yet much of the action seems to reflect political disputes between the duchy of Brabant and the county of Hainaut in the late twelfth century, so the descriptions of three tournaments can be regarded as reasonably accurate representations of contemporary practice.[16]

4   The *Turnier von Nantes* is a poem of 1,156 lines which should be understood as a political allegory, written in the second half of the thirteenth century by Konrad von Würzburg, a professional poet. Germanists have dated its composition from 1257 at the earliest to the 1280s at the latest, but the dating is unimportant for its depiction of tournaments. Most of the text tells of a stylised tourney at Nantes in Brittany between two groups designated as 'the Germans and the French' (*die Tiuschen und die Walhe*). The leader of the 'Germans' is a King Richard of England, who is probably to be identified with the historical Richard of Cornwall (1209–72), the second son of King John and for a time a claimant to the German throne; his followers are the kings of Denmark and Scotland, the dukes of Saxony, Brabant and Brunswick, the margraves of Brandenburg and Meißen, the landgrave of Thuringia and the count of Cleves. The 'French' are led by an unnamed king of France, and comprise the kings of 'Spain' (that is, Castile-León) and Navarre, the dukes of Brittany, Lorraine and Burgundy, and the counts of Bar, Blois, Artois and Nevers. Most of the poem is taken up with descriptions of the heraldry and equipment of the participants, but the remainder narrates the action of a conventional tourney.[17]

---

[16] *Rudolfs von Ems Willehalm von Orlens*, ed. Victor Junk (Berlin, 1906) [henceforth cited as *Willehalm von Orlens*, with references to lines]; Helmut Brackert, *Rudolf von Ems: Dichtung und Geschichte* (Heidelberg, 1968), pp. 58–93; William Henry Jackson, 'Warfare in the Works of Rudolf von Ems', in *Writing War: Medieval Literary Responses to Warfare*, ed. Corinne Saunders, Françoise Le Saux and Neil Thomas (Cambridge, 2004), pp. 49–75; Maximilian Benz, 'Heteronomien und Eigensinn. Die Werke Rudolfs von Ems im Spannungsfeld von Politik, Religion und Kunst', in *Mäzenatentum im Mittelalter aus europäischer Perspektive: Von historischen Akteuren zu literarischen Textkonzepten*, ed. Bernd Bastert, Andreas Bihrer and Timo Reuvekamp-Felber (Göttingen, 2017), pp. 105–24.

[17] 'Das Turnier von Nantes', in *Konrad von Würzburg, Kleinere Dichtungen* II, ed. Edward Schröder (Berlin, 1924), pp. 40–75 [henceforth cited as *Turnier von Nantes*, with references to lines]. On dating and interpretations, see: Helmut de Boor, 'Die

5   The most extensive information on tournaments in Germany appears in a work composed in the third quarter of the thirteenth century by Ulrich von Liechtenstein (d. 1275), a lord from the duchy of Styria. The *Frauendienst* (MHG *Vrowen dienst*), a title meaning the 'Service of Ladies', is a unique work which forms a first-person narrative of chivalric adventures containing many interpolated songs and other material.[18] While Germanists no longer regard the work as an autobiography, it must be noted that, unlike *Erec* and *Parzival*, Ulrich's adventures occur within a real historical framework and mention over 170 documented individuals.[19] Moreover, the main activity described in them is participation in different types of tournament. One of these is a new form of Ulrich's own devising, which can be described as a jousting tour, and it is this that has tended to attract the attention of researchers on tournament history, although the form

---

Chronologie der Werke Konrads von Würzburg, insbesondere die Stellung des Turniers von Nantes', *Beiträge zur Geschichte der deutschen Sprache und Literatur* 89 (1967), 210–69; Horst Brunner, 'Das Turnier von Nantes. Konrad von Würzburg, Richard von Cornwall und die deutschen Fürsten', in *De poeticis Medii Aevi quaestiones*, ed. Jürgen Kühnel et al. (Göppingen, 1981), pp. 105–27, reprinted in Brunner, *Annäherungen: Studien zur deutschen Literatur des Mittelalters und der Frühen Neuzeit* (Berlin, 2008), pp. 185–200; Heinz Thomas, 'Das Turnier von Nantes: Ein Lehrgedicht für Hartmann von Habsburg', *Beiträge zur Geschichte der deutschen Sprache und Literatur* 108 (1986), 408–25.

[18] Ulrich von Liechtenstein, *Frauendienst*, ed. Franz Viktor Spechtler, 2nd edn (Göppingen, 2003) [henceforth cited as *Frauendienst*, with references to strophes]. An English translation was published as *Ulrich von Liechtenstein's Service of Ladies*, trans. John W. Thomas (Chapel Hill, 1969), republished in condensed form (Woodbridge, 2004). As Thomas's translations of tournament terminology are sometimes very free, I have preferred to provide my own translations for passages quoted from this text.

[19] Heinz Dopsch, 'Zwischen Dichtung und Politik. Herkunft und Umfeld Ulrichs von Liechtenstein', in *Ich – Ulrich von Liechtenstein: Literatur und Politik im Mittelalter*, ed. Franz Viktor Spechtler and Barbara Maier (Klagenfurt, 1999), pp. 49–105; Gerald Krenn, 'Historische Figuren und/oder Helden der Dichtung? Untersuchungen zu den Personen im Roman Frauendienst', in *Ich – Ulrich von Liechtenstein*, pp. 105–32; Sandra Linden, 'Biographisches und Historisches: Eine Spurensuche zu Ulrich von Liechtenstein', in *Ulrich von Liechtenstein: Leben – Zeit – Werk – Forschung*, ed. Sandra Linden and Christopher Young (Berlin, 2010), pp. 45–98. There are extensive bibliographies of Ulrich's life and work: Klaus M. Schmidt et al., 'Bibliographie zu Ulrich von Liechtenstein', in *Ich – Ulrich von Liechtenstein: Literatur und Politik im Mittelalter*, pp. 495–509, and Sandra Linden, 'Kommentierte Bibliographie zu Ulrich von Liechtenstein', in *Ulrich von Liechtenstein: Leben – Zeit – Werk – Forschung*, pp. 535–86.

is quite atypical of the time.[20] However, in addition, there are extensive descriptions of tourneys at Friesach in Carinthia, Klosterneuburg in the duchy of Austria and Katzelsdorf in the duchy of Styria. Unfortunately these events are undated, but they can be regarded as accurate reflections of tourneys that took place in the southeastern parts of the Holy Roman Empire in the period roughly from 1220 to 1250.

Even though four of the five texts are works of complete fiction (while *Frauendienst* also contains elements of invention), all of them are invaluable in understanding how tourneys were organised and fought. This does not mean that we must uncritically accept everything narrated. Hartmann von Aue and Wolfram von Eschenbach could create a world of sumptuousness and luxury at the stroke of a pen, but in the real world tourneyers did not wear jewel-encrusted armour or carry shields studded with gold. However, these poets' descriptions of organisation and tactics had to be reasonably credible if they were to be at all convincing to patrons and audiences. They give far more detail than the Latin accounts, and precisely because they are told in vernacular language, they also reveal something of the mentality of tourneyers and the appeal of the contests they took part in.

The tourney was the original form of the tournament, in which two opposing forces, each consisting of as many as several hundred knights, fought on horseback over a large area in the course of a day. It originated as a consequence of changes in warfare occurring at the end of the eleventh century. The main fighting forces employed by almost all Western powers at this time were mounted knights equipped with helmets, shields and coats of mail and using spears and swords as their main weapons. The main tactic of a force of knights was the charge, but at the point of impact with their opponents they held their spears near the mid-point of the shaft, wielding them overarm in a stabbing motion. In the Bayeux Tapestry, dating from around 1080, the majority of the Norman knights depicted are shown using the weapon in this manner. Around the year 1100, however, knights developed a new technique: the spear was tucked under the right arm and aimed at an enemy's torso as the charge hit home. This tactical change increased the reach of the weapon, but more importantly, it enabled the knight to harness the speed and weight of his

---

[20] Discussion of Ulrich's two jousting tours is beyond the scope of this essay, but they are treated extensively in Alan V. Murray, 'Tourney, Joust, Foreis and Round Table: Tournament Forms in the *Frauendienst* of Ulrich von Liechtenstein', in *Pleasure and Leisure in the Middle Ages and Early Modern Age: Cultural-Historical Perspectives on Toys, Games, and Entertainment*, ed. Albrecht Classen (Berlin, 2019), pp. 365–94.

horse by concentrating these forces into the spear's point. This new technique proved so effective that the wooden spear soon became thicker and was given protection for the hand. It is conventional in English to refer to this heavier weapon as a lance, although the word *sper* was used for both in Middle High German.

The perfect charge occurred when a group of knights advanced in a very close formation several lines deep, gradually increasing speed to a gallop so that the impact of the entire group was delivered simultaneously. A charge performed well had a good chance of breaking through or dispersing an enemy formation and could thus secure a great initial advantage in any combat. However, it was also important that a unit which suffered such a shock could manage to regroup quickly, an eventuality which knights also needed to practise in order to be fully battle-ready. The tourney mimicked battle tactics, the only significant difference being that participants were not supposed to kill or injure their opponents. It was thus an activity in which two important military skills could be practised in peacetime: maintaining close and orderly formation while delivering a charge, as well as reforming after formations had broken up or retreated away from the enemy.[21]

These actions were not easy to execute. A knight had to ride while holding a shield on his left arm and a lance or sword in the right. The left hand also had to hold the reins, meaning that much of the control of the horse had to be done using the spurs. This was difficult enough, but it became more so because of the nature of knightly combat. The right hand was used to hold the lance fast or cut with the sword, while the shield arm had to parry such blows from opponents. Males from noble and knightly families normally learned to ride from an early age, but it is doubtful whether the multiple skills required in the tourney (as in war) were all learned at once, and in this connection it is worth looking in more detail at another form of military exercise, the *bûhurt* (with the associated verb *bûhurdieren*), which was known in Germany from the mid-twelfth century, although it may have been older than the tourney. Authorities are agreed that it involved riding in formation in the same manner as the tourney, but that it was far less warlike in character. The Germanist Harry Jackson has undertaken the most exhaustive study of the form, which has revealed the key characteristics that distinguished it from the tourney. The *bûhurt* was associated with joyful events such as weddings and knighting ceremonies, but was separate from any tourneys or jousts that were held on the same occasions. Participants always rode in formation, but without helms or

---

[21] Nickel, 'The Tournament: An Historical Sketch'; Rosemary Ascherl, 'The Technology of Chivalry in Reality and Romance', in *The Study of Chivalry*, pp. 263–311.

body armour. They always carried shields and one of the actions involved was using these to push back against opponents. In some cases, lances were also employed, but usually with blunted tips. Jackson states convincingly that 'one function of the *buhurt* was to provide training and exercise in such riding and to accustom men and horses to close physical contact'.[22] One could go further. Riding in formation was one step up from how most young men would have learned to ride, but in the tourney it was also necessary to do this while wielding a shield and lance, which required strength, dexterity and co-ordination. The *bûhurt* was a way of practising these basic requirements without the additional complication of hand-to-hand fighting, and the absence of swords, helmets and body armour meant that participants were obliged to concentrate on control of their mounts and maintaining formation. So just as the tourney was practice for war, so the *bûhurt* was practice for the tourney.

All of the accounts describe the magnificent appearance of the knights as they assembled to tourney. As far as can be established, tourneyers in this period used the same types of weapons and armour that were employed in war. The essential items were a hauberk (*halsberc*) made of mail, a helm and a lance and sword.[23] The saddle (with high cantle and pommel), stirrups, bridle, reins and spurs enabled the knight to sit securely and control his warhorse. However, the rest of their equipment was often more costly and elaborate than was normal on military campaigns.[24] Lances were painted in bright colours and, since many would be required, they were brought to the venue by squires in bundles, or greater numbers were carried by wagon.[25] A key element of decoration was heraldry. The armorial device of the bearer was shown on the shield, but also on the surcoat (*wâpencleit, wâpenroc*) and sometimes also on the horse trappings (*decke*) which were made of textiles. The crest (*zimîr*), that is the decoration on top of the helm, was often made of hardened leather or of metal horns, both offering an additional level of protection against sword

---

[22] William Henry Jackson, 'Lance and Shield in the *buhurt*', in *German Narrative Literature of the Twelfth and Thirteenth Centuries*, ed. Volker Honemann (Tübingen, 1994), pp. 39–51 (here 45).

[23] Claude Blair, *European Armour, circa 1066 to circa 1700* (London, 1958), pp. 19–36; Leslie Southwick, 'The Great Helm in England', *Arms & Armour* 3 (2006), 5–77. The articles by Jürgen Krüger, 'Das Rittertum', and 'Kampf und Krieg', in *Das Nibelungenlied und seine Welt*, pp. 70–75, 159–62 give excellent illustrations of knightly equipment of the period.

[24] *Frauendienst* 999–1001.

[25] *Erec* 735, 2335, 2351; *Parzival* 59,5, 61,23; *Willehalm von Orlens* 6402, 7436.

blows to the head. Alternatively it consisted of wings or plumes made from eagle or peacock feathers.[26] Sometimes the crest reproduced the arms on the shield, but often it was a distinctive figure, such as a beast. Surcoats might become torn or stained, while shields, which were mostly made of wood with some metal strengthening, might be hacked to pieces or discarded, and so crests were the most visible means of identifying combatants. Thus at Kanvoleis, Gahmuret recognises his own cousin Kaylet, king of Spain, by his ostrich crest.[27] In fact, before the tourney he assures Kaylet that he will assist him against his opponents, but in making this statement he uses armorial devices to designate the three main protagonists: an ostrich and serpent's head for Kaylet, a demi-griffon for Hardiz, king of Gascony, and an anchor for himself. Thus each tourneyer is personified by his crest.[28]

The areas in which German tourneys were fought seem to have been rather more restricted than in France, where contests were often held over a distance of several miles between two named villages. In the examples discussed, the events took place outside a town or castle, where there was a considerable infrastructure of accommodation and suppliers of food in addition to what knights might bring with them in the way of tents and provisions. These were certainly needed. In addition to the knight's warhorse (*ors*, *ros*), which was normally ridden only in battle or tournaments, a palfrey would be required for each knight, squire or groom to travel, with additional packhorses for equipment. A knight would require at least one servant to help him arm and have

---

[26] *Frauendienst* 244, 258–59, 998; *Willehalm von Orlens* 5997–6009; *Turnier von Nantes* 409–20, 442–43, 452–53, 488–91, 996–98; Blair, *European Armour*, pp. 181–83; Lutz Fenske, 'Adel und Rittertum im Spiegel früher heraldischer Formen und deren Entwicklung', in *Das ritterliche Turnier im Mittelalter*, pp. 75–160; Heiko Hartmann, 'Heraldische Motive und ihre narrative Funktion in den Werken Wolframs von Eschenbach', in *Wolfram von Eschenbach – Bilanzen und Perspektiven: Eichstätter Kolloquium 2000*, ed. Wolfgang Haubrichs, Eckart Conrad Lutz and Klaus Ridder (Berlin, 2002), pp. 157–81; Hartmann, 'Tiere in der historischen und literarischen Heraldik des Mittelalters. Ein Aufriß', in *Tiere und Fabelwesen im Mittelalter*, ed. Sabine Obermaier (Berlin, 2009), pp. 147–79; Haiko Wandhoff, 'Schwarz auf Weiß – Rot auf Weiß. Heraldische Tinkturen und die Farben der Schrift im Parzival Wolframs von Eschenbach', in *Die Farben imaginierter Welten: Zur Kulturgeschichte ihrer Codierung in Literatur und Kunst vom Mittelalter bis zur Gegenwart*, ed. Monika Schausten (Berlin, 2012), pp. 147–67.

[27] *Parzival* 50,1–6, 72, 29–30.

[28] *Parzival* 68,3–11: *dô sprach der künec von Zazamanc / 'dune dir mîn dienst hie zêren tuot. / wir sulen haben einen muot. / stêt dîn strûz noch sunder nest? / du solt dîn sarapandratest / gein sînem halben grîfen tragn. / mîn anker vaste wirt geslagn / durch lenden in sîns poinders hurt'*.

replacement equipment (such as lances) ready, and in most cases, another to look after the horses.[29] Of course, the greater lords are likely to have brought greater numbers of servants and other followers, such as musicians, who are often mentioned. If we accept Ulrich von Liechtenstein's figure of some 600 knights present at the tourney at Friesach, then a conservative estimate of the total numbers of attenders would be some 1,200 to 1,800 knights and service personnel accompanied by an even greater number of horses. Such numbers presented challenges of logistics, and a significant role in the running of tournaments was played by a class of people known as *kroyierer* or *grogierer*, literally 'cryers'. They acted like stewards at modern sporting events, directing participants to the right locations, but they are also recorded as going around summoning tourneyers and jousters at the start of the day and shouting encouragement during the combats.[30]

Tourneys might be impromptu events, as at Würzburg in 1127, but mostly they seem to have been arranged well in advance in order to attract the largest number of participants and give them ample time to prepare. Often they were held in connection with festivities such as weddings or knighting ceremonies.[31] This meant that large numbers of lords and knights had arrived at the venue of the tourney before it was due to take place. Many of them would be keen to try out their skills, and so the day before (or several days) was often devoted to jousting, the other main tournament form, which consisted of a series of combats between pairs of knights, as opposed to the mass combat of the tourney.[32] Our sources indicate that the MHG word *tjoste* was originally not restricted to tournaments; rather, it could denote any form of single combat, whether in warfare or not. Thus in *Erec* it is used to describe combats as diverse as attacks on the protagonist by a robber and a single combat in which Erec might forfeit his head to the grim and fearsome Red Knight Mabonagrin if he should

---

[29] Bumke, *Höfische Kultur*, 1: 236–40.

[30] *Parzival* 81,12–13; *Willehalm von Orlens* 6397–6400, 6462–71, 6745–53, 7453–69, 7821–23, 7965–71; *Frauendienst* 205,1–4, 220,1–3, 243,7–8, 256,1–8. The *kroyierer* are distinguished from squires (*knappen*) and pages (*garzûne*). This term is sometimes translated as 'heralds'. However, a herald was a relatively high-status individual whose main responsibility was matters involving coats of arms. These might involve officiating at tournaments, but known holders of the office date from later than the period under discussion. The *kroyierer* seem to have been a relatively low-status group of itinerants (*lantvarer*): Schultz, *Das höfische Leben zur Zeit der Minnesinger*, pp. 124–25.

[31] Bumke, *Höfische Kultur*, 1: 348–50.

[32] *Erec* 2421, 2455, 2774.

lose.³³ In *Parzival* it is often used of encounters between single knights in the countryside in which the initial charge with lances is followed by combat with swords.³⁴ On one occasion Wolfram uses the expression 'warlike joust' (*striteclicher tjost*) to make clear that he is talking about warfare rather than a tournament.³⁵

In the context of the tournament, however, jousting was relatively circumscribed in scope. Two knights charged each other with the aim of unhorsing their opponent or breaking a lance on him as an indication of having made a good strike; it is this aspect that is denoted by the verb *stechen*. They did not carry on fighting with other weapons if lances were broken, although lances could be replaced if more than one course was run. Jousters might agree a number of courses beforehand, or simply continue until one or both agreed to stop, or seek new challengers. Ulrich claims to have broken thirty lances in a single day's jousting at Friesach.³⁶ Hollywood films have produced a recurrent image of a highly regulated sporting event held in a designated ground surrounded by grandstands filled with cheering spectators, and a high-status presider and heralds directing proceedings and eventually acclaiming a victor. This may have been the pattern once the joust emerged as a discrete event, which was considerably later, but the jousting that preceded the tourney in the period under discussion here was largely informal, and provided entertainment for those assembled for the tourney, rather than non-participant spectators.³⁷

This preliminary jousting was often referred to as a 'vesper tournament' (*vesperie*) because it took place on the eve of the actual tourney.³⁸ However, it might go on for longer than a single day. The tourney at Friesach occurred on the occasion of a peace conference involving Leopold VI, duke of Austria (1198–1230), Bernhard II, duke of Carinthia (1202–56), and Heinrich IV of Andechs, margrave of Istria (d. 1228), which had been arranged in May on St Philip's Day. Unfortunately Ulrich does not specify the year, but the wealth of detail given by him indicates that it refers to real events that occurred during the period 1220–24.³⁹ It was also attended by many of the princes and lords

---

[33] *Erec* 3209, 3388, 6904, 6913, 7005, 9102.

[34] *Parzival* 679–80, 739.

[35] *Parzival* 43,15.

[36] *Frauendienst* 213,1–2.

[37] The circumstances and chronology of the joust appearing as a distinct tournament form in its own right are still not fully clarified and require further research.

[38] *Parzival* 86,21, 95,17; *Willehalm von Orlens* 7330–31, 7340–41, 7350, 7518–22, 8439, 8499–8500.

[39] Krenn, 'Historische Figuren und/oder Helden der Dichtung?', pp. 118–19.

of the southeastern part of the Holy Roman Empire along with their vassals. The various retinues present amounted to some 600 knights.[40] Many of these men clearly grew tired of kicking their heels while the principals were cooped up in negotiations, and so they started a series of jousts for their own entertainment. The jousters were not immune from injury; many suffered wounds, concussion or fractures.[41] However, this form of jousting consisted of a series of short encounters requiring limited bursts of energy and concentration, with the action involving striking with lances only. Those who were not wounded could easily continue later, and Ulrich states that the jousting went on for ten days. Only then did the princes insist that the jousting cease and a proper tourney be held on the following Monday.[42] When Willehalm receives the accolade of knighthood, his new status is immediately celebrated by the holding of a *bûhurt*, then after more festivities a tourney is announced. However, before it begins there is a considerable amount of jousting, which takes up approximately half the length of the entire description of the event.[43] Soon afterwards, another tourney is proclaimed, with a sparrowhawk as the prize for the best knight. Two thousand knights turn up, who are then divided into two sides, but they spend an entire day in jousting before the main event.[44] A third tourney is proclaimed soon after, but several of the lords who have assembled protest that it should not start until the arrival of others who are expected, so the intervening time is taken up with jousting.[45]

By far the most fanciful description of a tourney is given in Book II of *Parzival*, which contains a description of a tourney at the city of Kanvoleis proclaimed by Herzeloyde, queen of Norgals and Waleis, who has offered her own hand in marriage along with her two kingdoms to whoever is recognised as the victor. Prizes or other distinctions are known to have been given in tourneys, but Herzeloyde's offer is just as fantastic as the existence of her kingdoms.[46] Nevertheless, even this episode confirms the place of jousting as a preliminary event. While participants are still arriving there are already a number of jousts in progress.[47] Wolfram ingeniously has this jousting grad-

---

[40] *Frauendienst* 177–200.
[41] *Frauendienst* 209, 225, 236.
[42] *Frauendienst* 237–43.
[43] *Willehalm von Orlens* 5743–5884 (knighting and *bûhurt*), 6195–31, 6336–6488 (jousting), 6529–6826 (tourney).
[44] *Willehalm von Orlens* 7096–7770.
[45] *Willehalm von Orlens* 8379–8527.
[46] *Parzival* 60,9–17.
[47] *Parzival* 68,19–28.

ually draw in more and more of the retinues of the kings and lords present until a mass combat takes place. Herzeloyde is so impressed by Gahmuret's performance that she declares there is no need to hold the formal tourney, since he has distinguished himself above all others in the fighting.

Before the tourney could commence, the participants were divided up into two sides of roughly equal strength (a process described by the verb *teilen*).[48] The basic building blocks were the retinues of the princes and lords present, which would naturally be of varying sizes. The process can be illustrated by the division carried out for the Monday tourney at Friesach as described by Ulrich von Liechtenstein (Table 1), which is an important case in point because most of the retinue leaders can be identified as historical personages:[49]

The fact that each side in this case had exactly the same number of knights is perhaps suspicious, especially since it is unclear whether the number for each retinue includes its leader (who was present on the field), but the division shows the principle of fairness, and the totals give a reasonably realistic idea of the usual orders of magnitude. Each of the two sides was thus made up of a number of companies (*scharen*, *rotten*), each with its own commander (*rotmaister*), although the smaller retinues must have been combined with larger ones in order to avoid the possibility of any of them being overwhelmed by greater enemy companies. Thus Diepold of Vohburg, who had an unviable retinue of only twelve, seems to have been given some of Leopold of Austria's knights to make up a larger company.[50] On the day of the tourney it was usual for participants to attend mass, which is perhaps ironic given the Church's opposition to tournaments, but shows how little its prohibitions took effect.[51] The companies then paraded to the designated ground and formed up, sometimes accompanied by music.[52]

Friesach was notable for the large number of companies assembled. At Katzelsdorf, by contrast, there were only four companies in total, formed

---

[48] *Frauendienst* 1013–14, 1572–74, 1581–85; *Willehalm von Orlens* 6526–28, 6584–85, 7241–42, 8345–48.

[49] *Frauendienst* 246–54. Listing of the company commanders was carried out on the basis of the prosopographical information given by Krenn, 'Historische Figuren und/oder Helden der Dichtung?'.

[50] *Frauendienst* 246–54, 283–84.

[51] *Erec* 661–67, 2541–43; *Frauendienst* 255, 1012.

[52] *Frauendienst* 255–58; *Willehalm von Orlens* 6030–36; *Turnier von Nantes* 710–15.

Table 1. Numbers of Knights at the Friesach Tourney.

Duke of Austria's side	No. of knights	Margrave of Istria's side	No. of knights
Leopold VI, duke of Austria	100	Heinrich, margrave of Istria	60
Diebold, margrave of Vohburg	12	Bernhard II, duke of Carinthia	50
Albrecht III, count of Tirol	40	Meinhard III, count of Görz	55
Hugo von Taufers	23	count of Hainburg	32
Otto von Lengenbach	22	lord of Lebenau	25
Reinbert von Mureck	40	Hermann, count of Ortenburg	8
Hadmar von Kuenringe	31	Hartnit von Ort	36
Hermann von Kranichberg	20	Wulfing von Stubenberg	34
Wolfger von Gars	12		
Total	**300**		**300**

from a greater number of smaller retinues of vassals.[53] Each of the companies making up each side could manoeuvre independently; they might charge straight away against their opponents, or they could hold back in order to strike at the most favourable moment. However, knights did not always stay in formations; sometimes individuals rode out ahead of their companies in the hope of challenging others from their opponents.[54] Thus, the second tourney in *Willehalm von Orlens* begins with both Willehalm and Diebald von Gahgunie each charging out against each other and breaking lances; only then do the assembled companies clash.[55] At the tourney to celebrate his wedding Erec

---

[53] *Frauendienst* 1585.

[54] This practice was also known in warfare. See Martin H. Jones, 'Die tjostiure uz vünf scharn (*Willehalm* 362,3)', in *Studien zu Wolfram von Eschenbach: Festschrift für Werner Schröder zum 75. Geburtstag*, ed. Kurt Gärtner and Joachim Heinzle (Tübingen, 1989), pp. 429–41.

[55] *Willehalm von Orlens* 7643–48, 7652–60.

goes forth in order to carry out the 'first joust' (*daz er die ērsten tjost næme*); immediately two knights from the opposing side ride out against him. He unhorses both of them, and in total breaks twelve lances 'between the companies' (*enzwischen den scharn*). This practice, regularly described as jousting even though it occurred during a tourney, offered an opportunity to gain renown as any such deeds done would be more obvious in the open than in the close combat that often followed the initial charge.[56] However, it was often discouraged by commanders, as the temptation to seek personal glory could disrupt the ordered formations. Thus at Friesach, Ulrich describes how Hadamar von Kuenring shouted to his men as they were approached by the company of Wulfing von Stubenberg:

> 'Now form up close together!
> Do you see how that company is coming
> towards us with their lances?
> They want to prevent us from jousting,
> so be thankful for that.
> Let us not charge for too long,
> but get stuck into them.
> That will harm them and help us!'[57]

The purpose of such instructions was to be sure of delivering a disciplined and shattering charge against an opposing unit, and Ulrich's description of the start of the tourney at Katzelsdorf emphasises the importance of keeping close together, just as would be done in war:

> The prince of Austria's retinue
> Formed up chivalrously
> And the company of the lord of Maißau
> joined them there.
> Those in the company that was to begin the tourney
> Trotted alongside each other
> and kept together well,
> as one should do when facing enemies.[58]

---

[56] *Erec* 2415–34, 2584–91, 2600; *Turnier von Nantes* 746, 759.

[57] *Frauendienst* 263: *Nu drucket iuch zesamen gar! / seht ir, wie ritterlich diu schar / gegen uns dort stapfet mit den spern? / si wellent uns tyostirens wern, / des hab ir manlich herze danc. / nu machet den puneiz niht lanc und seht, daz wir si vast an komen, / daz mag in geschaden und uns gefromen!*

[58] *Frauendienst* 1586: *Des fürsten gesinde uz Oesterrich / die scharten sich do ritterlich, / zuo den sich scharn da began / von Missowe der vil biderbe man. / diu schar, diu den*

If a company could maintain a tight formation and build up a greater momentum than the opposing unit, the force of the collision (*puneiz*) might be so great that the opponents could be driven back in disorder or even broken through.[59] At Friesach Hartnit von Ort and his men successively drove through three opposing companies.[60] If both sides held firm, the effect of their clash might be that each company immediately fell back and tried to reform and turn around for a fresh charge.[61] This was not an easy manoeuvre to pull off, as they might be attacked by a fresh enemy squadron before good order could be restored.[62] In the majority of cases, however, it was likely that both formations broke up into a close combat mêlée (*mâlie*) fought with swords. The impact of the charge was such that many lances were broken; all of the texts mention how the splintered shafts (*trunzûne*) went flying all around. A lance which remained intact would be difficult to wield in the throng, and would best be discarded unless the knight intended to fall back and regroup immediately. Ulrich von Liechtenstein gives a good description of what occurred after two companies collided:

There was a great crash of lances,
and many a mighty thrust
with shields here and there
which caused swollen knees.
Many a brave man received
wounds and bruises from lances,
and suffered pain and injury
from grappling.

They pressed this way, they pressed that way,
and tried to turn about;
many had lost their helms;
while others tried to seize reins
in the great throng of knights.
Many a sword rang out on a helm
of those being attacked

---

turney solde heben, / si stapften bi einander eben / und habten sich zesamne wol, / als man ze rehte gegen vienden sol.

[59] *Frauendienst* 279, 1067; *Willehalm von Orlens* 6724–33, 6785–90.
[60] *Frauendienst* 269.
[61] *Frauendienst* 270.
[62] *Frauendienst* 271.

and many shields were broken apart
from the mighty blows.⁶³

Tourneying was a dangerous business, and much more so than jousting. The force of the initial impact would throw many knights from their horses, with the risk of trauma injuries, and once on the ground they were in danger of being trampled by the horses of friend and foe alike. In one of his many descriptions of hard-fought mêlées Rudolf von Ems describes how 'many a knight was felled, and trampled and struck' while many more are taken captive.⁶⁴ The main thing that distinguished the tourney from warfare was that opponents were not supposed to be killed or wounded, but captured. So while the charge practised riding in the formations required in battle, the opportunities for material gain were to be found in the mêlée fighting that followed it.

There were various methods of capturing opponents. Most commonly knights would strike an opponent with sword blows until he surrendered. The shield was often hacked into pieces.⁶⁵ Metal helms and coats of mail offered better protection, but one should not underestimate the psychological effects of repeated blows raining down on the head and body. Swords were used to deliver grim, fearsome strikes, which could be compared to hammer blows producing sparks from an anvil.⁶⁶ Sometimes close combat would develop into a form of grappling, in which a knight tried to wrestle an opponent to the ground or force off his helm, both of which would render him especially vulnerable.⁶⁷ This tactic can be seen in an illustration accompanying the poems of Heinrich I, duke of Anhalt, in the Codex Manesse, a song manuscript dating from around 1300. It shows three fully armoured knights striking three opponents with their swords as they try to hold them fast around their necks. Only one of the latter is wearing a helm; the implication is that the helms of

---

⁶³ *Frauendienst* 266–67: *Der spere chrach was da groz, / mit schilden manic grozer stoz / wart gestozen dort und hie, / da von geswellen muosten knie, / piule, wunden da gewan / von spern vil manic biderb man, / mit ringen tatens we ir liden, der wart vil manegez da verriden // Si drungen her, si drungen hin, / uf umbekeren stuont ir sin, / da manger helm vil ab brach; / den andern den man zoumen sach, / um den von rittern was gedranc. / manic swert uf helm erclanc, / vil schilde man da bresten sach, / von grozen stoezen das geschach.*

⁶⁴ *Willehlam von Orlens* 7698–99: *Da wart vil ritter ab gevalt, / getretten und gestossen.* Also lines 7690–7722 for many instances of captures.

⁶⁵ *Turnier von Nantes* 923–25.

⁶⁶ *Turnier von Nantes* 794–99: *dô sprungen fiures flammen / ûz helmen alsô grôze / als ûf dem anebôze / die gneisten von dem îsen, / golt und gesteine rîsen / begunde nider ûf den plân.*

⁶⁷ *Parzival* 73,18–28; *Turnier von Nantes* 920–21, 1080–81.

the other two have been forced off, while all six seem to have either lost their shields or discarded them, the better to get to grips with their opponents.[68]

A more specialised tactic, mentioned in the quotation above, was to seize the reins or bridle of an opponent's horse and lead it away, a practice known by the verb *zoumen* (< *zoum* 'bridle').[69] The *Turnier von Nantes* describes how in the mêlée knights try to seize the reins of their opponents, with many of them being knocked out of saddles and stirrups during the struggles.[70] A Frenchman seizes the bridle of the duke of Saxony, leads his horse away and ties it to a tree at the edge of the tourneying field.[71] At Friesach, Count Meinhard of Görz made straight for Leopold of Austria, grasped the bridle of his horse and managed to knock off his helm. The duke was in danger of being captured, but he was rescued by his ally Diepold of Vohburg, who was leading some of Leopold's men. Meinhard's company was now surrounded, but in turn Rudolf von Ras and Heinrich von Lienz broke through to reach him, and both sides retired to regroup.[72] Such tactics were not regarded as underhand. Indeed, it was perfectly acceptable for knights to converge on isolated opponents or smaller groups, or for multiple companies to launch joint attacks on single units.[73]

In some cases there was a demarcated safe area (*hamît* or *vride*) on each side where knights could ride to recover or re-equip themselves.[74] At Friesach Wolfger von Gars broke twenty lances and Dietmar von Liechtenstein broke twenty-five. They must have had plentiful replacements available on the day as well as squires visible and ready to hand them over when required.[75] During the tourney at Kanvoleis, Gahmuret rides back to such an area to find a fresh

---

[68] Heidelberg, Universitätsbibliothek, MS Cod. Pal. germ. 848, fol. 17r, available at https://digi.ub.uni–heidelberg.de/diglit/cpg848 [last accessed on 6 September 2019].

[69] *Willehalm von Orlens* 7665–69.

[70] *Turnier von Nantes* 824–27: *der eine den der ander disen / bî sîme zügel schiere greif. / dô wart vil manic stegereif / erlæret unde satelboge*. See also *Turnier von Nantes* 1060–61.

[71] *Turnier von Nantes* 828–33, 896–97.

[72] *Frauendienst* 283–84.

[73] *Frauendienst* 278.

[74] *Erec* 2630, 2703, 2765; *Parzival* 114,27; *Willehalm von Orlens* 7790–92, 7799.

[75] *Frauendienst* 289, 292.

horse and uses the opportunity to take off his helm.[76] By the 1180s the conical helmet with nose guard (as shown on the Bayeux Tapestry) was giving way to other types of helm which completely enclosed the head, with horizontal slits for the eyes and small holes for ventilation. A helm gave excellent protection but offered poor all-round visibility, and it became stifling for its wearer in the course of several hours' fighting. Erec withdraws from the tourney to rest for a time; he dismounts, removes his helm and loosens the mail coif worn under it in order to cool down; yet when he sees his own side retreating he rushes back into the fighting without the helm. This would have been a foolhardy deed and shows us one of the limits of a literary text.[77]

Captives were expected to give surety (*sicherheit*) and leave the field, making arrangements to have themselves ransomed once fighting had ceased.[78] At Friesach a lord of Königsberg was praised for having captured five knights, which suggests that this was a notable achievement.[79] Ulrich tells how most of the captives had to borrow money from the Jews of Friesach to redeem themselves.[80] Captured horses were often retained, however. Hartmann's narrator comments on the unusual conduct of Erec who, at his wedding tourney, releases the many horses he has taken without ransom, as he is fighting for fame rather than gain.[81] While jousting might go on for several days (as occurred at Friesach), after a day's tourneying the majority of knights and their horses would have been exhausted and many of them possibly injured. Thus a tourney normally only lasted for a single day.

The tourney originated as a form of training and exercising knightly retinues in the tactics that were most effective in warfare. However, in the way that it was practised there was much that ran counter to the demands of group discipline. The prospect of winning ransoms or capturing valuable warhorses was a major incentive for participants, but as far as the vernacular descriptions indicate, knights preferred to secure such gains as individuals or in small groups. Even those who disdained material gain might seek to enhance their reputations as knights on the tourney field, but their deeds could be best witnessed by fellow participants and spectators if they engaged in single combats, which explains the practice of jousting 'between the companies'. The increasing use of heraldry, which identified its unique bearer rather than the team,

---

[76] *Parzival* 75,23–25.
[77] *Erec* 2630–50.
[78] *Frauendienst* 306, 311; *Parzival* 85,5–8.
[79] *Frauendienst* 291.
[80] *Frauendienst* 311.
[81] *Erec* 2614–24.

is another indication of the focus on individual achievement. This shows that there was always an inherent tension in the tourney between a common need for discipline and an individual desire for honour or gain, and it was undoubtedly this contradiction that gave rise to the development of new forms in the course of the thirteenth century, such as the Arthurian-themed Round Tables and the *pas d'armes*, which showcased the prowess of individuals through jousting and offered a greater level of entertainment for spectators. There was more than one way of winning at tournaments.

2   *Por pris et por enor:* Ideas of Honour as Reflected in the Medieval Tournament

James Titterton

The anthropologist Julian Pitt-Rivers defined honour as an individual's 'estimation of his own worth, his *claim* to pride, but it is also the acknowledgment of that claim, his excellence recognized by society, his *right* to pride'.[1] Frank Stewart Henderson proposed an even simpler definition, describing honour as 'the right to be treated as having a certain worth'.[2] This 'right' must be accepted and acknowledged by others or else the individual will appear contemptible and ridiculous.[3] It must also be protected, even to the point of forcing others to acknowledge it through acts of violence, which Pitt-Rivers described as 'the ultimate vindication' of honour.[4] Failure to respond to such a challenge could itself strip the individual of their honour.[5]

Notions of honour also have a powerful normative influence on societies. Through ritual and ceremonial acknowledgement of certain individuals who possess this 'right', social and cultural norms are reinforced:

> Regardless of private feelings they serve to establish the consensus of the society with regard to the order of precedence; they demonstrate what is acceptable by reference to what is accepted. If the honour felt by the individual becomes honour paid by the society, it is equally the case that the honour which is paid by the society sets the standards for what the individual should feel.[6]

---

[1] Julian Pitt-Rivers, 'Honour and Social Status', in *Honour and Shame: The Values of Mediterranean Society,* ed. J. G. Peristiany (London, 1966), pp. 19–78 (p. 21).

[2] Frank Henderson Stewart, *Honor* (Chicago, 1994), p. 21.

[3] Pitt-Rivers, 'Honour and Social Status', p. 22.

[4] Pitt-Rivers, 'Honour and Social Status', p. 29.

[5] Stewart, *Honor*, pp. 64–69.

[6] Pitt-Rivers, 'Honour and Social Status', p. 38.

For example, a modern state awarding military medals for gallantry reinforces cultural values of courage, duty and self-sacrifice.

Although Pitt-Rivers and Stewart based their theories on studies of twentieth-century Andalusian and Bedouin culture, respectively, their conclusions provide a useful framework for discussing historical notions of honour. In this essay, I will discuss how the medieval tournament enabled the knighthood of western Europe to establish their 'right' to be treated as worthy; that is, to stake their 'claim to pride' before their peers. I will discuss the language and phrasing used by contemporary sources to describe honour in the context of a tournament, before considering the specific actions by which individuals or groups could demonstrate or claim honour.

The Language of Honour in the Medieval West

The literature of the medieval aristocracy is suffused with the language of honour. It portrays a culture obsessed with reputation, with individual and collective pride, with avoiding shame and taking forceful, frequently violent, revenge for insults. Yet this very ubiquity makes it difficult to study. There are many synonyms for honour and many ways of employing them.[7] For the purposes of this study, I have chosen to conduct a brief survey of the vocabulary used for honour in my main sources, followed by an analysis of the Old French word *pris*, a common synonym with particular relevance to tournament studies.

Yvonne Robreau has demonstrated just how complex medieval notions of honour could be through an exhaustive study of honour and shame in the fourteenth-century Lancelot-Grail Cycle. Honour is expressed as something 'interior', a matter of an individual's worth, that must be defended and protected from insults.[8] Yet it is also spoken of as an abstract commodity that can be gained or lost through actions.[9] Furthermore, honour can be a verb: one could 'do honour' to another, by surrendering to a superior opponent in combat, by welcoming them with appropriate ceremony or by giving suitable gifts.[10] There are also a number of other words with parallel or similar meanings, such as *gloire*, *nom*, *renom*, *los*, *hautesce*, *digneté* and *pris*.

---

[7] For a discussion of these difficulties, see Natasha Hodgson, 'Honour, Shame and the Fourth Crusade', *Journal of Medieval History* 39 (2013), 220–39 (p. 223).

[8] Yvonne Robreau, *L'honneur et la honte: Leur expression dans les romans en prose du Lancelot-Graal (XIIe–XIIIe siècles)* (Geneva, 1981), pp. 26–30.

[9] Robreau, *L'honneur*, pp. 30–37.

[10] Robreau, *L'honneur*, pp. 43–58.

All of these ideas can also be found in the literature discussed below. Chrétien de Troyes describes a knight who performed well in a tournament as one who possessed 'renown', or who had 'revealed his prowess'.[11] The anonymous poet who composed the epic poem celebrating the life of William Marshal, the great tournament champion of his age, depicts the young Marshal going to tournaments in order 'to seek' honour and 'winning' it by performing feats of arms.[12] *The Book of Deeds of My Good Lord Jean Le Maingre, called Boucicaut*, an anonymous prose biography of Boucicaut, marshal of France and a famous jouster (1366–1421), describes how he and his two companions 'received great honour from the king and knighthood of France' for the tournament they held at Saint-Ingelvert in 1390, in which they jousted against all comers.[13]

The use of *pris* in a tournament context is especially noteworthy for the present study. It is derived from the Latin *pretium*, which means 'money, wealth; worth, value, price' or 'reward; wages'.[14] This meaning was retained in Old French, where it could be used for the 'reward accorded to the victor in a chivalrous combat'.[15] It is the origin of the modern French *prix* and the English 'prize' and could be used in this sense in medieval tournaments.[16] Take, for example, the ordinances for a tournament to be held at Smithfield in London in 1390, recorded by Jean Froissart:

> And on the Monday, in the same place, sixty knights would come and joust in courtly fashion with blunted lances, and the one who jousted best among those without should expect to have for the *pris* a rich golden crown, and the one among those who were within who attended and jousted best would have a rich golden clasp.[17]

---

[11] Chrétien de Troyes, *Eric et Enide*, ed. Mario Roques (Paris, 1973), line 2162: *por ce que sa proecsce apeire*; line 2207: *Or fu Erec de tel renon*.

[12] *The History of William Marshal*, ed. A. J. Holden, 3 vols (London, 2006), I, line 2998: *Ert la venuz por son pris quere*; line 3012: *Qui onor conquert e gaaine*.

[13] *Le Livre des fais du bon messire Jehan Le Maingre, dit Bouciquaut, mareschal de France et gouverneur de Jennes*, ed. Denis Lalande (Geneva, 1985), p. 73: 'Si en sailli a tres grant honneur du roy et de la chevalerie de France'.

[14] 'Pretium', in Charlton T. Lewis and Charles Short, *A Latin Dictionary* (Oxford, 1879), p. 1442.

[15] 'Prix', in Robert Martin, *Dictionnaire du Moyen Français (1330–1500)* <http://www.atilf.fr/dmf/definition/prix> [Accessed 20 March 2018].

[16] 'Price, n.', in *OED Online* <http://www.oed.com/view/Entry/151135?> [Accessed 20 March 2018].

[17] *Oeuvres de Froissart: Chroniques*, ed. by Kervyn de Lettenhove, 25 vols (Osnabrück, 1967), XIV, p. 254: *Et le lundi seroient à celle meismes place les soixante chevalliers venans et jousteroient de lances à rochets courtoisement, et le mieulx joustant de ceulx de*

The word is not used exclusively for material objects, however. *Pris* also had a figurative meaning: 'value (moral, intellectual ...) attached to something or someone'.[18] The *Anglo-Norman Dictionary* gives the following possible definitions: 'esteem, renown; elite, flower, most esteemed one'.[19] This raises the question of how we should interpret statements such as the following, taken from the *History of William Marshal*:

> The Marshal, who had come there from another land to seek *pris* for himself, did such great feats of arms (this is the point), that there was no nobleman at the tournament, neither count nor baron nor youth, who did not wish to resemble him in feats of arms.[20]

We might interpret this as a statement that the Marshal came to the tournament to win prizes, such as the crown or clasp offered at Smithfield, but the mass tourneys of the twelfth century do not appear to have regularly awarded specific objects of this kind. According to the *History*, after a tournament held at Pleurs in 1178, a noblewoman presented Hugh III, duke of Burgundy, with a magnificent pike but he was unsure what to do with the fish. It was only when Philip I, count of Flanders, suggested that it be 'turned into a swan' and sent to the 'most worthy' competitor at the tournament that it became a 'prize' in the modern sense.[21] The material objects that competitors hoped to win at these events were no mere tokens: they were arms, horses and prisoners, to be sold or ransomed for cash. This distinction can be seen in a description of another tournament, held at Yonne c. 1178, from the *History*:

> It was plain to see that they could win much, but it was well-known, that whoever lost or won *pris*, that the Marshal had the *pris* and he had taken part of the booty too; but he very generously divided it with crusaders and

---

dehors c'est-à-entendre des chevalliers aroit pour le pris une couronne d'or très-riche, et celluy de dedens qui mieulx attendroit et jousteroit à l'examen des dames qui là présentes seroient en chambres et sur hours en accompaignant la royne d'Angleterre, et des hérauls qui ce verroient et jugeroient, auroit pour le pris ung fremail d'or très-riche.

[18] 'Prix', in Martin, *Dictionnaire du Moyen Français*.

[19] 'Pris', in *Anglo-Norman Dictionary (AND)*, online edition <http://www.anglo-norman.net/D/pris[1]> [Accessed 20 March 2018].

[20] *Marshal*, I, lines 2997–3002: *Li Mareschals, qui d'autre terre / Ert la venuz por son pris quere, / i fist tant d'armes, c'est la some, / Qu'el torneiement n'out halt home, / Conte, baron ne bacheler, / Qui d'armes nel volsist sembler.*

[21] The reference to a swan is probably a rather desperate rhyme by the poet: *un cigne* to rhyme with *plus digne*. *Marshal*, I, lines 3071–77.

prisoners, and released from their prisons many knights whom he had taken. He received great *pris* for what he did at that tournament.[22]

Here the poet draws a clear distinction between *le pris* (note the definite article) and more general booty, *gaaing*, of which the Marshal captured only part. A competitor could personally win or lose quantities of the intangible *pris* (surely a synonym for honour) but the one who was judged to be the best of them all was said to have 'won *le pris*'.[23] But winning *le pris* was itself determined by successfully defeating and capturing members of the opposing team, an effective means of gathering *pris* in the material sense. There is also a clear lexical link between *pris* and *prise*, the act of seizure or capture: one may seize honour and, indeed, seize it through the violent seizure of booty.[24] The Marshal then subsequently acquires even more intangible *pris* by generously dividing his material winnings with other competitors, as will be discussed below.

The meaning of *pris* appears to have evolved with the tournament. In the early period, it was an ambiguous term for both the booty that could be won on the field and the honour acquired through doing so, which would sometimes be acknowledged with a physical token. Later, when capturing booty ceased to be a dominant feature of the tournament, the honour and the token became synonymous. Froissart describes a tournament held at Paris in 1389 to celebrate the coronation of Isabel of Bavaria, queen of France:

> Now I wish to name for you the knights who were in that company and who called themselves the Knights of the Golden Sunbeam. And although this was the king's device for those days, it was worn by the king [Charles VI] and those who were without, and he jousted like the rest for a while, so that he himself might have a chance to win the *pris* through deeds of arms.[25]

---

[22] *Marshal*, I, lines 3553–62: *Molt gaaingnierent a veüe, / Mes bien fu la chose seüe, / Qui perdist ne qui que fust pris, / Que li Mareschal out le pris / E de gaaing rout il sa part; / Mais molt largement le depart / E as croisiez e as prisons, / E molt quita de lor prisons / Des chevalers qu'il aveit pris, / Qu'en li torna a grant pris.*

[23] A modern analogy might be the team member named as 'man of the match' or 'most valuable player'.

[24] 'Prise', *AND* online edition. Compare the historical English noun *prise*, which could mean both a 'blast on the hunting horn indicating that the quarry has been taken' and 'the seizure of something by a lord for his own use from his feudal tenants or dependants', both of which have connotations of forcefully capturing or taking something. 'Prise, n.1.', *OED Online* <www.oed.com/view/Entry/153675> [Accessed 21 March 2018]; 'Prise, n.2.', *OED Online* <www.oed.com/view/Entry/151534> [Accessed 21 March 2018].

[25] *Froissart*, XIV, p. 21: *Or vous vueil-je nommer par ordonnance les chevalliers qui estoient dedens, et s'appelloient les chevalliers du Ray du Soleil d'or. Et quoyque ce fuist pour*

Why was King Charles VI competing in this tournament, disguised amidst a company of knights? He had no need to win a physical *pris*; Froissart does not even specify if one was awarded there or not. Rather, the king wished to give the appearance (at the very least) of having competed with others on an equal footing to be accorded *le pris*, the honour of being judged the best jouster.[26]

We will now turn to an analysis of some of the specific ways in which the tournament enabled individuals to demonstrate their 'right to pride' or, to employ medieval terms, reveal their honour and gain honour for themselves.

Individual Honour and the Tournament: Men of Violence and Courtesy

Richard Kaeuper called prowess, the ability to fight courageously and skilfully with lance and sword, 'the demi-god in the quasi-religion of chivalric honour'.[27] If this was the case, then tournaments were its principal feasts. The first mass tourneys were almost indistinguishable from true warfare, with two teams of knights fighting one another across great areas of countryside. Later evolutions, although more strictly regulated and accompanied by more elaborate pageantry, were no less concerned with the public practice of violence.[28] The primary purpose of a tournament was to fight and this remained the principal means by which the competitors asserted their right to be treated as men of 'worth'.

The earliest descriptions of tournaments revel in the ferocity of mass combat. The author of *The History of William Marshal* described the behaviour that won his subject the magnificent pike of Pleurs:

---

ces jours la devise du roy, si estoit le roy de ceulx de dehors, et jousta comme les autres à orains, pour conquerre les pris par armes, se il en povoit avoir l'aventure.

[26] Unsurprisingly, the attendant ladies and heralds judged that the king had indeed been the best among those 'without', while 'the Hasle of Flanders', bastard brother to the duchess of Burgundy, was judged to have been the best of those 'within'. *Froissart*, XIV, pp. 22–23. For the purposes of this essay, and in view of the ambiguity of the term, I have chosen to leave *pris* untranslated throughout. It effectively conveys the violent, competitive aspects of masculine honour that were expressed in the tournament.

[27] Richard W. Kaeuper, *Chivalry and Violence in Medieval Europe* (Oxford, 1999), p. 130.

[28] Malcolm Vale, *War and Chivalry: Warfare and Aristocratic Culture in England, France and Burgundy at the End of the Middle Ages* (Athens, Ga., 1981), pp. 63–67.

William Marshal came there, well armed, great and strong and handsome, he fought among their men like a lion among cattle: whoever he struck had no protection, not from coif or helmet or ventail; he fought and hammered like a woodcutter upon oak trees.[29]

Henry of Laon, lamenting the decline of the tournament in France around the middle of the thirteenth century, described the knight fighting vigorously in a tournament as one who 'bathes in his own blood and sweat, this I call a high bath of honour'.[30] In an illuminating passage from Chrétien de Troyes's *The Knight of the Cart*, Guinevere, suspecting that the mysterious, all-conquering Red Knight at a tournament is Lancelot in disguise, commands him to 'do his worst'.[31] This he does by deliberately missing opponents with his lance, allowing himself to be struck and fleeing from his enemies: 'He would have rather died than do anything unless it seemed to be to his great shame, harm and dishonour, and he behaved as if he were afraid of everybody whom he saw approach.'[32]

The association of honour with skilful and courageous fighting continues in later sources. Geoffrey de Charny (d. 1356), a French knight and author of a treatise on chivalry, advocated that young knights should attend tournaments because 'they combine great expenditure, cost of equipment and expense [with] bodily hardship, bruises and injuries, and sometimes risk of death'.[33] Gutierre Diaz de Gamez stressed the physical power that his master, Pero

---

[29] *Marshal*, I, lines 2952–59: *Lors vint li Mareschals Willeaumes, / Bien armez, granz e forz e genz, / Si se feri entre lor genz / Com li lions entre les bués: / Qui il ateint ne li eut ués / Coife ne hialme ne ventaille; / Tot autresi i fiert e maille / Com li boscheron sor les cheines.*

[30] A. Langfors, '*Le dit des hérauts par Henri de Laon*', *Romania* 43 (1914), 216–25 (lines 62–64): *Car cil qui en tel point c'estuve / En son sanc et en sa suour, / Ce apel(e) je haut bain d'ounour.*

[31] Chrétien is engaged in wordplay here that is impossible to translate directly into English. The tournament teams were divided between those who fought for the Lady of Pomelegoi and those who fought for the Lady of Noauz. The cry of Lancelot's team would therefore be *au noauz* ('For Noauz!') but it could also mean 'do your worst'. Lancelot correctly interprets Guinevere's cryptic messsage as an instruction to do the latter, demonstrating both his true identity and his qualities as an attentive lover. Chrétien de Troyes, *Arthurian Romances*, ed. and trans. William W. Kibler and Carleton W. Carroll, rev. edn (London, 2004), p. 513.

[32] Chrétien de Troyes, *Le Chevalier de la charrete*, ed. Mario Roques (Paris, 1974), lines 5669–73: *por a morir rien ne feïst / se sa grant honte n'i veïst, / et son leit, et sa desenor, / et fet sanblant qu'il ait peor / de toz ces qui vienent et vont.*

[33] *The Book of Chivalry of Geoffroi de Charny: Text, Context, and Translation*, ed. and trans. Richard W. Kaeuper and Elspeth Kennedy (Philadelphia, 1996), p. 86: *car*

Niño, count of Buelna, displayed when jousting against the French knight Jean de One at Paris c. 1405:

> And at the moment that [Pero Niño] broke his lance the bodies of the two horses met, and Jean de One and his horse rolled to the ground. They ran up and lifted up the knight, who had fallen in so rude a fashion that he was in peril of death, and his horse with him. In this fall he put his arm out of joint, and was for many days a cripple.[34]

The winning of honour through courageous and violent action was fundamental to the tournament. They were violent competitions in which success was awarded to those who were judged to be the most skilfully violent. This reflects their probable origins in the ritualised combats between bachelor knights that often preceded pitched battles or were arranged to break up the monotony of siege warfare in the eleventh and twelfth centuries.[35] These combats, conducted in full view of their peers, were arguably a better way for the young men to enhance their reputation than the confused and desperate business of true warfare, in which individual demonstrations of prowess were (ideally) subordinated to the need to fight as an effective unit.

This desire for distinction and recognition of one's feats of arms contributed to the early development of heraldry, and the associated office of the herald, so that individuals could be identified during the tourney.[36] See, for example, Chrétien's depiction of the tournament between Pomelegoi and Noauz in *The Knight of the Cart*, in which the spectating knights help the ladies to identify individuals by the emblems on their shields:

> Pray do you see the one with a band of gold bendwise across the middle of his shield? That is Governal de Roberdic. And do you also see the one behind him, who has set an eagle and a dragon side by side upon his shield?

---

il convient grans mises, grans estofes et grans despens, travail de corps, forisseures et bleceures, et peril de mort aucune foiz.

[34] Gutierre Diaz de Gamez, *The Unconquered Knight: A Chronicle of the Deeds of Don Pero Niño, Count of Buelna*, ed. and trans. Joan Evans (Woodbridge, 1928), p. 146.

[35] Dominique Barthélemy, 'The Chivalric Transformation and the Origins of Tournament as Seen through the Norman Chroniclers', *Haskins Society Journal* 20 (2009), 141–60 (pp. 154–56).

[36] Adrian Ailes, 'The Knight, Heraldry and Armour: The Role of Recognition and The Origins of Heraldry', in *Medieval Knighthood, IV: Papers From The Fifth Strawberry Hill Conference 1990*, ed. Christopher Harper-Bill and Ruth Harvey (Woodbridge, 1992), pp. 1–22 (pp. 18–19); Michel Pastoureau, 'La diffusion de armoiries et les débuts de l'héraldique', in *La France de Philippe Auguste: Le temps des mutations*, ed. Robert-Henri Bautier (Paris, 1982), pp. 737–60 (p. 741).

That is the king of Aragon's son, who came to this land to win *pris* and honour.[37]

As these individual emblems evolved into heritable 'coats of arms', so they added an additional dimension to the question of honour in the tournament. By the mid-thirteenth century, a competitor's arms no longer identified him solely as an individual but as the member of a family, with its own history and 'right to pride'.[38] Michel Pastoureau has identified how the lower ranks of the nobility adopted arms that resembled those of great families in the hope of catching some reflected glory.[39] Over the course of the Middle Ages, the 'right' to bear arms would become the key feature that distinguished nobility from commoner and permitted one to enter the 'honour group' of chivalry.[40] This theme of defending and maintaining another's honour (whether an individual or a group) is one that I shall return to later.

Demonstrating prowess could certainly earn an individual honour but, ideally, he needed to be more than just a great warrior. Courtesy, refinement and good manners were also important. At the tournament at Pleurs, we are told that the assembled noblemen 'held [William Marshal] to be without peer, for they could not find his peer in fair words or deeds; nor anybody less boastful about his doings, about anything he said or did'.[41] At the Pentecost tournament held outside Edinburgh in Chrétien's *Eric and Enide*, Eric distinguishes himself and is described in terms similar to those used by the Marshal poet:

> Now Eric was of such renown that nobody else was spoken of; no man had such good grace, he who resembled Absalom in face and Solomon in speech, who resembled the lion in ferocity and equalled Alexander in giving and distributing.[42]

---

[37] Chrétien, *Le Chevalier*, lines 5773–82: *Veez vos or / celui a cele bande d'or / par mi cel escu de bernic? / C'est Governauz de Roberdic. / Et veez vos celui aprés, / qui an son escu pres a pres / a mise une aigle et un dragon? / C'est li filz le roi d'Arragon / qui venuz est an ceste terre / por pris et por enor conquerre.* For the translation of *bernic* as 'bendwise', see Gerard J. Brault, *Early Blazon: Heraldic Terminology in the Twelfth and Thirteenth Centuries with Special Reference to Arthurian Literature* (Oxford, 1972), p. 120.

[38] Maurice Keen, *Chivalry* (London, 1984), p. 126.

[39] Pastoureau, 'La diffusion de armoiries', p. 754.

[40] Keen, *Chivalry*, p. 128.

[41] *Marshal*, I, lines 3155–59: *Par els fu tenuz a non per, / Kar l'om n'i trovast pas son per / De bien dire ne de bien faire; / Ne mains vantant de son afaire, / De rien ke die ne que face.*

[42] The Biblical Absalom, son of David, was described as a paragon of male beauty: 'In all Israel there was not a man so highly praised for his handsome appearance

Modesty was also important. Chrétien scorns the king of Ireland's son for presuming that he would be regarded as the best competitor at the tournament between Pomelegoi and Noauz: 'The king of Ireland's son thought, without hesitation and without defence, that he would have all the renown and all the *pris;* but he was painfully wrong for there were many who were his equal'.[43] In contrast, at the tournament held at the Castle of Maiden's Rock in Malory's *Le Morte Darthur*, Lancelot tries to refuse being given 'the honoure and the gré [prize; first place; reward]' by his fellow competitors. He insists that, as Trystram 'hath bene lenger in the fylde than I, and he hath smyttyn downe many mo knyghtes this day than I have done', he should be given it instead but this only proves to the rest that Lancelot is indeed 'the beste knyght' present.[44]

The time to demonstrate these qualities was not on the field but at the feasts, dancing and other social events that invariably accompanied tournaments. The holding of these feasts and the ability to behave appropriately at them were regarded as a mark of noble distinction.[45] It should be noted that these courtly qualities only enhanced the honour of a skilful warrior: they were not a substitute for prowess. Competitors at a tournament, whether historical or literary, were regarded as honourable because they possessed fine manners in addition to their ability to unhorse an opponent in combat.

While the demonstration of violence and courtesy were largely consistent across the history of the tournament, the ability to display that other key chivalric quality, *largesse*, the 'magnificent, great-hearted generosity' that set the nobility apart from the avaricious commoners, changed significantly.[46] In the early tourney, where competitors could earn themselves a fortune by ransoming captives, individuals might demonstrate their *largesse* by freely sharing their spoils. We have already seen how the Marshal won *grant pris* at Yonne by

---

as Absalom. From the top of his head to the sole of his foot there was no blemish in him' (2 Samuel 14.25. Douay-Rheims edition). Chrétien, *Eric et Enide*, lines 2207–14: *Or fu Erec de tel renon / qu'an ne parloit se de lui non; / nus hom n'avoit si boene grace / qu'il sanbloit Ausalon de face / et de la lengue Salemon, / et de fierté sanbla lyon, / et de doner et de despandre / refu il parauz Alixandre.*

[43] Chrétien, *Le Chevalier*, lines 5709–13: *Li filz de roi d'Irlande pansee / sanz contredit et sanz desfansse / qu'il ait tot le los et le pris; / mes laidemant i a mespris / qu'asez i ot de ses parauz.*

[44] Sir Thomas Malory, *Le Morte Darthur: or The Hoole Book of Kyng Arthur and of His Noble Knyghtes of The Rounde Table*, ed. Stephen H. A. Shepherd (London, 2004), p. 445.

[45] Joachim Bumke, *Courtly Culture: Literature and Society in the High Middle Ages*, trans. Thomas Dunlap (Los Angeles, 1991), pp. 191–99.

[46] Kaeuper, *Chivalry and Violence*, pp. 193–98.

sharing his winnings and magnanimously freeing many of the knights whom he had captured.[47] Elsewhere, the poet tells us that the Marshal was unconcerned whether or not he took booty at tournaments: 'He never strove for booty, but strove so hard to do fair deeds that he did not care about booty. He won something of greater value, for he who wins and seizes honour makes a richer bargain'.[48] Chrétien makes a similar claim about Eric's conduct at the Pentecost tournament:

> Eric did not want to strive to take horses or knights, but to joust and do fair deeds to reveal his prowess; he made the ranks of the opposing side tremble, his prowess gladdened those who were alongside him; he took horses and knights in order to defeat them more completely.[49]

It is tempting to dismiss such statements as so much chivalrous humbug. Competitors were clearly very much interested in acquiring wealth at tournaments. Later in his tale, the Marshal poet proudly relates how his subject, working together with Roger de Jouy, captured 103 knights in a single year.[50] Nor was this acquisitiveness confined to the rough-and-ready era of the mass tourney. Geoffrey de Charny prepared a series of questions about proper chivalrous conduct, to be debated by members of the Order of the Star, an order of chivalry founded by John II of France in 1352. Every question relating to jousts, and the majority of those relating to the tourney, is concerned with the winning of horses or who should pay compensation to whom for an injured horse.[51] Yet those high-minded statements of Chrétien and the Marshal poet reveal something about the chivalrous ideal of *largesse*: it was as much an attitude of mind as it was a standard of behaviour. Booty and wealth were the just and natural rewards for one who performed 'fair deeds', i.e., fighting with skill and courage. The important thing was not to appear concerned about the material reward. The ideal knight was one who faced victory and defeat, riches

---

[47] *Marshal*, I, lines 3558–62.

[48] *Marshal*, I, lines 3007–12: *Unques al gaaing n'entendi, / Mais al bien faire tant tendi / Que del gaaing ne li chalut. / Il gaainna qui mielz valut / Quer molt fait cil riche bargainne / Qui onor conquert e gaaine.*

[49] Chrétien, *Eric et Enide*, lines 2159–67: *Erec ne voloit pas entandre / a cheval n'a chevalier prandre, / mes a joster et a bien fiere / por ce que sa proescse apeire; / devers lui fet l'estor fremir, / sa proesce fet resbaudir / cez devers cui il se tenoit; / chevaux et chevaliers prenoit / por cez de la plus desconfire.*

[50] *Marshal*, I, lines 3409–25.

[51] *Charny's Men-at-Arms: Questions Concerning the Joust, Tournaments, and War*, ed. and trans. Steven Muhlberger (Wheaton, Ill., 2014), pp. 82–87.

and poverty, with equanimity. Greed and covetousness were for merchants and peasants, not noblemen.

As mass tourneys became less popular, however, and the joust became the dominant form of the tournament, there were fewer opportunities for competitors to take captives or gain honour by sharing their plunder. At the same time, jousting equipment became more specialised and the associated pageantry more elaborate, which meant that competition was placed beyond the means of less affluent men.[52] In later tournaments, *largesse* was demonstrated in the expensive staging, costumes and entertainment that accompanied the combats.[53] Gutierre Diaz de Gamez lauded Henry III of Castile for his generosity when holding tournaments to mark feast days:

> When the Church celebrated such a festival, he had prepared fair feasts and processions, and furthermore ordered jousts and tourneys and sports with canes; then did he bestow arms and horses, rich dresses and harness for those who should appear therein, and especially when there came to his court ambassadors of foreign princes.[54]

Henry of Laon complained that, in his time, lords no longer displayed the *largesse* that had once been customary at tournaments but that they were now more concerned with financial and legal disputes:

> But formerly the high lords of the land who had done homage to Prowess maintained themselves widely and freely, full of honour and love of battle, from vespers to morning. They gave rich feasts and prized knights, at least those who were related to them; and also they recognised the arrival of a poor young man of *pris*, they took their shield at once and hung it next to their banner.[55]

---

[52] Larry D. Benson, *Malory's Morte Darthur* (London, 1976), p. 166; Ruth Mazo Karras, *From Boys to Men: Formations of Masculinity in Late Medieval Europe* (Philadelphia, 2003), p. 58.

[53] Alan Young, *Tudor and Jacobean Tournaments* (London, 1987), p. 22.

[54] Gamez, *Unconquered Knight*, pp. 39–40.

[55] David Crouch's translation of *maintenent* (lines 126) as 'now' suggests that Laon considered the taking of the shield to be somehow dishonourable. I have chosen to understand *maintenent* as meaning 'immediately', indicating that, formerly, lords were quick to adopt the 'young men of *pris*' into their household. I believe this fits the sense of this section better, as it is followed by the line: *Or sont changiees leur manieres*. For Crouch's translation, see David Crouch, *Tournament* (London, 2005), pp. 188–93. Langfors, 'Henri de Laon', lines 116–27: *Mais jadis li haut ber de terre, / Qui firent a prouece homage, / Se maintenoi[e]nt lié et large, / Plain d'ounour et plain de hutin, / [Et] a vespree et a matin / Dounoi[e]nt les riches mengiers / Et pri[s]oi[e]nt les*

Perhaps the greatest display of *largesse* of this kind was the Field of Cloth of Gold, the staggeringly extravagant tournament of 1520 in which Henry VIII of England and Francis I of France attempted to outdo one another, not only in feats of arms but also in the lavishness of their retinues, their costumes and accommodation. To give only one of the numerous examples of *largesse* demonstrated at the Field, Henry had a fountain constructed in front of his temporary palace, 'gylte with fyne golde [...] whiche by the conduyctes in therth ranne to all people plenteously with red, white, and claret wyne'.[56]

These were some of the ways that competitors at the tournament could establish their 'right to pride' as individuals: by fighting well, by displaying good manners and by behaving generously, whether that be sharing plunder or distributing gifts. Honour was not just a matter for the individual knight, however. Their behaviour could also influence the 'rights' of other individuals and the social groups to which they belonged.

Collective Honour and the Tournament: Ladies and Kingdoms

Even when they competed as teams in the mass tourney, knights fought for their individual honour. This appears to have been a limited commodity. In *Le Morte Darthur*, while competing at the aforementioned tournament at the Castle of Maiden's Rock, Palomides openly weeps because Trystram is fighting so valiantly 'that he shoulde gete but lytyll worship that day'.[57] This desire for individual recognition, to stand out among one's peers, has been linked to the decline of the tourney as the dominant form of tournament and to the rise of the joust, with its greater emphasis on individual skill.[58] Yet there was also a collective dimension to the tournament and that included collective honour. We have already noted how knights could bring honour to their family by bearing their hereditary coat of arms at a tournament.

One of the most significant ways in which an individual knight's honour could affect another's at a tournament was his relationship with women. Women could not participate in the violent action but were nevertheless key

---

chevaliers, / Au mains tous ciaus de leur ys[sue]; / Et si savoi[e]nt la venue / D'un povre baceler de pris, / Maintenent ert ces escus pris / Et pendus delés leur banieres.

[56] Edward Hall, *Triumphant Reign of Henry VIII, the XII Year* (London, 1809), p. 605.
[57] Malory, *Morte Darthur*, p. 442.
[58] Crouch, *Tournament*, pp. 119–20.

figures, particularly in matters of honour. Siegfried Christoph's analysis of chivalric attitudes to female honour is worth quoting at length:

> In order to properly honor a knight, the woman must herself be a person of honor. In this way, women are drawn into the domain of honor, as peers who are capable of recognizing and acknowledging honorable deeds ... In this way, women have a considerable influence upon who and what is eligible for honoring ... For a woman to honor an unworthy object would be tantamount to jeopardizing her own honor.[59]

From the earliest records of the tournament, we find women acting as prize-givers, handing out the tokens that signified who had won the most honour that day. A letter from the English baron Roger fitz Walter inviting William d'Aubigny to attend a tournament at Stanford in 1215, preserved in Roger of Wendover's *Flowers of History*, refers to a bear being awarded for just this reason: 'He who does the best there will receive a bear, which a certain lady will send to the tournament'.[60] In later tournaments, the women are explicitly depicted as judges, collaborating with the heralds to determine which of the competitors was the most worthy. For example, the *pris* at the Smithfield tournament of 1390 were to be awarded 'according to the scrutiny of the ladies who would accompany the queen of England in her chambers and on the platforms, and of the heralds who would come and judge'.[61]

René d'Anjou's *Traictié de la forme et devis d'ung tournoy*, which describes an ideal tournament, portrays the prize-giving as an elaborate ceremony in which 'one of the ladies and two damsels' parade three times around the hall, carrying the prize under a veil, before stopping 'before the one to whom they wish to give *le pris*'.[62] The *Traictié* also features an unusual ceremony held the day before the combats, in which the ladies view the crests of the competitors and identify those who have 'spoken ill' (*mesdit*) of them, in order that they

---

[59] Siegfried Christoph, 'Honor, Shame and Gender', in *Arthurian Romance and Gender: Selected Proceedings of the Seventeenth International Arthurian Congress*, ed. Friedrich Wolfzettel (Amsterdam, 1995), pp. 26–33 (p. 31).

[60] Roger of Wendover, *Chronica sive flores historiarum*, ed. Henry O. Coxe, 5 vols (London, 1841–44), III, 322: *Qui melius ibi faciet, habebit ursum, quem domina quaedam mittet at torneamentum.*

[61] *Froissart*, XIV, p. 254: *à l'examen des dames qui là présentes seroient en chambres et sur hours en accompaignant la royne d'Angleterre, et des hérauls qui ce verroient et jugeroient, auroit pour le pris ung fremail d'or très-riche.*

[62] René d'Anjou, 'Traictié de la forme et devis d'ung tournoy', in *Oeuvres complètes du roi René*, ed. T. de Quatrebarbes, 2 vols (Angers, 1844–46), II, 1–44 (here pp. 37–38): *et en ce point feront troys tours à l'environ de la sale, puis se arresteront davant cellui auquel ils vouldront donner le pris.*

might be punished for their dishonourable conduct the next day.[63] Here we see noblewomen acting as the arbiters of honour in the otherwise masculine world of the tournament.

Knights might compete in tournaments for the honour of ladies: not to establish or reveal their own honour, but that of women. Perhaps the most famous example is Ulrich von Liechtenstein (d. 1275), who undertook his famous 'Venus Tour' in order to honour his anonymous mistress.[64] According to Ulrich, when his lady heard of his plan, she said it 'will surely do him good and he will win a rich reward in praise from many a lady and lord'.[65] Ulrich used the tour to honour not only his own lady but to encourage other knights to honour women in general. In the challenge he sent out as 'Queen Venus', Ulrich promised to give a gold ring to any knight who broke a lance against him, which the victor was to send 'to the lady whom he loves most', but if Ulrich unhorsed somebody they would be required 'to bow toward the four ends of the world in honour of a woman'.[66]

There are many other, less flamboyant, examples of this kind of service. Geoffrey de Charny advised his readers to 'honour, serve and greatly love those goodly ladies and others whom I hold as ladies, who also do good deeds, and through whom are made knights and goodly men-at-arms'.[67] This appears to have been the motivation for John Holland, earl of Huntingdon, who, having already run the set number of courses against the French champions at Saint-Inglevert in 1390, 'requested to run a lance one more time for love of his

---

[63] René d'Anjou, 'Traictié', p. 21.

[64] For a comprehensive study of tournaments in Ulrich's *Frauendienst*, see Alan V. Murray, 'Tourney, Joust, Foreis and Round Table: Tournament Forms in the *Frauendienst* of Ulrich von Liechtenstein', in *Pleasure and Leisure in the Middle Ages and Early Modern Age: Cultural-Historical Perspectives on Toys, Games, and Entertainment*, ed. Albrecht Classen (Berlin, 2019), pp. 365–94.

[65] *Ulrich von Liechtenstein's Service of Ladies*, trans. John W. Thomas (Woodbridge, 2004), p. 47; Ulrich von Liechtenstein, *Frauendienst*, ed. Franz Viktor Spechtler, 2nd edn (Göppingen, 2003), 467,4–5: *si ist im guot, / im wirt darumbe ein sölher solt / daz im die biderben werdent holt.*

[66] *Ulrich von Liechtenstein's Service of Ladies*, p. 50; Ulrich von Liechtenstein, *Frauendienst*, p. 105 (Brief B): *swelch ritter gegen ir kumt und ein sper wider si enzweie gestichet, dem gibt si ze miet ein guldin vingerlin; daz sol er senden dem wibe, diu im diu liebest ist. ... Stichet min vrowe Venus deheinen ritter nider, der sol envier enden in die werlt nigen einem wibe ze eren.*

[67] *Charny*, p. 94: *Et bien doit l'en honorer, servir et tres bien amer icelles tres bonnes dames et autres que je tien toutes a dames, qui ainsi font les bons, et par elles sont faiz chevaliers et les bonnes genz d'armes.*

lady'.[68] The *chapitres* for Antoine de Bourgogne's *pas d'armes*, 'The Knight of the Oppressed Lady', held in 1462, presented the *pas* as a competition for the right to defend a lady's honour. Antoine took on the role of a foreign knight who had come to the duke of Burgundy's court to hold a *pas* in order to find the knight best able to defend an anonymous noblewoman from her enemy. The victor would serve as 'an example and encouragement to all other knights to uphold ladies' causes'.[69]

In addition to competing for the honour of another individual, knights also competed as members of social groups, such as chivalric orders or subjects of a particular region or kingdom. In the twelfth century it was customary for competitors at a tournament to divide into two teams along broadly regional lines. In 1168, at a tournament held between Gournay and Ressons, Baldwin V, count of Hainaut, chose to break with tradition and side with the French against the Flemings and men of Vermandois, on account of his enmity with Philip I, count of Flanders. Philip was so angry at Baldwin's behaviour that 'having arranged his men as if for a serious battle, the horsemen as well as the foot soldiers, [he] resolved to engage the French and men of Hainaut'.[70] In the thirteenth and fourteenth centuries, jousts were arranged between teams of English knights and Scottish or French knights during truces between their respective kingdoms, such as the famous Saint-Inglevert tournament of 1390.[71] Froissart records that the three French champions were welcomed into Paris after the tournament: 'for they had valiantly born and safeguarded the honour of the kingdom of France'.[72]

National honour could be enhanced not just by competing in national 'teams' but by hosting tournaments. 'Diplomatic' tournaments were a regular feature of international relations in the later Middle Ages, allowing princes

---

[68] *Froissart*, XIV, p. 110: *Encoires de recheif requist le conte de Hostidonne à courir une lance pour l'amour de sa dame.*

[69] 'Chapitres of the Bastard of Burgundy as the Knight of the Oppressed Lady for a *pas d'armes*, 25 February 1462', in Ralph D. Moffat, 'The Medieval Tournament' (unpublished Ph.D. thesis, University of Leeds, 2010), pp. 258–65 (pp. 260–61).

[70] Gilbert of Mons, *La chronique de Gislebert de Mons*, ed. by Léon Vanderkindere (Brussels, 1904), p. 97: *Comes autem Flandrie, nimia accensus ira, cum suis hominibus tam equitibus quam peditibus quasi ab bellum ordinatis gravius Francis et Hanoniensibus occurrere cepit.*

[71] Richard Barber and Juliet Barker, *Tournaments: Jousts, Chivalry and Pageants in the Middle Ages* (Woodbridge, 1989), pp. 34–42.

[72] *Froissart*, XIV, p. 151: *car vaillamment ils s'estoient portés et avoient gardé l'onneur du royaulme de France.*

to impress foreign dignitaries with their wealth and sophistication.[73] In 1415 English ambassadors were entertained by a tournament in Paris and in 1428 Burgundian ambassadors were honoured with a tournament in Lisbon.[74] At the heart of the Field of Cloth of Gold, the most famous and elaborate of all diplomatic tournaments, was a Tree of Honour entwined with a hawthorn and a raspberry, representing the nations of England and France which were to be jointly defended in the tournament.[75]

Another example of how notions of collective honour influenced the practice of tournaments was the practice of limiting entry to those of proven noble descent. This practice appears to have begun sometime in the fourteenth century and was particularly widespread in Germany and the Low Countries.[76] Not only was entry to the tournament restricted to those of noble descent, but any of the competitors who were found to have acted dishonourably were subjected to ritual humiliation. At a tournament held in Heilbronn in 1481, punishable offences included living in a town, engaging in trade or marrying a commoner.[77] René d'Anjou gives detailed lists of the offences and punishments for the competitors at his ideal tournament, which included speaking ill of ladies, breaking a promise or lending money at interest.[78] Like much of the chivalric ritual and performance in the later Middle Ages, these regulations asserted the right of the aristocracy to maintain their preeminent position in society, preventing the increasingly wealthy and influential gentle amd mercantile families from participating in their exclusive 'honour group'.[79]

---

[73] Barber and Barker, *Tournaments*, pp. 168–69.

[74] Richard Barber, *The Knight and Chivalry* (Woodbridge, 1995), p. 215.

[75] Joycelyne G. Russell, *The Field of Cloth of Gold: Men and Manners in 1520* (London, 1969), pp. 112–13.

[76] Mario Damen, 'Tournament Culture in the Low Countries and England', in *Contact and Exchange in Later Medieval Europe: Essays in Honour of Malcolm Vale*, ed. Hannah Skoda, Patrick Lantschner and R. L. J. Shaw (Woodbridge, 2012), pp. 247–65 (pp. 259–63).

[77] Barber, *Knight and Chivalry*, pp. 221–22.

[78] René d'Anjou, 'Traictié', p. 22.

[79] Barber, *Knight and Chivalry*, p. 222; Karass, *Boys to Men*, p. 24.

Conclusion

Tournaments reflected several key ideas about honour in medieval aristocratic culture. They gave competitors the opportunity to demonstrate their worthiness, to justify their 'claim to pride', through their courtly and sophisticated behaviour at the feasts and dances that accompanied a tournament. They were a space to demonstrate the open-handed generosity that was expected of a chivalrous individual, whether by sharing out the booty from a successful tourney or providing lavish entertainments at a stylised *pas d'armes*. Noblewomen could bestow honour on the male competitors by acting as prize-givers, while the men could bring honour to women by competing in their name. An individual might bring honour to his family by wearing his hereditary arms or bring honour to his nation, either as a valiant competitor or a generous host. In later centuries, the very act of participating in a tournament was a mark of noble honour that set the individual apart from the commonality and placed them among the social and (supposedly) moral elite of their age.

Throughout the Middle Ages, one aspect of the tournament remained pre-eminent: the connection between masculine honour and prowess. Consistently, in both historical records and literature, knights gained and demonstrated their honour by fighting courageously in the tournament itself. There was no better way to gain honour and no amount of generosity or courtesy would compensate for cowardly behaviour. As Pitt-Rivers observed, in societies governed by honour, 'respect and precedence are paid to those who claim it and are sufficiently powerful to enforce their claim'.[80] This is something that William Marshal or Ulrich von Liechtenstein would have understood just as readily as Boucicaut or Francis I. Whatever other rewards might be had at a tournament, the honour gained by demonstrating one's strength and courage remained the greatest.

---

[80] Pitt-Rivers, 'Honour and Social Status', p. 24.

3 Richard II of England and the Smithfield Tournament of October 1390: An Instrument to Establish Royal Authority

James Beswick

> A formal tournament was held at Smithfield on 10 October, providing the nobles and gallant knights of many areas a reason for visiting London ... The tournament lasted three days, on the first of which the honours were awarded to the king.[1]

The spectacle of the tournament was surely at its height when the monarch of a nation was involved, as King Richard II of England was at Smithfield in October 1390. Certainly, the image of Richard's involvement in a tournament may be unfamiliar to a modern reader, unaccustomed to a martial presentation of the much-maligned king.[2] Nevertheless, Richard offered his own patronage of tournaments on several occasions, and in October 1390 held one of the grandest and most successful tournaments of his reign.

Tournaments themselves were great chivalric occasions throughout the medieval world, where individual prowess could be demonstrated for all to see. Arranged and organised for the nobility, they encapsulated and embodied the images and ideals of knighthood and chivalry, and might also include women and people of lower social groups as spectators. Despite a growing appreciation

---

[1] *The Westminster Chronicle 1381–1394*, ed. and trans. Leonard. C. Hector and Barbara F. Harvey (Oxford, 1982), p. 451: *Item Xmo. Octobris apud Smethefeld errant slompnia hastiludia; qua de causa de pluribus partibus ad civitatem London comites et valentes milites accesserunt ... Durabant namque ista hastiludia per tres dies; laus quoque prime diei domino regi fuit concessa.*

[2] This essay will not attempt to add to the debate on Richard's character, for which see: Nigel Saul, *Richard II* (London,1997); James L. Gillespie, 'Richard II: King of Battles?', in *The Age of Richard II*, ed. James L. Gillespie (Stroud, 1997), pp. 139–64; Christopher Fletcher, *Richard II: Manhood, Youth, and Politics, 1377–99* (Oxford, 2008).

for show and display, however, the tournament was not a vainglorious pursuit of the nobility. It could also be a weapon of politics, where plans, schemes and reputations could be made or destroyed, and even lives lost. It could be used to challenge the power of a monarch and embed factionalism at court. But it could also be an instrument used to help establish royal authority and bring tangible benefits to any monarch who could wield this instrument correctly. To demonstrate this, I will briefly explore the politicisation of the tournament in England before examining the Smithfield tournament of 1390 in detail. By examining the participants in the tournament, the symbolism incorporated into the event, and the nature of Richard's own involvement, it is possible to see how he attempted to manipulate the tournament and wield it for his own purposes. It was not simply a spectacle, but a manifestation of power.

The exact date of the origin of tournaments is not known, but they were well established by the mid-twelfth century.[3] Almost from the outset, tournaments were politicised events in England. During the civil wars between King Stephen (1135–54) and the Empress Matilda (1139–67) tourneying took place between the two respective sides. For example, during the siege of Winchester in 1141, Matilda's knights would leave the city daily in order to tourney against those from the besieging force. Stephen even prohibited the staging of at least two tournaments because of the potential political fallout.[4] It was due to this politicisation of tournaments, as well as to unite the two factions of the civil wars, that during his own reign Matilda's son Henry II (1154–89) imposed a complete ban on tournaments within England.[5] This was an integral part of Henry's policy to re-establish royal authority and ensure that the control and patronage of tournaments fell under the crown.[6] It was this ban that paved the way for the formal licensing of tournaments in England by Richard I in 1194. England became the only kingdom in Europe

---

[3] David Crouch, *Tournament* (London, 2005), pp. 1–16.

[4] *History of William Marshal*, ed. A. J. Holden, trans. S. Gregory, 3 vols (London, 2002–2006), 1, lines 1207–12; Juliet Barker, *The Tournament in England, 1100–1400* (Woodbridge, 1986), p. 8; Crouch, *Tournament*, p. 9.

[5] William of Newburgh, 'Historia Rerum Anglicarum', in *Chronicles of the Reigns of Stephen, Henry II, and Richard I*, ed. Richard Howlett, 4 vols (London, 1885), 2: 422–23; Richard Barber and Juliet Barker, *Tournaments: Jousts, Chivalry and Pageants in the Middle Ages* (Woodbridge, 1989), p. 19.

[6] For the early years of Henry II's reign and the re-establishment of royal authority see, Emilie Amt, *The Accession of Henry II in England: Royal Government Restored, 1149–1159* (Woodbridge, 1993); Graeme J. White, *Restoration and Reform, 1153–1165: Recovery from Civil War in England* (Cambridge, 2000).

at this time where the monarchy had almost complete control over tournament activity.[7] Such control inherently politicised the tournament, for if the monarch controlled tournament activity, then it could be an arena where the nobility could challenge such control and authority.

It was during the reigns of John (1199–1216), Henry III (1216–72) and Edward II (1307–27) that tournaments were used to undermine and challenge the power of the monarch, providing a pretext to meet and discuss grievances and formulate political or military opposition to the king. For example, in 1228 Pope Gregory IX's papal legate in England was ordered to excommunicate any tourneyer, because it was believed that the barons were meeting 'on the occasion of tournaments' (*sub occasione torniamentorum*) to conspire against Henry III.[8] In the reign of Edward II, a tournament held at Dunstable in 1309 was used to draw up the eleven grievances put forward against the king at the April Parliament of the same year.[9] Lords opposed to the king could also use such occasions to bring together large retinues to execute their political aims, as in 1215 when rebellious barons gathered their armies to oppose King John.[10] A similar pretext was used in 1312, when a section of the nobility opposed to Edward II gathered in order to capture and murder his favourite, Piers Gaveston, earl of Cornwall.[11] These kings regularly reverted to prohibitions, which were often sent to specific lords, forbidding their participation in a tournament. However, such prohibitions were often ignored, as in 1248 when William de Valance held a tournament at Northampton in defiance of a general prohibition by Henry III.[12] Such acts were damaging to a king's authority as it demonstrated his lack of power and control. When a king lost control of the tournament, it could be used by his opponents and the disillusioned as a powerful weapon against him.

Yet in the right hands tournaments could be exploited and manipulated to unite the nobility under the person of the king and further that king's authority.

---

[7] For a complete discussion of this practice, see Barker, *Tournament in England*, pp. 11–12, 53–56.

[8] *Foedera, Conventiones, Litterae etc.*, ed. Thomas Rymer, 4 vols (London, 1739), 1: 301.

[9] John R. Maddicott, *Thomas of Lancaster, 1307–1322* (Oxford, 1970), pp. 95–103.

[10] Ralph de Coggeshalle, *Chronicon Anglicanum*, ed. Joseph Stevenson (London, 1875), pp. 172–73.

[11] Monk of Malmesbury, *Vita Edwardi Secundi*, ed. Noël Denholm-Young (London, 1957), p. 23.

[12] Matthew Paris, *Chronica Majora*, ed. Henry R. Luard, 7 vols (London, 1872–82), 5: 83.

It was during the reigns of Edward I (1272–1307) and Edward III (1327–77) that the danger of the tournament to royal power was diminished and harnessed for their own purposes. By participating in and sponsoring tournaments, both kings ensured that they could not be exploited by opponents, as had happened in the reigns of Henry III and Edward II. Furthermore, both kings used the tournament to celebrate themselves and their military successes. Edward I held tournaments at Nefyn and Caernarfon in 1284 to celebrate his victories over the Welsh, and at Falkirk in 1302 to celebrate victory over the Scots.[13] Likewise, after his successes in France in 1346–47, Edward III held jousts at Reading, Eltham, Windsor, Lichfield, Bury St Edmunds and Canterbury. French and Scottish captives, including King David II of Scotland, were often present. A decade later Edward III held another tournament at Smithfield, this time with John II, king of France, as his prisoner and guest.[14] Evidently both Edward I and Edward III were using the tournament as a form of propaganda to glorify themselves, their reigns, and their victories. Despite both of these kings using tournaments to their advantage, there were times when prohibitions on tournaments were enacted. However, unlike John, Henry III, and Edward II, both kings had the power to enforce such a prohibition.[15]

Given that Edward III was able to manipulate the tournament for his own ends, as well as offer it patronage, it is no coincidence that the Order of the Garter was established at a tournament in Windsor on 23 April 1349, with St George as its patron saint.[16] Membership was restricted to only twenty-six knights, including the king as sovereign of the order. Juliet Vale has suggested that this number was chosen to create two evenly matched tournament

---

[13] *Chronicles of the Reigns of Edward I and Edward II*, ed. William Stubbs, 2 vols (London, 1882), 1: 104; *Annales Monastici*, ed. Henry R. Luard, 5 vols (London, 1866), 4: 489; Monk of Malmesbury, *Vita Edwardi Secundi*, p. 6.

[14] Barber and Barker, *Tournaments*, pp. 34–35; *Eulogium Historiarum*, ed. Frank Haydon, 3 vols (London, 1858–63), 3: 227.

[15] For example, Edward I prohibited tournaments while on campaign in Scotland, after desertions from the army in 1302 and 1306. See *Calendar of Close Rolls: Edward I, 1302–7*, ed. Henry Maxwell Lyte, 5 vols (London, 1908), 5: 66; *Calendar of Fine Rolls: Edward I, 1272–1307*, ed. Henry Maxwell Lyte, 2 vols (London, 1911), 1: 543–44. Edward III issued a general prohibition during the Parliament of Northampton in 1328, to encourage attendance. See *Calendar of Close Rolls: Edward III, 1327–30*, ed. Henry Maxwell Lyte, 3 vols (London, 1908), 1: 382.

[16] For further discussion on the founding of the order see D'Arcy J. D. Boulton, *The Knights of the Crown: The Monarchical Orders of Knighthood in Later Medieval Europe, 1325–1520* (Woodbridge, 1987), pp. 96–117.

teams, yet this is by no means certain.[17] Regardless, Edward had established a company where the bonds and allegiances of the tournament team became inexorably linked to loyalty to the sovereign.

The Smithfield tournament of 1390 was one of the grandest chivalric occasions of the reign of Richard II. It began on Sunday 9 October with twenty knights of the Order of the Garter being led by twenty women, all of whom were clad in the white hart livery of Richard, from the Tower of London to Smithfield. On the following day these knights undertook jousts against 'all manner of knights who should wish to come' and challenge them.[18] The jousting continued for the following two days, and after each day, prizes were given to the knights who had jousted best, as judged by the ladies attending the tournament. These ladies were themselves also judged on their dancing and merrymaking and awarded prizes by the knights.[19] This merrymaking took place at great feasts that were held in the evenings and constituted a major part of the event, continuing afterwards at Windsor castle. To encourage participation at the event, participants were accorded twenty-eight days of safe conduct.[20]

Richard's reign up until this point had been one of minority and political turmoil, and within ten years of acceding to the throne Richard faced a challenge to his royal authority. There had already been the crisis of the Peasants' Revolt in 1381, which Nigel Saul has described as 'the largest and most serious outbreak of popular unrest in England in the Middle Ages'.[21] The uprising was in part a response to a series of poll taxes collected during the years 1377–81.[22] However, it was in 1386 that the real challenge to royal authority began. At the so-called 'Wonderful Parliament', Richard's chancellor, Michael de la Pole (c. 1330–89), was removed from his position by the demand of

---

[17] Juliet Vale, *Edward III and Chivalry* (Woodbridge, 1982), pp. 88–91.

[18] 'To Cry a Joust [Smithfield Tournament 1390]', in Ralph D. Moffat, 'The Medieval Tournament: Chivalry, Heraldry and Reality: An Edition and Analysis of Three Fifteenth-Century Tournament Manuscripts' (unpublished PhD thesis, University of Leeds, 2010), pp. 250–52: *qui vouldront la venir pour Jouster*; *The Brut or The Chronicles of England*, ed. Friedrich W.D. Brie (London, 1906), pp. 343–44.

[19] 'To Cry a Joust', p. 252: *Et a la dame ou damoiselle qui mieulx dancera ou qui menera plus Joyeuse vie les troys Jours deua[n]tditz qui est a entendre le Dimenche le lundj et le mardj sera donne par lesditz cheualiers vng fermail dor.*

[20] 'To Cry a Joust', pp. 251–52.

[21] Saul, *Richard II*, p. 56.

[22] For a fuller discussion on the uprising, see Saul, *Richard II*, pp. 56–82; Rodney Hilton, *Bond Men Made Free: Medieval Peasant Movements and the English Rising of 1381* (London, 1973).

Parliament, and impeached for peculation in office.[23] Yet the challenge was compounded when a continual council, as well as a conciliar commission, was appointed to hold power for a year. Richard and his councillors had effectively been removed from government.[24]

Richard's response to this was to meet with judges at Shrewsbury and Nottingham in August 1387, asking ten questions regarding the legality of his exclusion from government by Parliament. The judges ruled against Parliament, stating that those responsible should be punished 'as traitors'.[25] In order to protect themselves from such repercussions, five lords known as the Appellants took control of Richard's person, and defeated his favourite, Robert de Vere, earl of Oxford and duke of Ireland, at Radcot Bridge.[26] At the ensuing Parliament in 1388, known as the 'Merciless Parliament', there was a purge of royal councillors and favourites, with Michael de la Pole sentenced to death, Robert de Vere exiled, and Richard's guardian and chamber knight, Sir Simon Burley, executed amongst others.[27] The Appellants then took control of the governance of the realm and Richard was once more excluded. Royal authority was at an all-time low, the political community was fragmented, and the future appeared to be bleak for Richard. Yet in 1389 he declared himself of age and took the government into his own hands.[28] The Smithfield Tournament was

---

[23] Once more taxation was an underlying cause in Pole's impeachment, after suggesting a tax twice the usual amount. *Knighton's Chronicle* claims there was immediate uproar in response to this suggestion. See *Knighton's Chronicle 1337–1396*, trans. Geoffrey H. Martin (Oxford, 1995), p. 354; Saul, *Richard II*, pp. 156–62. For a full study on the impeachment see John S. Roskell, *The Impeachment of Michael de la Pole, Earl of Suffolk, in 1386* (Manchester, 1984).

[24] *The Westminster Chronicle*, pp. 166–74; Gerald Hariss, *Shaping the Nation: England 1360–1461* (Oxford, 2005), pp. 462; Saul, *Richard II*, pp. 161–64.

[25] The questions are given in *The Westminster Chronicle*, pp. 196–202, and *Knighton's Chronicle*, pp. 394–98. See Stanley B. Chrimes, 'Richard II's Questions to the Judges, 1387', *Law Quarterly Review* 72 (1956), 365–90; Dione Clementi, 'Richard II's Ninth Question to the Judges, 1387', *English Historical Review* 86 (1971), 96–113.

[26] The five Appellant lords were Richard's uncle, Thomas of Woodstock, duke of Gloucester (1355–97), Richard FitzAlan, earl of Arundel (1346–1397), Thomas Beauchamp, earl of Warwick (1338–1401), Henry Bolingbroke, earl of Derby (1367–1413), and Thomas Mowbray, earl of Nottingham (1366–99). For further discussion of the events leading to Radcot Bridge, see Saul, *Richard II*, pp. 185–90.

[27] *The Westminster Chronicle* provides a comprehensive account of the Parliament, including a breakdown of each individual charge (pp. 235–335).

[28] Richard claimed that until this point, he and the realm had been under the control of others, overburdened by taxation, but now that he was mature, he would provide good governance. See *The Westminster Chronicle*, pp. 390–92.

Richard's opportunity to show to domestic and international audiences a spectacle that demonstrated the power and wealth of England. It also provided a chance to reassert royal authority under Richard's personal rulership and heal the wounds of a turbulent past.

Those who participated in the tournament were crucial to Richard's attempts to establish royal authority. It was the knights of the Order of the Garter who represented Richard and made up the 'home team' in the event. The order comprised some of the most powerful lords in England, such as John Holland, earl of Huntingdon, as well as those renowned for chivalry, such as Sir Peter Courtenay. However, more importantly, all of the Appellant lords who had recently opposed Richard were Garter knights, as were others such as Sir John Devereux, who had been part of the continual council.[29] By using these lords, his enemies of the preceding years, as the 'home team', Richard was clearly attempting to reconcile them with him. English kingship had become reliant on conciliation between king and nobles, in part due to the growing power of Parliament in the granting of taxation and other rights.[30] If a king wished to be powerful and establish his own authority, he needed the support of his greater nobility. Richard was using the event at Smithfield to get his nobility back on side, and thereby extend his authority and power. By having these lords act as his representatives, Richard was demonstrating and outwardly projecting to the kingdom the renewed unity of the nobility under his own personal kingship.

The nature of the tournament was equally important to Richard's attempts to portray unity under his kingship. It was not exclusively dedicated to demonstrating knightly prowess. Unfortunately, there is no course-by-course description of the jousting at the tournament, like that given by Froissart for the jousts at Saint-Ingelvert earlier in the year.[31] Instead Froissart gives a stock account of the Smithfield tournament, claiming that 'everyone exerted himself

---

[29] For a complete list of the Garter knights, see: Grace Holmes, *The Order of the Garter: Its Knights and Stall Plates 1348 to 1984* (Windsor, 1984), pp. 121–22. The only Appellant absent was Henry Bolingbroke, who was on crusade in Prussia. His absence was probably a result of disagreements with Gloucester, and not animosity between him and Richard. See Francis R. H. Du Boulay, 'Henry of Derby's Expeditions to Prussia 1390–1 and 1392', in *The Reign of Richard II: Essays in Honour of May McKisack*, ed. Francis R. H. Du Boulay and Caroline M. Barron (London, 1971), pp. 153–55.

[30] Parliament had of course taken control and governance of the realm away from Richard in 1386.

[31] Jean Froissart, *Chronicles of England, France, Spain, and the Adjoining Countries*, trans. Thomas Johnes, 2 vols (London, 1862), 2: 434–46.

to the utmost to excel: many were unhorsed and more lost their helmets'.[32] Such phrasing is standard for Froissart, especially when he is not sure of what actually occurred. It also gives credence to the argument that demonstrating prowess was not the main intention of the tournament, as there was no single or collective demonstration of prowess for Froissart to discuss. It appears that for the first two days of the tournament, Richard's twenty knights were to take the field at Smithfield with six lances each, and 'deliver all manner of knights who should wish to come there to joust'. On the final day sixteen squires were to take the field and they would then 'deliver' all knights and squires who also wished to come and joust.[33] This was at least how the tournament was intended to proceed as described in an invitation which set out the rules and proceedings to be followed, and which was circulated throughout England, Scotland, Hainaut, Germany, Flanders and France to encourage participation.[34] However, in the absence of a course-by-course description of the event, as well as Froissart's own inaccuracies, it is likely that this text is the most reliable source for the tournament.[35]

Safety was a key consideration for Richard, as the jousts themselves were highly regulated. Participants were not to joust with sharpened lances, but with 'lances [that] shall have reasonable coronels'.[36] Lances with coronels were blunted and more likely to break upon impact, and they were also less likely to pierce armour and thus were far less dangerous than sharpened lances. To ensure fairness and safety it was decreed that anyone who 'jousted with unreasonable coronels' should 'lose his horse and harness'.[37] All participants were to 'joust in high saddles', which gave the rider greater support, making them less likely to be unhorsed during a joust.[38] The direction concerning saddles further suggests that Froissart was using a stock phrase when discussing the

---

[32] Froissart, *Chronicles*, 2: 479: *Lors commen cerent les joustes grandes, belles, et qui honnourablement furent joustees.*

[33] 'To Cry a Joust', pp. 251–52: *deliurer toutes manie[re]s de ch[eua]l[ie]rs qui vouldront la venir pour Jouster.*

[34] Froissart, *Chronicles*, 2: 478.

[35] An example of Froissart's inaccuracies in describing the event is the assertion that sixty, rather than twenty knights took part (*Chronicles*, 2: 477). However, this assertion is not supported by any other source and it seems very unlikely that the tournament would have tripled in size from its inception to its execution.

[36] 'To Cry a Joust', p. 251: *Et que les lances aient Rasisonnables Roques.*

[37] 'To Cry a Joust', pp. 252: *Et qui Joustera lesditz troys Jo[u]rs de non Raisonnables Roques perdra son cheual et son harnoys.*

[38] 'To Cry a Joust', p. 251: *Jousteront en haultes selles.*

tournament, as it makes it unlikely that 'many were unhorsed'. This emphasis on safety in the planning of the event was to prevent any serious injuries or deaths during the tournament. An accidental death could have easily jeopardised Richard's attempts at unifying the nobility under his leadership and even created a feud. Thus, by limiting the jousts, Richard ensured that the projection of unity he was attempting to display to the realm was not put at risk.

The tournament included a considerable element of festivity, as the contemporary sources make clear.[39] Impressive prizes were given out at the end of each day to the knights who distinguished themselves, and grand merrymaking ensued in the evenings. Both Richard and John of Gaunt, duke of Lancaster (1340–99), the king's uncle, held 'magnificent' feasts as part of the tournament, first in London and then moving to Windsor.[40] The reason for such grand festivities was to help build bonds between Richard and the nobility who attended. John of Gaunt was the most powerful lord in England, but from 1385 he had been estranged from Richard, pursuing his own ambitions in Iberia and Aquitaine, and thus had been absent from English politics. Gaunt's sponsorship of one of the feasts demonstrated his own reconciliation with Richard, as well as a return to the politics of the realm as Richard's most powerful supporter.[41] The tournament was also notorious for causing an international crisis as Richard inducted William, count of Ostrevant (1365–1417), into the Order of the Garter as he tried to create alliances on the continent. William and Richard were kinsmen, and William's native Hainaut had aided the English during the early Hundred Years' War. However, in 1385 William had married the daughter of Philip the Bold, duke of Burgundy (1342–1404), sealing an alliance with the French. William's induction into the Order of the Garter in 1390 was thus regarded by them as a betrayal. *The Westminster Chronicle* claims that the affair 'caused some gnashing of French teeth', while Froissart asserts that 'the king of France and his council were much angered' by it.[42] The affair might suggest that Richard was not as eager for peace as has often been suggested by modern scholars. It was certainly a tactic Richard

---

[39] Froissart describes the tournament as a *feste* (*Chronicles*, 2: 478), as does 'To Cry a Joust' (p. 252). *The Brut* regularly describes it as a *fest and Iustes* (feast and joust) (p. 343).

[40] Froissart, *Chronicles*, 2: 479–80: *moult grant, sumptueux et merveilleusement bien*.

[41] Saul, *Richard II*, pp. 131–34. Saul claims that after his reconciliation, Gaunt 'gave Richard his full backing throughout the remainder of his active career' (p. 240).

[42] *The Westminster Chronicle*, pp. 452–53: *propter quod frendent Francigene ipsum comitem cum cachinno turpiter irridentes eo quod fecisset homagium et fidelitatem regi Anglorum*; Froissart, *Chronicles*, 2: 480–81: *le roy de France et son conseil estoient infourmés*.

used to create alliances, as he also created William, duke of Guelders (1364–1402), a Garter knight earlier in the year.[43] Regardless, by ensuring that the tournament was one of festivity, Richard was undoubtedly using it to heal the wounds of the past, and to create bonds, unity, and alliances both domestically and internationally.

The festive nature of the tournament had the added benefit of presenting the grandeur and largesse of England under Richard's kingship, showing the prosperity that Richard would bring now that he controlled the governance of the realm. It was a show of his royal magnificence, a statement to domestic and international audiences alike.

Sheila Lindenbaum agrees that Richard intended to use the tournament as a way of creating unity within English political society. However, she argues that Richard was unsuccessful in this, pointing to what she considers to be the exclusion of certain groups, such as the citizens of London, in the planning and viewing of the event, which 'stayed firmly in the hands of the king'.[44] She also claims that the employment of a nightwatch is further evidence of this.[45] Yet Lindenbaum's analysis neglects the fact there had already been a tournament at Smithfield in May, earlier in the year, also under the patronage of Richard, which had been attended by 'innumerable members of the populace'.[46] If the tournament is considered as an instrument to demonstrate and create unity, the use of nightwatchmen was not an oppressive act. Rather, it was a sensible action to ensure that the unity of the occasion could not be disrupted. This may well have been synthetic, to create the illusion of unity, but it still had the effect that Richard desired. Furthermore, Richard's monopoly over the planning of the event gives greater credence to the argument that he was intending and hoping to use the event for his own benefit, which was to reconcile the nobility towards him and thereby assert his royal authority. Lindenbaum's criticisms of Richard's actions at the Smithfield tournament of October 1390 are rendered less significant because he had already addressed the issues at the Smithfield tournament of May 1390.

Symbolism was a crucial element in the Smithfield tournament and Richard's attempts to establish royal authority. It was there that Richard used the white hart badge for the very first time. The device, a pun on Richard's own name, was to become the symbol most closely identified with him, yet it was

---

[43] *The Westminster Chronicle*, pp. 434–35.

[44] Sheila Lindenbaum, 'The Smithfield Tournament of 1390', *Journal of Medieval and Renaissance Studies* 20 (1990), 1–20.

[45] Lindenbaum, 'Smithfield Tournament', p. 18.

[46] *The Westminster Chronicle*, pp. 432–33: *ac popularibus infinitis*.

also a symbol of chivalric honour.⁴⁷ Richard had the twenty Garter knights liveried with this personal badge, as well as the twenty ladies leading those knights. By having these participants wear his personal badge, Richard was once more showing and demonstrating his power in a symbolic way. The Garter knights were some of the most powerful and chivalric lords in all of England, and included some of Richard's former opponents. Badges and livery at this time were used to demonstrate that those wearing them were in that lord's service, and so having these lords wear his personal badge and livery showed them to be part of Richard's affinity.⁴⁸ He was not only demonstrating this dominance to the lords themselves, but to the realm as a whole. It is because of this that *The Brut* describes the lords as being part of the royal household, stating that 'those on the king's side wore a uniform: on their coats, armour, shields, horses and trappings were white harts ... This hart was the king's livery which he gave to the lords and ladies, knights and squires, so his *household* could be distinguished from other people.'⁴⁹ Richard's authority and power at this time had not recovered from the challenges of the 1380s, but this tournament was meant to project an image of royal power and dominance, even if that was not Richard's true position. The hope was that such a demonstration would have a tangible impact on Richard's real power and authority.

Yet the use of the livery was not just about showing and symbolising dominance over the lords and Richard's former enemies. It was equally about creating companionship and appealing to chivalric honour. The livery and badge were a further example and presentation that the lords (even those formerly opposed to Richard) were now unified and reconciled under his personal kingship. It was to highlight the fact that the wounds of the past had been healed and that all had come together under Richard himself.

The central use of the Order of the Garter, as well as the white hart device, was a symbolic move by Richard, in an effort to exploit his heritage as well as

---

⁴⁷ Eleanor Scheifele, 'Richard II and the Visual Arts', in *Richard II: The Art of Kingship*, ed. Anthony Goodman and James Gillespie (Oxford, 1999), pp. 255–69; Helen Barr, *Socioliterary Practice in Late Medieval England* (Oxford, 2001), p. 83; Michael Bath, 'The White Hart, the *cerf volant*, and the Wilton Diptych', in *Third International Beast Epic, Fable and Fabliau Colloquium* ed. Jan Goossens and Timothy Sodmann (Köln, 1981), pp. 25–42; James L. Gillespie, 'Richard II's Cheshire Archers', *Transactions of the Historic Society of Lancashire and Cheshire* 125 for 1974 (1975), 1–39.

⁴⁸ Saul, *Richard II*, pp. 200, 265–66.

⁴⁹ *The Brut*, pp. 343–44: *And pay of the kinges syde were alle of on sute: her cotis, her armyour, schelde3, & her hors & trapure, alle was white hertis ... þe which hert was þe kingi3 lyveray þat he yaf to lorde3 & ladie3, kny3tis and skquiers, for to know his housholde from oþer peple.* [my emphasis].

chivalric honour. Edward III had used tournaments, chivalry and the Order of the Garter to glorify himself and his foreign wars, but he also used them to 'help bring the nobility together' and to 'inspire knights and magnates, and bind them to him' by allowing them to share in this glorification, which helped to further extend his authority over them.[50] By using the knights of the Order of the Garter as his representatives, Richard was emphasising his heritage, harnessing and using the memory of Edward III embodied by the Garter to further his own power and authority. Members had to swear obedience and loyalty to the king of England as Sovereign of the Order. Thus, Richard was reminding the companions of their oaths to himself as king.[51]

From the mid-fourteenth century ideals of chivalry had strongly emphasised loyalty to the crown as an imperative trait in the chivalric ethos.[52] By holding the greatest chivalric event of his reign to date, by having the most chivalrous knights participate, and by having them wear the white hart as a sign of chivalric honour, Richard was clearly stating that he was the master of English chivalry and that chivalric loyalty was owed to him. He was appealing to the chivalric ethos of each knight participating, but also of those watching the spectacle, to garner greater loyalty and support, and in turn further his own authority. By showing himself to be the head of English chivalry this also had the further advantage of ensuring that patronage of tournaments remained in Richard's hands, as nobles would look to him for sponsorship and not others.

The Smithfield tournament was also a chance for Richard to create an image of manhood for himself. He had declared himself of age the year before the tournament, in 1389, aged twenty-two. However, as recently as 1388, at the Merciless Parliament, Richard was still being considered as a youth. During the political turmoil of that year the Lords rebuked Richard for his 'youthful duplicity' and 'misgovernance', warning him to correct his mistakes and rule better in the future. Richard conceded to the Lords and agreed 'to be guided by their wholesome advice'.[53] One of the key reasons for the execution and

[50] Scott L. Waugh, *England in the Reign of Edward III* (Cambridge, 1991), p. 130.

[51] Boulton, *The Knights of the Crown*, pp. 118–38.

[52] This can be clearly seen in Geoffroi de Charny's *Book of Chivalry*, with statements such as 'for the faith and loyalty which they owe to their lord cannot be better demonstrated than by serving him and assisting him loyally'. See Richard W. Kaeuper and Elspeth Kennedy, *The Book of Chivalry of Geoffroi de Charny: Text, Context, and Translation* (Philadelphia, 1996), p. 89: *car la foy et loyauté qu'ilz doivent a leur seignur ne peut ester miex monstree que de li server et aidier loyaument*.

[53] Saul, *Richard II*, pp. 175–205; *The Westminster Chronicle*, pp. 226–28: *Ad hec stupefactus rex ait se velle ipsis prout decuit in licitis obtemperare et eorum salubri consilio*

purge of Richard's councillors and household, at the end of the Parliament, was because they were considered to have 'taken advantage of Richard's tender age' and offered him youthful counsel.[54] Smithfield provided Richard with the prime opportunity to prove his manhood in a martial setting. Kingship in the late fourteenth century had become interlinked with ideas of manhood and masculinity, to the extent that a good king was seen to be a manly king.[55] One key area of proving manhood throughout the Middle Ages was through martial deeds.[56] The *Westminster Chronicler* claims that the proposal for holding the tournament came from William, duke of Guelders, who was 'anxious' to see Richard 'accoutred for combat'.[57] The suggestion here is that Richard had not hitherto been seen in a state ready for battle and that it would be beneficial for Richard to show himself in such a way. The chronicler asserts that Richard won the honours of the first day, and even Froissart claims that 'King Richard entered Smithfield magnificently accompanied by dukes, lords, and knights, for he was the chief of the tenants of the lists'.[58] By taking part in the tournament, leading the Garter knights, and even performing well, Richard was revealing his martial prowess to confirm his manhood in the eyes of his subjects. By thus proving his manhood, Richard could project an image of good kingship.

How far was the Smithfield tournament successful in re-establishing the royal authority of Richard II? In 1388 Richard's authority was at an all-time low, as the Appellant lords took over the governance of the realm. However, by the mid-1390s, Richard's personal authority was at an all-time high.[59] There was immediate success in re-establishing and furthering royal authority after the Smithfield tournament. Throughout the 1390s Richard retained more than eighty-two knights in his personal service, when previously he had retained

---

gubernari.

[54] Saul, *Richard II*, pp. 175–205; Anthony Tuck, *Richard II and the English Nobility* (London, 1973), pp. 121–34.

[55] Katherine J. Lewis, *Kingship and Masculinity in Late Medieval England* (London, 2013), pp. 1–23. For a full study on Richard's manhood, and its impact on kingship, see Christopher Fletcher, *Richard II: Manhood, Youth, and Politics, 1377–99* (Oxford, 2008)

[56] Ruth Mazo Karras, *From Boys to Men: Formations of Masculinity in Medieval Europe* (Philadelphia, 2003), pp. 1–10, 20–28.

[57] *The Westminster Chronicle*, pp. 450–51: *nam dux Geldr' dum esset hic in Anglia multum affectavit videre regem nostrum armatum.*

[58] Froissart, *Chronicles*, 2: 479: *Aprés nonne s'en vint le roy d'Angleterre sur la place arméz et bien acompaigniés de ducs, de contes et de grans seigneurs, car il estoit de ceulx de dedens.*

[59] Saul, *Richard II*, pp. 235–69.

just seven. More than half of these were retained between 1391 to 1392, the years immediately after the tournament.[60] The men retained were substantial figures within their own communities. Most were lords of several manors or more, such as Sir Gerard Braybrooke and Sir William Sturmy. Richard also attracted men such as Sir Simon Fellbrigg, Sir William Arundel and Sir Edward Dallingridge to his service. All of them had previously been retained by Appellant lords and may have even been part of the military opposition to Richard in 1387.[61] Clearly Richard's personal authority had risen considerably from what it had been in the 1380s, to encourage retainers of his former enemies to choose his lordship over theirs. If Richard were still a weak king after 1390, then these men would have continued to remain in the service of the Appellants, as Richard's own lordship would not have been attractive. Thus, it is no coincidence that these men were retained after the Smithfield tournament, where Richard was able to show to the realm an image of good lordship and good kingship.

This increase in retaining had an additional effect as more of Richard's affinity were returned as members of Parliament. In the first Parliament of 1390 Richard had thirteen members of his affinity returned, but this number had almost doubled to twenty-two for the Parliament of 1391.[62] This in turn gave Richard a greater influence and control of Parliament. From 1391 the Commons granted Richard the wool subsidy and tonnage and poundage at the full rate. He was also granted a half tenth and fifteenths, with another full tenth and fifteenth if he was to go to war.[63] In previous years the Commons had been reluctant to grant taxation, but now as a monarch steadily growing in power and authority, Richard was able to get more out of them, with taxation in 1393 being granted 'to honour the person of the king'.[64]

In conclusion, it can be said that the tournament in medieval England was not just a pastime of the nobility that was vainglory and hollow. The development of the tournament in England was distinctive from that in continental Europe in that it was politicised almost from its outset. It became an important part of royal ceremony, an instrument that could have powerful effects within the realm. Wielded correctly, the tournament was a tool by which monarchs could establish and further their royal authority, as Richard II did

---

[60] Harriss, *Shaping the Nation*, p. 470.
[61] Saul, *Richard II*, pp. 266–67.
[62] Saul, *Richard II*, p. 261.
[63] Harriss, *Shaping the Nation*, p. 474; Tuck, *Richard II and the English Nobility*, p. 144.
[64] *Rotuli Parliamentorum, 1278–1503*, ed. John Strachey et al., 4 vols (London, 1767–77), 3: 301–2.

with Smithfield in 1390. Richard used the tournament to demonstrate the reconciliation between himself and the nobility. He used the Garter knights and lords as the key participants in the event, many of whom were Appellant lords who had previously been his enemies. He took a symbolic approach to their participation by ensuring that they all wore his own personal badge and livery of the white hart. This was to demonstrate to all present that they were under Richard's control, part of his affinity for the tournament, and reconciled with the king. The use of the Garter knights was also a way for Richard to use his heritage, and the prestige of his grandfather, Edward III, to consolidate power in his own reign. Richard was attempting to appeal to notions of loyalty to the crown inherent in the chivalric ethos to his own advantage. By holding a great chivalric event, and using the most chivalric knights, he was demonstrating that he was the ruler of English chivalry and that loyalty was owed to him. Furthermore, by leading these knights himself, and winning the honours of the first day, Richard was trying to prove his manhood in a martial setting, and in so doing, project an image of manliness and good kingship. Richard's attempts to use the tournament to further his authority had tangible effects as it allowed him to attract more knights and country gentry to his service, as his lordship was seen to be more attractive. This in turn allowed Richard to gain greater power over Parliament, especially the Commons, as several taxes were granted to him in 1391. It is in the years after 1390 that Richard's authority was considered at its height, and the Smithfield tournament was one of the tools used by him to make that happen.

4   *Alle myn harneys for the justes:* Documents as a Source for Medieval Jousting Armour

Ralph Moffat

William, Baron Bergavenny, was so familiar with his jousting equipment that he could, in his will of 1408, simply refer to it as his *h[ar]neys*.[1] In the same way John, Earl Warenne, left *tout mon hernoys p[u]r le Jouster* (all my harness for jousting) to his son in 1347.[2] For Bartholomew, Lord Burghersh, in 1369 these were *les armes entier p[u]r les joustez q[ue] fuist pur mon corps* (all the jousting arms that were for my body).[3] A Leicestershire knight's possessions were laconically recorded as *Justy[n]gherneys* in 1374.[4] The term *harness*, of obscure origin, became synonymous with the armour borne by warriors. As a horse is strapped and buckled into its harness, so too is the man into his. Bearing such contemporary familiarity in mind, is it possible to unpick some detail and provide a deeper insight into the specialised equipment used by jousters? In this essay I seek to prove that this can be done – to some extent – and that through an examination of such documents as wills, inventories and household payments a picture will emerge of both the dynamic evolution and stagnant decay of this jousting 'harness'. These sources are all the more important to the study of the origins and development of the joust as very little material culture has passed down to us.[5] They also provide solid dating evidence, unlike many other textual sources such as romances and poems.

---

[1] London, Lambeth Palace Library, MS Register of Archbishop Arundel 2, fol. 156r.
[2] York, Borthwick Institute, MS Abp Reg 10 (William Zouche 1342–52), fol. 316v. Mr Nathan Williams was most generous with his assistance locating this and other York documents.
[3] London, Lambeth Palace Library, MS Register of Archbishop Whittlesey, VA6, fol. 98r–v.
[4] London, British Library, MS Sloane Charter XXXI 2: Inventory of the effects of Sir Edmund Appleby, Appleby Magna, Leicestershire, 1374.
[5] The fragments of jousting arms and armour excavated from a German castle cannot be solidly dated. See P. Hans-Werner and D. Breiding, 'An Important Find of

Firstly, a frank admission. Akin to the amusing theatrical prelude to the *Pas d'armes* of the *Perron Phae*, I consider myself merely to be the *nain* standing on the shoulders of the *geans* who have gone before. I have mined a rich seam of references and chased down numerous footnotes from the glossarists Du Cange and Gay, and such scholars of arms and armour as Meyrick, Baron de Cosson, Viscount Dillon, Way, Laking, Beard, ffoulkes, Mann, Norman, Anglo, and Blair. I have endeavoured – wherever possible – to make my own transcriptions of original documents and have thus, as that sage knight Philippe de Mézières advises, imbibed directly from the fount rather than from its streams.[6]

The Joust: A Heads Up

From contemporary sources such as regulations and chronicle descriptions, the purpose of the joust is clear. To gain victory the jouster had to shatter a solid wooden lance on his opponent. The body was a suitable target but the prize was the head.[7] This can also be demonstrated in artwork. In an early fourteenth-century manuscript miniature the jousters lower their lances to strike, while a mirror case from the same period shows a good lance-strike to the head (Figures 1 and 2).

The lance had to be broken with such force as would be required to cause the lancehead to penetrate the head or body, thereby inflicting a fatal blow.[8] Jousts were an extremely important part of celebratory events in this era; a world-weary knight advised his young sovereign:

Late-14th & Early-15th-Century Arms and Armour from Haus Herbede, Westphalia', *Journal of the Arms & Armour Society*, 19 (2007), 1–28.

[6] Philippe de Mézières, *Le Songe du Vieil Pelerin*, ed. G. W. Coopland, 2 vols (Cambridge, 1969), 2: 224: *es ruisseaux comme elle fait en sa propre fontayne*.

[7] For example, Professor Noel Fallows has translated the regulations promulgated in 1330 by Alfonso XI of Castile and León in his *Jousting in Medieval and Renaissance Iberia* (Woodbridge, 2010), pp. 209–11. Rather garbled versions of the rules of John Tiptoft, earl of Worcester, for *justes of peace royall* of 1466 survive in London, British Library, MS Harley 2358, fols 9r–11v, and in later manuscript copies. See also Tobias Capwell's lavishly illustrated *Arms and Armour of the Medieval Joust* (Leeds, 2018), pp. 21–23.

[8] For the lance shaft having to be broken at the correct point, see Ralph D. Moffat, 'The Medieval Tournament: An Edition and Analysis of Three 15th-Century Tournament Manuscripts', (unpublished Ph.D. thesis, University of Leeds, 2010), pp. 61–62.

Fig. 1. Illustration of a miniature from the Codex Balduini Trevirensis, German, c. 1300.

Fig. 2. Ivory mirror case (detail), French, early fourteenth century.

... and especially avoid jousting. I am not saying that if some great foreign king or prince comes to visit you, or at any great nuptials or celebrations, you cannot joust (running to break) four or five lances to honour the company. But do not joust (to break) fifty or sixty or one hundred lances as you are accustomed to do.[9]

To avoid such unpleasantries as severe injuries and fatalities, innovation of equipment was a stark necessity. Adaptions to the lance fittings, protective body armour and saddle can be traced in these documents – sources that pre-date written regulations and the surviving artefacts.

The Jousting Lance and Its Fittings: Coronel, Grapper and Vamplate

To reduce the chance of injury, a new type of lancehead came into use, the coronel. As its name suggests, it is crown-shaped with sharp prongs. The prongs were designed to catch on an opponent's harness causing the lance to break when the strike was true (Figure 3).

The grapper or (in its earlier name) grate was affixed to the lance behind the grip. This device was a disk-shaped attachment that prevented the lance from shooting back under the arm on impact. It also helped prevent injury to the jouster's arm and hand from the rebounding force of his own lance.

Combining the French word *avant* (fore) and the English 'plate', the vamplate was a disc- or cone-shaped piece of metal fitted over, and nailed to, the lance shaft to provide protection against incoming lance strikes (Figure 4).

The first document found (so far) to record these lance fittings was written in 1322. It is an inventory of the goods of Sir Roger Mortimer, earl of March, in his castle at Wigmore, Herefordshire, and also in the abbey there. Here listed are: *j g[r]ate iij vaumplates* and *j coronali p[ro] iustis*. That these items are lance fittings is clear as they are listed just after 'iron heads for lances' (*capitib[u]s ferr' p[ro] lanceis*).[10] As the fourteenth century unfolds more of this equipment reveals itself in the documents. There survives a long and detailed account of Edward III's heaumer (plate armourer) Gerard of Tourney, covering a period from 1 April 1337 to 20 September 1341. In this, we

[9] Philippe de Mézières, *Songe du Vieil Pelerin*, 2: 212: *et par espicial de jouster. Je ne dy pas, que s'il venoit aucun roy ou tresgrant prince estrange pour toy visiter, ou aucunes grans nopces et sollennelles, que tu ne peusses bien jouster quatre ou cinq lances pour la compaignie honourer, et non pas jouster ou l ou lx ou c lances comme tu as acostume.*

[10] Kew, The National Archives (TNA), E 154/1/11B. I extend my thanks to Ms Barbara Wright for sharing her images of this document.

Fig. 3. Miniature from the Sherborne Missal. English, illustrated by John Siferwas between 1396 and 1407.

Fig. 4. Vamplate, German, mid sixteenth century.

see numerous payments for equipment for *les Justes* for that fanatical jouster King Edward, his entourage and visiting dignitaries. These lance fittings are consistently bought together: *iiij Grates & iiij auant plates xx s xij Coronal*s and *iiij auantplates iiij Grates & vj Coronals vij li xij s ij Coronals ij s.*[11] In an article published in 1854 is an inventory of the armoury of Dover Castle of 1361. Regrettably, the original has yet to be traced. In this are: *deux avantplates* and

---

[11] TNA, E 101/338/11.

ij. cornals, j. grate pur joutes.¹² The account of the Constable of that same castle for 1369 to 1371 lists two *vantplatis* along with two *coronal'* and one *gr[a]te p[ro] hastilud'*.¹³ An inventory of the Tower of London of 1372 lists fifteen lance staves without vamplates along with the other fittings: *iiij grates xv stufs lanc' sine auantplat' [...] xxxij Coronaux*.¹⁴ By the later part of the century, such fittings were ubiquitous and the documents in which they are found are discussed below.

Body Defences for the Jouster

With the development of the jousting lance and its fittings a concomitant change in the body defences can be demonstrated. This equipment will be investigated in the order in which the jouster would be armed by his attendant squire.

Torso Defences: Pair of Plates, Poitrine and Breastplate

From the end of the thirteenth century a common torso defence was the pair of plates, often simply referred to as 'plates'. By riveting iron or steel plates of various size to a canvas or leather foundation, armourers crafted a flexible and reliable defence. In some instances left uncovered, plates were usually faced with fabric of some kind. That pairs of these were made specifically for jousting is evidenced by the listing of *ij paires de plattes a jouster* in the inventory of the castle armoury of William, count of Hainaut, at Mons of 1358. These are clearly differentiated from those for use in war: *ij paires de plattes de wiere*.¹⁵ Gerard of Tourney's account of payments for Edward III's armour of 1337 to 1341 lists the *Poit[ri]ne p[u]r Justes* in four instances.¹⁶ This word means 'breast' in French and it is not too foolhardy to interpret this as an early form of breastplate. Six *poitrines a jouster* were in the aforementioned Mons castle armoury in 1358.

---

[12] A. Way, 'Accounts of the Constables of the Castle of Dover', *Archaeological Journal* 11 (1854), 381–88. Thanks are due to Dr Adrian Ailes and Dr Paul Dryburgh for their generous assistance in attempting to locate this document.

[13] TNA, E 101/29/38, mm 1–2. I am grateful to Dr Dryburgh for locating this document.

[14] TNA, E 101/397/10, mm 1–3.

[15] Mons, Archives de l'État, Chartrier des archives de la ville, no. 146.

[16] TNA, E 101/338/11.

The largesse of Edward the Black Prince can be appreciated in his Register. It records his numerous gifts of arms and armour from 25 January 1351 to 24 January 1366. Amongst these are *j peir plates p[u]r les justes & j brestplate*. These were received at the time of the 'joust which the Earl of March had cried after the fête at Windsor in the thirty-second regnal year' (*a les Justes q[ue] le Counte de la March' fist crier ap[re]s la feste de Wyndesore lan du regne le Roi xxxij*). This provides a firm date of some short time after St George's Day (23 April) 1358.[17] In Dover castle armoury in 1361 there was *j. brustplate pur Justes* and the *brestplate p[ro] hastilud'* in the account of this same castle of 1369 to 1371 is most probably the same one.[18] More gifts from the Black Prince's Register hint at the possibility of the jousting breastplate having been borne over the pair of plates thus providing a secondary layer of protection. One *peir plates p[u]r les justes & j brestplate* were given together and, intriguingly, another participant received one 'pair of plates covered with cloth of gold, and one breastplate, and one pair of vices' (*j paire plates couertz oue drap door [sic] & j Brestplate & j paire vices*).[19] Might these 'vices' be some means by which the breastplate was affixed over the pair of plates? At present, there are no similar sources which might serve to shed any more light on this word.

Arm and Hand Defences

Manifer: *Main-de-Fer*

By combining the flared cuff of the plate gauntlet with the lower-arm and elbow plates (vambrace and couter) skilled armourers came up with a solid one-piece defence for the left arm: the 'iron hand'. Viscount Dillon eloquently refers to 'the main de fer, its name at once explaining its nature, and uncorrupted by long usage'.[20] No examples from the period under discussion survive but some idea of their construction and appearance is provided by existing fifteenth-century manifers (Figure 5).

As with the poitrine, the earliest instance so far documented is in Gerard of Tourney's account of 1337 to 1341. Two shillings are spent on furbishing two (*p[u]r le Fourbir de ij maindefer ij s*) and the same amount for the purchase of another two *maindefer*.[21] The mention of 'furbishing' is noteworthy. Rather

---

[17] TNA, E 36/278.

[18] Way, 'Account of Dover Castle', p. 188; TNA, E 101/29/38, mm 1–2.

[19] TNA, E 36/278.

[20] Viscount Dillon, 'An Armourer's Bill, temp. Edward III', *The Antiquary* 20 (1890), 148–50 (p. 148).

[21] TNA, E 36/278.

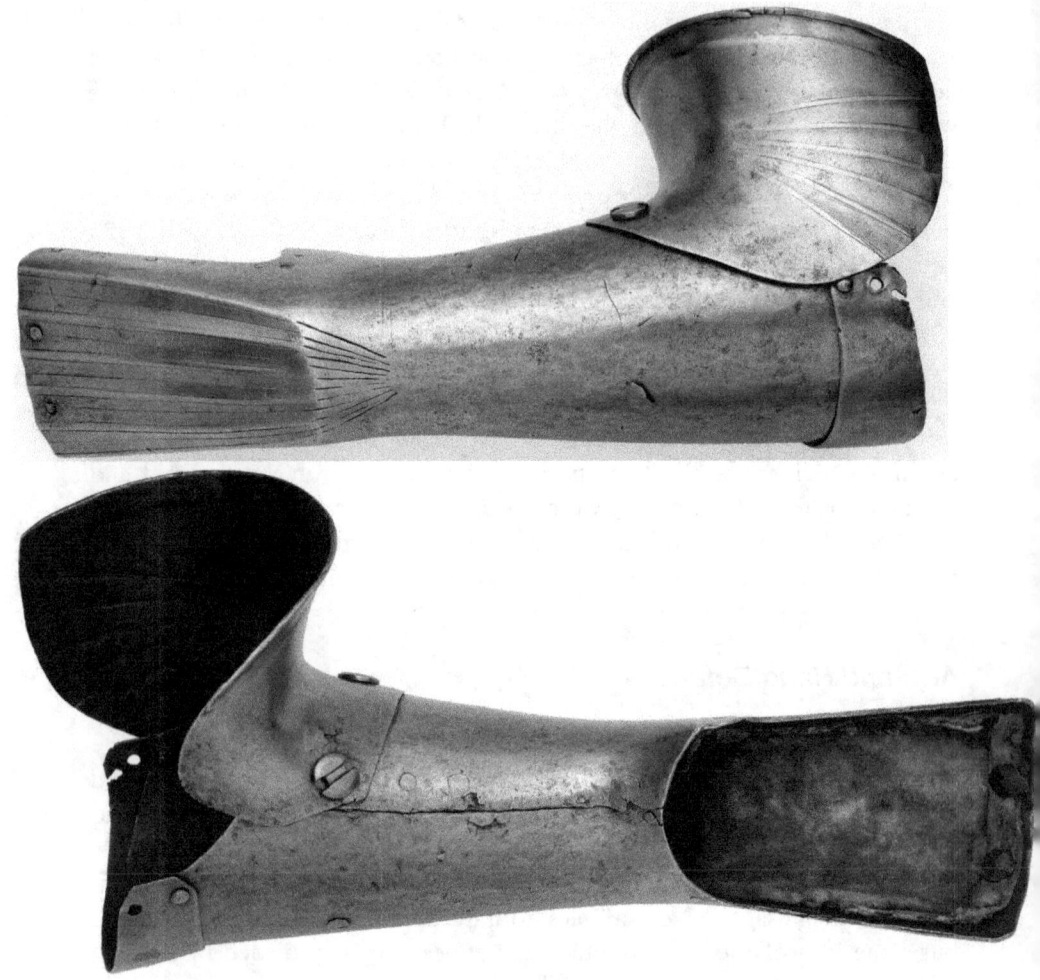

Fig. 5. Manifer, German, c. 1490.

than a newly-made piece, this suggests that a manifer that had previously been in use is here re-serviced. As will be argued below, a lack of descriptive features or sense of novelty is indicative of the use of such equipment prior to its appearance in the record. Manifers next appear – in the sources consulted – in the inventory of a Nottinghamshire knight of 1355. Two are listed after his jousting saddle, helms and shield: *j sel p[u]r lez justes ij helmes j escu ij meyndeffers*.[22] An inventory of the Tower of London of 1372 records a *mayndefer*

[22] Nottingham, Nottingham University Library, MS Mi I 40: Goods of Sir Baudwyn Fryvill, location not recorded.

with other jousting kit.²³ References to manifers proliferate in such sources as inventories of effects of Englishmen towards the end of the century. In 1387 Sir Simon Burley had six *mayndefers* with *vj vamplates v grates & xij cornals*.²⁴ John Dounton, keeper of armour to Henry, earl of Derby (the future Henry IV), kept a detailed account between 1393 and 1394. Dounton purchased a new manifer for his lord for jousts and also made payments for the riveting and repair of another (*j mayndefer nou' empt' p[ro] d[omi]no p[ro] hastilud' … p[ro] Clouura vni' mayndefer & p[ro] mu[n]dac[i]o[n]e eiusd[e]m*). One was also purchased for the earl's teenaged half-brother Thomas Beaufort.²⁵ Two *mayn de fers* were inventoried amongst *lez p[ar]cell' del h[er]noys* of Richard, earl of Arundel, in 1397.²⁶ The five *maindeferr'* belonging to Thomas, duke of Gloucester, in the same year were for *p[u]r ioustes de pees*.²⁷ An inventory dated January 1399/1400 records six *maynfers* and seventeen vamplates at Dartington Hall, Devon. These, along with his two *justynsad'* and *helmes*, are the meagre legacy of John Holland, earl of Huntingdon, a skilled jouster who was much celebrated in his day.²⁸

Polder-Mitton

The manifer served as a good protection for the jouster's left arm and hand. What then, for the right? The lance's vamplate offered some defence for this area but it is possible to chart a new development in the household accounts of Henry, earl of Derby, of 1393/4. Arm defences for the right forearm were purchased for jousting. Each pair of these vambrace are described as 'with one wing': *j par' vantbras cu' j ala p[ro] hastilud' vj s* and *j vantbras cu' vna ala p[ro] hastilud' vj s*.²⁹ This entry can be interpreted as meaning that the vambrace has a protruding section extending over the vulnerable inside of the elbow to deflect lance strikes. It can be strongly argued that we have here the progenitor of the polder-mitton. From the French for 'shoulder of mutton', existing polder-mittons do bear an uncanny resemblance to that cut of meat. An anonymous Frenchman writes of the arms and armour employed in France in 1446.

---

23 TNA, E 101/397/10, mm 1–3.
24 Oxford, Bodleian Library, MS Eng.hist. b.229, fol. 9r.
25 TNA, DL 28/1.
26 TNA, E 163/6/13.
27 TNA, E 136/77/4. Jousts of peace and war are discussed below.
28 TNA, C 145/278/37.
29 TNA, DL 28/1.

Under the section *La faczon de leur harnoys de Jouste* he provides a detailed description:

> On the right hand ... from the gauntlet to beyond the elbow, in lieu of a vambrace, is a (piece of) armour called a polder-mitton. This is made wide around the elbow and expands downwards and around the crook of the elbow. It is made thus so that, in bending (the arm) when one places the lance in the (lance) rest, the curve of the said polder-mitton covers the crook of the elbow for a good palm in height.[30]

Evidence for the adoption of the word into English is found in a manuscript dating to the mid-fifteenth century. This celebrated work contains striking miniatures of jousting scenes as well as a rare depiction of a warrior in the process of being armed by his squire. In the section on the *Abilment for the Justus of the Pees* a *maynfere* and a *rerebrasce a moton* [sic] are permitted.[31]

There are many fine examples of this defence surviving from the fifteenth century; illustrated here is one from Glasgow Museums' collection (Figure 6). The artist of a beautiful French manuscript of *c.* 1470 (now in the British Library) has clearly depicted a single-piece polder-mitton in a dramatic jousting scene (Figure 7). And, although not depicted in a jousting context, some impression of the form this piece may have taken comes from a drawing made by an anonymous Tuscan artist around 1435 (Figure 8).

It is not too far-fetched to seek the development of new pieces of armour at this time. The pauldron, a more fully-developed plate shoulder defence, is to be found in the possession of Richard, earl of Arundel, in 1397 and in the Tower of London in 1413. Pairs were purchased for the Earl Marshal in 1414 and for Thomas, duke of Clarence, in 1418.[32]

---

[30] Paris, Bibliothèque nationale de France, MS fr. 1997, fols 63r–79r (fol. 76r): *a la main droite ... depuis le gantellet Jusques oultre le code en lieu de auant braz y a vne armeure qui se appelle espaulle de mouton laquelle est faczonnee large endroit le code Et se espanouist aual Et endroit la ploieure du braz se Reuient ploier par faczon que quant len a mis la lance en larrest la dicte ploieure de la dicte espaulle de mouton couure de puis la ploieure du braz vng bon dor en hault.*

[31] New York, Pierpont Morgan Library, MS M.775, fol. 123v. For a detailed investigation, see Viscount Dillon, 'On a Ms. Collection of Ordinances of Chivalry of the 15th Century Belonging to Lord Hastings', *Archaeologia* 57 (1900), 29–70.

[32] TNA, E 163/6/13 and E 361/6/11d; Berkeley, Berkeley Castle Archives, Muniment D1/1/30; London, Westminster Abbey, MS Muniment 12163, fol. 12r.

Fig. 6. Polder-mitton, probably Flemish, mid-fifteenth century.

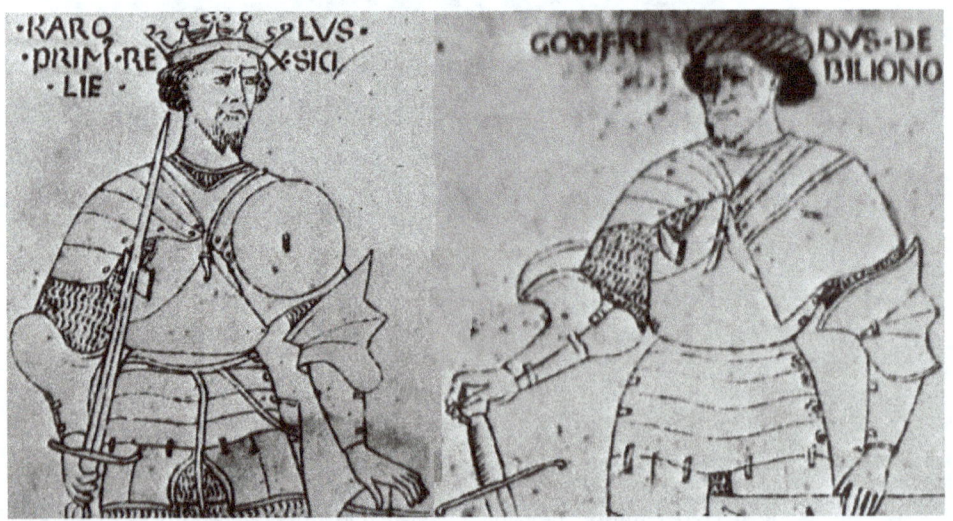

Fig. 7. MS miniature, French, c. 1470.

Fig. 8. Detail of an illustration from the *Libro di Giusto*, Tuscan, c. 1435.

Fig. 9. Stained glass panel, German, c. 1380–1400.

Reinforces for Helms

There are numerous fourteenth-century depictions of reinforcing plates strapped and buckled across the front of the jousting helm. From the Bodleian Library's lavish *Romance of Alexander* of c. 1338–44 and Gelre Herald's vibrant armorial to images in stained glass (Figure 9), its function was clearly understood by these artists.

Jack Scott of Glasgow Museums identified a (now lost) example of a helm and reinforce found in the environs of the tower house of Castlemilk to the south of the city of Glasgow, recorded in an engraving in a publication of 1793 (Figure 10).[33]

Such pieces are to be found in the documents. In 1358 the count of Hainaut had six jousting helms and six bevors: *vj hiaumes a jouster et vj baiuieres*.[34] The bevor (from French *baver*: to dribble, slaver from the mouth) is a plate defence for the lower face and throat. Only fifteenth-century bevors survive and are undoubtedly of a different form. This later type is borne with the sallet (helmet): headgear not usually associated with jousting. To return to the fourteenth century, the second earl of Salisbury received from the Black Prince one helm with mantling garnished with silver and one bevor-strap in the same suite for the jousts held in 1358: *j heaume oue vn cower garniz dargent & j seint[u]re al Barber del seute garniz dargent*.[35] The word *bevor* appears to give way to the simple 'piece' or *pièce*. Thus there are *ij peces p[ro] j helm d[omi]ni* purchased between 1392 and 1393 for Henry, earl of Derby, and two *peses de healmes* amongst the jousting armour of Thomas, duke of Gloucester, in 1397.[36] I have argued elsewhere that variants of the word 'piece' have been used by writers to denote a reinforcing plate borne over such armour as the pair of plates from the early fourteenth century.[37]

---

[33] J. G. Scott, 'Two 14th-Century Helms Found in Scotland', *Journal of the Arms & Armour Society* 4 (1962), 68–71 (p. 71); D. Ure, *The History of Rutherglen and East-Kilbride* (Glasgow, 1793), fig. 1 opp. p. 60.

[34] Mons, Archives de l'État, Chartrier des archives de la ville, no. 146.

[35] TNA, E 101/338/11.

[36] TNA, DL 28/1 and E 136/77/4.

[37] Ralph Moffat, 'The *Manner of Arming Knights for the Tourney*: A Re-Interpretation of an Important Early 14th-Century Arming Treatise', *Arms & Armour* 7 (2010), 5–29 (p. 6 and p. 18 for discussion). This article investigates London, British Library, Add. MS 46919, fols 86v–87v: *Ad bellu' ... plates de alemayne ou autres cu' p[e]ceb[us]* (For war ... German [steel] plates or others with the piece).

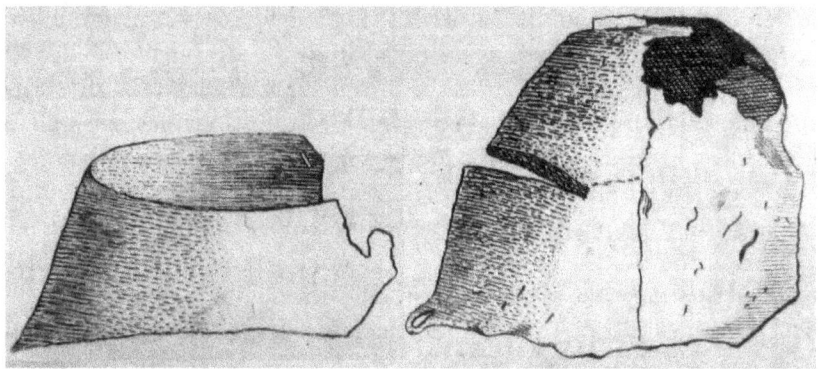

Fig. 10. Engraving of an early fourteenth-century helm and reinforce, 1793.

Keepers of Armour and Armour Makers

Large, solid steel defences such as breastplates, manifers and polder-mittons could certainly have been crafted by armourers working in England in the early fourteenth century. An ordinance regulating tournaments in England was decreed at the siege of Stirling (mid-April to 24 July 1304) and copied at Dartford (Kent) in 1331. Named amongst those of *la cite de loundr[e]s* hiring out equipment were *les healmer[er]s* – helm-makers: an early name for plate armourers.[38] Indeed, in their regulatory 'articles' of 1347 the Heaumers of the city categorise themselves as men who craft 'heaumerie and other armours that are forged with the hammer' (*heaumerie & autr[e]s arm[ur]s q[ue] sount forgez de martel*).[39]

By the late fourteenth century there is solid evidence for the production of jousting armour in England. In 1378 the neighbours of a London armourer, Stephen atte Fryth, complained of the vibrations caused by the sledgehammers used to work great pieces of iron into such armour as breastplates: *cu[m] grossis malleis diu[er]sas magnas pecias ferri ... op[er]and' & faciend' inde diu[er]sas armat[ur]as vid[e]l[ice]t Brestplates*.[40] Stephen atte Fryth held the position of *armurer mons' le Roy* in 1397 and in 1413 was mentioned as 'the late' armourer of King Richard II: *nup[er] armatori Reg' Ric[ard]i se[cun]di*.[41] His replacement under Henry IV, John Dounton, had been keeper of Henry's armour for many years, even accompanying his employer on crusade in

---

[38] Cambridge, Gonville & Caius College Library, MS 424/448, p. 89.
[39] London, London Metropolitan Archives, Letter-Book F, fol. 142v.
[40] London, London Metropolitan Archives, Plea & Memoranda Roll A10.
[41] TNA, E 136/77/4 and E 361/6/11d.

Prussia.⁴² In 1402 Dounton secured a lifelong pension after holding the office of Armourer of the King's Body within the Tower of London (*loffice de Armorer pur v[ost]re corps deinz v[ost]re Tour de londres a t[er]me de sa vie*).⁴³ The seriousness with which he took his professional responsibilities is evidenced by his forking out 40s to a *Joyno[u]r* for one armoire bought for the Office of the Lord's Armourer (*j armariolo empt' p[ro] officio armat[u]re d[omi]ni*); an intriguing example of a medieval filing cabinet.⁴⁴ Dounton had purchased armour – including that for jousting – from Stephen atte Fryth and other London armourers such as John Grove, John Sendall and Richard Peacock in the 1390s.⁴⁵ These professionals knew each other and trusted in the quality of the specialised equipment crafted by their peers; standing as a testament to the skill of these men. Theirs was the harness on which the very lives of the jousters depended.

The Jousting Saddle

The Queen of Nubia sent her young squire to the court of the Princess of Great Britain so that 'he may learn how the chivalrous knights of your court train their sons and youngsters to stay in the saddle' (*pur lui enseigner coment les chiualerouses chiualers de v[ost]re court soloient enseigner lour filz & enfauntz de lour assaier as selles tenir*). Although her letter was written at the 'Marvellous Manner of Mount Sanai', this Nubian queen is more likely to have been a courtier of Queen Philippa of England in the 1350s.⁴⁶ For as mounted combat with lances began to take place in a more controlled manner than the turbulent stramash of the tournament, changes in the construction of the saddle were under way. The invitation to the royal jousts at Smithfield in 1390 insists

---

⁴² *Expeditions to Prussia and the Holy Land Made by Henry Earl of Derby*, ed. Lucy Toulmin Smith (London, 1894), p. 257.

⁴³ TNA, SC 8/268/13392.

⁴⁴ TNA, DL 28/1.

⁴⁵ TNA, DL 28/1. For the Groves, see Ralph Moffat, 'Armourers and Armour: Textual Evidence', in *Encyclopedia of Medieval Dress and Textiles of the British Isles, c. 450–1450*, ed. Gale R. Owen-Crocker, Elizabeth Coatsworth and Maria Hayward (Leiden, 2012), pp. 49–52.

⁴⁶ Edinburgh, Edinburgh University Library, MS 83, fols 95v–96r. I extend my thanks to Professor Nigel Ramsay and Ms Louise Gardiner for bringing these fascinating challenges to my attention.

that competitors should joust 'in high saddles' (*Jousteront en haultes selles*).[47] The saddler of Henry, earl of Derby, was tasked with *emendac[i]o[n]e alt[er]ius sell' alt' de staur' p[ro] hastilud' pac'*: mending another high saddle from store for the joust of peace.[48]

A detailed study of the saddle is provided elsewhere in this volume. It need only be said here that constructional differences are evident in these written sources. In a legal wrangle of 1350 between the London saddle-makers and fusters (saddletree-makers) there is mention of the *arson p[u]r tournement*, *arson p[u]r Justes* and *arson p[u]r destrers*: wooden saddletrees for tournaments, jousts and destriers (war horses).[49] Amongst 'all manner of other appurtenant harness' (*ou to' maner' autr' herneys apurtenantz*) of an English knight in 1355 was *j sel p[u]r lez justes*.[50] Another English knight's saddle and shield (*sella scuto*) were inventoried as *Justy[n]gherneys* in 1374.[51] Mons castle was home to six *sielles a Jouster* and as many *sielles de Ch[eua]l[ie]rs a tournois* (knights' saddles for tourneys).[52] The level of protection afforded by the saddle was clearly different depending on the realm from which one hailed. Our anonymous French writer of 1446 states that 'in the said Realm of France they arm themselves in legharness when they joust' (*oudit Royaulme de france se arment de harnois de Jambes qua[n]t Ilz Joustent*).[53] The jousting knights in the miniature from the Sherborne Missal (Figure 3) have long-fronted saddles, negating the need for plate leg defences.

The Vocabulary of Jousting Equipment

It is significant that there is no suggestion whatsoever by the men who compiled these documents that this jousting equipment was new or in any way unfamiliar to them. Explanatory language *is* to be found in similar sources elsewhere. One chronicler relating the action of a duel in 1350 explained to his readers that one of the fighters suffered a punch in the face from knuckledusters on his opponent's gauntlets 'called *gadelinges*' in

---

[47] Leeds, Royal Armouries Library, MS 0035 (I.35), fol. 13r; Moffat, 'The Medieval Tournament', p. 251.
[48] TNA, DL 28/1.
[49] London, London Metropolitan Archives, Plea & Memoranda Roll A6.
[50] Nottingham, Nottingham University Library, MS Middleton Mi I 40.
[51] London, British Library, MS Sloane Charter XXXI 2.
[52] Mons, Archives de l'État, Chartrier des archives de la ville, no. 146.
[53] Paris, Bibliothèque nationale de France, MS fr. 1997, fol. 77r.

current parlance (*eos moderni vocant gadelinges*).⁵⁴ A notary itemising the goods of a ship at Plymouth around 1400 considered it necessary to explain that the thirty pairs of plates were *called* brigandines: *xxx paria de platys voc' briganteirs*.⁵⁵ In Durham priory in 1404 was 'one hauberk called a jazerant' (*j lorica vocat' gessera[u]nt*).⁵⁶ The goods of Henry, archbishop of York, in 1423 included *vno pectoral' al' brestplat'*: one chest-piece otherwise known as a breastplate.⁵⁷

By contrast, there is some evidence for novel introductions. For example, arm defences 'of the new manner' were purchased for Edward III between 1337 and 1340 (*vne peire de rerebraz & auantbraz fourbiz p[u]r le corps le Roi de la nouelle man[er]e*).⁵⁸ Five hundred soldiers of a French invasion force of 1385 were issued with basinets that were 'good and suitable of the new style' (*bon et souffisant de nouuelle facon*).⁵⁹

The argument must also be made that these documents required a great deal of accuracy in the terminology employed by their producers. They were of a type that was (and still is) legally binding. In 1322 the goods of the earl of March were delivered to the earl of Arundel by indenture on the orders of the king: *lib' Comiti de Arundel' p[re]cepto d[omi]ni Regis & p[er] indentur'*.⁶⁰ Testators had to ensure that the beneficiaries of their wills would receive the correct bequests. They are also working documents that would pass from one pair of hands to another with each itemised piece ticked off the list. For example, the parcels of armour Stephen atte Fryth inventoried in 1397 were delivered to another armourer: *Lez p[ar]celles de armur' quex Stephan' atte Freth ... ad deliure a Joh[a]n' Torr'*.⁶¹

---

⁵⁴ *Chronicon Galfridi le Baker de Swynebroke*, ed. E. M. Thompson (Oxford, 1889), p. 113.

⁵⁵ TNA, C 145/296/10. For more information on the brigandine, see I. Eaves, 'On the Remains of a Jack of Plate Excavated from Beeston Castle, Cheshire', *Journal of the Arms & Armour Society* 13 (1989), 81–154.

⁵⁶ Durham, University Library, Durham Cathedral Muniments, GB-0033-DCD. For the jazerant, see *Encyclopedia of Medieval Dress and Textiles*, pp. 293–95.

⁵⁷ York, York Minster Archives, L1/17/2.

⁵⁸ TNA, E 101/338/11.

⁵⁹ Paris, Bibliothèque nationale de France, MS latin 16928, fol. 199r.

⁶⁰ TNA, E 154/1/11B.

⁶¹ TNA, E 136/77/4.

Storage and Upkeep

A knight advised his monarch to make a long truce with a warlike neighbouring kingdom in the hope that *thair armyng sall worth ald / And be rottyn, distroyit, or sald*.⁶² This was certainly the fate of much of this jousting harness. Its having been listed along with many old and worn out items indicates the gear to have been stored for some time. Roger, earl of March (b. 1287), had been involved in martial pursuits for many years. He was twenty-two years old when he took part in the Dunstable tournament of 1309. The inventory of his effects of 1322 is an account of the 'dead stock': *comp' de mortuo stauro*.⁶³ The same term – *Mortu' stauru'* – is applied to the jousting equipment in Dover castle between 1369 and 1371. It was piled up with a great deal of other weapons and armour categorised as worn out and of no value (*debil' & null' valor'*).⁶⁴ Some of the armour of Henry, earl of Derby, and a jousting saddle were retrieved from store (*de staur'*) in the 1390s.⁶⁵ 'Old fashioned' vamplates were in Mons castle in 1358 (*ij Rondelles a jouster de le [sic] viese maniere*).⁶⁶ After the execution of the treasonous Henry, Lord Scrope, in 1415, his old jousting saddles (*ij veillis justing sadils*) were accounted for.⁶⁷ The *iij olde Justing' sadell' peinted of diu[er]s werkys* and *x olde Justing sadell' parcell' broken' for the pese* in the Tower of London in 1455 would have been very old indeed.⁶⁸ All of this evidence should be interpreted as demonstrative of these items having been in use for some time before their appearance in the documentary record. The chronology of the development of specialised equipment for the joust needs be reconsidered.

Jousts of Peace and Jousts of War

The investigation into the nature of equipment for jousts of peace, for jousts of war and simply 'for war' must be reserved for another time. Some indication of the complexity can be seen in the sources of the later fourteenth century. Two

---

⁶² *The Bruce / John Barbour*, ed. A. A. M. Duncan (Edinburgh, 1997), p. 347.

⁶³ TNA, E 154/1/11B.

⁶⁴ TNA, E 101/29/38, mm 1–2.

⁶⁵ TNA, DL 28/1.

⁶⁶ Mons, Archives de l'État, Chartrier des archives de la ville, no. 146. For *rondelle* as the French term for vamplate, see Moffat, 'The Medieval Tournament', pp. 40–43.

⁶⁷ Original document cited in C. L. Kingsford, 'Two Forfeitures in the Year of Agincourt', *Archaeologia* 70 (1920), 71–100 (p. 73).

⁶⁸ TNA, C 66/480/7.

lanceheads for jousts of war and six coronels for jousts of peace (*ij ferr' lanc' p[ro] hastilud' guerre & p[ro] vj Coronalx p[ro] hastilud' pac'*) were purchased for Henry, earl of Derby, between 1393 and 1394. Payment was also made for 'one newly-furbished pair of plates made both for (jousts of) peace and for war' (*p[ro] j par' plates nou' furbis' fact' tam p[ro] pac' q[u]am p[ro] guerra*).[69] Richard, earl of Arundel, had three helmets: *bacynetz p[u]r iousts de guerr'* in 1397 and, in that same year the basinet, steel collar and pairs of plates *p[u]r ioustes de guerr'* of Thomas, duke of Gloucester, were inventoried with his *healmes p[u]r ioustes de pees*.[70] In his somewhat circumlocutory bequest of 1408, William, Baron Bergavenny, left *myn best h[ar]neys for to ben armyd Inne Als welle for the were [i.e. war] as for the pees with alle myn other h[ar]neys for the justes of pees w[i]t[h] all other harneys þat longyth to werr'*.[71] So utterly confused was Sir John Cornwall by the challenge to mounted and foot combat he had received from a team of French knights around 1400 that he suggested that two complete harnesses (*deux paires de harnas entiers*) should be crafted and sent as a model to ensure the parity of the arms of both parties.[72]

Conclusion

These surviving documents are tiny pinpricks of light in the umbrous shroud of the unknown. There are, undoubtedly, many more yet to be found. We must look backwards from the earl of March's inventory of 1322 to seek evidence of novelty and use of detailed explanation – 'in the new manner', 'called a', etc. – perhaps then the story of the origins of the joust can be told more fully. The fourteenth century, as we have seen, was both a time of stagnation – with much old and worn-out equipment – and a dynamic period of evolution with such developments as the polder-mitton.

This evolution can be shown to have caused a shift in attitude amongst some fourteenth-century commentators. For them the hurly burly of the mass tournament was done and had given way to a less hazardous and more individualistic show of prowess. In his devotional work of 1354 Henry, duke of Lancaster, envisioned the tormented Christ as having his nose battered and broken like a man who frequently took part in tournaments: *come un home qe*

---

[69] TNA, DL 28/1.
[70] TNA, E 163/6/13 and E 136/77/4.
[71] London, Lambeth Palace Library, MS Register of Archbishop Arundel 2, fol. 156r.
[72] London, British Library, Add. MS 21357, fol. 4r.

va moelt a ces turnois ... le nees grandement defolez et debrisez.[73] For the soldier and chronicler Jean le Bel, William Montagu was a strong and hard knight who had lost an eye in a tournament. Tellingly, in the same sentence Le Bel informs us that Sir William had found such favour with Edward III that he was ennobled as earl of Salisbury.[74]

The joust, on the other hand, was a different matter. John Bromyard, a Dominican friar who died around 1352, fulminated against those 'who have their armour gilded and frivolously decorated' and 'wield large and heavy lances in the joust – which others do not, or cannot wield – and strike both horse and rider to the ground'. All this was inspired, he raged, by nought but 'naked vanity' (*ita de uanitate nuda*).[75] The aforementioned duke of Lancaster openly confessed that he had stretched out his stirrups in the joust not for virtuous purposes, but was motivated purely by the 'vile sin of lust'.[76]

By the 1440s, Alonso, bishop of Burgos in the kingdom of Castile, would rail against knights who concentrated their efforts on:

> having many arms or in changing the conformation of them and devoting one's energy to discovering new pieces of armour and giving them new names so that if our ancestors arose from the dead they would not understand them.[77]

Descendants as well as ancestors find themselves in this same predicament. As more sources come to light our understanding will improve. We can but hope that many more documents and even examples of early jousting arms and armour will be discovered.

---

[73] Henry of Lancaster, *Le Livre de Seyntz Medicines*, ed. E. J. Arnould (Oxford, 1940), p. 138.

[74] *Chronique de Jean le Bel*, ed. J. Viard and E. Déprez, 2 vols (Paris, 1904–5), 2: 110–11: *fort chevalier et dur, et perdist ung œul à l'un de ces tournoys et acquist si grand grace envers le roy qu'il le fist conte de Salebri.*

[75] J. Bromyard, *Summa praedicantium ...*, 2 vols (Venice, 1586), 2: verso of p. 110: *arma sua emunt, & deaurant, & superfluè se ornant ... q' in hastiludio grossam & quadratam portauit lanceam, qualem nullus alius portauit, vel portare potuit, & quod equum & ascensorem proiecit in terra[m].*

[76] *Livre de Seyntz Medicines*, ed. Arnould, p. 72: *estrenai jeo si les estruz a les joustes ... ceo est en droit male entente de cel vile pecché de leccherie.*

[77] Fallows, *Jousting in Medieval and Renaissance Iberia*, pp. 70–71: *en tener muchas armas ni en mudar el tajo de ellas y poner su trabajo en hallar nuevas formas de armaduras y poner nombres nuevos, que si nuestros antecesores se levantasen no los entenderían.*

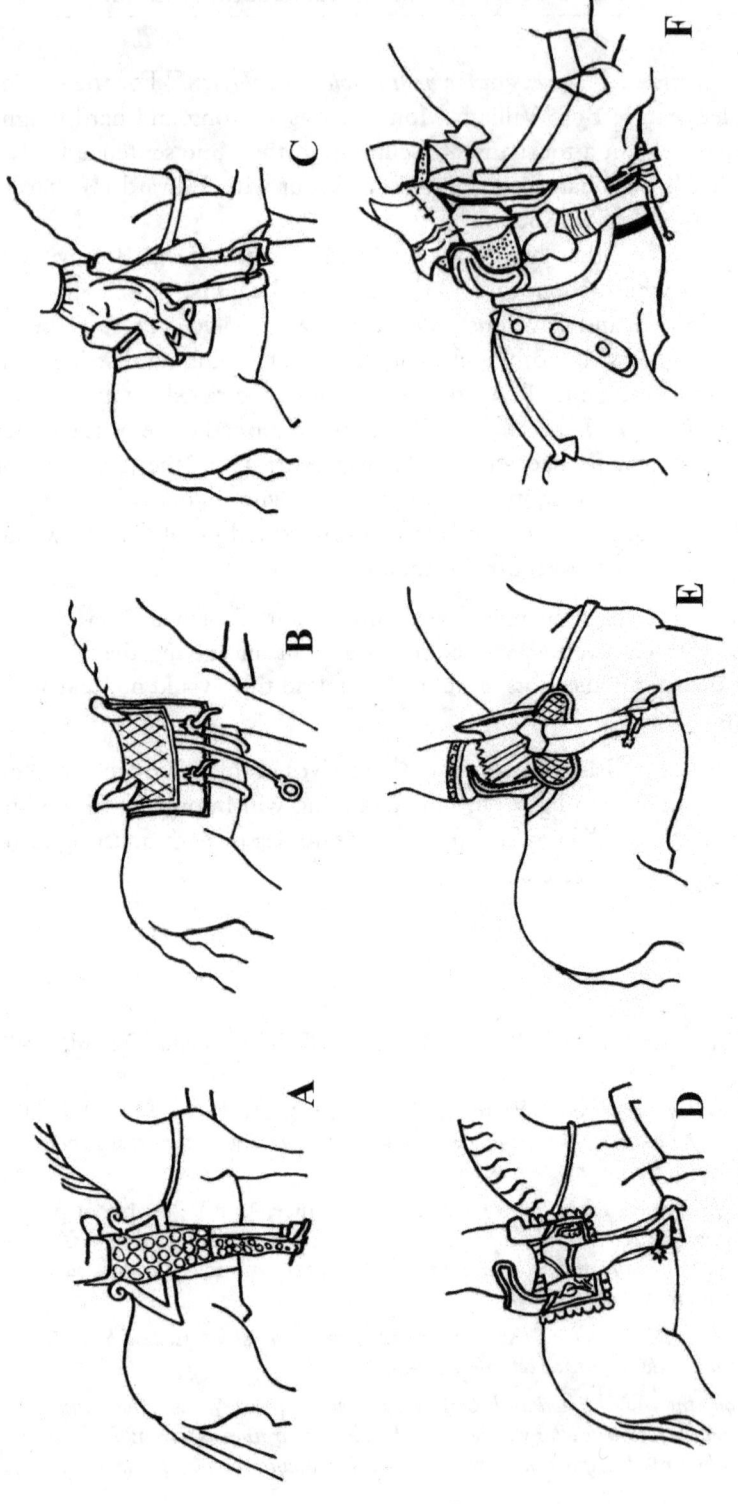

Fig. 1. Main styles of war saddle used in western Europe between the eleventh and fifteenth centuries. A = eleventh century; B = twelfth century; C = thirteenth century; D = fourteenth century; E = fourteenth century (high); F = fifteenth century (author's illustration).

5 The Tournament Saddle

Marina Viallon

The saddle was an essential part of the knight's equipment, as its role was fundamental for the efficiency of the fighting horseman. It was the direct link between horse and man. The latter needed it to be able to make the most of the advantages and qualities of his mount: strength, speed and mobility, without reducing in any way his fighting skills. During the eleventh century in Western Europe, knights developed a specific fighting technique – the charge with the couched lance. This led to the development of a new war saddle by the end of the twelfth century. Far from being a mere change of fashion, this new saddle was the ultimate improvement of a dominant war technique that lasted for more than five centuries. This saddle differed from travelling or hunting saddles, which were designed for other purposes. As the first tournaments in the twelfth century used regular war equipment, their participants also used regular war saddles, which continued in use until the end of the age of the tournaments in the seventeenth century. Nevertheless, from the fourteenth century onwards, some saddles were designed exclusively for the tournament, with features that would make them totally inappropriate in other contexts.

In the Middle Ages a saddle comprised a wooden saddle-tree, composed of four elements: two saddle bows (the pommel at the front, the cantle at the back) and two sidebars, the only elements of the tree in direct contact with the horse's back on either side of its spine. To these sidebars were usually attached the stirrups and leather straps to which the belly girth was buckled. Over this rigid structure there were soft elements, mainly made of leather: the seat (usually stuffed with hay or animal hair) and the saddle flaps. At the back and the front, buckles could be found for the fixation of crupper straps and breast straps, securing the saddle to the horse.

Evolution of the War Saddle

The saddle used by knights up to the first half of the twelfth century was not very different from that represented in the famous Bayeux Tapestry, dated to around 1080 (Figure 1a). Its general shape consisted of a basic seat between two low saddle-bows. Both pommel and cantle were flat and relatively narrow and while they helped the rider to maintain himself on the horse, they could not prevent him from falling on either side. The seat was covered with leather or fabric saddle-flaps descending on the horse's belly to protect the wooden structure and to cover the girth and stirrup buckles, preventing them from being damaged and keeping them from bruising the rider's legs. This type of saddle was attached with a single girth and secured by a simple breast-strap to prevent it from sliding backwards. During the twelfth century, however, the war saddle underwent a notable evolution (Figure 1b), and by the end of the century its shape had been transformed into a type used until the sixteenth century, and known as the high-bow saddle (Figures 1c–f).

We do not know exactly when and where this saddle with high pommel and cantle was developed. It may have been during the 1180s, but it was certainly established by the last decade of the twelfth century and was used by all Western European knighthood. Its basic shape was a straight seat elevated at least about ten centimetres above the horse's back, and flanked by high and wide saddle bows. Sometime later, the curved cantle would also enclose the rider's hips. The pommel appears slightly curved towards the front, allowing the knight to stretch his legs forwards more comfortably. Very good representations of it can be found in illuminations of the Morgan Bible, while the Bamberg Horseman gives us an exceptional three-dimensional example.[1] More than merely allowing the knight to be safer during combat, this new saddle was the result of several decades of research to improve the couched lance technique itself in order to make the great cavalry charge the most feared and dominant battlefield tactic of the time.

Unlike combat with the sword or other single-hand weapons, lance combat as it had evolved in the twelfth century was an exclusively cavalry technique, using the horse's strength and speed as two essential components of its efficiency. The saddle was the only physical link between knight and horse, and the new saddle type transformed the union of man and horse into a terrible war machine that dominated the battlefield for three centuries. The efficiency of the blow also depended on the position of the lance-bearer. The new lance technique certainly compelled the rider to find a more suitable position, leading to the development of a new saddle securing him in that position. As shown in many late twelfth- and thirteenth-century illuminations, the knight aimed at his opponent by bending his upper body forward and stretching his

---

[1] New York, Pierpont Morgan Library, MS M.638 (Paris, c. 1240–50). This manuscript is known variously as the 'Morgan Bible', 'Maciejowski Bible' and 'Crusader Bible'. The Bamberg Horseman (Ger. Bamberger Reiter), a sculpture, c. 1230 in Bamberg cathedral, Germany.

straight legs towards the horse's shoulders, making an angle where the point was locked in the cantle. Helped by the curved cantle securing his hips, the knight was able to keep his body balanced, essential for a good aim, and above all, locked in. He was able to take the shock of his own weapon, as well as being less easily unhorsed by an opponent. If the main concern of this type of fighting saddle in the Middle Ages was personal security, it also allowed knights to give stronger and more efficient blows, particularly with the lance, and allowed them to resist opposing riders similarly equipped.[2]

Despite some minor developments, such as a more curved cantle found from the fourteenth century onwards (Figure 1d), this was the main type of war saddle used in Western Europe until early modern times. As a result of changes in warfare, this saddle was progressively abandoned during the first half of the sixteenth century, to be replaced by a lower type inspired by the *jineta* saddle (Muslim light cavalry saddle), and the medieval type survived mainly as a tournament saddle. It seems to have completely disappeared around the mid-sixteenth century.

The First Tournament Saddles

It was during the early fourteenth century, when specialised arms and armour such as reinforcing plates and blunted weapons started to be used in tournaments, that the first tournament saddles appeared, their main purpose being to give the rider additional protection and security. It seems that the first tournament saddles were simply war saddles with the addition of specific elements. Interesting examples can be seen in some of the illuminations from the Manesse Codex (Figure 2).[3]

The jouster's thighs are protected by elongated padded cushions attached to either side of the pommel. Indeed, the thighs, whether mailed or otherwise,

---

[2] The Mallorcan knight Ramon Llull describes the metaphorical significance of the knight's weapons and equipment in his *Llibre de l'orde de cavalleria* (1275). Concerning the saddle, see: Ramon Llull, *Llibre de l'Ordre de Cavelleria*, ed. M. Gustà (Barcelona, 1980), p. 71: *La sella en que cavalca lo cavaller per significar seguretat de coratge e carrec de cavalleria; car enaixi con per la sella cavaller esta segur sobre son cavall, enaixi seguretat de coratge fa estar de cara lo cavaller en la batalla, per la qual seguretat esdeve ventura amiga de cavalleria* ('The saddle in which the knight is riding signifies the safety of courage and the task and burden of chivalry; because as in his saddle the knight is kept safe on his horse, the same way the safety of courage makes the knight face the battle, for the said safety helps him in adventure, the friend of chivalry.').

[3] Heidelberg, Universitätbibliothek, MS Pal.germ. 848 (German, c. 1310–40).

Fig. 2. Albrecht Marschall von Rapperswil winning a joust, Manesse Codex, fol. 192v, Zürich, c. 1310–40.

were particularly exposed to opponents' weapons (lances or swords) and many tournament saddles had features protecting this area.[4]

An early and impressive representation of a saddle especially designed for a tournament can be found on an equestrian statue of Cangrande I della Scala, lord of Verona, made around 1335 (Figure 3).

This sculpture, originally placed at the top of Cangrande's funerary monument next to the church of Santa Maria Antica of Verona, represents the lord and his horse fully equipped to fight in a tourney using lance and sword.[5] The most interesting element of the portrayed equipment is the saddle. Both cantle and pommel are very high, to protect the lower chest (stomach) and the loins. Two lateral panels, of *cuir bouilli* (hardened leather), are represented as being attached between the pommel and the long cantle's extensions. These panels would protect the knight's thighs similarly to the cushions seen in the Manesse Codex. Hence Cangrande is seen completely enclosed in his saddle, making it impossible for him to fall from his horse but also protecting his vital organs. Even when they were not completely enclosed as here, these very efficient saddles are certainly the reason why we see so many falling horses in tournaments. Rider and mount being almost inseparable, a too-violent lance blow to the knight would have toppled both man and horse to the ground. However, even though it had many advantages, such a saddle would never have been used in battle. In war, for practical reasons but also for his own safety, the knight had to be able to move freely in his saddle, turning backwards, and above all to mount and dismount easily and without help, and to free himself from the saddle if his horse was killed under him. Most of the time, tournament saddles were differentiated from war saddles by long cantle wings fully enclosing the hips and a very long and protective pommel. Certain variant forms of these evolved into very elaborate and distinctive types.

---

[4] The high and wide pommels of late medieval fighting saddles, often reinforced with steel plates, had the same properties. Pietro Monte describes them in his *Collectanea* (*De sellis quibus milites gravis armature utuntur*): Pietro Monte, *Petri Montii exercitiorum, atque artis militaris collectanea in tris libros distincta* (Milan, 1509), ch. 89 [unpag.]. In the same chapter, he mentions that the lateral parts of the pommel protecting the knees are called *urtus* in the vernacular. *Urtus* is probably a Latinisation of the French word *hourt*, also used by René of Anjou in his *Book of Tournaments*, about 1465, for describing a wide padded element suspended from the saddle, protecting both the rider's legs and the horse's chest.

[5] The original is preserved in the Museo Civico di Castelvecchio, Verona.

Fig. 3. Funerary statue of Cangrande della Scala, lord of Verona, c. 1335.

The High Saddle

One of the most impressive and specific types of saddle created for the tournament was the one generally called the 'high saddle' (*Hohenzeug* in German), for it raised the rider between 15 and 30 centimetres above the horse's back.[6]

[6] Note that the rider is not sitting on the saddle.

The Tournament Saddle

Fig. 4. Tourneyers on high saddles, after a drawing in a boxwood sketchbook attributed to the circle of Jacquemart de Hesdin, France, third quarter fourteenth century, Morgan Library, New York (author's illustration).

The first high tournament saddles appeared at the same time as some war saddles also began to 'rise' in the regions under German influence, around 1360. A drawing in a sketchbook attributed to the circle of Jacquemart de Hesdin, executed in the third quarter of the fourteenth century (Figure 4), shows two knights in tournament equipment, one with a lance, the other with a sword, both riding the new saddle.[7]

The seat itself is very high, and positions the rider, using the 'standing style', with his bottom pressed against the cantle, and his knees at the level of the horse's back. For the rider on the right, the pommel's extensions are long enough and curved inwards to protect the legs against lance blows. However, the knight using the sword does not have a very protective pommel; perhaps this was a variant designed for tourneys using swords only. The cantle's wings almost completely enclose the rider's hips, but are not fixed to the pommel, preventing him from falling sideways but allowing the man to mount and dismount by himself.[8] The statue of Mastino II della Scala in Verona, dated to the 1350s, shows a similar saddle but with the use of what appear to be removable belts between pommel and cantle, enclosing the rider completely (Figure 5).[9]

---

[7] Despite being drawn next to each other, these two riders are independent figures and are not meant to be part of the same tournament.

[8] Certainly with difficulty, and possibly with the help of mounting steps.

[9] These belts are only visible on early photographs of the sculpture. They broke, with part of the pommel, before the original statue entered the collection of the Museo

Fig. 5. Funerary statue of Mastino II della Scala, lord of Verona, c. 1351–60.

The use of belts, straps or ropes for securing the rider on the saddle was then generally forbidden by tournament rules, for the obvious advantage they gave. Such explicit interdictions are found up to the early modern period, as in the *ordonnance* published for the tournament of the Field of Cloth of Gold (1520).[10] In the case of Mastino II, the exceptional use of these belts could be explained by the flat pommel, which is less restraining than the curved one drawn by Jacquemart de Hesdin. This first form of tournament high saddle, obviously designed to give maximum protection and security in lance combat, seems to have stayed almost unchanged until the end of the fourteenth century.[11] A relief preserved in the Germanisches Nationalmuseum in Nuremberg for example, representing St George slaying the dragon, shows the saint riding this type of high saddle.[12] On this sculpture, which can be dated to between 1370 and 1380, the pommel's wings extend over the full length of the legs to the feet. The appearance of such impressive saddles can be explained by the development of a special type of war saddle in the second half of the fourteenth century (Figure 1e).

During this period, some saddles were significantly higher, with a narrower seat. The result was that instead of being seated on the seat with the lower part of the back pressed against the rear saddle-bow, the rider had to place his bottom *on* the cantle, with the upper part of his thighs enclosed by the cantle's wings. Riding with straight legs, he stood rather more than he sat. This elevated position is perfectly described by King Duarte of Portugal in his treatise written in 1438:

> This style is based on riding firm on the stirrups with the legs extended and not being seated on the saddle, but having the body balance helped by the saddle-bows, the pommel and the cantle. Those who used this riding style have learned it in the old time.[13]

---

di Castelvecchio, Verona.

[10] *L'ordonnance et ordre du tournoy, joustes et combats à pied et à cheval* (Paris, 1520), p. 6.

[11] Lances were used in both tourneys and jousts. It is often impossible to say when seeing an illustration of a knight alone whether he was equipped for a joust or a mêlée using lances. Later representations confirm the use of high saddles in tourneys.

[12] Nuremberg, Germanisches Nationalmuseum, Inventory number Pl. O. 3458.

[13] Paris, Bibliothèque nationale de France, MS Portugais 5, fol. 102r–103v: *Terceiro andar firmado nas strebeiras e pernas dereitas e no seendo dentro na sella, mas recebendo alguna ajuda dos arçones. E as em que assy cavalgam som aquellas em que antygamente auyam acostumados en esta terra dandar sobre cavallos.* Translation from Duarte I of Portugal, *The Royal Book of Jousting, Horsemanship and Knightly Combat: A Translation into English of King Dom Duarte's 1438 Treatise 'Livro Da Ensinança De Bem*

He says also that 'the feet are to stay very firm on the stirrups and you are never to be seated on the saddle, as that would result in loss of elegance, loss of agility and loss of body quietness and would make you less strong'.[14] Indeed, raised on the stirrups, the rider was less subject to the horse's movements, and his lance's blow could be more accurate, and so more efficient. Not having anything to restrain his back, the rider was prevented from falling backward by pressing his upper legs against the pommel. As a result the legs were placed less forward than we see in the thirteenth century, more under the rider's body. The cantle kept him from falling sideways. To fight in this position the knight had to be an excellent and skilful rider and be trained from childhood to manipulate both the lance and sword on this rather uncomfortable seat.[15] Therefore such specific equipment was the mark of an elite who could afford to spend hours training on horseback to be perfectly at ease in using this new technological advancement. Moreover, the introduction of this new type of saddle around 1360 was contemporaneous with a change in civilian and military dress. The new fashionable clothing fitted closely to the body and accentuated the waist and the knight's slender legs formed by years on horseback, symbol of his social status.[16] In general, northern Italians and Germans seemed to have been particularly fond of very high seats until around 1400, one good example being the statue of Bernabò Visconti in Milan, sculpted in 1363.[17] His saddle is so high that his feet are at the level of the middle of his

---

Cavalgar Toda Sela', trans. Antonio Franco Preto (Highland Village, Tex., 2005), p. 23.

[14] Paris, Bibliothèque nationale de France, MS Portugais 5, fol. 103: *E as pees ben firmes e nunca seer na sella por que faz perder afremosura e soltura e assessego e ajuda seer menos forte*. Duarte I of Portugal, *The Royal Book of Jousting*, p. 23. Later he also says that in addition to being 'the best way of avoiding defeats and falls' (*por que scusan muyto os reveses e ocayr*), this position 'will also give your riding additional elegance and handsomeness' (*ofaz mais solto e mais fremoso*).

[15] Both warhorse and war saddle were used only during battle. For travelling to the battlefield the knight used a travelling horse with a more comfortable civilian saddle.

[16] Stella M. Newton, *Fashion in the Age of the Black Prince* (Woodbridge, 1980), p. 54. The late fourteenth-century war saddle and the new fighting position emphasised this new thin body shape and especially the legs, which were thereafter enclosed by articulated plates. Being handsome and elegant in the saddle as a knight had a real social importance for the nobility in the Middle Ages and was considered in armour fashion as well. See Paul Martin, *Armour and Weapons* (London, 1968), p. 58.

[17] Bonino da Campione, Monument to Bernabò Visconti (1323–85). The monument comes from the now demolished church of San Giovanni in Conca, Milan. Today

horse's belly. The *Hohenzeug* is actually the tournament version of this new saddle, and by the end of the fourteenth century it had become very popular in most of the Germanic regions, from Northern Italy to Flanders.

Around 1400 there was a small but significant evolution in the tournament high saddle. This new type is distinguished by the cantle's wings being completely fixed to the pommel, forming two loops, which the rider had to pass his legs through. It would certainly have been very difficult (and not very elegant) for the knight to get on this saddle, and he probably needed the help of a squire and very high steps. Then the rider was so high that the squires who had to equip him with his helm and shield had to be themselves on horses. Moreover, many representations of jousts on high saddles in the early fifteenth century show at least one knight being equipped by his squires when he is already mounted. The rider mounted his saddle with only his cuirass and, possibly, his arm defences. The remainder of his equipment (helm, targe, gauntlets, lance) was fastened on by his squires who were themselves on horses. No leg armour was required, as the saddle protected him down to the toes. On a 1402 fresco in Runkelstein castle, showing a tourney with lances, riders stand straight on their stirrups, their legs completely protected by the saddle with the horses equipped with shaffrons and peytrals in *cuir bouilli* painted like the saddle.[18]

An exceptional example of this type of saddle, preserved in the Royal Armouries Museum in Leeds, gives us further information about its nature and construction (Figure 6).

Made in the first quarter of the fifteenth century, it consists of a large pommel forked for the horse's back, with both sides elongated towards its shoulders. The wooden saddle-tree is entirely covered with large pieces of rawhide, a means of strengthening the structure that is still used on today's western saddles. On the parts that are visible (front of the pommel, sides of the loops, rear of the cantle), some traces of the *gesso*, formerly painted, still remain. The seat is a narrow bar with two large rings connected to the edges of the pommel, surrounding the rider's legs, and it does not have a cantle. With nothing restraining his back, the rider had to press his legs and knees against the pommel's extensions to keep his balance.[19]

On the surface of the saddle there are a significant number of weapon impacts, mostly concentrated on the left side, where the two riders met each other. The most impressive are those blows given by lances with coronel heads

---

it is preserved in the Museo d'arte antica in the Castello Sforzesco, Milan.

[18] Schloss Runkelstein (Roncolo), Bozen/Bolzano, Italy.

[19] For a detailed study of this object, see Marina Viallon, 'A German High Tournament Saddle in the Royal Armouries, Leeds', *Arms & Armour* 12 (2015), 103–23.

Fig. 6. Tournament high saddle, first quarter fifteenth century, German. Leeds, Royal Armouries, VI.94.

that missed their targets and ended their course against the rawhide of the saddle, some having torn it and the wood underneath over several centimetres. A coronel was a type of lance head shaped as a three- or four-pointed crown. Used exclusively in tournaments, it prevented the lance from piercing the armour while its points helped it to break by catching the asperities of the target. However, given the strength of the blow, they were still dreadful weapons. Without the protection of his armour and his saddle, these lances could have easily injured or killed a man.

Many sword cuts, mostly located on the upper edge of the object, reveal that the saddle was obviously used in several tourneys utilising this weapon.

But perhaps this saddle was also used in tourneys imvolving both lances and swords. Here again, the violence of the combat is apparent as these cuts were made by swords sharp enough to easily make a cut four centimetres deep in one of the thick wooden edges. Indeed, tourneys could be very violent, as illustrated on another fresco from Runkelstein castle showing a ferocious fight with clubs. In this example the combatants are using high tourney saddles, with shorter leg defences and without the closed rings. Some of them are even trying to remove their opponent's helms while others beat those who have already lost theirs. This iconography showing sharp swords helps us to understand the marks on the Leeds saddle.

During tournaments with high saddles, the precarious seat gave an ever-higher degree of difficulty, as aiming properly with a lance from a galloping horse with such equipment was a real challenge, requiring much practice, and it was a way to demonstrate knights' abilities. However, the important number of impact-marks also highlights the necessity of such a protection. Hard as a shield, and actually made from the same materials, the saddle did its job protecting its rider from his opponents' misaimed blows.

Around 1415, whilst maintaining all its characteristics (very high seat with enclosing sides and protection for the abdomen and legs), this saddle was further improved. From then on, the horse's peytral was attached to the pommel's sides, covering the rider's feet, and in consequence some saddles could be made somewhat shorter. Saddle and peytral gave a unifying protection from the rider's belly to the horse's chest. It is exactly the same principle as the *hourt* described by René of Anjou in his *Book of Tournaments*, which he justifies by saying: 'the *hourt* is good to protect the horse or destrier from being hit in the fray, and it also protects the legs of the tourneyers from blows'.[20] In his text René also explains that he created this imaginary event using ideas taken from tournaments from all over Europe. Peytrals used with high saddles in the Holy Roman Empire probably inspired the type of *hourt* he created. During tourneys and jousts in the open (without a tilt barrier), it was not uncommon for horses to run into each other, and without this protection riders would also have run the risk of trapping their legs between two horses. Another improvement in this third generation of high saddle was the addition of hinges at the rear of the cantle, allowing the loops to open (Figure 7).

These were secured to the pommel by removable pins. Several examples of this kind are still visible in some museums, especially in Germany as, for

---

[20] René d'Anjou, *Le Livre des Tournois du Roi René de la Bibliothèque nationale*, ed. F. Avril (Paris, 2010), p. 36: *lequel hourt est bon pour garentir le cheval ou destrier despauler contre le hurt quant on vient de choc, et preserve aussi la jambe du tournoyeur de toute estorses, ...*

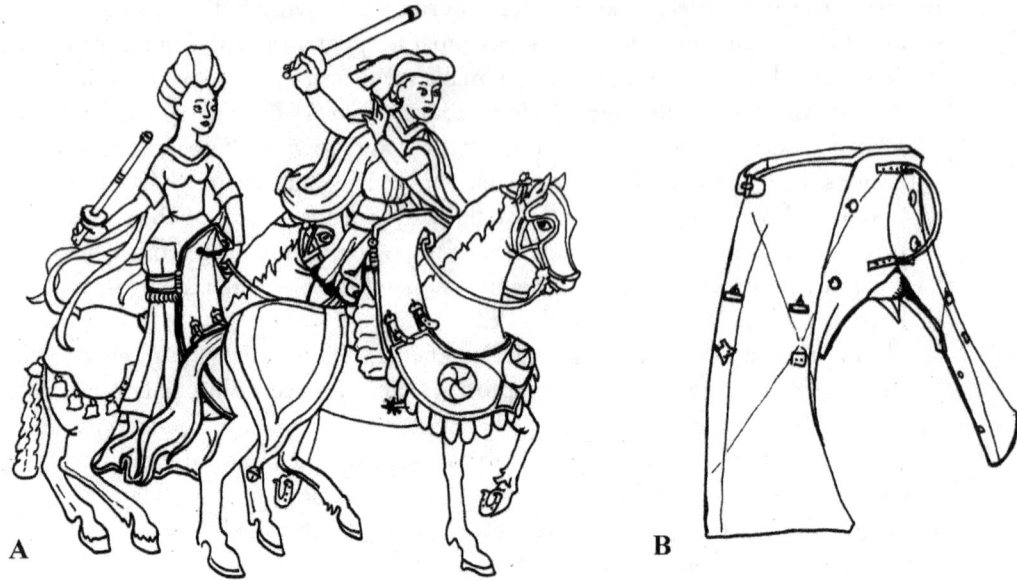

Fig. 7. Hinged tournament high saddles. A = detail of a mid-fifteenth-century Flemish tapestry showing Greeks and Amazons fighting a *Kolbenturnier* (tourney with maces). After *Hercules Initiating the Olympic Games*. Glasgow, The Burrell Collection. B = High saddle for the tourney, second half fifteenth century, preserved in the Germanisches Nationalmuseum, Nuremberg. (author's illustrations).

example, the one preserved in the Germanisches Nationalmuseum in Nuremberg (Figure 7b). These continued to be used until the end of the fifteenth century and iconography tends to indicate that they were mostly used in tourneys even if some illustrations show them being used for jousts as well.[21]

This tournament with the high saddle seems to have become obsolete around 1500. However, Maximilian I, king of the Romans and Holy Roman Emperor (1459–1519), who liked to create (or recreate) various types of tournaments with their own specific equipment, presented the *Hohenzeuggestech* as part of his illustrated *Triumph* (1512–19).[22] As he did in other cases, Maximilian reinvented this old form of tournament by keeping the spirit of it,

---

[21] A typical example is seen in the joust between Freydal (Maximilian I) and Hans von Werdenberg, represented on folio 98 of the manuscript of *Freydal*, the tournament book of Emperor Maximilian I: Vienna, Kunsthistorisches Museum, Inv.-Nummer 5073 (c. 1512–15).

[22] Hans Burgkmair, *The Triumph of Maximilian I: 137 Woodcuts by Hans Burgkmair and Others*, ed. and trans. Stanley Appelbaum (New York, 1964), p. 47.

and creating a *Gestech* 'in the style of', but in many details the equipment was different. The saddle itself, even if its cantle cannot be seen because of the rider's skirt, does not seem as high as the old high saddles were, and the cantle's tips are not closed. Only the front of it recalls the fifteenth century. A metallic pommel, with a handle for the reins at the front, is riveted to a wide peytral in *cuir bouilli*. I have found no evidence of this kind of *Gestech* after the *Triumph*; thus it seems that it was definitely abandoned after Maximilian's death.[23]

Low Saddles

In the fifteenth century there was another type of tournament saddle in the German Empire called the low or flat saddle (*niedriger Sattel*; *selle rase* in French sources). Most of the low saddles that have survived are dated from the first half of the fifteenth century and were made in Central Europe and decorated with inlaid bone elements. This type of saddle probably originated in the kingdom of Hungary. Its shape evolved from the traditional Hungarian saddle which was itself descended from the Mongolian saddle. It was used for travelling, hunting and fighting in war alongside another type with a high cantle inspired by the western war saddle.[24]

A similar low saddle can already be seen on a bronze sculpture of St George made in 1373. It is difficult to know if the saint is meant to be represented on a tournament saddle or on a traditional Hungarian war saddle.[25] Nevertheless it is not impossible that at that time Hungarians employed such low saddles in their tournaments, even if there is no evidence of this kind of use before the fifteenth century.

Sigismund of Luxembourg (1368–1437), king of Hungary, became king of the Romans in 1410 and Holy Roman Emperor in 1433. His reign saw the spread of the Hungarian low saddle across the German Empire, and Sigismund used splendidly decorated examples as diplomatic gifts, such as the saddle in the Royal Armouries collection that is thought to have been offered

---

[23] This late type of *Hohenzeuggestech*, not being recorded anywhere else during the last years of Maximilian's life, may not have actually have taken place.

[24] An example of this type of 'Westernised' Hungarian saddle was made c. 1455 for Ladislaus Postumus, king of Hungary and Bohemia (r. 1440–57). See Vienna, Museum, A.64.

[25] In the later Middle Ages, St George was frequently represented with tournament equipment, especially saddles. The original St George statue by the Cluj craftsmen Martin and Gheorghe is in St Vitus Cathedral, Prague. A 1904 copy is in St Michael's church, Cluj-Napoca, Romania.

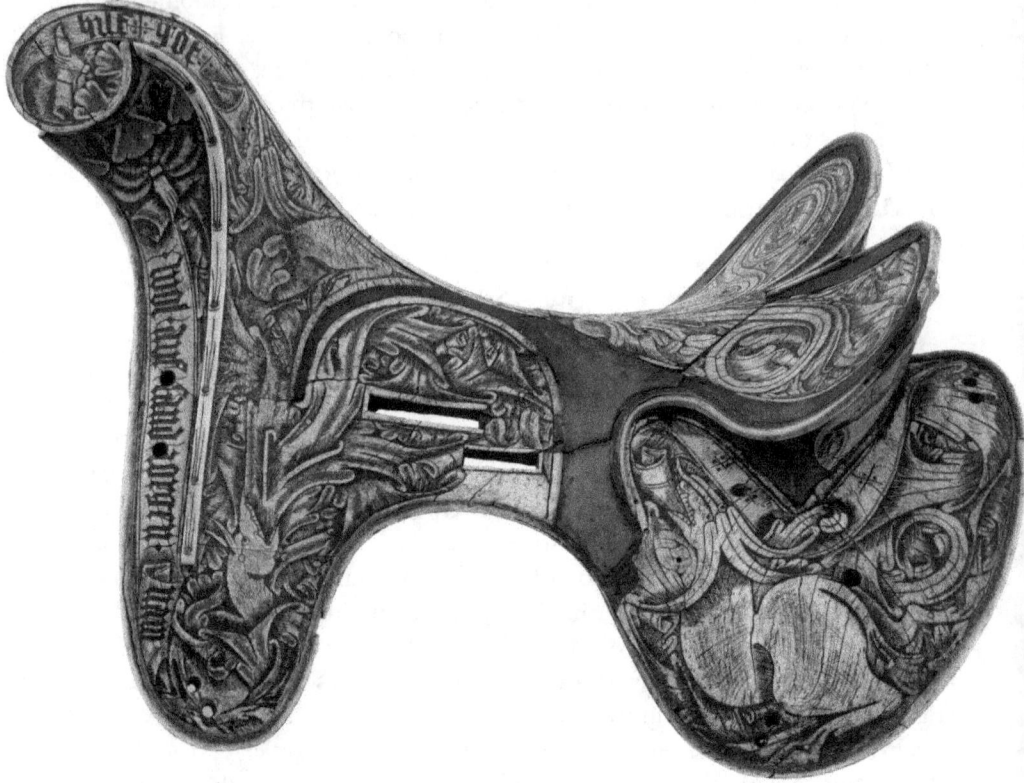

Fig. 8. Saddle, possibly Hungarian, 1410–40. Tower of London, Royal Armouries, VI.95.

by Sigismund to King Henry V of England (1387–1422) during his visit to London in 1416 (Figure 8).[26]

The pommel of this saddle is narrow and curled at the top; the seat, close to the horse's back, is slightly curved and terminates in a low and flat cantle forming two semi-circles. Two slots, the lower for the girth, the upper for the stirrups, are present on each side of the bars. Several pairs of holes were used to fix the buckles for the breast and crupper girths and the leather panels. This luxurious example is covered with bone elements carved with an intricate decoration, partly painted, showing the dragon associated with St George.

[26] Karen Watts, 'Une selle médiévale d'Europe centrale au Royal Armouries Museum', in *Armes et cultures de guerre en Europe centrale, XVe–XIXe siècle* (Paris, 2005), pp. 47–64 (p. 47).

The Tournament Saddle

This saddle is part of a group of about twenty surviving saddles, probably made in Hungary between 1410 and 1440. As with the example in the Royal Armouries, these saddles are all made of wood partially covered with black leather and inlaid with bone decoration that was originally painted. Contemporary iconography, such as the St George painted by Rogier van der Weyden (c. 1425–35) (National Gallery of Art, Washington, D.C.), or several fifteenth-century German prints, shows the few missing elements, such as large leather flaps hanging from the sides of the saddle to protect the rider's legs from rubbing against the girth's buckles.[27] Thus, unlike the other tournament saddles examined here, this one does not give any protection, nor does it prevent the rider from falling if he loses his balance. Indeed, in the rest of Western Europe this shape of saddle-tree was not designed for the tournament, or even for war, but it was the classic shape for a civilian riding saddle found in many representations throughout the fifteenth century. Their wooden structures were, however, covered with soft materials and leather, while the saddle-tree is virtually directly visible on low tournament saddles. This flat seat, more padded on civilian saddles, was originally designed for being seated at ease for travelling long journeys on horseback.

Contemporary evidence proves nonetheless that saddles like the one from the Royal Armouries, or at least their simpler models, were indeed used in tournaments. A nice example is given by an illumination from the Tross'sche Fragment (1430–40), representing a knight receiving the prize at a tournament (Figure 9).[28] Behind him his horse is equipped with a low saddle decorated with bone bands and with leather saddle flaps on the sides. Near the horse, his squire carries the knight's banner and his tournament weapons: a targe, a lance with a coronel head and a mace. This equipment indicates that he took part in a tourney using lances and maces. It means that during the same period, high saddles and low saddles were used in similar tourneys, and probably in jousts as well. The use of flat saddles in tournaments would have increased the difficulty and the danger of the combat. These saddles were ridden in the elevated position described by Don Duarte, as we see in Van der Weyden's St George already cited.

---

[27] Several German prints dating from the second half of the fifteenth century show St George mounted on a flat bone saddle while killing the dragon. See, for example, a print by Master E.S., made in the third quarter of the fifteenth century: Vienna, Albertina, Inv. No. DG1926/760.

[28] The Tross'sche Fragment was a fragmentary manuscript of poems preserved in the Berlin Staatsbibliothek, and destroyed during bombing of the city in 1945.

Fig. 9. Schenk Konrad von Limpurg receiving the prize at a tournament, Tross'sche Fragment, 1430–40.

Most of the bone saddles still preserved today, even though highly decorated, are perfectly functional, and could have been used in such events.[29] Iconography, however, shows simpler saddles, which were certainly those more commonly used but less beautiful, and they have not survived. Such gorgeous objects could also have been used for parades and other feasts surrounding actual combat during tournaments.

Another type of low saddle was developed at the end of the fifteenth century, perhaps as an evolution of the Hungarian low saddles previously discussed. These low saddles, developed in the Holy Roman Empire during the time of Maximilian I, are little different from their predecessors and were used in a very Germanic form of tournament, the *Rennen*. Equivalent to the joust of war, the latter was traditionally run in war armour, but by the time of Maximilian it had become a game as sophisticated as the joust of peace (*Gestech*), with very specialised weapons and armour. More violent than the *Gestech*, the main

---

[29] Some saddles of the group are clearly not functional, like an example that lacks the slits and holes for the girthing and trappings: Budapest, Magyar Nemzeti Museum, Inv. 55.3119.

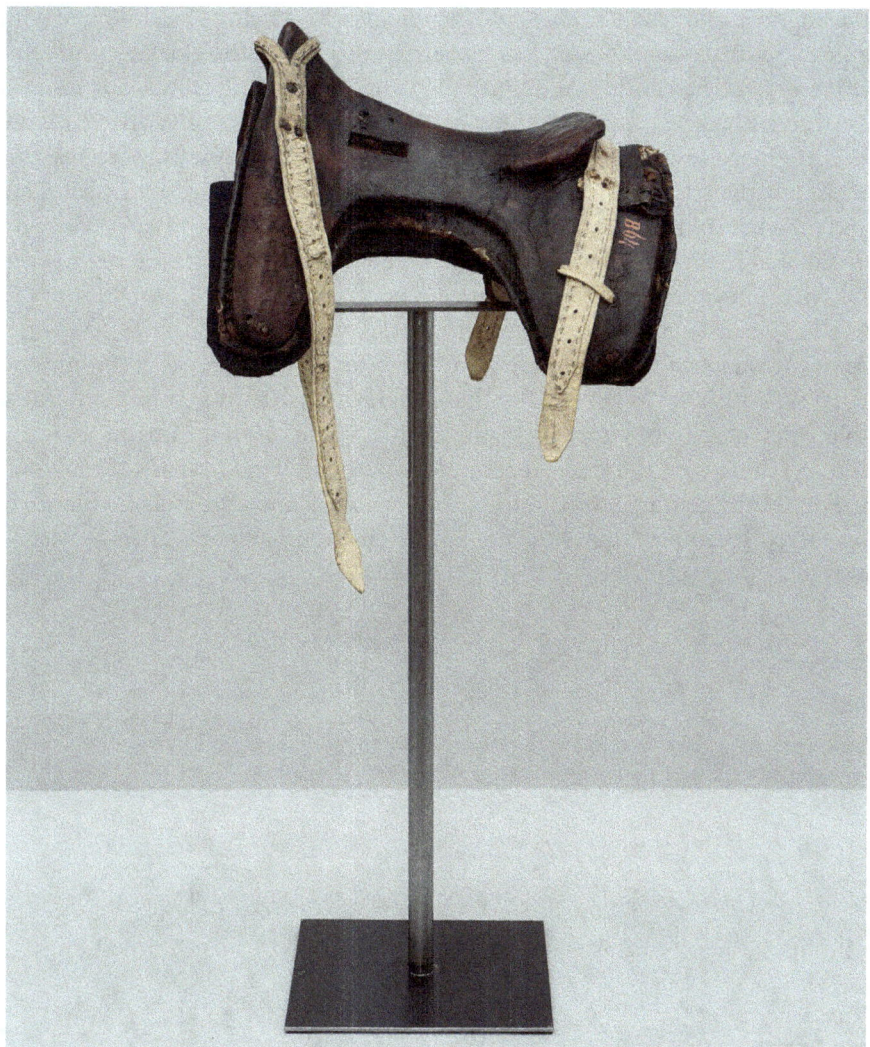

Fig. 10. Low saddle for the *Rennen* used in the tournaments of Maximilian I. South German, late fifteenth century, Vienna, Kunsthistorisches Museum, B.64.

purpose of the *Rennen* was to unhorse an opponent and to aim at some specific points of the armour with a head-blow scoring the most. Lances had a single blunt-pointed head and were not designed to break like those in the *Gestech*. Difficulty was increased by using these saddles without a cantle, making it a challenge for the rider to stay on his horse after a blow. German tournament books show two main types of low saddles. The first type, which can be seen in the engravings of the *Triumph of Maximilian I*, had a simple saddle tree with a pommel that was more or less present, mostly used for blocking the reins (Figure 10). The cantle was slightly defined but certainly could not restrain anything. The second type had a small pommel but no cantle at all (Figure 11). Its long leather seat was completely flat and its only purpose was for attaching the stirrups. Several examples of such saddles, used by Maximilian and members of his court, are still preserved at the Kunsthistorisches Museum of Vienna. These saddles were ridden with bent legs, allowing the rider to keep his balance by pressing them against the horse's belly. The *Rennen* armour did not have cuisses and poleyns for protecting the thighs and knees. When a *hourt* (*Stechsacke*) was not used, two independent thigh-defences (*dilgen*) were hung on both sides of the saddle. These engravings show that sometimes these thigh-defences were attached to the saddle, while on other images they are shown falling with the rider. These saddles were used in Germany throughout the sixteenth century until tournaments evolved into carousels in the early seventeenth century. They were the last specific tournament saddles in use.

Fig. 11. Ernst von Braunschweig in a *Rennen* (detail), from 'Tournament Book of the Electors of Saxony'. Image from the facsimile edition: *Der Sächsischen Kurfürsten Turnierbücher*, ed. Erich Haenel (Frankfurt, 1910), p. 31.

Conclusion

From the fourteenth century onwards, the first tournament saddles were primarily designed to give more safety to the rider, but soon extraordinary forms were designed. On the one hand the high saddles increased the difficulty of riding and fighting. On the other hand, the low saddles gave no protection to the knight. The demand for these saddles spread across the Empire because knights liked the extra challenge they brought to jousts and tourneys, making the victors worthier of admiration. It must also be noticed that these saddles were used only in regions of Germanic influence, known for having invented and practised the most varied forms of tournaments in Europe. Thus, alongside the rich fabric, the fantastic and colourful crests, the music and the settings, there is no doubt that these special saddles added something incredible to the great spectacle of tournaments in the late Middle Ages.

6 Between Sport and Theatre: How Spectacular was the *Pas d'armes*?

Catherine Blunk

Picture medieval knights and squires charging towards each other on horseback, striking helmets or shields and breaking lances: it is spectacular. Men in shining armour striking each other with swords or poleaxes, and groups of men exchanging blows in a mêlée must have been spectacular as well, even if their weapons were blunted. Noblemen performing deeds of arms in *pas d'armes* during the fifteenth century competed in all three types of combat. Yet it is generally thought by those familiar with the *pas d'armes* that it was more spectacular than other jousts and *emprises* due to its theatricality.[1]

Definitions of the *pas d'armes* commonly indicate that theatrical production is one of its defining features. The following passage, for example, is emblematic of definitions found both in general studies on medieval chivalry and in specialised analyses of *pas d'armes*: 'This form of deed of arms, sprung from the custom of a knight holding a bridge or gate against all comers, is attested as early as the eleventh century and probably has Germanic roots. In the fifteenth century, such deeds took on the form of state theater – though

---

[1] On the difference between an *emprise* and a joust, see Philippe Contamine, 'Les tournois en France à la fin du Moyen Âge,' in *Das ritterliche Turnier im Mittelalter: Beiträge zu einer vergleichenden Formen- und Verhaltensgeschichte des Rittertums*, ed. Josef Fleckenstein (Göttingen, 1985), pp. 425–49. Jousts were held for entertainment or diversion and did not require as much advanced planning as an *emprise*. In contrast, an *emprise* (or *entreprise*) consists of deeds of arms (on horseback or on foot, fought with lances, swords or poleaxes, most commonly between two individuals) planned carefully in advance by one or more noblemen, called the *entrepreneur(s)*, having issued a written challenge via a king of arms or herald. An object, such as a bracelet or collar, often worn by the *entrepreneur* or *entrepreneurs* until they accomplish their deeds of arms, is also called an *emprise*. A *pas d'armes* is thus a form of *emprise*.

the combat was no less real or intense.'² The second sentence suggests that although the *pas d'armes* consisted of real combat (and indeed people were hurt and occasionally killed), an accompanying theatrical production or performance was one of its defining properties. The introduction to the most recent critical edition of a *pas d'armes* states that a *pas d'armes* is half theatre, half sport, a theatrical representation with elaborate decoration and rich costumes, careful staging, and dialogues written in advance.³ However, examination of the accounts of twenty-three events commonly found in corpora established by scholars investigating *pas d'armes* reveals that, while many did in fact feature such theatrical representation, the descriptions of several of these events mention little or no theatrical production at all. Is it appropriate to define a *pas d'armes* by saying that it was a type of medieval tournament whose spectacular character was enhanced by theatrics, including actors in character and in costume performing dialogue, careful stage production, and decoration according to a fictional scenario developed in its governing document? Even if the theatrical productions did exist, why did the authors of so many of their accounts choose not to mention or emphasise them? What did they emphasise instead, and how can the answers to these questions inform our understanding of the *pas d'armes*? More generally speaking, to what extent was the *pas d'armes* more spectacular than other *emprises* or peace-time deeds of arms?

The corpus studied here is set out in the chart below, which includes the court and the year in which the events took place. The chart is divided into two columns indicating the theatricality of each event according to its extant accounts. The descriptions of the events in the right column do not indicate, I would argue, a type of production meeting the above definition. The question marks identify events that I am not certain were *pas d'armes*.⁴

---

[2] Ken Mondschein, 'Chivalry and Knighthood', in *Handbook of Medieval Culture: Fundamental Aspects and Conditions of the European Middle Ages*, ed. Albrecht Classen (Berlin, 2015), pp. 159–71 (here 167).

[3] *Le Pas du Perron Fée*, ed. Chloé Horn, Anne Rochebouet and Michelle Szkilnik (Paris, 2013), pp. 8–9: 'Un pas est une manifestation mi-théâtrale, mi-sportive…'. On the sport-like quality of *pas d'armes* and other jousts, see Sébastien Nadot, *Le Spectacle des joutes: Sport et courtoisie à la fin du Moyen Âge* (Rennes, 2012).

[4] On the jousts in Nancy and Châlons-sur-Marne (now Châlons-en-Champagne), see Catherine Blunk, '*Faux pas* in the Chronicles: What Is a *Pas d'armes*?', *The Medieval Chronicle* 11 (2017), 87–107.

Events whose accounts clearly describe theatrical production	Events whose accounts mention little or no theatrical production
Paso de la Fuerte Ventura, Castile, 1428	*Passo Honroso*, Castile, 1434
Pas de la Gueule du Dragon, France, 1446	*Paso de Valladolid*, Castile, 1440
Pas de la Joyeuse Garde, Anjou, 1446	*Pas de l'Arbre Charlemagne*, Burgundy, 1443
Pas de la Bergère, Provence, 1449[a]	*Pas (?) de Nancy*, Lorraine, 1445[b]
Pas (?) du Chevalier au Cygne, Burgundy, 1454[c]	*Pas (?) de Châlons-sur-Marne*, France, 1445
Pas du Pin aux Pommes d'or, Aragon, 1455[d]	*Pas du Géant à la Blanche Dame du Pavillon*, Anjou, 1446
Pas (?) du Compagnon à la Larme Blanche, Burgundy, 1458[e]	*Pas du Chevalier Aventureux*, Berry, 1447
Paso de Jaén, Castile, 1461	*Pas de la Belle Pèlerine*, Burgundy, 1449
Pas du Perron Fée, Burgundy, 1463	*Pas de la Fontaine des Pleurs*, Burgundy, 1449
Pas de l'Arbre d'or, Burgundy, 1468	*Paso de Madrid*, Castile, 1460
Pas de la Dame Sauvage, Burgundy, 1470	*Pas de la Dame Inconnue*, Burgundy, 1463
	Pas de Sandricourt, France, 1493

[a] This *pas* was organised by René, duke of Anjou, who also held the titles of count of Provence and duke consort of Lorraine, among others.

[b] This event was likewise organised by René d'Anjou.

[c] I am unconvinced by the extant accounts of the jousts held for the Feast of the Pheasant that this event should be called the *Pas du Chevalier au Cygne*, but since I cannot be certain, I include it in this column as well; the event was unquestionably theatrical.

[d] Gaston IV, count of Foix, was the entrepreneur of this *pas* held during a visit to his father-in-law, Juan II, king of Navarre, who became king of Aragon in 1458.

[e] Chastellain repeatedly calls this event a *joustes* and *feste*. He explains that he does not recount it at length because it was only for fun: 'comme j'ay dit, que ce n'estoit que esbatement, et non pas chose qui touchoit a parfond honneur'. Georges Chastellain, *Chronique: Les Fragments du Livre IV révélés par l'Additional Manuscript 54156 de la British Library*, ed. Jean-Claude Delclos (Geneva, 1991), pp. 129–32.

The term *pas d'armes*, evoking a knight defending a passage, charges this type of tournament with a fictional quality at the outset, which approaches its full potential in the theatrics associated with the events listed in the left column of the chart. The fiction of defending a passage is sometimes developed in the *chapitres* or *lettre d'armes*, a written document detailing the terms and rules of the *pas* circulated to publicise it and solicit noblemen to accept the challenge. The rules were enforced by judges who were responsible for determining the winners of each encounter and the overall champion or champions of the *pas*. The Burgundian chronicler Olivier de La Marche, who describes many Burgundian *pas d'armes*, often includes their *chapitres* in his accounts, as he does for the *Pas de la Dame Sauvage*. In the allegorical *chapitres* of this *pas*, we learn of the *entrepreneur*, the Chevalier à la Dame Sauvage, who wanders in a wasteland called Youth until he falls in love with a wild woman, the Dame Sauvage, covered on all parts of her body by the most beautiful blonde hair to be seen. The knight asks this wild woman to retain him as her servant, but she refuses until he earns renown through chivalric exercises. The Chevalier à la Dame Sauvage composes the *chapitres* in direct discourse, and includes detailed information about the logistics of the *pas*, such as the location of the stands, the types of combat and weapons involved, and the prizes to be awarded. The *chapitres* retain elements of the fictional scenario as well. For example, the knight asks the lady to provide two young women to attend the event.

La Marche clearly indicates that the fictional scenario is amplified by theatrics during the *pas d'armes* itself. The two young women participate in a type of theatrical production accompanying the *pas* that enacts, to a certain extent, its fictional scenario. Two trumpeters wear wild-men costumes as do two other men leading two hackneys bearing the two young women. The Dame Sauvage herself is not portrayed by an actress, but rather her portrait appears on a shield to be awarded as one of the prizes. The venue features decorations based on the theme of the *pas*: the door through which the *entrepreneur* enters, the balcony over it, and the *entrepreneur*'s pavilion are decorated with trees and greenery. The account does not indicate enactments of fictional scenes or the exchange of dialogue, but the characters participate in ceremonial activities. La Marche tells us that they accompany the *entrepreneur* in and out of the lists, and they also help with prizes. The wild men and women are all wearing very well made golden hair, and it was very strange to see.[5]

---

[5] *Traicté de la forme et devis comme on faict les tournois*, ed. Bernard Prost (Paris, 1878), p. 71.

The entrepreneur does not appear in costume. On the first day his horse's caparison bears the motif of the *pas*, but he competes in different attire on other days. La Marche does not refer to him as the Chevalier à la Dame Sauvage throughout his account. Rather, he most often calls him *l'entrepreneur* or *le chevalier entreprener*, and occasionally he calls him by name. It should be noted that La Marche attended the *pas* himself and reports his own speech. At the beginning of the *pas* he presents the *entrepreneur* to the duke, saying that the young ladies of the Dame Sauvage send their respects and presents him as the knight of their mistress. He speaks once again at the conclusion of the *pas*, thanking the duke on behalf of the *demoiselles de la Dame Sauvage* for the honour he has bestowed on 'Glaude de Vaudray, son serviteur vostre subject'.[6] The *entrepreneur*'s identity thus shifts from his fictional identity as a knight in the service of the Dame Sauvage to his real identity as a subject of Charles the Bold, duke of Burgundy, underscoring the splendour of the court. This *pas d'armes* clearly features a theatrical production alongside the combat: the *entrepreneur* and actors bear the names of fictional characters, they wear costumes based on the fictional scenario of the *pas* outlined in the *chapitres*, the venue is decorated with its thematic motifs, and the author of the *pas* account inserts himself into the fiction of the *pas* through direct discourse during the event. Furthermore, La Marche underscores the spectacular quality of the *pas* by noting the numerous spectators and even their reactions to the competition.

The *Pas de la Joyeuse Garde* also features theatrical production. Although the author of its most complete description does not include the *chapitres* or summarise them (although he claims to), he does explain that the fiction of the *pas* is based on the story of Lancelot and the defence of the pillar (or *perron*) at the Joyeuse Garde.[7] This fictional defence is enacted as each visiting competitor arrives to joust, as follows: the visiting nobleman accepts the challenge by forcefully striking a shield hanging on the *perron*, often knocking it down. This agitates a dwarf, who goes to the castle to solicit help. A lady emerges with one of the noblemen defending the *pas*, escorts him to the lists, and the two joust. In contrast to the *Pas de la Dame Sauvage*, the various ladies who escort men from the castle do not bear fictional names. They either embody a type, or they are identified by their actual names, as are the noblemen competing in the *pas*.

---

[6] *Traicté de la forme et devis*, p. 93. 'Claude de Vauldrey, her servant your subject' [author's translation].

[7] *Das Turnierbuch für René d'Anjou (Le Pas de Saumur): Vollständige Faksimile-Ausgabe im Originalformat der Handschrift Codex Fr. F. XIV Nr. 4 der Russischen Nationalbibliothek in St. Petersburg: Kommentarband/mit Beiträgen*, ed. N. Elagina, J. Malinin, T. Voronova and D. Zypkin (Moscow, 1998), pp. 67–113 (here 67).

Although the author also frequently alludes to the topos of fighting for the love of a lady, this pretext is never expressed in a story. There is no mention of a specific knight or squire falling in love with a fictional lady, at least from what we can tell from the poem describing the event or the short chronicle passages that mention it.[8] These and the remaining extant accounts of the events in the left column of my chart describe theatrical representation that develops beyond a fictional scenario reflected in the *chapitres*, decorations, and thematic motifs displayed on horses' caparisons or *entrepreneurs*' shields or other attire.

If such theatrical production was indeed absent from the events in my right-hand column – roughly half of the *pas d'armes* typically examined –, or if it was simply deemed not significant enough by their authors to describe it, what was significant about these *pas d'armes* to the authors of their texts? To determine this, I would advocate a definition of the *pas d'armes* which considers the textual nature of their extant accounts. Most *pas d'armes* texts exhibit conventional features. Briefly stated, these can be grouped into three main categories: preparation, entries and combat. If festivities, such as a prize ceremony or banquet, took place after the *pas*, these are also described. Whether found in independent formats, chivalric biography, or chronicle, whether in verse or prose, in French or Castilian, the clear majority of accounts bear – at a minimum – traces of this conventional imprint.[9]

The conventional features recognisable in so many *pas d'armes* accounts derive from earlier texts. Authors tell us this themselves. They indicate that they sought sources written at *pas* by heralds or other experts when composing their descriptions. For example, La Marche, in his account of the *Pas de l'Arbre*

---

[8] Mathieu d'Escouchy, *Chronique*, ed. G. du Fresne de Beaucourt, 3 vols (Paris, 1863–64), 1: 107–8, and Guillaume Leseur, *Histoire de Gaston IV, comte de Foix*, ed. Henri Courteault, 2 vols (Paris, 1893), 1: 194–96.

[9] More *pas d'armes* accounts in this corpus exhibit conventional elements than indicate theatrical production. Two unconventional accounts appear in Spanish chronicles: the *Paso de Jaén* and the *Paso de Valladolid* in, respectively, *Hechos del condestable don Miguel Lucas de Iranzo (crónica del siglo XV)*, ed. Juan de Mata Carriazo (Madrid, 1940), pp. 58–69 and *Crónicas de los reyes de Castilla desde Alfonso el Sabio hasta los católicos don Fernando y doña Isabel*, ed. Cayetano Rosell, 3 vols (Madrid, 1875–78), 68: 567. We do not know enough about the *Pas du Géant à la Blanche Dame du Pavillon* and the *Pas du Chevalier Aventureux* accounts to know if they were conventional, although I would cautiously guess that they were. These accounts are lost to us because they were supposedly filled with 'boring' joust and tournament descriptions that were analogous to other scenes copied from the original, now lost manuscript. See 'Le Manuscrit original de l'Histoire de Gaston IV, comte de Foix, par Guillaume Leseur: additions et corrections à l'édition de cette chronique', ed. Henri Courteault, *Annuaire-bulletin de la Société de l'histoire de France* 43 (1907), 180–81.

Charlemagne, explains that he consulted all the texts written by kings of arms and heralds present to write his account.[10] Some of the authors were heralds themselves. Other texts indicate that scribes recorded *pas* at the time of the event, such as the *scrivanos* seated with the judges, king of arms and herald in the *Passo Honroso* and the *clercs* depicted in the manuscript of the *Pas de la Joyeuse Garde* seated with paper, writing.[11]

The *chapitres* or *lettres d'armes* are an example of a heraldic document. Monstrelet says that he has included a copy of the *chapitres* for the *Pas de l'Arbre Charlemagne* in his chronicle, but he is not the original author. *Lettres d'armes* also exist for other types of *emprises*, but it may be that the presence of a fictional pretext outlined in *chapitres* is unique to the *pas d'armes*. It is true that some of the *pas* I have listed above which do not indicate a theatrical production nonetheless do mention a fictional pretext for the *pas*, either in *chapitres* or elsewhere. Even so, we should not confuse the presence of a fictional scenario expressed in the *chapitres* with an indication of fully developed theatrical production. In addition to the *chapitres*, other conventional elements include descriptions of requests for permission to hold the *pas*, publication of the *chapitres* and preparations of the venue, as we shall see.

One of the most significant features of *pas d'armes* accounts is a repetitive description of what the competitors and their horses wear as they enter the lists to compete. These descriptions are very similar to those found in chronicles to describe entries into cities, such as royal entries. The heraldic colours, coats of arms, helmets, crests, caparisons, banners and mottoes commonly described revealed the identities of participants and their noble status which was necessary to compete. Recognising and describing these armorial bearings was a herald's speciality. These elaborate (and often spectacular) garments should not be confused with costumes (whose purpose was to conceal identities). *Entrepreneurs'* attire often bore the motifs of a fictional theme, and occasionally they fought incognito, as in the *Passo Honroso*. But the knights and squires accepting the challenge are rarely depicted wearing costumes.

Conventional combat descriptions feature formulaic, repetitive and precise reports (often of each course or blow) and identify the winner and often prizes. It is logical that heralds or scribes would have been concerned with capturing the precise details of each encounter and would have devised formulaic

---

[10] Olivier de La Marche, *Mémoires d'Olivier de La Marche, maître d'hôtel et capitaine des gardes de Charles le Téméraire*, ed. Henri Beaune and Jules d'Arbaumont, 4 vols (Paris, 1883), 1: 291.

[11] Pero Rodriguez de Lena, *El passo honroso de Suero de Quinones*, ed. Amancio Labandeira Fernandez (Madrid, 1977), p. 101; *Das Turnierbuch für René d'Anjou (Le Pas de Saumur)*, fol. 10v.

patterns to note them. One goal of participating was to earn renown; a herald's recording and publication of his accounts made that possible. In his *capítulos*, Suero de Quiñones, the entrepreneur of the *Passo Honroso*, states, 'So that the benefit and advantage which shall be gained in the said deeds of arms may not be concealed from anyone, the heralds who shall be there shall provide a signed statement, to anyone who should request it, concerning the truth that he shall wish to request about what he did.'[12] Chroniclers such as La Marche, who later used these types of texts to compose their more permanent accounts, may also have attended the events themselves and sometimes added their personal recollections; by studying these variations we can deduce what each author found significant or what corresponded to the wider project of his text. It would also make sense that heralds were not often interested in recording information about spectators.

It was partially through the examination of a work of fiction, *Jehan de Saintré*, that I was able to identify these conventional elements.[13] This is an informative text, given that its author, Antoine de La Sale (c. 1398–1470), was an expert in tournaments. The story recounts how a young widow at the French court undertakes the project of making a renowned knight of a young page, Jehan de Saintré. She carefully teaches him how to participate and organise several *emprises*. For example, his first *emprise* takes place against a knight named Enguerrand in Barcelona, and he later competes against a Polish knight in another *emprise* at the French court. One of Saintré's *emprises* is a *pas d'armes*, and La Sale is careful to make it textually distinct from the accounts of Saintré's other *emprises*. Its entry and combat descriptions are repetitive and formulaic; La Sale demonstrates his command of this type of heraldic writing. The texts describing Saintré's other *emprises* exhibit narrative features more characteristic of tournament descriptions in romance. For example, they alternate descriptions of fighting in the lists and spectators' activities and discourse in the stands (especially those of women) in a way that is rarely seen in *pas d'armes* accounts. In Saintré's *pas*, spectators are not mentioned. Furthermore, examination of the extant manuscripts of *Jehan de Saintré* shows that the account of Saintré's *pas d'armes* features a distinctive textual layout in

---

[12] Pedro Rodriguez de Lena, '*El Passo Honroso* de Suero de Quiñones: Selected Passages', in Noel Fallows, *Jousting in Medieval and Renaissance Iberia* (Woodbridge, 2010), p. 405: *Por que a ninguno non sea escondido el bien o ventaja que en las dichas armas fará, los farautes que lo demandare, lo que con verdad cerca [de lo] qui fizo demandar querrá.*

[13] Antoine de La Sale, *Jehan de Saintré*, ed. Joël Blanchard and Michel Quereuil (Paris, 1995), pp. 308–20.

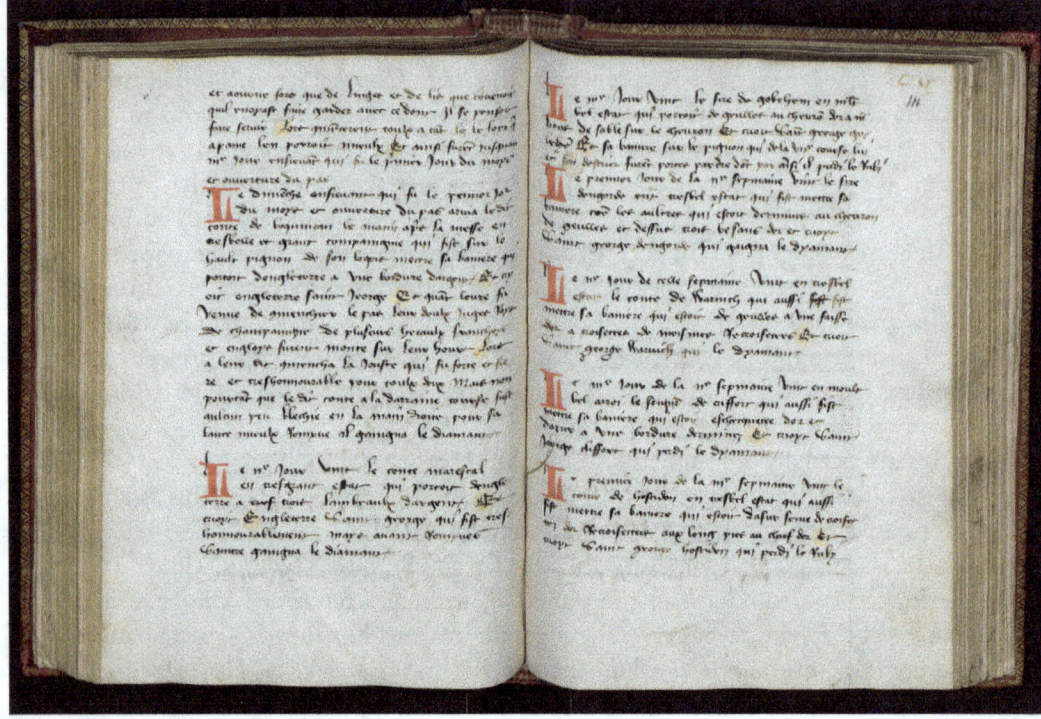

Fig. 1. The textual layout of the *pas d'armes* account in *Jehan de Saintré*. Brussels, KBR, MS 9547, fols. 110v–111.

most of the manuscripts (Figure 1).[14] This *mise en page* also distinguishes this *emprise* from others in which Saintré competed.

La Sale does not pretend to copy *chapitres* into his text, but rather has the female protagonist dictate them to Saintré when she instructs him to hold a *pas*.[15] This female character does not, however, attend the *pas*, and the narrator does not mention any female presence at it. The entry and combat descriptions follow a strict pattern that includes which day of the *pas* is being described (first, second, etc.), the name of the nobleman accepting the challenge, the description of the arms on his banner, his 'cry' (for example *Engleterre! Saint George!*), and the prize won.

The narrator recounts Saintré's organisation of the *pas* at length. He describes how this knight in training obtains horses, armour, caparisons and

[14] Brussels, KBR, MS 9547, fol. 111.
[15] Michelle Szkilnik, *Jean de Saintré: Une carrière chevaleresque au XVe siècle* (Geneva, 2003), p. 76.

Fig. 2. Construction of the venue for Saintré's *pas d'armes*. Brussels, KBR, MS 9547, fols. 109v–110.

twelve outfits, how he has a herald publicise the *pas*, and how he requests that a truce between the French and English be respected for the duration of the event. He describes the construction of houses for the participants and stands for the judges and heralds. This is so significant that it merits an illustration in one of the two extant illuminated manuscripts (Figure 2).[16] Saintré hosts a dinner for the heralds before the *pas* and is praised even before the competition begins.

Nevertheless, La Sale, who was a judge at the theatrical *Pas de la Joyeuse Garde* ten years earlier, does not create any theatrical production for his character's *pas* and strips it of even the most basic dramatic symbolism, such as the hanging shields that competitors touch to accept the *emprise*, thematic decorations or a fictional scenario. His emphasis is on the positive interaction between the participants: Saintré is an excellent host to his English guests. His houses include lovely rooms, wardrobes, tables, tapestries and all the necessities.

---

[16] Brussels, KBR, MS 9547, fol. 109v.

Saintré is attentive to kings of arms and heralds, showering them with gifts. It is for this attention and successful preparation that Saintré is lauded, not for his combat skills or for a successful theatrical execution that impresses spectators. The preparations ensure the competitors' and judges' comfort and enjoyment; spectators are not even mentioned. Following the *pas*, La Sale has his characters – English and French noblemen usually at war with each other – exchange *honneurs et reverences* better than they could have if they had been brothers.

Accounts of four non-fictional *pas* bear similar features to La Sale's narrative: the *Passo Honroso*, the *Pas de l'Arbre Charlemagne*, the *Pas de la Belle Pèlerine*,[17] and the *Pas de la Fontaine des Pleurs*.[18] None describe what I would consider a theatrical performance staged alongside combat. La Marche, who described the three Burgundian *pas*, does however indicate that each is founded on a theme. All are named for monuments where the *pas* were held: at a tree named Charlemagne,[19] the Pilgrim's Cross and a Fountain of Tears. The *Passo Honroso* takes place at a bridge near the pilgrimage route to Santiago de Compostela.[20] The text of the *Pas de la Belle Pèlerine* indicates a fictional scenario developed from the cross. Its *chapitres* outline an elaborate fictional scenario in which the Dame de la Belle Pèlerine seeks help on her pilgrimage to Rome.[21] The Chevalier à la Pèlerine is happy to help her but must defend a *pas* first. When Suero de Quiñones, the *entrepreneur* of the *Passo Honroso*, requests permission for his *empresa*, he explains that he has been imprisoned by a lady and wears an iron collar around his neck.[22] The *chapitres* of the extremely long account state

---

[17] The chapitres of the *Pas de la Belle Pèlerine* are found in Escouchy, *Chronique*, 1: 244–63.

[18] The chapitres of the *Pas de la Fontaine des Pleurs* are found in Escouchy, *Chronique*, 1: 264–73. The *Pas de La Fontaine des Pleurs* also appears in three other texts: La Marche, *Mémoires*, 2: 141–204; 'Le Livre des faits du bon chevalier Messire Jacques de Lalaing', in *Œuvres de Georges Chastellain*, ed. Baron Kervyn de Lettenhoven, 8 vols (Brussels,1863–67), 8: 188–247, and Jean Le Fèvre de Saint-Rémy, 'Epître', ed. François Morand, *Annuaire-Bulletin de la Société de l'histoire de France* 8 (1884), 177–239.

[19] La Marche, *Mémoires*, 1: 284. The chapitres of the *Pas de l'Arbre Charlemagne* appear in Enguerran de Monstrelet, *La Chronique d'Enguerran de Monstrelet*, ed. L. Douët-d'Arcq, 6 vols (Paris, 1857–62), 6: 68–73. Monstrelet refers to l'Arbre Charlemagne as l'Arbre des Hermittes.

[20] Pedro Rodriguez de Lena, '*El Passo Honroso*', p. 73.

[21] The *Pas de la Fontaine des Pleurs* also takes place along a pilgrimage route. La Marche, *Mémoires*, 2: 143.

[22] Wearing such an *emprise* is not unique to the *pas d'armes*.

that any lady passing the place of his *passo* must have a knight or nobleman fight for her in order to pass, or she will lose her right glove.[23] The author describes a few women who do indeed wish to pass without companions to fight for them, but it is not clear whether they belong to a fictional, scripted performance.[24] Could it be that later fictional depictions of this topos – such as at the *Pas de la Gueule du Dragon* – were inspired by real practice?[25]

Neither the *chapitres* nor the authors of the texts describing the *Pas de la Fontaine des Pleurs* and the *Pas de l'Arbre Charlemagne* mention any fictional scenarios motivating these *emprises*, although in one account the Dame des Pleurs supposedly gives the judge, Toison d'Or, a golden robe at the end of the *Pas de la Fontaine des Pleurs*.[26] Very few costumes are associated with these events. Only in the *Pas de la Belle Pèlerine* do the *entrepreneur*'s squires dress as pilgrims, and his three companions dress as Lancelot, Tristan and Palmades. On the other hand, La Marche does mention decorations at all three *pas*, such as thematic motifs embroidered on *entrepreneurs*' apparel and tents. In fact, some of the decorations at these *pas* were quite elaborate, as we shall see.

The *entrepreneur* of the *Passo Honroso* has a statue or picture of a herald erected on the road to the *passo* indicating the way, but no decorations based on the theme of fighting for the love of a lady are mentioned in the preparations. However, the preparations highlight another significant theme: religion. The author describes a pavilion with religious paintings and sculptures used to hold three daily masses throughout the *passo*. The *Pas de l'Arbre Charlemagne* also features religious paintings, such as *ymaiges* of God, the Virgin Mary and St Anne, and a stone cross featuring a picture of a crucifix before which knelt a *presentacion* of the *entrepreneur*, Pierre de Bauffremont, the Seigneur de Charny. This picture, like that of the herald in the *Passo Honroso*, indicates the way to the *pas*.[27] The *entrepreneur* Jacques de Lalaing had a pavilion placed in front of the Fontaine des Pleurs, on top of which was an *image* of the Virgin Mary. Under and to the left of this picture was the Dame de La Fontaine des Pleurs, with her hand near her eye to wipe away tears. Large blue tears fell into a fountain flowing onto three shields hung on a unicorn's neck. The tears fell through *trois tuyaux*; these three pipes indicate that the lady was not

---

[23] Pedro Rodriguez de Lena, '*El Passo Honroso*', p. 92.

[24] Pedro Rodriguez de Lena, '*El Passo Honroso*', pp. 183–84.

[25] *Das Turnierbuch für René d'Anjou (Le Pas de Saumur)*, pp. 68–69.

[26] The judge, Toison d'Or, was in fact Jean Le Fèvre de Saint-Rémy, the author of the account. La Marche, in his version of the *pas*, says that the robe was from the entrepreneur. Jean Le Fèvre de Saint-Rémy, 'Epiître', p. 233.

[27] La Marche, *Mémoires*, 1: 291–93.

portrayed by an actor but was a statue or automaton. The pavilion was guarded by a real person, not a fictional character, the herald Charolais, every first day of the month for a year.[28] The men accepting the *pas* would touch one of three shields to accept the challenge. La Marche calls these features of the venue a *mistere*. It is clear that he refers to the objects representing the two women, the unicorn, the fountain of tears and the two shields when he uses this word, because he explains how the men ceremoniously removed the *mistere* for the very last time at the end of the *pas* and specifically identifies these objects.[29] He also says these things were strange and new in the region.[30]

The *Pas de la Belle Pèlerine* was unusual in that it was not very successful: only two men participated. Although he describes no actors portraying fictional characters, La Marche obeys the fictional pretext by referring to the *entrepreneur* as *le chevalier à la pelerine*, at least early in the *pas*. Later, the *entrepreneur* decides to fight without his visor and to remove the decorations bearing the motif of the *pas* (embroidered pilgrims' staffs) from his tent, leaving only the arms of Luxembourg on display. At this time, La Marche starts to call him the Seigneur de Haulbourdin.[31] Therefore in La Marche's text the importance of the theatrical persona of the *chevalier à la pèlerine* lies more in underscoring the shift from the entrepreneur fighting with his visor closed to fighting with it open than in calling attention to an elaborate stage production, if one existed.

Instead of hiding identities through fictional characters, the true identities of Charny and his twelve companions are the subjects of the decorations at the *Pas de l'Arbre Charlemagne*. Instead of being decorated with motifs from a fictional theme, the lists are decorated with two tents for his twelve companions covered with their coats of arms and mottoes. Charny's side is covered with four banners bearing his arms. La Marche remarks that this was something 'very triumphal' to see.[32] He describes at length Charny's *pompes et préparacions*, including a house for the judges and heralds overlooking two lists, and a ramp or steps used to help the competitors. The beneficiaries of these preparations are the participants themselves, not spectators. La Marche indicates that the three nearby castles Charny prepares are part of the *mistere*, but he does not suggest that they are supposedly part of a fictional storyline. He also says that

---

[28] 'Le Livre des faits du bon chevalier Messire Jacques de Lalaing', pp. 201–2; Jean Le Fèvre de Saint-Rémy, 'Epître', p. 213.

[29] La Marche, *Mémoires*, 2: 202.

[30] La Marche, *Mémoires*, 2: 147. The precise region is not specified.

[31] La Marche, *Mémoires*, 2: 131.

[32] La Marche, *Mémoires*, 1: 297.

after the *pas* the kings of arms and heralds assembled from all over to honour *le mistere* and to bring in (again in ceremonial fashion) the two shields that had hung from the Arbre Charlemagne for the duration of the *pas*.[33]

Like Saintré's fictional *pas* therefore, the accounts of the above *pas* do not describe theatrical productions enacted at the events, but they do indicate governing themes and impressive decorations. They share with La Sale's fictional *pas* a strong emphasis on the organisational skills necessary to host a *pas d'armes*. Saintré's *pas d'armes* is presented as a rite of passage for a knight in training; La Marche calls a *pas* a *noble espreuve*.[34] The *Passo Honroso* recounts Suero de Quiñones' preparations in minute detail, and the description of Saintré's preparations of the venue recall those of Charny at the *Pas de l'Arbre Charlemagne*. As in the Brussels *Saintré* manuscript, Lalaing's venue merits a miniature (Figure 3).[35]

The authors emphasise the competitors' true identities and especially their status as *nobles gentilshommes*. Even though Lalaing and Haulbourdin supposedly compete incognito, their true identities are not really hidden. Lalaing dines with the other competitors regularly throughout the *pas*. Such dinners are an important custom of the *passo* at the *Passo Honroso*, and one of the castles at the *Pas de l'Arbre Charlemagne* was prepared for such parties held after each competition. These gatherings were for men only; like Saintré's *pas*, these texts constitute a masculine space, and it is possible that the actual events did as well. Few spectators are mentioned at these *pas*, and the few who are mentioned are men. In fact, the *chapitres* of the *Pas de la Fontaine des Pleurs* discourage spectatorship, because they restrict men from watching the competition until after they have competed.[36] The niece of Charles, duke of Orléans (1395–1465), does arrive at this *pas* along with many men and women, but nobody competes during their stay, so they are not spectators. It is important to remember that these *pas* were intended to take place over long periods of time. Barber and Barker point out the less spectacular nature of *pas d'armes*: 'The *Passo Honroso* and other passages of arms had little pageantry about them, though they were carefully refereed and recorded by heralds; these, rather than the spectacular ceremonial jousts, were tournaments for the connoisseur.' Regarding the *Passo Honroso* specifically, they say: 'There was about two hours' worth of jousting each day, which hardly made it an exciting occasion for

---

[33] La Marche, *Mémoires*, 1: 233.
[34] La Marche, *Mémoires*, 2: 120. A 'noble test' [author's translation].
[35] Paris, Bibliothèque nationale de France, MS fr. 16830, fol. 124.
[36] La Marche, *Mémoires*, 2: 174–75.

Fig. 3. The image of the Virgin Mary, the Lady of Tears fountain, and the herald Charolais at the *Pas de la Fontaine des Pleurs*. Paris, Bibliothèque nationale de France, MS fr. 16830, fol. 124.

onlookers: it was entirely for the benefit of the knights involved.'[37] The emphasis in these texts is on ceremony (which underscores proper comportment and a prince's control), encouraging harmonious relationships, thoughtful deliberations and solutions to disagreements. Touching each other's hands and being friends or like brothers are recurrent motifs. Although the author of the *Passo Honroso* is frank about competitors who behave poorly, he nonetheless writes of the love the men had for the *entrepreneur* and each other.

The descriptions of the remaining *pas* on the right side of my chart mention little or no theatrical production. The *chapitres* of the *Pas de la Dame Inconnue* describe a fictional scenario, but they contain no instructions to build theatrical sets and no mention of characters who will perform certain duties at the *pas*.[38] The account of the *Paso de Valladolid* is quite short as well, and its author does not mention theatrics.[39] The account of the *Paso de Madrid* is very short. It mentions a wild man who refuses to let ladies pass unless their men agree to run six courses, but there is no way to know if this is simply a scenario outlined in the *chapitres*, some sort of statue guarding the passage, or a more theatrical production featuring an actor.[40]

The texts recounting the jousts at Nancy in 1455 mention neither a fictional scenario nor any theatrical production, but King Charles VII of France (1403–61) wore the arms and crest of Lusignan, and René d'Anjou (1409–80) dressed as Godfrey of Bouillon, hero of the First Crusade.[41] Mathieu d'Escouchy focuses on participants' attire of *diverses couleurs et riches paremens* at Châlons-sur-Marne, which closely followed the jousts at Nancy, but he does not mention disguises. At the very late *Pas de Sandricourt* (1493), some combat takes place in areas with names taken from fiction, but this does not

---

[37] Richard W. Barber and Juliet R. V. Barker, *Tournaments: Jousts, Chivalry, and Pageants in the Middle Ages* (Woodbridge, 2000), p. 8. Given La Marche's attention to *serimonies*, I would disagree that they had little pageantry about them.

[38] 'La Joute de la Dame Inconnue – La joute du Sire de Commines et du Sire de Jonvelle à Bruges', ed. Baron Kervyn de Lettenhove, *Compte Rendu des séances de la Commission Royale d'Histoire*, ser. 3, 11 (1870), 473–82.

[39] *Crónicas de los reyes de Castilla*, 68: 567.

[40] *Crónicas de los reyes de Castilla*, 70: 112–13.

[41] Guillaume Leseur, *Histoire de Gaston IV, comte de Foix*, ed. Henri Courteault, 2 vols (Paris, 1893), 1: 129–93; Mathieu d'Escouchy, *Chronique*, 1: 49–51; La Marche, *Mémoires*, 2: 50–63; 'Le Livre des faits du bon chevalier Messire Jacques de Lalaing', pp. 38–69. See also note 4, above. On the possible motivations behind these choices, see Christian de Mérindol, *Les fêtes de chevalerie à la cour du roi René: Emblématique, art et histoire (les joutes de Nancy, le Pas de Saumur et le Pas de Tarascon)* (Paris, 1993), pp. 16–22.

constitute a fictional scenario.[42] One visitor from Normandy is led into the lists by a 'shepherdess', but he is not the *entrepreneur*. Otherwise, the author, a herald, mentions nothing about people portraying characters or any theatrical production. He does describe the festivities, meals and dances, and the venue, in such detail that it is hard to believe that he would not have described the theatrical production if there had been one. Unusually, he emphasises female attendance and talks about what the spectators would have seen, so this lends the event a spectacular, festive quality. But concerning the competition, his emphasis is on noblemen gathering on good behaviour to take part in chivalric exercises. The manuscript containing the accounts of the *Pas du Géant à la Blanche Dame du Pavilion* and the *Pas du Chevalier Aventureux* has been lost, and the limited information we have (essentially lists of the participants) comes from notes taken on the manuscript in the seventeenth century.[43] It would be premature to draw conclusions about defining characteristics of the *pas d'armes* without having more evidence that these events contained significant theatrical imprints.

I have focused my analysis on theatrical representations associated with the entries into the lists or combat. To be fair, however, I should mention a theatrical representation of a sort that took place during the post-*pas* festivities at the close of the *Pas de la Fontaine des Pleurs*. Lalaing held a banquet for the men competing in the *pas*. Set in the centre of tables at the banquet were two *entremets* or dioramas representing the *pas*. In *Le Livre des faits de Jacques de Lalaing*, passages in verse recount direct discourse between Lalaing, the Virgin and the Dame de la Fontaine des Pleurs.[44] Reading this text, the modern reader may wonder if these *entremets* were a theatrical play; it is almost as if the author wished to evoke such a performance on the page. La Marche is clear in his *Mémoires*, however, that Lalaing's verses were writings placed on one of the *entremets* at the feet of the figure representing him, and he says nothing of the women's messages.[45] Still, we might think of these *entremets* as theatrical production of a sort. Instead of being accompanied by theatrical production, the *pas* itself becomes the subject of a theatrical production – albeit in miniature and inanimate forms – at the banquet following the *pas*. In any case, it seems to represent a development in what is indicated by the term *mistere*; La Marche

---

[42] Orléans le Héraut, *Le pas des armes de Sandricourt, relation d'un tournoi donné en 1493 au château de ce nom*, ed. Augustin Vayssière (Paris, 1874).

[43] 'Le Manuscrit original de l'Histoire de Gaston IV', 43:2: 201–7.

[44] 'Le Livre des faits du bon chevalier Messire Jacques de Lalaing', pp. 239–46.

[45] La Marche, *Mémoires*, 2: 201.

specifies that the *entremets* are a part of it.[46] As for a fictional scenario governing the *pas*, one appears at the very end in two versions of the *pas*. Following his banquet with the men, Lalaing invites the local women to a banquet of their own, and the Dame de la Fontaine des Pleurs supposedly writes them a letter in which she explains that the knight defending the *pas* did so because of her tears and to honour the pilgrimage to Rome and Jubilee year.[47] This is informative, because it suggests that the fictional scenarios accompanying *pas d'armes* may not have been of interest to male participants. La Marche does not include this fiction, and he does not mention the dinner Lalaing hosts for the women, but does say that women spoke about him favourably and called him a good knight.[48]

Held between 1449 and 1450 at Chalon-sur-Saône, the *Pas de la Fontaine des Pleurs*, with its mechanical *Dame des Pleurs* and its theatrical *entremets* at the final dinner, may represent a pivotal moment, at least for Burgundian *pas d'armes*. Let us recall that La Marche notes this was new in the region. It is therefore worth considering whether we can speak of an evolution in the *pas d'armes* held at the court of Burgundy. The *Pas de la Belle Pèlerine* was held the same year Lalaing's *pas* began. The Burgundian *pas* which followed were all very theatrical. The *Pas de la Dame Sauvage*, discussed above, was held twenty years later than Lalaing's *pas*, but the theatrical *pas* that preceded Lalaing's *pas* were not Burgundian. At least one very theatrical *paso* existed as early as 1428 (the *Paso de la Fuerte Ventura*), so this format was not a Burgundian invention.[49]

The *pas d'armes* was not static and existed in a variety of forms over many decades in several courts. This makes it difficult to identify its defining characteristics. If we suspect that most *pas* featured theatrical production even though so many texts did not emphasise them, finding more witnesses could lend the evidence needed to support this assertion. Conventional *pas d'armes* accounts have the disadvantage of not accurately indicating certain features that did not interest heralds or even authors adapting heralds' texts, such as how many spectators (especially women) watched the events. It is hard to determine how spectacular an event was without having reliable information about its

---

[46] La Marche, *Mémoires*, 2: 202. 'Ainsi fut le banquect achevé, et le mistere d'icelluy pas'.

[47] 'Le Livre des faits du bon chevalier Messire Jacques de Lalaing', pp. 245–46, Jean Le Fèvre de Saint-Rémy, 'Epître', p. 237.

[48] La Marche, *Mémoires*, 2: 203.

[49] *Refundición de la Crónica del halconero*, ed. Fernan Pérez de Guzmán, Lope de Barrientos and Juan de Mata Carriazo (Madrid, 1946), pp. 59–62.

audience. Finding more archival evidence of the type found by Rose-Marie Ferré concerning the costs of the *Pas de la Joyeuse Garde* would help identify expenses associated with theatrical sets, costumes and decorations.[50]

Nevertheless, we can conclude from focusing on the non-theatrical features of the *pas d'armes* that many authors did emphasise that the *pas d'armes* was more complex than an extravagant, nostalgic spectacle organised to demonstrate a prince's wealth, power and splendour. Modern Olympic games feature tremendously costly, complex and theatrical opening and closing ceremonies based on a theme. The Olympics engender peaceful interaction between nations, and perhaps in five hundred years scholars will analyse the symbolism of their ceremonies and the expenditures endured by various host cities. But during the events, in their immediate aftermath, and the decades shortly thereafter, I would suggest that the athletes' performances interest people the most. Sports reporters and other experts record precise details of each event at the time of games, and shortly thereafter other authors, such as journalists or screenwriters, compose narratives, sometimes to offer compelling stories of athletes' remarkable exploits and to set positive examples for young athletes to aspire to. I perceive the same motivating concerns in *pas d'armes* texts. How spectacular was the *pas d'armes*? As deeds of arms, they were all spectacular, but theatrical production may have only made some of them more spectacular than others. First and foremost, however, all *pas d'armes* accounts described amicable physical competition between noblemen from a variety of European courts.

---

[50] Rose-Marie Ferré, 'Les ecclésiastiques et les fêtes profanes à la cour de René d'Anjou: L'exemple du *Pas de Saumur*', in *L'artiste et le clerc: Commandes artistiques des grands ecclésiastiques à la fin du Moyen Âge (XIVe–XVIe siècles)*, ed. Fabienne Joubert (Paris, 2006), pp. 351–70.

7 Art Imitating Life Imitating Art? Representations of the *Pas d'armes* in Burgundian Prose Romance: The Case of *Jehan d'Avennes*

Rosalind Brown-Grant

Scholarship on the *pas d'armes* over the last thirty years or so has definitively laid to rest the idea that this type of literary-inspired tournament is in any way symptomatic of the decadence or infantilism of the chivalric culture of the late Middle Ages, as earlier commentators such as Johan Huizinga once claimed.[1] Thus, for example, Michel Stanesco has attributed the popularity of the *pas d'armes* in fifteenth-century Anjou and Burgundy to a genuine desire on the part of the late medieval nobility to emulate their literary avatars, a process he dubs the *enromancement* ('romanticisation') of daily life.[2] Jean-Pierre Jourdan, for his part, has shown how these spectacles of elite sporting prowess were integral to the political life of the period, being organised as part of larger occasions such as marriages, peace treaties and ceremonial entries at which the nobility conducted its essential business and affirmed its identity as an

---

[1] Johan Huizinga, *The Waning of the Middle Ages: A Study of the Forms of Life, Thought and Art in France and the Netherlands in the Fourteenth and Fifteenth Centuries* (London, 1924). See also Raymond Kilgour, *The Decline of Chivalry as Shown in the French Literature of the Late Middle Ages* (Gloucester, Mass., 1937); and Jean Rychner, *La littérature et les moeurs chevaleresques à la cour de Bourgogne (Leçon inaugurale 30 janvier 1950)* (Neuchâtel, 1950).

[2] Michel Stanesco, *Jeux d'errance du chevalier médiéval: Aspects ludiques de la fonction guerrière dans la littérature du Moyen Âge flamboyant* (New York, 1988), p. 23. See also Armand Strubel, 'Le *pas d'armes*: Le tournoi entre le romanesque et le théâtral', in *Théâtre et spectacle hier et aujourd'hui. Moyen Âge et renaissance: Actes du 115e Congrès national des Sociétés savantes (Avignon, 1990), Section d'histoire médiévale et de philologie* (Paris, 1991), pp. 273–84. All translations of quotations from primary and secondary sources are my own.

exclusive social group.³ Furthermore, as Christiane Raynaud observes, being timed to coincide with key dates in the liturgical calendar, these events could also be an encouragement to undertake crusade, the very highest application of chivalric prowess for serious military and spiritual ends,⁴ as in the case of the famous *Pas de la Fontaine des Pleurs* of 1449–50 that was organised by the Burgundian knight Jacques de Lalaing during the year of the jubilee in Rome.⁵

As the ultimate late medieval example of life imitating art,⁶ the *pas d'armes* are based on often elaborate literary scenarios, with the idea of amorous service to a mysterious Lady acting as a pretext for the tournament itself.⁷ While

3   Jean-Pierre Jourdan, 'Le symbolisme politique du pas dans le royaume de France (Bourgogne et Anjou) à la fin du Moyen Âge', *Journal of Medieval History* 18 (1992), 161–81. See also Jennifer R. Goodman, 'Display, Self-Definition, and the Frontiers of Romance in the 1463 Bruges Pas du Perron Fée', in *Persons in Groups: Social Behavior as Identity Formation in Medieval and Renaissance Europe*, ed. Richard C. Trexler (Binghamton, N.Y., 1985), pp. 47–54; Évelyne van den Neste, *Tournois, joutes, pas d'armes dans les villes de Flandre à la fin du Moyen Âge (1300–1468)* (Paris, 1996); and Sébastien Nadot, *Le spectacle des joutes: Sport et courtoisie à la fin du Moyen Âge* (Rennes, 2012).

4   Christiane Raynaud, 'Fêtes d'armes et dévotions au XVe siècle', in *The Medieval Chronicle IV*, ed. Erik S. Kooper (Amsterdam, 2006), pp. 127–46.

5   Unless otherwise stated, all references to the account of this *pas d'armes* are taken from the chivalric biography of Jacques de Lalaing edited in Emmy Springer, '*Les Fais de messire Jacques de Lalain* de Jean Lefèvre de Saint-Rémy' (unpublished Ph.D. thesis, Université de Paris III, 1982), hereafter abbreviated to *JL*. On this particular *pas d'armes*, see Georges Doutrepont, '*Le Livre des faits du bon chevalier messire Jacques de Lalaing*: Une biographie romancée du XVe siècle', *Journal des savants* (1939), 221–32; Alice Planche, 'Du tournoi au théâtre en Bourgogne: Le Pas de la Fontaine des Pleurs à Chalons-sur-Saône, 1449–1450', *Le Moyen Âge* 81 (1975), 97–128; Élisabeth Gaucher, '*Le Livre des Fais de Jacques de Lalain*: Texte et image', *Le Moyen Âge* 95 (1989), 503–18; Michelle Szkilnik, 'Mise en mots, mise en images: *Le Livre des Faits du bon chevalier Jacques de Lalain*', *Ateliers (Cahiers de la Maison de Recherche, Université Charles de Gaulle-Lille 3)* 30 (2003), 75–87; Rosalind Brown-Grant, 'Narrative Voice and Hybrid Style in Burgundian Chivalric Biography', *Cahiers de recherches médiévales et humanistes* 22 (2011), 25–41; and Brown-Grant, 'Commemorating the Chivalric Hero: Text, Image, Violence, and Memory in the *Livre des faits de messire Jacques de Lalaing*', in *Violence and the Writing of History in the Medieval Francophone World*, ed. Noah D. Guynn and Zrinka Stahuljak (Cambridge, 2013), pp. 169–86.

6   See Yin Liu, 'Richard Beauchamp and the Uses of Romance', *Medium Aevum* 74 (2005), 271–87; and Michelle Szkilnik, 'Que lisaient les chevaliers du XVe siècle? Le témoignage du *Pas du Perron Fée*', *Le Moyen Français* 68 (2010), 103–14.

7   Jean-Pierre Jourdan, 'Le thème du Pas et de l'Emprise. Espaces symboliques et rituels d'alliance en France à la fin du Moyen Âge', *Éthnologie française* 22 (1992),

some *pas* are inspired by fairly generic romance motifs such as combat by a ford or a bridge against foes such as shepherds or wild men,[8] others draw on specific literary texts, though not always with great fidelity to the original source. Thus, for example, the *Pas de l'Arbre d'or* of 1468, organised by Anthony, the Great Bastard of Burgundy, as part of the celebrations of the marriage of his half-brother Charles the Bold to Margaret of York, borrows the figures of the *Dame de l'Isle Celee* ('Lady of the Secret Island') and the giant Garganeus from Aimon de Varennes' thirteenth-century *Roman de Florimont*, whilst Jacques de Lalaing's *Pas de la Fontaine des Pleurs*, for which he is hailed as a *nouvel Ponthus* ('new Ponthus'), makes reference to the eponymous hero of the early fifteenth-century *Roman de Ponthus et Sidoine*.[9]

What has been less explored in recent studies on the *pas d'armes* is the question of whether this process of imitation could work both ways. In other words, did the real *pas d'armes* of the mid to late fifteenth century influence in turn the imaginative literature of the day, particularly the highly popular pseudo-historical romances featuring heroes who were the putative ancestors of actual late medieval families? In order to detect such an influence, one would need to be able to distinguish the different levels of imitation whereby art (the late medieval romance) imitated life (the late medieval *pas d'armes*) which itself imitated art (the romances of earlier centuries), in a kind of *mise en abime* effect. One possible example of this is Antoine de La Sale's romance *Jehan de Saintré* (1456), which, as both Michelle Szkilnik and Catherine Blunk have shown, recounts the hero's fictional *pas d'armes* by employing the

---

172–84; Jourdan, 'Le thème du pas d'armes dans le royaume de France (Bourgogne, Anjou) à la fin du Moyen Âge: Aspects d'un théâtre de chevalerie', in *Théâtre et spectacle hier et aujourd'hui*, pp. 285–304. See also Anthony Annunziata, 'Teaching the *pas d'armes*', in *The Study of Chivalry: Resources and Approaches*, ed. Howell Chickering and Thomas H. Seiler (Kalamazoo, Mich., 1988), pp. 556–82; and Annette Lindner, 'L'influence du roman chevaleresque français sur le pas d'armes', in *Les sources littéraires et leurs publics dans l'espace bourguignon (XIVe-XIVe siècles)*, ed. Jean-Marie Cauchies, *Publications du Centre Européen d'Études Bourguignonnes* 31 (Neuchâtel, 1991), pp. 67–78.

[8] See, for example, the *Pas d'Armes de la Bergère*, held in Tarascon in 1449: Harry F. Williams, '*Le pas de la bergère*: A Critical Edition', *Fifteenth Century Studies* 17 (1990), 485–513. For an analysis of this event, see Jane H. M. Taylor, '"Une gente pastourelle": René d'Anjou, Louis de Beauvau et le *Pas d'armes de la bergère*', in *René d'Anjou, écrivain et mécène (1409–1480)*, ed. Florence Bouchet (Turnhout, 2011), pp. 197–208.

[9] For the comparisons with Florimont and Ponthus, see Nadot, *Le spectacle des joutes*, pp. 175–77. See also Annunziata, 'Teaching the *pas d'armes*', and Lindner, 'L'influence du roman chevaleresque'.

same tropes of heraldic discourse that were used in contemporary tournament accounts, chronicles and chivalric biographies to commemorate the actual *pas d'armes* of those such as Jacques de Lalaing.[10] Although scholars have often stressed the uniqueness of *Saintré* compared with other prose romances produced around the same time,[11] I will argue here that the example of the *pas d'armes* episode in the Burgundian romance of *Jehan d'Avennes* likewise constitutes a clear example of this process of art imitating life imitating art in the late medieval period.

Jehan d'Avennes was written sometime between 1460 and 1467, thus slightly post-dating *Saintré*, and it forms the first part of a trilogy that also contains the stories of his supposed granddaughter, the *Fille du comte de Ponthieu* ('Daughter of the Count of Ponthieu'), and her supposed great-grandson, Saladin, the latter in a blatant attempt to appropriate the glory of this historical figure for a Burgundian dynasty.[12] The hero, Jehan, is introduced as an unruly youth of high birth who has to be inducted into the ways of chivalry by a lady, the Countess of Artois, with whom he falls deeply in love. Inspired by his passion, Jehan attempts to secure the lady's affections by performing an impressive series of chivalric exploits, which include a tournament, two judicial combats, a *pas d'armes* and three actual wars (against the Emperor of Germany, the English, and the Saracens in Spain, respectively). Although, on belatedly discovering that his beloved is in fact already married, Jehan suffers a bout of madness and flees to a forest, the couple are finally reunited when her first husband dies and the two of them marry, having a fine *descendance* that eventually leads to the aforementioned 'Fille' and Saladin. The complete

---

[10] Michelle Szkilnik, *Jean de Saintré: Une carrière chevaleresque au XVe siècle* (Geneva, 2003), pp. 71–94; and Catherine Blunk, 'La vois des hiraus: the Poetics of Tournament in Late Medieval Chronicle and Romance' (unpublished Ph.D. thesis, University of Wisconsin-Madison, 2008), pp. 258–366.

[11] For example, Szkilnik, *Jean de Saintré*, but see Rosalind Brown-Grant, *French Romance of the Later Middle Ages: Gender, Morality, and Desire* (Oxford, 2008) which also takes issue with this view of seeing *Saintré* as unique in questioning the link between love and arms in these fifteenth-century romances.

[12] All quotations from this text are taken from the following edition: *L'Istoire de tres vaillans princez monseigneur Jehan d'Avennes*, ed. Danielle Quéruel (Villeneuve d'Ascq, 1997); all page references to this text (hereafter abbreviated to *JA*) will be given in parentheses in the body of this essay immediately after the quotation and translation, as for other primary texts cited. For a literary analysis of *Jehan d'Avennes*, see Brown-Grant, *French Romance*, pp. 44–54.

trilogy is preserved in two paper manuscripts: Paris, Bibliothèque de l'Arsenal, MS 5208 and Paris, Bibliothèque nationale de France (BnF), MS fr. 12572.[13]

Three main parallels can be drawn between the presentation of the *pas d'armes* sequence in *Jehan d'Avennes* and that found in the tournament accounts, chronicles and chivalric biographies of the mid fifteenth century, despite some key differences between them that are specific to the romance genre. These parallels concern, first, the staging of the *pas*; second, the chivalric ethos that underpins the combats; and third, the self-reflexivity of the *pas* as a self-conscious form of chivalric role-play.

As regards staging, before even embarking on a *pas d'armes*, a real or fictional knight (known as the *entrepreneur* of the *pas*) has to ensure that he has the necessary authorisation from his sovereign prince to organise such an event. Thus, just as his real-life counterpart, Philippe de Lalaing (Jacques' younger brother) who organised the *Pas du Perron fée* in Bruges in 1463 is described as seeking permission from his lord, Duke Philip the Good of Burgundy,[14]

---

[13] The Arsenal manuscript contains only three miniatures in total (executed in *grisaille*), one at the head of each of the three sections of the trilogy, which have been attributed to either Jean Le Tavernier d'Audenarde or to the Girart de Roussillon Master (often identified as Dreux Jehan): on these different attributions, see *JA*, introduction, p. 8; the website *Un corpus de manuscrits illustrés aux anciens Pays-Bas (1400–1550)* created by Hanno Wijsman to complement his *Luxury Bound. Illustrated Manuscript Production and Noble and Princely Book Ownership in the Burgundian Netherlands (1400–1550)* (Turnhout, 2010) <http://www.cn-telma.fr/luxury-bound/manuscrit2582/>; and the website created to accompany *Miniatures Flamandes 1404–1482*, ed. Bernard Bousmanne and Thierry Delcourt (Paris, 2011), the catalogue of an exhibition held in Paris and Brussels in 2011–12 <http://expositions.bnf.fr/flamands/pedago/pp_201205_flamands_003.pdf>. The latter manuscript is extensively illuminated in pen and wash by the Wavrin Master, an artist who specialised in illustrating romances, active in Lille in the 1450s and 1460s, and is so-called after his chief patron Jean de Wavrin, a chronicler, bibliophile and counsellor at the Burgundian court. On this artist, see Pascal Schandel, 'Le Maître de Wavrin et les miniaturistes lillois à l'époque de Philippe le Bon et de Charles le Téméraire', 3 vols (unpublished Ph.D. thesis, Université des Sciences Humaines de Strasbourg, 1997); Pascale Charron, *Le Maître du Champion des dames* (Paris, 2004), pp. 243–57; Pascal Schandel, 'Le Maître de Wavrin', in *Miniatures flamandes*, pp. 358–66; Rosalind Brown-Grant, 'Laughing *At* or *With* the Text: The "Wavrin Master" as Illuminator of Burgundian Prose Romance', *Cahiers de recherches médiévales et humanistes* 30 (2015), 407–19 (text), 455–59 (colour plates); and Rosalind Brown-Grant, *Visualizing Justice in Burgundian Prose Romance: Text and Image in Manuscripts of the Wavrin Master (1450s-1460s)* (Turnhout, 2020).

[14] See *Le pas du perron fée (Édition des manuscrits Paris, BnF fr 5739 et Lille BU 104)*, ed. Chloé Horn, Anne Rochebouet and Michelle Szkilnik (Paris, 2013), p. 97,

so Jehan d'Avennes asks for the go-ahead from his lord, the King of France (*JA*, pp. 74–75). This issue of authorisation is very important because, as Jean-Pierre Jourdan reminds us, no matter what the literary pretext for a *pas* was, in terms of being presented as amorous and chivalric service to a Lady, the actual person who was the main sponsor and beneficiary of a *pas* was in fact the *entrepreneur*'s sovereign, who would not only put up substantial money for the event but also bask in its reflected glory.[15] Whilst Philip the Good is, then, all too willing to provide Jacques de Lalaing with *or, chevaulx, harnas et baghes* ('gold, horses, armour and baggage') for his *Pas de la Fontaine des Pleurs* (*JL*, p. 329) the King of France readily supplies Jehan d'Avennes for his event with *pavillons, chevaux, or et argent* ('pavilions, horses, gold and silver') (*JA*, p. 75).

Another reason for a lord's readiness to authorise one of his subjects to organise a *pas d'armes* is that it would allow him not only to find out who his best knights were, should he need to know this in preparation for an actual war, but also to gauge the strength of those outside his court who might become his enemies, given that those knights authorised to accept an *entrepreneur*'s challenge would not always belong to the same courtly entourage as him.[16] In both Jacques de Lalaing's real *pas* and Jehan d'Avennes' fictional one, a number of non-Burgundian knights thus take up the challenge: while Lalaing fights, among others, a Sicilian knight (Jean de Boniface) and a Savoyard squire (Jacques d'Avanchier) (*JL*, pp. 342–48, and 374–81, respectively), Jehan pits himself exclusively against English knights such as the Duke of Gloucester and the Earl of Salisbury (*JA*, pp. 79–80). Indeed, our romance hero explicitly states that his aim is to *esprouver honnestement la proesse d'Engleterre* ('openly test the prowess of the English', *JA*, p. 74), given that he will later meet many of these English knights again at a tournament sponsored directly by the King of France in Compiègne and also on the field of battle in the reconquest of English-held parts of southwestern France.

The means by which the *pas d'armes* is publicised to its intended group of challengers in both historical and romance examples is a formal letter of arms composed and disseminated by a herald at the *entrepreneur*'s request.[17]

---

hereafter abbreviated to *PPF*.

[15] Jean-Pierre Jourdan, 'Les fêtes de la chevalerie dans les états bourguignons à la fin du Moyen Âge: Aspects sociaux et économiques', in *Jeux, sports et divertissements au Moyen Âge et à l'âge classique: Actes du 116e congrès national des Sociétés savantes (Chambéry, 1991), Section d'histoire médiévale et de philologie* (Paris, 1993), pp. 257–77. See also Nadot, *Le spectacle des joutes*, pp. 243–72.

[16] Nadot, *Le spectacle des joutes*, pp. 273–310.

[17] On the role of heralds, see Torsten Hiltmann, 'Information et tradition textuelle: Les tournois et leur traitement dans les manuels des hérauts d'armes au XVe siècle',

Chronicle and tournament accounts of real *pas* frequently transcribe the letters of arms verbatim as historical documents attesting to the veracity of the chronicler or herald's version of events;[18] hence both Jacques and Philippe de Lalaing's letters of arms are faithfully reproduced in the specific accounts that record their respective *pas d'armes* (*JL*, pp. 312–26 and *PPF*, pp. 98–106).[19] It is much more unusual to find this also happening in a romance like *Jehan d'Avennes* where the inclusion of his albeit fictional document (*JA*, p. 78) creates a distinct *effet de réel* in imitation of its historiographical counterparts, all the more so as it is preceded in the narrative by two other similar documents, all of them termed *mandements* ('letters'). One of these is sent by the King of France to publicise his tournament at Compiègne (*JA*, p. 73), the other is sent by the Emperor of Germany to rally his knights to make war on France so as to avenge the death of his brother from the injuries sustained in an earlier judicial combat fought against the hero (*JA*, pp. 76–77).

As Sébastien Nadot notes, acceptance of the terms of a *pas d'armes* was a matter of honour: once the challenge had been taken up, a challenger was obliged to present himself for combat at the appointed time and to observe the terms on which the combat was to be run.[20] The letters of actual *pas* were thus not only very lengthy affairs, running to several folios, but also semi-legal documents,[21] as can be seen in their use of set formulae involving the future tense regarding the stipulations of how the combat will be conducted.[22] Though much shorter than most historical letters of arms, the one found in

---

in *Information et société en occident à la fin du Moyen Âge: Actes du colloque international tenu à l'Université du Québec à Montréal et l'Université d'Ottawa (9–11 mai 2002)* (Paris, 2004), pp. 219–31; and Hiltmann, 'Un État de noblesse et de chevalerie sans pareilles? Tournois et hérauts d'armes à la cour des ducs de Bourgogne', in *La Cour de Bourgogne et l'Europe: Le rayonnement et les limites d'un modèle culturel. Actes du colloque international tenu à Paris les 9, 10 et 11 octobre 2007*, ed. Werner Paravicini with Torsten Hiltmann and Frank Viltart (Ostfildern, 2013), pp. 253–88.

[18] See Rosalind Brown-Grant, 'Narrative Style in Burgundian Chronicles of the Later Middle Ages', *Viator* 42 (2011), 233–82.

[19] The letter of arms of Jacques de Lalaing's *pas* is also transcribed in Mathieu d'Escouchy's account of this event in his chronicle, which gives no other information about it: see Mathieu d'Escouchy, *Chronique*, ed. G. du Fresne de Beaucourt, 3 vols (Paris, 1863–64), 1: 264–73. Olivier de La Marche, in his much longer account of the individual combats that took place during Jacques' *pas*, does not, however, reproduce this letter: see Olivier de La Marche, *Mémoires*, ed. Henri Beaune and J. d'Arbaumont, 4 vols (Paris, 1883–88), 2: 142–204.

[20] Nadot, *Le spectacle des joutes*, p. 149.

[21] Szkilnik, *Jean de Saintré*, p. 74, terms them 'quasi juridiques'.

[22] See Szkilnik, *Jean de Saintré*, pp. 74–75.

Jehan d'Avennes nonetheless uses exactly the same contractual style: *trouvera ... entrera ... qui sera vaincu ... sera tenu de donner ung rubi* etc. ('will find ...will enter ... who will be beaten ... who will be obliged to give a ruby', *JA*, p. 78). Furthermore, although the actual scenario of the *pas* outlined in Jehan d'Avennes' letter of arms is much less elaborate than that in its historical equivalents (a point I will return to below), the rhetorical tropes used are identical to those found in the account of Jacques de Lalaing's *pas*.[23] We thus find the same invocation to God and the Virgin (*JL*, p. 312; *JA*, p. 78), the same reference to the illustrious institution of chivalry and the desire of knights to increase their renown (*JL*, p. 312; *JA*, p. 78), and almost exactly the same presentation of the *entrepreneur* as a knight of suitably high birth: *un chevalier, noble de toutes lingnes et sans reproce* (*JL*, p. 312); *ung chevalier noble de toutez lignez et sans reproce* (*JA*, p. 78) ('a noble knight on all four sides of his lineage and without reproach'). Similarly, each letter introduces the *entrepreneur* in his chivalric incognito – Jacques de Lalaing as the *Chevalier du pas* ('Knight of the *pas*') and Jehan d'Avennes as the *Chevalier Blanc* ('White Knight') – and affirms that the *pas* has obtained the imprimatur of the *entrepreneur*'s sovereign: *par l'intermédiaire du tres excellent et puissant prince, son tres redoubté seigneur Philippe duc de Bourgogne* ('by the intercession of that most excellent and powerful prince, his most esteemed lord Philip, Duke of Burgundy', *JL*, pp. 312–13); *par le congié et licence de tres hault, excellent et tres poissant prince, le roy de France* ('by the permission and authorisation of the most high, excellent and powerful prince, the King of France', *JA*, p. 78). They also both choose as the location of the event one that has a certain symbolic and/or strategic importance[24]: in the case of Jacques de Lalaing's *pas*, a fountain situated on the island of Saint-Laurent in the town of Chalon-sur-Saône, which divides the River Saône into two large channels[25]; and, in that of Jehan d'Avennes, *sur la frontiere d'Engleterre en la forest, auprés d'une plaine qui est environ la ville de Bordeaux* ('on the border with England in a forest, near to a plain that is close to the town of Bordeaux') (*JA*, p. 78). Finally, each fixes the date and duration

---

[23] On the typical format of the letter of arms, see Nadot, *Le spectacle des joutes*, pp. 151–53.

[24] See Jourdan, 'Le thème du pas d'armes dans le royaume de France (Bourgogne, Anjou) à la fin du Moyen Âge: aspects d'un théâtre de chevalerie', pp. 286–87.

[25] Known in the medieval period as Saint-Laurent-lès-Chalon, the island is now a suburb of Chalon-sur-Saône. As Olivier de La Marche explains in his account of Jacques' *pas* (*Mémoires*, 2: 143), this choice of location was determined by the fact that it was on the route for knights travelling to the jubilee in Rome from France, England, Spain and Scotland, hence maximising the potential number of competitors willing and able to take up his challenge.

of the *pas* with a similar attention being paid to the symbolism of the number 'one'[26]: Jacques' *pas* is to run for one year, at a rate of one day of combat per month, whereas Jehan's more modest *pas* starts on the first of April, at a rate of one combat per day for fifteen days, with the *entrepreneur* being ready to start the combat at the hour of 'prime' on each day.

One of the two main differences between the historical and fictional *pas* in terms of their staging is that the stipulations about the way in which the combats will be conducted in, for example, Jacques de Lalaing's letter of arms, are far more elaborate than those in Jehan d'Avennes'. According to the former, the challenger must touch one of three different coloured shields held up outside the *entrepreneur*'s tent in order to signify which type of combat he has chosen (with lances, poleaxes or swords) and twenty-five separate *chapitres* ('chapters') then go on to explain the different rules applied to each of them (*JL*, pp. 317–26). By contrast, the stipulations of Jehan d'Avennes prescribe only one course of lances with sharpened weapons, and, if neither opponent is unhorsed by the other, the fight is to continue on foot with swords until one of them is beaten (*JA*, p. 78). Moreover, unlike the real *pas d'armes*, such as Jacques', at which many of the combats were judged by the Burgundian king of arms, Toison d'or ('Golden Fleece'), no separate judge is allowed for in Jehan's fictional *pas*. Instead, his succinct but precise letter of arms is taken as decisive in any dispute between the two combatants as to the outcome of any particular encounter, with the hero courteously but firmly stressing on two of the days of combat that his opponent is honour-bound to abide by *la maniere contenue en mon mandement* ('the way in which it is described in my letter') (*JA*, p. 83) and *le contenu de ma publication* ('the contents of my letter') (*JA*, p. 85) which, of course, he graciously agrees to do.

The other main difference between historical *pas d'armes* such as those of the Lalaing brothers and Jehan d'Avennes' romance version is the lack of an explicit scenario of service to a Lady in the latter.[27] The scenario outlined in Philippe de Lalaing's *Pas du Perron fée* (*PPF*, pp. 157–63) is probably the most elaborate of them all, involving the *entrepreneur* being kept prisoner by a fairy until he can prove himself worthy through his feats of arms of being

---

[26] See Jourdan, 'Le thème du Pas et de l'Emprise'; and Jean-Pierre Jourdan, 'Le perron de chevalerie à la fin du Moyen Age: aspects d'un symbole', in *Seigneurs et seigneuries au Moyen Age: Actes du 117e Congrès national des Sociétés savantes (Clermont-Ferrand, 1992), Section d'histoire médiévale et de philologie* (Paris, 1993), pp. 581–98.

[27] See Danielle Quéruel, 'Tournois et romans d'aventure en Bourgogne au XVeme siècle', in *Le Tournoi au Moyen Âge. Actes du colloque des 25 et 26 janvier 2002*, ed. Nicole Gonthier (Lyon, 2003), pp. 45–57.

released from the magical *perron* itself which, rather marvellously, is described as mechanically opening and closing each day to allow the *Chevalier du pas* to enter and exit the field of combat. Yet, the absence of such a scenario in Jehan's letter of arms should not necessarily invalidate our seeing his *pas* as being influenced by its historical avatars in adopting the pose of serving a Lady, especially as numerous other real *pas* are also much more reticent in this respect, such as that held at Saint-Inglevert in 1390.[28] Rather, given that Jehan's stated aim is to engage in *armez secretez* ('secret feats of arms') (*JA*, p. 97) by scrupulously maintaining his chivalric incognito throughout the fifteen days of the *pas*, instead of a direct reference to his lady-love in his letter of arms the various symbolic actions that he performs during the *pas* offer constant and clear reminders of his amorous motivation for fighting. He thus fixes a golden figurine of her to his helm (*JA*, pp. 83–84), composes poems and songs in her honour (*JA*, p. 91), and gives velvet hats to his servants with *Vive la Belle* ('Long live the Beautiful Lady') embroidered on them in pearls (*JA*, p. 96).

The second type of parallel I want to draw between the historical and the fictional *pas d'armes* in *Jehan d'Avennes* concerns the chivalric ethos of the combats where, once again, there is clear congruence between them. In this respect, I have to disagree with Michelle Szkilnik's claim that *Jehan de Saintré* alone depicts the hero as a Jacques de Lalaing-type whose *pas* is an elite sporting event undertaken in a spirit of international brotherhood. This is supposedly in contrast to other fifteenth-century prose romances which simply rehash Arthurian clichés in their depiction of the hero consistently asserting his physical dominance over his opponents as if in mortal combat.[29] In my view, the parallels between Jacques and Jehan are in fact quite compelling: each is depicted devoutly hearing mass each day before the combat begins; each enters and exits the field of combat according to a set ritual (Jacques leaves the Carmelite church where he spends the night before the fight and crosses the river in a boat whereas Jehan has himself armed and disarmed each day in his own pavilion); and most importantly, each takes every care not to wound or worse, kill, his opponent. As Jourdan has argued, this latter issue is crucial since the very idea of the *pas* is to score points rather than to maim or

---

[28] On this event, organised by Jean II Le Maingre, known as Boucicaut, see Annunziata, 'Teaching the *pas d'armes*', pp. 564–67; and *The Chivalric Biography of Boucicaut, Jean II Le Meingre*, trans. Craig Taylor and Jane H. M. Taylor (Woodbridge, 2016), pp. 48–52. See also Jean-Pierre Jourdan, 'Le thème du pas dans le royaume de France (Bourgogne, Anjou) à la fin du Moyen Âge: l'emergence d'un symbole', *Annales de Bourgogne* 62 (1990), 117–33 (here 123).

[29] Szkilnik, *Jean de Saintré*, pp. 87–89.

fight to the death, failure to take sufficient care in the combat being very much to the discredit of the knight lacking the appropriate skill.[30]

Although some chronicle or tournament accounts of the bouts in actual *pas d'armes* are very short, as in Philippe de Lalaing's *Pas du Perron fée*, where the narrator simply records the number of times the *entrepreneur* struck his opponent with his lance or his sword, those in the case of Jacques de Lalaing go into real technical detail. For example, in the fight against Jean de Boniface, Jacques is described as grabbing his opponent's poleaxe, hitting him three times on the visor with the point of his own weapon, seizing the crest on his helm and using this to make him fall to the ground (*JL*, pp. 346–47). Likewise, each of the fifteen bouts fought by Jehan d'Avennes is rendered in a similar level of detail, with three of them being deemed worthy of illustration in the BnF manuscript (out of a total of seventeen images for the whole text).[31] The first of these images, all of which follow the narrative very closely in depicting Jehan dressed in white in his guise as the *Chevalier Blanc*, shows the hero fighting against the Duke of York (fol. 34) (Figure 1). Emphasising the initial even-handedness of the bout through the symmetrical composition of the

---

[30] Jourdan, 'Les fêtes de la chevalerie dans les états bourguignons', pp. 264–67.

[31] The full cycle of images is as follows: frontispiece showing the author consulting the source of the text which he claims to have translated from Latin (fol. 1); Jehan killing a serpent (fol. 18v); Jehan fighting a judicial combat against the Emperor of Germany (fol. 24); combat at the *pas* against the Duke of York (fol. 34); combat at the *pas* against the Seigneur de Duras (fol. 37v); combat at the *pas* against the Seigneur de Beaumont (fol. 42v); knights assembling for the tournament at Compiègne (fol. 48v); interview between Jehan and the Countess of Artois (fol. 64v); the King of France leading his army out of Rheims to fight the Emperor of Germany (fol. 69); Jehan d'Avennes fighting a judicial combat against the Seigneur de Rochefort (fol. 83); Jehan fighting in war against the English (fol. 89v); a messenger arriving at the court of the King of France to broker peace with the English (fol. 93); Jehan fighting in war against the Saracens in Spain (fol. 100); Jehan fighting in war against the Saracens in Spain (fol. 106v); interview between Jehan and the Countess of Artois at which she tells him that she is married (fol. 112); Jehan meeting the Countess of Artois in the forest where they are reconciled (fol. 115); dancing at the wedding feast of Jehan and the Countess of Artois (fol. 119v). The importance of the miniatures illustrating the *pas d'armes* is demonstrated by there being no other sequence of three images all devoted to the same episode in the narrative; the skilful restraint and sporting prowess displayed by the hero in the *pas* can also be contrasted with his use of far deadlier violence in the three images devoted to war (fols. 89v, 100, 106v) where he slays his enemy on the battlefield. On the relative scarcity of images of *pas d'armes* in both romance and historiographical sources, see Guillaume Bureaux, 'Pas d'armes et vide iconographique: Quand le texte doit remplacer l'image (XVe siècle)', *Perspectives médiévales: Revue d'épistémologie des langues et littératures du Moyen Âge* 38 (2017) <https://peme.revues.org/12792>.

Fig. 1. Jehan d'Avennes fights the Duke of York. *Jehan d'Avennes*, Paris, Bibliothèque nationale de France, MS fr. 12572, fol. 34.

Fig. 2. Jehan d'Avennes fights the Seigneur de Duras. *Jehan d'Avennes*, Paris, Bibliothèque nationale de France, MS fr. 12572, fol. 37v.

Fig. 3. Jehan d'Avennes fights the Seigneur de Beaumont. *Jehan d'Avennes*, Paris, Bibliothèque nationale de France, MS fr. 12572, fol. 42v.

image, the depiction of each knight hitting the other's shield with his lance mirrors the reflexive verbs used in the text to underscore this reciprocation of blows that redounds to each man's honour: *s'entresaluerent lez deux chevaliers … et … s'entredonnerent si grans coups sur lez escus* ('the two knights *greeted each other* … and … *dealt each other* such great blows on their shields', *JA*, pp. 82–83, my emphases). The other two miniatures, by contrast, show the exact moment when the hero gains the upper hand. The representation of the fight against the Seigneur de Duras (fol. 37v) (Figure 2) has the two knights on foot with Jehan having just struck the decisive blow against his man, who lies on the ground, his sword having fallen from his hand. Jehan's body position, as he holds his sword with the point facing down and backwards away from the defeated knight, visually translates his respect and care for his opponent which Duras, despite having been slightly wounded, duly acknowledges, as the narrator states that *il le prinst en pacience et amoureusement se rendy* ('he took it in good part and lovingly surrendered', *JA*, p. 87). The third miniature, which portrays Jehan fighting against the Seigneur de Beaumont (fol. 42v) (Figure 3), also illustrates the clinching blow dealt by the hero as well as his dexterity. Having shattered his own sword and needing to put his shield above his head to protect himself from his opponent's blows, Jehan takes advantage of the fact that Beaumont's sword has become stuck in the shield in order to grab him round the waist so hard that, if he wanted to, he could throw him to the ground, at which point his opponent surrenders (*JA*, pp. 93–94).

The final parallel that I want to draw here between the accounts of real *pas d'armes* and the fictional one in *Jehan d'Avennes* is their use of self-reflexivity as a way of signalling to the reader that the performance of a *pas* is self-conscious role-play and not just an unthinking rehash of earlier literary models.³² In the chivalric biography of Jacques de Lalaing, the fiction of the *pas* is mostly maintained, with the rubrics generally respecting the knight's incognito but slipping occasionally to reveal that the *Chevalier du pas* is in fact none other than *messire Jacque de Lalain* (see, for example, *JL*, p. 342), as does the narrative when one of the guards of the lists reprimands the hero for his chivalric zeal and addresses him by his real name: *Messire Jacques, c'est assez! Il vous doit souffire* ('Messire Jacques, that's enough, you must content yourself with that') (*JL*, p. 359).³³

In *Jehan d'Avennes*, this self-reflexivity is heightened by the extraordinary lengths that the hero goes to in order to keep his *armes secretez*. Not only does he courteously but firmly refuse to feast with the English knights after each day's combat but he even enlists the help of two passing knights from Picardy to liaise between him and his opponents by bringing them tasty dishes to eat at the banquets and giving them all prizes at the end. However, the rubrics

---

³² On this issue of self-reflexivity in the *pas d'armes* whereby all those involved either as participants or as spectators are shown consciously playing along with the fictitious framing of the event, see the editors' discussion of the prologue attached to the version of the *Pas du Perron fée* recorded in Lille, Bibliothèque universitaire, MS 104 (*PPF*, p. 27): 'Il est clair que le duc et toute sa cour se prêtent gracieusement au jeu imaginé par Philippe et la manière dont le prologue habille la réalité (report de la date du pas, lecture des chapitres devant la cour, installation du perron, explications du nain aux chevaliers désireux de toucher les écus) de détails merveilleux (rôle et pouvoir supposés de la dame) révèle l'artifice de cette mise en scène.' ('It is clear that the duke and all the members of his court graciously play along with the game dreamt up by Philippe, and the way in which the prologue dresses up reality (the putting back of the date of the *pas*, the reading out loud of all the *chapitres* before the court, the setting up of the *perron*, the dwarf's explanations to the knights wanting to touch the different shields) with more supernatural elements (the role and the powers supposedly wielded by the Lady) points up the artifice involved in this *mise en scène*.')

³³ In his account of Jacques' *pas*, which lacks the rubrics found in the version contained in the chivalric biography, Olivier de La Marche (*Mémoires*, 2: 161) reveals this self-consciousness on the part of the combatants by recalling Jean de Boniface's 'surprise' at finding out that he had been fighting a disguised Jacques all along: *Quant le chevallier ouy nommer messire Jaques de Lalain, son compagnon, et il le recongneut, il luy fit moult grand honneur et chere, et s'embrasserent, et ainsi furent icelles armes accomplies* ('When the knight heard the name of messire Jacques de Lalaing, his companion in arms, and recognised him, he treated him with great honour and delight; they embraced each other and so it was that the combat ended.')

of the BnF manuscript, which are written in the same hand as the rest of the text, consistently refer to the hero by his proper name, stating: *Comment monseigneur Jehan ... porta par terre / obtint le pas / vainqui a l'espee* ('How monseigneur Jehan brought [his man] to the ground / was the victor in the fight / beat [his man] in the sword fight'). Through this constant pulling back of the hero's mask, as it were, the reader of *Jehan d'Avennes* is made very aware of the fact that this is a literary character playing out a contemporary form of combat. Indeed, this self-conscious performance, which almost borders on self-parody, is not unique to the hero. Another rather nice *clin d'œil* in this romance to the conventions of the contemporary *pas d'armes* is the description of the Duke of Gloucester that could have come straight out of the account of the *Pas du Perron fée* which revels in detailing all the heraldic and chivalric accoutrements of the combatants. Not only is this character portrayed as being decked out in his *heaulme de nouvelle facon, garny d'un lupard d'or seant sur le sommet et environné de deamans, fremaulz, saphirs et rubis* ('helm in the latest fashion, decorated with a golden leopard perched on the top and surrounded by diamonds, clasps, sapphires and rubies'), but he enters and exits the lists accompanied by no less than *deux Morez et [un] naim qui portoit son cor* ('two Moors and a dwarf who carried his horn', *JA*, p. 84), these being the 'must-have' accessories for any self-respecting participant in a late medieval *pas d'armes*![34]

To conclude: the whole episode of the *pas d'armes* in *Jehan d'Avennes* is presented as a self-consciously ludic 'time-out' from his other chivalric pursuits, one that the hero organises whilst waiting for the King of France's tournament at Compiègne to begin and before war kicks off against the Emperor of Germany, both of which were announced in the *mandements* ('letters') that preceded that heralding the *pas* itself. The close parallels that can be drawn between the real accounts of fifteenth-century Burgundian *pas d'armes* and this fictional one in terms of staging, chivalric ethos and self-reflexivity, all go to show that art could indeed imitate life imitating art in this period of medieval French literature. Intended to be read as a form of pseudo-history, these romances, like the tournament accounts, chronicles and chivalric biographies with which they have so much in common, thus aimed to hold up to

---

[34] See, for example, *PPF*, p. 129: *Aprés ce que mouseigneur Adolf de Clevez oult clos ledit pas, le chevalier fut mené par son nain devant les juges ... Et tantost que ledit chevalier fut rentré dedens ledit perron, vindrent trois hommes mores abilliés a la fachon du païs, vestus chascun des couleurs donc les les escus estoient qui pendoient audit perron* ('After monseigneur Adolph of Cleves had brought the aforesaid *pas* to a close, the knight was led by his dwarf in front of the judges ... And no sooner had the knight gone back inside the aforesaid *perron* than three Moors appeared dressed in the manner of the country, each wearing the colours of the shields that had been hanging on the aforesaid *perron*.')

their audience of noble initiates a mirror through which to admire the arts of chivalry as performed by some of its most illustrious practitioners in one of its most extravagant and elaborate manifestations, the spectacular *pas d'armes*.[35]

---

[35] On the numerous links between these different genres, see Rosalind Brown-Grant, 'Narrative Style in Burgundian Prose Romances of the Later Middle Ages', *Romania* 130 (2012), 355–406; Brown-Grant, 'Narrative Voice and Hybrid Style in Burgundian Chivalric Biography'; and Brown-Grant, 'Narrative Style in Burgundian Chronicles'.

8 The Foot Combat as Tournament Event: Equipment, Space and Forms

Iason-Eleftherios Tzouriadis

In the fifteenth and sixteenth centuries, foot combat became an often popular event in tournaments, with notable monarchs of the period participating in and excelling at it. In contrast with jousting and its variations (which were more widely practised, and seen as more prestigious than foot combat), and other forms of mounted competitions, there has been little dedicated research on the various aspects and details of foot combat. This situation is understandable considering the dearth of sources on foot combat competitions compared with the other forms of events of the tournament, as well as the lack of consistency in those sources. Fighting 'at the barriers' as a synonym for foot combat works in the same manner as 'the lists' is used to refer to mounted competitions. In the case of foot combat, the barrier refers to the format of the competition that became popular in the sixteenth century, where contestants fought with various weapons over a separating construction. The popularity of foot combat tournaments coincided with (and was most likely affected by) changes and transitions in martial culture which also had an impact in the conduct of war as well as with the development of martial culture in civic environments with the introduction and increasing popularity of fencing guilds that in their own turn would hold their own competitions.

It is difficult to trace the precise origin or purpose of foot combat competitions because they included many other aspects of the medieval tournament: practice for war, combat sport and spectacle. In the study of foot combat competitions, the comparison with jousting is inevitable. While the latter can be seen as a measure of the prowess of a martial elite which reflects the use of cavalry in military contexts, the former is an expression of core martial skills associated with infantry warfare. This approach is what may lead one to depict foot combat as less chivalric but this is not necessarily true. The deeds in challenges of foot combat of famous knights such as Jacques Lalaing, Richard Beauchamp, earl of Warwick, and many more were already celebrated by the end of the fifteenth century. Accounts from throughout the fifteenth century give examples of *pas d'armes*, challenges and judicial duels between knights fought on foot. Foot combat competitions and games for foot soldiers were popular in different Italian cities in the same period and special equipment was designed and used for these activities, such as specially padded helmets and gloves.[1]

It is likely that the origin of foot combat lies in these challenges, games and judicial duels. However, it is impossible to determine when the transition to structured competition occurred, or whether foot combat tournaments evolved from duelling. The contemporary depictions of duels and challenges, their format and the spaces in which they were fought in the early to mid fifteenth century bear a striking resemblance to the same aspects found in illustrations of foot combat competitions from the sixteenth century. The relationship between the format and structure of tournament conduct and judicial duel or trial by combat has been stressed by Vale.[2] The competitive duel that the foot combat resembles was certainly a gripping narrative model for the spectator. Though jousting combines several impressive skills, foot combat could evoke a common literary trope where two heroes compared their skill in arms.

The aim of this essay is to discuss the aspects of foot combat that defined it as a structured event within tournaments in Western Europe from the end of the fifteenth to the end of the sixteenth century. The specialised defensive and offensive equipment of the participants needs to be examined particularly through extant examples, while there needs to be an examination of the rules that dictated the conduct of the competition and the space in which it was to be fought. By addressing these subjects, the changing formats and role of foot combat can be analysed.

The chronological frame of this essay is the late fifteenth and the sixteenth centuries. There are several reasons for this choice. First and foremost, surviving evidence, such as written sources, iconography and extant examples of equipment for what fits the aforementioned definition of foot combat tournaments primarily comes from this period. Second, foot combat acquired strict formats for formal competition in this period, moving away from the ideas of

---

[1] Richard Barber and Juliet Barker, *Tournaments: Jousts, Chivalry and Pageants in the Middle Ages* (Woodbridge, 2000), pp. 83–84; William Heywood, *Palio and Ponte: An Account of the Sports of Central Italy from the Age of Dante to the XXth Century* (London, 1904), pp. 118–19.

[2] Malcolm Vale, *War and Chivalry: Warfare and Aristocratic Culture in England, France and Burgundy at the End of the Middle Ages* (London, 1981), p. 76.

duelling or sparring. Finally, this timeframe saw radical changes in the conduct of warfare throughout Europe.

The fifteenth and sixteenth centuries were a period of ongoing military conflict across Europe. Technological innovation and transition affected military technology. Simultaneously, changes in military thinking, as well as in social structures, affected military organisation and changed the conduct of war.[3] The use of combined arms (infantry, cavalry and artillery) became common practice for European armies of the period. The fourteenth century had already marked the end of the dominant role of cavalry on the battlefield.[4] The following two centuries saw an increase in the importance of infantry, as well as drastic changes in the composition of armies, with the transition to more widespread use of professional soldiers. Standing armies composed of professional troops began to emerge in Europe, sometimes with the addition of foreign or domestic mercenaries. By the end of the fifteenth century the Swiss *Reisläufer* and the German *Landsknechts*, professional hired soldiers that served as regular infantry and fought in numerous campaigns, were considered to be military elites because of their martial impact.[5] Cavalry was still effective, but in this period it was used in conjunction with infantry armed with staff weapons, crossbows, harquebuses or other early firearms, and artillery. As a result of drilling and training, infantry was better able to repel cavalry charges and launch coordinated attacks.[6] This was the result of ongoing changes in infantry warfare that already started from the late thirteenth century and intensified during the fourteenth and fifteenth centuries.[7] This shift in effectiveness and impact from cavalry to infantry and the increasing

---

[3] Bert S. Hall, *Weapons and Warfare in Renaissance Europe: Gunpowder, Technology, and Tactics* (Baltimore, 1997), pp. 234–35; Frank Tallett and D. J. B. Trim, '"Then Was Then and Now is Now": An Overview of Change and Continuity in Late-Medieval and Early-Modern Warfare', in *European Warfare: 1350–1750*, ed. Frank Tallett and D. J. B. Trim (Cambridge, 2010), pp. 1–26.

[4] Vale, *War and* Chivalry, pp. 100–5.

[5] John R. Hale, *War and Society in Renaissance Europe: 1450–1620* (Baltimore, 1985), p. 38.

[6] David Eltis, *The Military Revolution in Sixteenth-Century Europe* (London, 1995), pp. 44–46; Clifford J. Rogers, 'Tactics and the Face of Battle', in *European Warfare: 1350–1750*, pp. 203–35 (here 208–24); A. Logan Thompson, 'The Decline of the Armoured Knight Part 1: The Rise of the Halberd and the Emergence of Gunpowder', *Classic Arms and Militaria*, May 1998, pp. 34–37.

[7] Kelly DeVries, *Infantry Warfare in the Early Fourteenth Century: Discipline, Tactics and Technology* (Woodbridge, 2006); John France, *Western Warfare in the Age of the Crusades: 1000–1300* (London, 1999), p. 28.

importance of the latter can be interpreted as one of the main reasons for the inclusion of foot combat in tournaments during the period under examination.

Written sources and art relating to tournaments prior to the third quarter of the fifteenth century deal, in their majority, with the competition of knights on horseback and the various forms and events of the medieval tournament as this developed. The status and importance of the participants in society and the battlefield were strengthened by the roles in which they took part in these competitions. Learning to fight on foot was part of the training of martial elites, but in the context of a tournament, where pageantry was a key element, this was insignificant as fighting on foot carried no lustre. In the early sixteenth century the *pas d'armes* and other forms of tournaments held in France, England, Italy and Germany included a variety of events such as jousting, foot combat, and thematic events such as storming a fortress.[8] Sources from throughout the sixteenth century in Western Europe attest to the inclusion of foot combat events of various formats in tournaments.

Foot combat in tournaments did not cease at the end of the sixteenth century, but it did change. Whereas certain examples of practice in the fashion of previous decades can be detected in such events in the seventeenth century, the conduct, equipment and, most importantly, context had changed. Changes in European societies, courts and military elites saw a decline in the popularity of the tournament, and with it the foot combat competitions. In places such as Switzerland, Germany, Iberia and Sweden, foot combat competitions were already being organised in civic environments from the end of the sixteenth century as a form of civic sport, or as exhibitions by fencing guilds. The equipment and rules of conduct also changed significantly.[9] It is difficult to decide to what extent these competitions and martial displays can be considered as foot combats in the way in which they were conducted in previous decades, but they are surely a continuation, transition and byproduct of the same martial tradition. The inclusion of foot combat in tournament events is a testament not only to the ongoing relationship and communication between tournaments and war, but also to the changing face of warfare and the way in which it affected all activity and cultural elements with a martial basis.

---

[8] Francis H. Cripps-Day, *The History of the Tournament in England and in France* (London, 1918), p. 125.

[9] Sydney Anglo, *The Martial Arts of Renaissance Europe* (New Haven, 2000), pp. 170–71.

A Brief Definition of Tournament Foot Combat

Before proceeding to discuss foot combat in tournaments it is important to provide a definition of the subject, so that the reader is aware of what the term implies for future reference. Broughton provided two strict definitions. According to the first, in the 'foot tournament' combat was conducted over a barrier and the participants had to either mutually splinter lances on the opponent or exchange blows with swords on each other's helmets. Blows to the legs would in both cases lead to disqualification, due to the absence of leg armour.[10] The second term Broughton defines is the *fussturnier*, which is described as a form of tournament used in the late fifteenth century between teams or troops that fought across a barrier, where each combatant had to break lances with both hands on all of their opponents and deliver a specific number of strikes with swords. Because combatants did not wear leg armour, all strokes below the belt were deemed invalid.[11] It is unclear why Broughton produced two similar definitions and why he used the German term *fussturnier*. Both of these definitions are narrow and specific, and do not reflect the various formats of foot combat in tournaments. This highlights the need for a clear and inclusive definition. Foot combat tournaments can be defined as a form of competitive, usually secondary, event taking place in the context of a wider tournament event. They were fought between competitors on foot, one-on-one or in paired teams. These participants competed in a predetermined format that dictated the arms and armour used, the space and surrounding equipment (such as fences and barriers), and the winning conditions of the competition (such as landing a number of blows on the opponent on allowed body areas). Sometimes the rules also specified the prizes that could be won. Judges present determined the winner or punished contestants who broke the rules and regulations. The audience varied depending on the format: in some cases only other participants were allowed to be present, or in the case of court events, they were restricted to courtly society. In some cases they were open to the general public, particularly in events taking place in a city square or other civic environments. From here onwards the term foot combat will be used to refer to such combat in the context of tournaments, and not to indicate any form of combat occurring between foot-soldiers on the battlefield or any other context, unless so noted.

---

[10] Bradford B. Broughton, *Dictionary of Medieval Knighthood and Chivalry: Concepts and Terms* (New York, 1986), p. 209.

[11] Broughton, *Dictionary*, p. 215.

Much like the portrayal of foot combat as a tournament event in primary sources and art, research on the subject has been scarce. The usual trend in secondary literature specific to the medieval tournament is to mention foot combat in passing (if at all), with a few exceptions. Unlike understudied subjects that are ignored simply due to the lacklustre effect of adjacent topics (for the example the sword being a common object of study while other weapon groups are comparatively understudied), the relationship of the tournament and foot combat is not as simple. Primary sources rarely provide more than a few sentences of information, and not all tournaments include foot combat, whether in the fifteenth or sixteenth century. Tournament books that so lavishly illustrate jousting do not always portray foot combat, and when they do it is usually to a disproportionately smaller degree. To find many of the foot combat depictions that will be discussed later in this essay one must often look into various forms of art, from manuscript illuminations and woodcuts in printed books to paintings and tapestries from the examined period. Thankfully, modern scholars do often take foot combat into account as part of the development of the wider tournament tradition, and usually highlight aspects of foot combat related to their specific research topic. The most thorough work on foot combat by far is Dillon's article which thoroughly explores the different sources that provide snippets of information on foot combat competitions, particularly from the fifteenth century.[12] His study is a thorough examination of foot combat, particularly of its early forms in the fifteenth century, and this essay will attempt to group together some of the aspects of foot combat competitions Dillon scattered in his essay, such as the competition space and equipment. Authors dealing overall with the medieval tournament, such as Barber and Barker or Clephan, dedicate some discussion to foot combat but do not go into the same detail as they do on subjects such as the tourney or jousting.[13] More detailed work has been produced on the practical use of weapons in foot combat rather than on their form or on the context of their use.[14]

---

[12] Harold A. L. Dillon, *Barriers and Foot Combats* (London, 1905).

[13] See Barber and Barker, *Tournaments*; Robert Coltman Clephan, *The Medieval Tournament* (New York, 1995; reprint of *The Tournament: Its Periods and Phases*, London, 1919); Christopher Gravett, *Knights at Tournament* (Oxford, 1998). Mentions of foot combat in these works vary in length and are scattered throughout the text.

[14] For the use of weapons in foot combat in the fifteenth and sixteenth centuries, see Sydney Anglo, '*Le Jeu de la Hache*: A Fifteenth-Century Treatise on the Technique of Chivalric Axe Combat', *Archaeologia* 109 (1991), 113–28; Claude Gaier, 'Technique des combats singuliers d'après les auteurs "bourguignons" du XVe siècle', *Le Moyen Âge* 91 (1985), 415–57; *L'Art chevaleresque du combat: Le maniement des armes*

Arms and Armour of the Foot Combat

Arms and armour were an essential part of the equipment and the identity of the warrior. Specialised armour designed for tournaments had already appeared at the end of the thirteenth century, developed to be used in the early forms of jousting that were already emerging. Extant examples survive of tournament armour from the beginning of the fifteenth century that aimed to minimise the physical dangers that came as natural with the participation in a martial sport that included a combination of significant speed, force and weapons. Tournament-specific armour was reinforced either by being thicker or with the addition of extra protective pieces, which made it heavier. Usually the helmet was locked to the cuirass with a variety of mechanisms to limit head movement upon impact. These modifications and specific needs gave these harnesses and pieces of equipment a distinctive look compared with their equivalent for field use. Foot combat was no exception to this, and in the period examined, during which foot combat reached the pinnacle of its popularity, specific equipment developed for this type of competition as well.[15]

A brief description and depiction from an English manuscript from the middle of the fifteenth century gives valuable information on the equipment of a participant in foot combat, as well as the practicalities of wearing it.[16] It is important to mention that the context of the fight in this case is judicial combat. However, the equipment depicted, both defensive and offensive, which is depicted spread out on a table, such as the great basinet, the axe and the *ahlspiess*, is roughly the same that would be used in foot combat tournaments in the following decades, as can be observed in the cases of later depictions and extant equipment.

The variations of the defensive equipment of the foot combat can be developed and discussed on two axes: the helmet designs geared towards increased

---

à travers les livres de combat (XIVe-XVIe siècles), ed. Daniel Jaquet (Neuchâtel, 2012). The case of *Le Jeu de la Hache* discussed by Anglo is of particular interest because it appears to instruct the reader on how to compete in an armoured judicial duel with axes in a predesignated space. The form of the combat is nearly identical to foot combat with the same weapons. The revised edition, dating and discussion provided by Dupuis and Deluz on *Le Jeu de la Hache* also places it in the same chronological context of the late fifteenth century where foot combat systematically appears as part of tournaments. See Olivier Dupuis and Vincent Deluz, '*Le Jeu de la Hache*: A Critical Edition and Dating Discussion', *Acta Periodica Duellatorum* 5 (2017), 3–62.

[15] Donald J. La Rocca, *How to Read European Armour* (New York, 2017), p. 90.

[16] Harold A. L. Dillon, 'On a MS Collection of Ordinances of Chivalry of the Fifteenth Century, Belonging to Lord Hastings', *Archaeologia* 57 (1900), 29–70 (here 44).

protection, and the design of specific parts of the harness. Much as in the case of armour specifically designed for jousting, the helmet was often the most distinctive piece of armour designed exclusively for foot combat. Helmets were a visual focal point of the armour (because they were on eye level and they often had intricate decorations and designs), but most importantly they had to protect the head and neck of the wearer.

The great basinet appears to have been a popular helmet design for foot combat in the late fifteenth and early sixteenth centuries. It is large, with an integrated neck part that locks onto the cuirass, and has a convex visor that sometimes has a reinforcing ridge in the middle. Sir Giles Capel's great basinet from the first quarter of the sixteenth century has a large visor with numerous rectangular holes creating chevron patterns.[17] This would protect the wearer from most thrusting blows and would also allow good overall vision. The neck of the armour is solid and restrictive and is designed to lock onto the breastplate. A gilded great basinet that belonged to Maximilian I, Holy Roman Emperor, is attached to the cuirass in a similar manner, but the visor has a different design, also designed for foot combat.[18] A central ridge reinforces the brow and top of the helmet, and an inner vertical grill adds additional protection to the horizontal eye opening. Decreasing the risk of the long horizontal eye slit in great basinets often meant that the opening would have to be really narrow.[19] An observation of the shape of the bulkier and rounder extant examples of the great basinet helmets certainly bears some resemblance to the shape of some of the helmets used for the *Kolbenturnier*, a type of mounted competition that was conducted with clubs or blunted swords.[20] The existence of nearly grill-shaped framework visors on helmets such as that from the tonlet armour of Henry VIII of England reinforces this resemblance.[21] There is no proof of a link in the design of the two types of helmets other than that they were both used in different types of tournament.

Even though it first appears in the first quarter of the sixteenth century, the close helmet became the most popular form of helmet in foot combat from

---

[17] Foot combat helmet of Sir Giles Capel, New York, The Metropolitan Museum of Art, 04.3.274.

[18] Foot combat armour, Vienna, Kunsthistorisches Museum, B 71.

[19] An example of this is a German great basinet dated to 1500: Berlin, Deutsches Historisches Museum, W 1014.

[20] Two helmets for the *Kolbenturnier* from the Metropolitan Museum of Art in New York highlight this observation. The first has an iron frame covered partially by canvas whilst the second is steel resembling even more certain foot combat bascinets. See New York, The Metropolitan Museum of Art, 40.135.3 and 29.158.37.

[21] Tonlet armour, Leeds, Royal Armouries, II.7.

the second half of the sixteenth century onwards. This is most likely connected to changes in the format of foot combat as a whole and the introduction of different rules and formats that shifted to the use of offensive equipment other than what the great basinet was intended to face. Compared with great bascinets, close helmets offered less protection for the neck of the user, but had increased protection on the front sides of the head and visor. They allowed greater mobility and certainly their design was more elegant. The close helmet usually offered two or three layers of protection on the front of the face with different visors and protective parts moving on the same side pivots. An Italian foot combat close helmet from the third quarter of the sixteenth century has all of the above characteristics.[22] The helmet closes and locks on the turning collar of the gorget and allows increased peripheral motion.[23] A German armet from 1560 has a bellow visor that resembles the design of some visors of previous great basinets for foot combat, in what is perhaps a stylistic aesthetic combination of certain features of the two most popular helmets for foot combat competitions (Figure 1).[24] Some close helmets for foot combat had incorporated neck protection that added an extra layer on top of the gorget.[25] This extra neck protection is articulated and not locked into place as in the great basinets previously discussed.

A comparison of helmets for mounted tournaments and helmets for foot combat, especially great basinets, makes certain observations possible. In both cases the neck is treated as a crucial element in the design of the object and it is necessary that, supported by armour, it stays locked in place. This is certainly understandable in the case of jousting where a breaking lance could land with tremendous force onto someone's neck or head. Therefore, impact on the area of the head and the neck had to be minimised. The throat, as a sensitive part of the human body, was also covered and protected with no gaps allowed. However, the existence of the same principles in foot combat armour reveals that the threat of hits on the head or neck were as significant as for jousting. Besides the obvious threat to the throat, sustained strikes to the head or neck with swords, axes and spears could cause serious injury.[26] Mobility (particularly of the neck in the case of great basinets) and visibility were

---

[22] Close helmet, Philadelphia, Philadelphia Museum of Art, 1977-167-128.

[23] A gorget is a collar that supports and helps distribute the weight of the cuirass, and at the same time protects the neck of the wearer.

[24] Portions of an armour, Leeds, Royal Armouries, II.173.

[25] Close helmet, New York, The Metropolitan Museum of Art, 14.25.548.

[26] For a discussion on the forces applied with the thrusting motion of staff weapons and their penetrative capabilities see Iason-Eleftherios Tzouriadis, 'The Typology

Fig.1. Portions of an armour, German, 1560. Leeds, Royal Armouries, II.173.

sacrificed for the sake of safety. The lack of visibility is an indirect indication of the martial skill required of the competitors.

Besides the head-specific protection that developed for foot combat, certain types of harness specifically developed for this type of competition appeared during the period. The most distinctive in shape is tonlet armour, a harness that includes a deep metal skirt which gives the armour its name. Extant examples demonstrate an interesting variety in the shape, structure and length of the tonlet. The overall shape could be straight or flared, its length varying, with its lower part reaching to the middle part of the thigh to covering the knees. It could also be solid or more usually articulated. The tonlet allows freedom of movement and increased protection on the upper leg and abdomen area, particularly considering that its purpose was to be usually used with large two-handed swords that would not be able to strike underneath it. Perhaps the exemplar tonlet armour is Henry VIII's harness used for the Field of Cloth of Gold in 1520.[27] The tonlet is deep and wide and has nine articulated layers. A gilded tonlet armour of Maximilian I has a shorter skirt and large pauldrons covering most of the upper cannon (the upper part of the arm protection) and part of the cuirass, both on the front and back.[28] The overlapping plates provide extra protection and are fitted over the lower part of the helmet. A Milanese tonlet armour in the Italian style from the last quarter of the fifteenth century has wide curves and an eight-layer articulated skirt.[29] The harness belonged to Claude de Vaudrey, a member of the Burgundian court, and Maximilian I won it from him during a foot combat which is illustrated in *Freydal*.[30] A suit of foot combat armour belonging to Archduke Ferdinand of Tirol from 1547 has a tonlet made of two parts joined together at the sides.[31] It goes down to the middle of the thigh and is flared outwards. The front part of the tonlet is a downwards extension of the breastplate and bears the same decorative patterns. Based on extant examples, it can be said that tonlet armour was in use from the last quarter of the fifteenth century and remained in fashion for the

---

and Use of Staff Weapons in Western Europe c. 1400–c.1550' (unpublished Ph.D. thesis, University of Leeds, 2017), pp. 262–70.

[27] Tonlet armour, Leeds, Royal Armouries, II.7. See also Claude Blair, 'King Henry VIII's Tonlet Armour', *Burlington Magazine* 125 (1983), 16–20.

[28] Foot combat armour, Vienna, Kunsthistorisches Museum, B 71.

[29] Tonlet armour, Vienna, Kunsthistorisches Museum, B 33.

[30] *Freydal. Des Kaisers Maximilian I. Turniere und Mummereien*, ed. Quirin von Leitner 2 vols (Vienna, 1880–82), 1, fol. 39.

[31] Tonlet armour of Archduke Ferdinand II of Tirol made by Jörg Seusenhofer and Hans Peckhammer. Vienna, Kunsthistorisches Museum, HJRK A 638.

first half of the sixteenth century. Iconographic examples from even earlier depict harnesses that could be identified as short tonlets.

One of the most iconic armour designs made for the foot combat is the one that fully encloses the body of its user, leaving no parts exposed. Parts of the body such as the thighs, which in field or jousting armour would be protected by the saddle, were in this case fully covered.[32] This type of armour was designed for competing with larger weapons such as the axe or the two-handed sword. The most impressive example of this was the harness produced for Henry VIII in 1520 but never finished or used.[33] Intricate articulated plates cover all surfaces including the inside of joints, the armpits and buttocks. A similar Italian extant armour made earlier in the first quarter of the sixteenth century has decorative patterns that reflect contemporary fashion.[34] These rare harnesses are proof that the technology that went into the equipment of foot combat was sometimes a reflection of the peak of armour production of its time, and the needs of the competition pushed technical boundaries in new directions.

Finally, harnesses for foot combat changed radically after the third quarter of the sixteenth century when the introduction of protective barriers between opponents prevented hits below the waist. The prohibition of low strokes and the existence of the barrier made leg armour redundant, although some thigh protection attached to the cuirass would still exist. A prominent example of this style is a suit of armour by Anton Peffenhauser made in 1591 (Figure 2).[35] The armour, part of a set of twelve matching harnesses, is problematic because it is composed from different parts of the different armours from that set of twelve. However, it is important to mention that none of them have leg armour and therefore they were designed for fighting over a barrier. A lavishly etched, engraved and partially gilded foot combat armour from 1590 does not even have tassels or any other form of protection below the abdomen.[36]

The defensive equipment used for foot combat was developed and advanced in a reciprocal relationship with the corresponding weapons that were used in these competitions. Unlike the often distinctive and specialised armour that developed for foot combat, the weapons used for these competitions reflected the military realities of their period. Sometimes modifications were made to these weapons in order to increase the safety of the competitors by blunting

---

[32] *The Last Knight: The Art, Armor, and Ambition of Maximilian I*, ed. Pierre Terjanian (New York, 2019), p. 96.

[33] Foot combat armour, Leeds, Royal Armouries, II.6.

[34] Foot combat armour, Paris, Musée de l'Armée, G.178.

[35] Foot combat armour, Leeds, Royal Armouries, II.186.

[36] Foot combat armour, Philadelphia Museum of Art, 1977-167-37.

Fig. 2. Foot combat armour composed of pieces of different armours from a set of twelve of Christian I, Elector of Saxony, German, 1591, by Anton Peffenhauser. Leeds, Royal Armouries, II.186.

them. Several types of swords and staff weapons were used throughout the late fifteenth and sixteenth centuries, with certain visible trends.

The most distinctive weapon used in foot combat before the introduction of the separating barrier was the axe, which saw use throughout the second half of the fifteenth and at least the first quarter of the sixteenth century. It found its way from the battlefield to judicial combat, then to foot combat, and finally became a ceremonial object, and is arguably the earliest identifiable weapon used in foot combat competitions. First, the terms used for this weapon group have to be briefly discussed. Often all weapons that roughly fall into this category are described in scholarship with a multitude of interchangeable terms such as pollaxe, poleaxe, polearm, polax or simply axe. This is a source of confusion as many of these weapons do not even have an axe element. The recommended overall term for this weapon group is axe-hammers, divided into subgroups depending on the offensive technical features of the examined object.[37]

The pollaxe is a two-handed hybrid weapon designed to be used for cutting, thrusting, bludgeoning and pulling. Its head is complex, with one side bearing an axe which can have a convex or straight blade, a vertical spike on the top which can be bladed and usually of quadrangular or triangular shape, and on the opposite side of the axe either a hammer usually of flat or ribbed ending or a downwards facing beak. The *bec-de-corbin* is also a hybrid weapon, designed for bludgeoning, thrusting and pulling. It differs from the pollaxe in that instead of an axe blade one side always has a small coronel-shaped hammer with three or four prongs. Opposite the hammer a beak extends downwards. The weapon usually has a vertical spike of varying length extending the axis of the shaft. Single-handed versions of this weapon were also used in foot combat.[38] Both sub-groups (the pollaxe and the *bec-de-corbin*) appear to have certain additional features on the shaft, such as reinforcing metal strips, the langets (metal that extend on the shaft) as well as other protective features that vary from object to object. A highly detailed manuscript illumination from the second half of the fifteenth century demonstrates the variety in the shape of axe-hammers available for foot combat in this period.[39] Whereas the two combatants fight in an enclosure using axe-hammers of the *bec-de-corbin* type, guards observing the fight are holding a variety of staff weapons such as bills, spears and axe-hammers of the pollaxe type, as well as a weapon resembling a standard halberd. An extant example of a pollaxe from Burgundy

---

[37] Tzouriadis, 'The Typology and Use of Staff Weapons', pp. 226–40.

[38] Los Angeles, J. Paul Getty Museum, MS 114 (2016.7), fol. 123r.

[39] London, British Library, MS Harley 4375, fol. 171v.

resembles those depicted in the Beauchamp Pageant, an illustrated biography of Richard Beauchamp, earl of Warwick, and is dated to the middle or third quarter of the fifteenth century.[40] The head has an axe of a slightly convex shape. On the opposite side it has a hammer which flairs outwards towards its percussive point and a small downwards beak grows from it. Finally, it has a vertical leaf-shaped bladed spike. It is secured on the shaft with two pairs of langets. Several similar pollaxes survive from the second half of the fifteenth century. A pollaxe from the last quarter of the fifteenth or the beginning of the sixteenth century has a straight axe-head, a flat hammer with three protruding prongs, and a reinforced vertical spike (Figure 3).[41] Extant examples of *bec-de-corbins* perfectly reflect the depictions of this type of weapon from the middle of the fifteenth century onwards.[42] A *bec-de-corbin* from the second quarter of the sixteenth century with a coronel-shaped hammer is not much different in form and is an excellent example of this type of weapon that was in use in its later years (Figure 4).[43] It is interesting to observe that often axe-hammers, particularly of the pollaxe type depicted in foot combat scenes, have one or two protective rondels. These sometimes survive on extant examples when made of metal. Leather rondels rarely survive beyond traces on similarly rare original shafts from the fifteenth century. The reasons behind their extinction on surviving objects is the difficulty of preserving the material, as well as the replacement of many of the original shafts in centuries that followed their use. Rondels do not appear to be an integral part of the axe-hammer in iconography but they are common and would offer extra protection, especially in the context of sporting competition. Weapons of this group were popular in foot combat until the middle of the sixteenth century.

The *ahlspiess* appears to be another staff weapon sometimes used in foot combat. The weapon had a long quadrangular or triangular head used for

---

[40] Pollaxe, New York, The Metropolitan Museum of Art, 14.25.302. The examples from the Beauchamp Pageant have many of the structural elements already mentioned. *Pageant of the Birth, Life and Death of Richard Beauchamp Earl of Warwick K.G., 1389–1439*, ed. Harold A. Dillon and W. H. St John Hope (London, 1914), p. 75.

[41] Pollaxe, Leeds, Royal Armouries, VII.1509.

[42] An exemplar weapon of this category used and represented in late fifteenth- and early sixteenth-century depictions is dated to the last quarter of the fifteenth or first quarter of the sixteenth century and is possibly Italian. It has a three-pronged coronel-shaped hammer and a reinforced vertical spike and back-spike, which both indicate its use against armoured targets. *Bec-de-corbin*, New York, The Metropolitan Museum of Art, 14.25.465.

[43] *Bec-de-corbin*, Leeds, Royal Armouries, VII.1510.

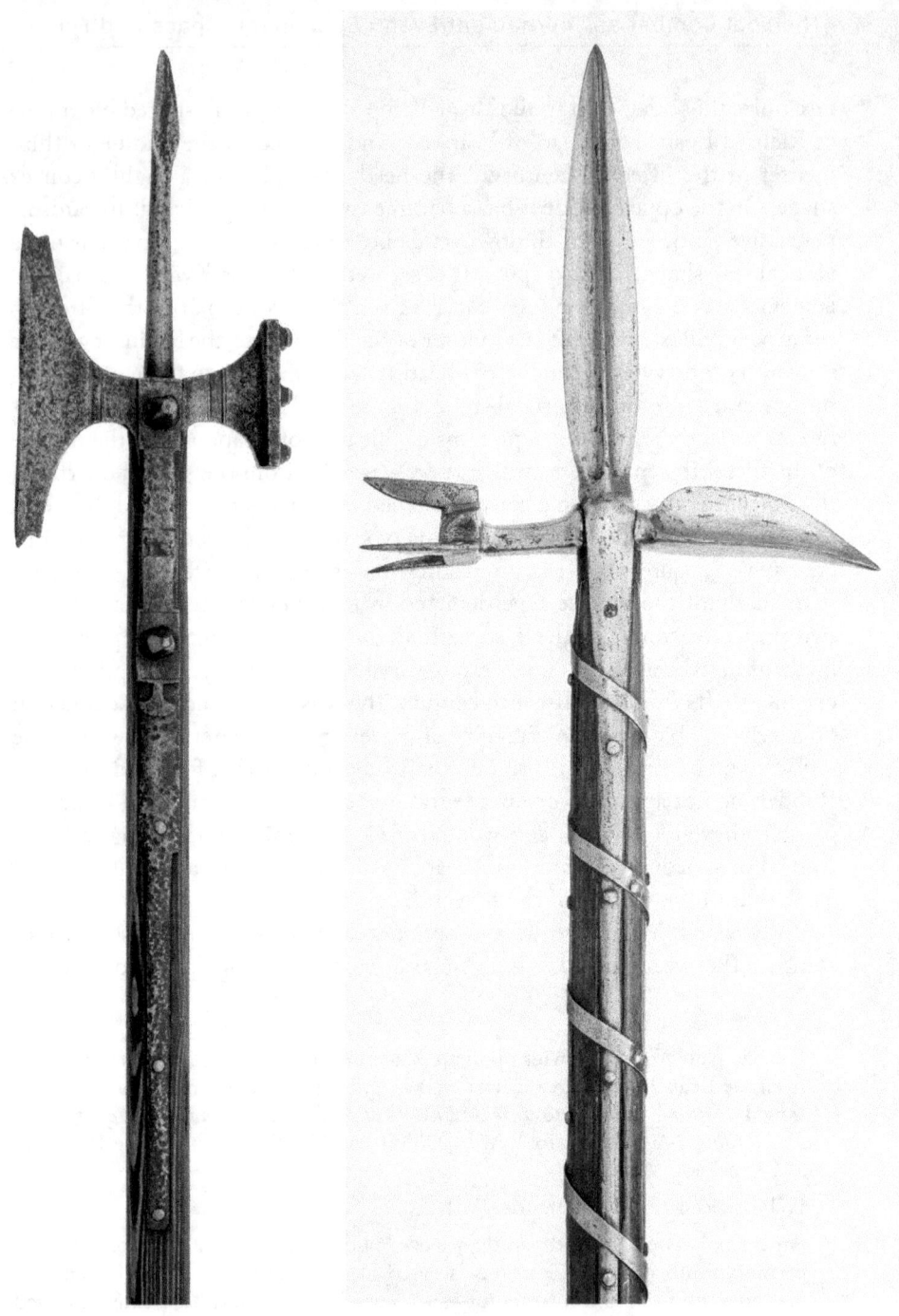

Fig. 3. (left) Pollaxe, English, 1475–1510. Leeds, Royal Armouries, VII.1509.

Fig. 4. (right) *Bec-de-corbin*, English, first half of the sixteenth century. Leeds, Royal Armouries, VII.1510.

thrusting.⁴⁴ At the base of the long metal head a metal rondel could usually be fitted to protect the upper hand and also to increase thrusting force as a pushing point. Evidence of this is usually limited to iconographical elements. The consistency of its occurrence in pictorial evidence over the second half of the fifteenth and the first quarter of the sixteenth century is proof of its use during stages of foot combat competitions. The *ahlspiess* is part of a knight's equipment being prepared for foot combat as depicted in a manuscript from the middle of the fifteenth century.⁴⁵ In his pageant from 1485 Richard Beauchamp can be found using the *ahlspiess* against his opponent.⁴⁶ It is notable that the weapon in this case has a spike at its lower end. The *ahlspiess* definitely declined in popularity during the sixteenth century, but evidence of its use can still be found at least in the first quarter. Two detailed examples of the *ahlspiess* used in foot combat are presented in *Freydal* where Maximilian is shown fighting against Wolfgang von Polhaim and Hanns Traunpicz, members of his court.⁴⁷ The weapons used by the Holy Roman Emperor resemble extant examples from the late fifteenth century more closely, with shorter and thicker heads than their more slender and popular counterparts from the late fifteenth and sixteenth centuries. The *ahlspiess* appears to have been the first weapon that was excluded from foot combat, at some point in the first half of the sixteenth century.

Unsurprisingly, the sword, the weapon mostly associated with military elites in medieval and early modern Europe, was also used in foot combat. Its two-handed and single-handed forms and variations were used throughout the period. However, whereas the two-handed sword appears to have been more popular in the late fifteenth and first half of the sixteenth century, single-handed variations appear to have been favoured after that. The use of the two-handed sword in foot combat coincided with its development within the wider martial tradition in Europe as the exemplar weapon in fighting systems and in the training of weapons.⁴⁸ Besides their military counterparts, which would also be used in some competitions, certain two-handed swords designed

---

⁴⁴ For the different forms and nomenclature regarding the *ahlspiess*, the *candeliere* and the *breschspiess* see Tzouriadis, 'The Typology and Use of Staff Weapons', pp. 148–58.

⁴⁵ Dillon, 'Hastings', p. 44.

⁴⁶ *The Beauchamp Pageant*, p. 27.

⁴⁷ *Freydal*, pp. 23, 147.

⁴⁸ Roberto Gotti, Daniel Jaquet and Iason-Eleftherios Tzouriadis, *European Martial Arts: From Vulcan's Forge to the Arts of Mars* (Botticino, 2019), p. 132.

for foot combat had rebated edges.⁴⁹ In the sixteenth century the traditional arming sword had transitioned in most places in Europe into what is referred to as the sidesword, an often slightly more slender weapon than its predecessor, with a variety of hilt forms that could have protective elements such as rings and bars for the user's fingers and hand. It would be safe to assume that in cases where the participants in foot combat used single-handed swords in the sixteenth century, they would be using sideswords.⁵⁰ There are, however, depictions that suggest that simpler forms of single-handed swords would also have been in use during this period.⁵¹ Most iconographical examples of tournaments as well as rules from the early sixteenth century onwards suggest that single-handed swords were in use, especially after the introduction of the barriers. It is unlikely that rapiers were used in foot combat, at least not in the period examined. The repeated blows on armour required in most tournament formats would take a toll even on the heavier and thicker swept-hilt rapiers in use from the end of the sixteenth century (Figure 5).⁵² Their use should not be categorically excluded because of the slow transition from the late sidesword to the early rapier and therefore of a period where the form of this type of sword was fluid. Towards the end of the period and later, single-handed swords used in foot combat were often rebated and their tips were rounded (Figure 6).⁵³

---

⁴⁹ *Henry VIII: Arms and the Man, 1509–2009*, ed. Graeme Rimer, Thom Richardson and J. P. D. Cooper (Leeds, 2009), p. 120.

⁵⁰ Portraits of nobles and depictions of participants in foot combat from the sixteenth century often include sideswords, many with complex hilts. An Italian example of a knight who has taken his tournament armour off shows a decorated sidesword with finger rings and a bar to protect the knuckle. It is interesting that the knight also has a device to support his leg which is suffering from some sort of injury. See Giovanni Batista Moroni, 'Il Cavaliere dal Piede Ferito' (London, The National Gallery, NG1022).

⁵¹ Alan Young, *Tudor and Jacobean Tournaments* (London, 1987), pp. 32–33.

⁵² Portraits of noblemen from the last quarter of the sixteenth century sometimes depict their subjects with elements of foot combat armour and wearing a rapier. It is more likely that the case for this was because the sword had already become an essential accessory of a gentleman's attire and image, rather than to use it in combat at the barriers as their waist-high armour would suggest. In a portrait of Robert Radcliffe, earl of Sussex, from the last quarter of the sixteenth century, he is depicted holding a pike and an early swept-hilt rapier whilst wearing armour for foot combat at the barriers. Marcus Gheeraerts the Younger, 'Portrait of Robert Radcliffe', Leeds, Royal Armouries, I.36.

⁵³ Tournament sword, Leeds, Royal Armouries, IX.1217.

Fig. 5. Painting, *Portrait of Robert Radcliffe*, English-Flemish, about 1593, by Marcus Gheeraerts the Younger. Leeds, Royal Armouries, I.36.

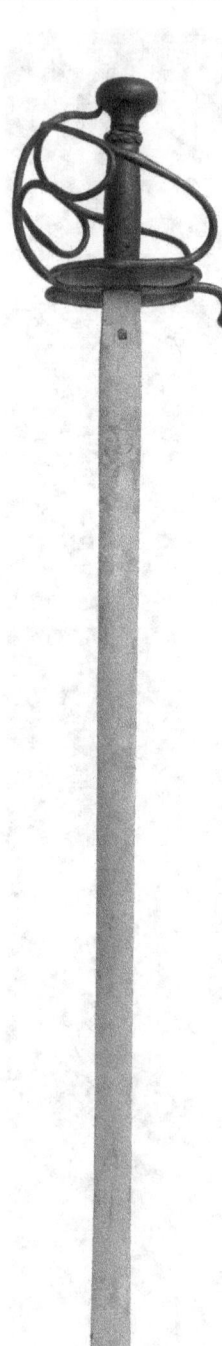

The pike was a form of particularly long spear that became the dominant infantry weapon of European battlefields in the sixteenth and seventeenth centuries. Its use affected the conduct of war particularly in the sixteenth century. The shaft was long and either straight or thicker in the middle. The head was usually a short quadrangular spike fitted on the top of the shaft with a socket whilst sometimes short langets (elongated metal strips), extended from the socket and were nailed to the shaft. At the bottom of the pike another smaller spike was placed primarily to act as an anchor against enemy charges. The weapon was large and hard to use and its size varied greatly depending on the place and time of origin, but it became the standard weapon of most European armies in one form or other. Extant examples rarely have the original shaft, and those that do may have had it shortened, either during their period of use or later for display and storage purposes. This makes the study of the technical characteristics of pikes difficult, as the length of this weapon is the one feature that matters the most. From the second quarter of the sixteenth century pikes became increasingly popular in foot combat, especially after the introduction of the barrier, and by the end of the sixteenth century they were probably the most commonly used weapon. It is interesting to observe that this trend further enhances the alignment of offensive equipment used in infantry warfare and foot combat. Shorter spears of various sizes were used, especially in the beginning of the examined period, as weapons of initial engagement and often hurled at the opponent.

Fig. 6. Tournament sword, German, mid-seventeenth century. Leeds, Royal Armouries IX.1217.

Besides the aforementioned weapons numerous others can be found in odd iconographic examples of foot combat. The partizan, the glaive, the flail, the halberd, the dagger and shields of various sizes were used in illustrations of competitions from the period. Maximilian I's *Freydal* is a good example as the Holy Roman Emperor is depicted using all of the above weapons and more. The variety in weaponry for hand-to-hand combat in the late fifteenth and sixteenth centuries was extraordinary. However, foot combat focused on only a small selection of the equipment available. We can only speculate why these limitations persisted for such a long period. The likeliest reasons revolve around the safety of the competitors, the ease of production and availability of equipment, as well as keeping up with the trends of the military reality. The various axes and the two-handed sword slowly gave way to the pike and the single-handed sword.

Rules and Conduct

Just as in any form of competition, rules were essential to foot combat. They dictated the format of the competition, the space in which the combat would be fought, the equipment that would be used, and most importantly, what would be allowed as performed actions as well as the winning conditions. By examining some of the surviving sets, we can filter and investigate common themes and requirements of foot combat.

Two different types of foot combat were fought during the tournament held to celebrate the marriage of Louis XII of France to Mary, sister of Henry VIII, in Paris in 1514.[54] Participants could choose the format of competition they would fight in by touching different coloured shields. Gold and silver corresponded to jousting with sharp and blunt lances respectively, and black and tawny to the two formats of foot combat. Black was chosen for fighting over a barrier with an unspecified weapon and tawny for fighting with a targe and spear which would continue with two-handed swords once the spear was thrown. The latter format is nearly identical to the practices depicted and described in the so-called '*Gladiatoria*' manuscripts from the middle of the fifteenth century, which share the same artistic style and cover similar aspects of armoured combat involving a progression in the use of different weapons.[55]

---

[54] Cripps-Day, *The History of the Tournament*, pp. 125–26.

[55] See *Gladiatoria: New Haven, MS U860.F46 1450*, ed. Dierk Hagedorn and Bartlomiej Walczak (Herne, 2015), whose essays highlight the unique nature of this group of manuscripts and tackle various research aspects such as the language used, the equipment depicted and the format of combat.

The foot combat format described in these manuscripts starts with the combatants throwing spears while holding small shields, then moving to the use of two-handed swords, and finally to the use of daggers while wrestling. What is interesting regarding this format is that the combatants depicted have most likely previously fought on horseback, as is suggested by the shape of their shields, which are targas with slots for lances and are sometimes depicted in these manuscripts attached to the shoulders of the combatants. Additionally, the context in which the combat is presented is that of a judicial duel. This theme is used as the canvas to illustrate the techniques and motions of the two combatants. It is likely that this form of judicial combat was popular, and had survived to the early sixteenth century as an alternative form of foot combat.

On 22–23 June 1520, during the Field of Cloth of Gold held between Henry VIII of England and Francis I of France, the two kings and their retinues competed in foot combat. Surviving details mention that the barrier was three feet high with cross bars at each end, and long enough to allow the simultaneous competition of ten pairs of men.[56] This chosen format dictated fighting over barriers two by two. First the contestants fought with sharp spears that had been rebated for the competition, then, after the spears were broken, the contestants kept on fighting with the broken shafts. This was followed by hurling them at their opponent and even thrusting with their arms as if they were still handling spears. Following this, the contestants competed with two-handed swords.[57]

The rules and prizes given at a foot combat tournament over a barrier held in England, to celebrate the arrival of Philip II (1556–98), king of Spain, in 1544 reveal details about the format and judging of the competition.[58] The

[56] Edward Hall, 'The Triumphant Reigne of Kyng Henry the VIII', in *Lives of the Kings*, ed. Charles Whibley (London, 1904), pp. 213–14; *Calendar of State Papers and Manuscripts Relating to English Affairs Existing in the Archives and Collections of Venice and in Other Libraries in Northern Italy*, III, *1520–1526*, ed. Lubbock Rawdon Brown (London, 1869), pp. 28–29; Oxford, Bodleian Library, MS Ashmole III6, fol. 102v; *Letters and Papers, Foreign and Domestic, of the Reign of Henry VIII*, vol. 3 part 1, ed. J. S. Brewster (London, 1867), p. 311.

[57] Joycelyne G. Russell, *The Field of Cloth of Gold: Men and Manners in 1520* (London, 1969), pp. 140–41.

[58] Clephan, *The Medieval Tournament*, p. 125 (transcription of 'Ashmolean, MS. 845, 171a; and Harl. MS., Codex 69, Art. 20', that is: Oxford, Bodleian Library, MS Ashmole 845, part 2, and 'The booke of certaine triumphes', London, British Library, MS Harley 69): *1. He who cometh forth most gallantly, though without superfluities, shall have a rich brooch. 2. The best stroke with the pike shall have a ring with a ruby. 3. The best strike with the sword shall have a ring with a diamond. 4. He that fighteth most valiantly shall have a ring with a diamond. 5. The prize of all together in*

competitors used pikes and swords, and the quality of strikes was judged. Penalised actions included hitting the opponent below the belt, wearing a type of gauntlet that would lock the weapon in the hand or other type of weapon-fastening equipment, being disarmed, and refusing to show the sword one is using to the judges. These are indications that the safety of the participants was a constant concern and that safe conduct was promoted through awarding prizes for it or by penalising dangerous actions. Additionally, such rules reveal that the gear of the contestants was checked beforehand by officials to ensure that the appropriate equipment was used. Potentially, these rules imply that some competitors would use inappropriate equipment in order to gain an advantage. The rule regarding the hand not touching the barrier was most likely implemented for distancing and safety purposes. Fighting gallantly but without endangering one's self was also seen as something prize-worthy, demonstrating that, in addition to the objective criteria of hitting a specific target or not doing certain actions, a type of attitude was encouraged while competing. It is noteworthy that in the hierarchy of prize-worthy criteria this is the first condition mentioned.

An account of the rules of a foot combat tournament held in the town of Kassel in central Germany in 1596 provides detailed information on how the competition was to be conducted.[59] The rules state that all competitors should be of noble birth, and that they must enter the competition with armour that is usually used in foot combat. Equipment that would lock the weapon in the user's hand is not allowed and neither are decorative pieces on the helmet. The latter rule might appear strange, but considering that the helmet is presented as the optimal target the lack of decorative elements appears sensible so that the judges can better see delivered blows. No one should use spears and swords that have not been approved by the judges, which is an indirect indication of a pre-combat checking to ensure that no one could cheat or endanger their opponent by using illicit equipment. The number of thrusts and strikes for each competitor is set at three with the spear and five with the sword, and they should all be aimed at the head. Prizes were awarded for spears broken on the head. By contrast the rules list a series of actions that disqualify anyone from gaining a prize. They included thrusting below the belt, striking the barrier,

---

> rank at the foyle was a ring of gold with a rich diamond. He that giveth a stroke a stroke with a pike from the girdle downwards shall win no prize. He that shall have a close gauntlet or anything to fasten his sword to his hand shall win no prize. He whose sword falls out of his hand shall win no prize. He that striketh his hand in fight on the barriers shall win no prize. Whosoever shall fight and not show his sword to the judges shall win no prize.

[59] Munich, Bayerische Staatsbibliothek, MS Cod.icon. 27(1), fol. 19r.

breaking the spear anywhere other than the opponent, getting too close to the barrier and touching it with the body, and using the barrier for support. Additionally, using the sword with both hands is not allowed (which implies that one-handed swords were used), and hitting with the flat of the blade completely disqualified a competitor from gaining a prize. If anyone lost their weapon they could not replace it, but if they broke their weapon on their opponent they were to be handed a replacement. The most severe penalties were for being pushed to the ground by a sword or spear, which led to an immediate exclusion of the person pushed from the competition. This shows that footwork and balance were considered fundamental and valued as much as good strikes. An important rule that highlights something about the format of this competition stated that the competitors could not step backwards with both legs or dodge thrusts or strikes. This seemingly insignificant rule effectively means that the flow of action only included offensive actions and parries. Finally, the most important of rules is reserved for the end, stating that whatever was not covered in this article of rules was at the discretion of the judges.

The Kassel rules for foot combat appear to have elements that can be found in all previous accounts. This by no means suggests that there was knowledge of previous foot combats; rather, the similarities between some of the requirements in the aforementioned competitions show the existence of a foot combat tradition in which similar practices and sensibilities are found in different places. The safety of the competitors, respect towards judges, and often a fixed number of strikes are elements that appear throughout these competitions.

Barriers, Fences and Judges

One aspect of foot combat that is rarely addressed is the surroundings of the competitors in the narrower sense. The space and the relevant other features in which the foot combat was conducted affected the conduct of the combat itself, and were nearly as important to the format of the competition as the offensive and defensive equipment used. Additionally, judges and referees were prominently mentioned in rules, and often their positioning in or next to the competition space was important for the progression of the event.

In the fifteenth century foot combat tournaments were often conducted in a fenced enclosure (usually made of wood and rope), within the area of a wider event.[60] In the second half of the fifteenth century the stylized depiction of

[60] The enclosure is sometimes referred to as *champ clos*, and was most likely there to both limit the space of the competition as well as, presumably to protect spectators,

judicial duels and challenges often shows them inside such well-defined enclosures.[61] This type of space, or at least the method by which the foot combat space was designated, remained in use throughout the sixteenth century. One of the most detailed depictions of a foot combat space from the middle of the sixteenth century shows the fighting space to be square with a double enclosure.[62] A multi-storey construct for the judges and the sovereign can be seen in the centre of one side of the outermost fence. The fences are solid and create a passageway for heralds and supporting judges to move in. They also appear to protect members of the audience. A manuscript illumination from the last quarter of the fifteenth century depicts the fence of a foot combat enclosure with movable horizontal parts that were used as doors.[63]

In the sixteenth century it became common for the competitors to be separated by a horizontal barrier, which varied in form. In a depiction of foot combat with pikes from the third quarter of the sixteenth century, in which the contestants are fighting wearing armour that does not cover their legs, the barrier is cylindrical and supported on two trestle-like constructs.[64] They appear to have elements built into them that would prevent the barrier from moving or falling down if struck by blows from above. Blows from below were not allowed in this type of competition, and in such cases the barrier would move out of place, thus signalling an illegal strike. An interesting design from the last quarter of the sixteenth century has a long quadrangular barrier separating the two contestants, supported on each side by tall columns.[65] It is safe to assume that all three parts would be made of wood. The height of the horizontal piece is at the level of the thighs of the contestants but the unnecessarily tall supporting sides might suggest that the height was adjustable. The same sketch has a detail that highlights an interesting potential aspect of foot combat competitions in this period. Next to each of the vertical supports of the barrier there is a basket of spare swords that resemble those that the competitors are using. This suggests that while weapons were provided at the event, their quality was poor and replacements were needed. Another potential explanation is that the swords were made of wood and thus broke easily on the competitors' armour, but there is not enough supporting evidence for this. The

---

much like the tilting yard. See Braden Frieder, *Chivalry and the Perfect Prince: Tournaments, Art, and Armor at the Spanish Habsburg Court* (Kirksville, 2008), p. 11.

[61] For an example of this, see London, British Library, MS Harley 4375, fol. 171v.
[62] London, College of Arms, MS M.6, fol. 62.
[63] New York, Pierpont Morgan Library, MS M.775, fol. 277v.
[64] Detail depicting foot combat, Florence, Uffizi Gallery, The Valois Tapestries.
[65] Young, *Tudor and Jacobean Tournaments*, p. 32.

grounds of the foot combat tournament in Kassel in 1596 are an example of the space of conduct of competitions in urban environments at the end of the period.[66] The town square serves as the wider natural enclosure and the spectators are locals. Judges and officials observe from a tent-like construct, whilst competitors waiting to fight and assistants to the judges are closer to the centre of the square where a long barrier is set between the two competing sides. This demonstrates that the size of the specialised equipment could be tailored to the needs of the competition. Spectators are watching, either standing around the perimeter of the square or from balconies, turning the combat sport of the nobility into an urban spectacle. This development shows a significant shift in the nature of foot combat, namely the existence of an outside crowd, whereas in previous cases the spectators would be either simply the other competitors or the members of a court. Finally, one of the most unique features appearing in an illumination of a tournament during Elizabeth I's reign is a protective wire mesh placed between the queen's podium and the combatants who fight over a barrier.[67] This separating barrier is depicted as solid, and was most likely made of wooden planks. The mesh would protect the queen from flying fragments from broken weapons and wood, and appears in two occasions in the same drawing with the combatants fighting first with spears and then with swords. The addition of this technical feature, designed to protect a viewer, is a direct indication of foot combat as a spectacle and even has some resemblance with modern protective equipment in stadiums.

The physical position of the judges during the foot combat tournament is also worth discussing. Considering that their role was to impose certain rules, they would have to be positioned close to the combatants, which of course could be hazardous, not only due to the possibility that they might accidentally be hit by one of the blows the combatants were exchanging, but also due to wooden or metal shrapnel potentially breaking off the combatants' equipment and injuring them. There are no direct guidelines on this matter, but important information can be extracted from iconography. In the cases of enclosed spaces, particularly in the fifteenth century, judges appear to be standing on balconies or other sheltered constructions adjacent to and slightly elevated above the space where combat is fought.[68] The principle of the judges watch-

---

[66] Munich, Bayerische Staatsbibliothek, MS Cod.icon. 27(1), fol. 17v.

[67] Young, *Tudor and Jacobean Tournaments*, pp. 78–79.

[68] See London, British Library, MS Harley 4375, fol. 171v. Examples of elevated wooden constructions that are part of a wider solid enclosure can be found in all illustrations of the Beauchamp Pageant depicting challenges and tournaments. These depictions also inform us of the nature of the attending courtly crowd that

ing the foot combat from an elevated construction persists in the sixteenth century, perhaps sometimes with the addition of more complicated sheltered structures.[69] In a manuscript illumination from the first half of the sixteenth century, combatants fight in an enclosure in pairs (without a barrier), while the judge and the spectators watch from three elevated sheltered structures made of wood.[70] In some cases, assistants to the judges stood inside the enclosure. In the case of a double enclosure, assistants and other relevant personnel would stand on the passageway between the two fences leaving them closer than the rest of the audience but also somewhat protected from stray blows.[71] After the introduction of the barriers in foot combat, assistants would stand usually on each side of the barrier, a popular practice that persisted throughout the sixteenth century. In most of the referenced examples, and generally in most depictions showing foot combat, judges are present watching alongside other figures. Besides the participants engaged in combat, these figures include judging assistants, heralds and contestants waiting to compete. The latter can be identified from their equipment, usually standing close to where the action is taking place. However, it is important to note that sometimes these armoured figures were there to intervene in case combat became too violent or if one of the participants was injured.[72] The aforementioned assistants are often depicted with staves, which acted not only as an indication of status but also could be used to separate participants if necessary.

Maximilian I and Foot Combat

Foot combat tournaments were popular in sixteenth-century England, particularly during the reign of Henry VIII (1509–47). There was a brief period of time during the reigns of Edward VI (1547–53) and Queen Mary (1553–54) when tournaments including foot combat were in abeyance, but there was a significant resurgence and increase in their popularity during the reigns of

---

observed from elevated positions, as well as of the presence of heralds. *The Beauchamp Pageant*, pp. 10, 27, 43, 58, 59, 62, 67.

[69] London, The College of Arms, MS M.6, fol. 62.
[70] Los Angeles, J. Paul Getty Museum, MS 114 (2016.7), fol. 98v.
[71] London, The College of Arms, MS M.6, fol. 62.
[72] A depiction of such an example shows armoured guards and waiting participants with glaives intervening to stop one of the competitors in a foot combat tournament from attacking his opponent after the latter had dropped his pollaxe. London, British Library, Cotton MS Nero D. IX, fol. 46.

Mary and Philip (1554–58) and Elizabeth I (1558–1603).[73] However, no sovereign can be associated more with tournaments in general as well as with foot combat than Maximilian I, king of the Romans and Holy Roman Emperor. The second half of the fifteenth century marked a resurgence of interest in chivalric ideals and associated practices amongst the German martial elites. This created a fertile environment for tournaments and for Maximilian to pursue self-glorification through them and through the creation of a chivalric identity, particularly as expressed through his three pseudo-biographical books: *Theuerdank*, *Freydal* and *Weisskunig*.[74] The emperor is often shown competing in various tournaments and challenges in these books, and always prevails.

In the sections of his books that include foot combat, one can observe how Maximilian is performing discernible actions and techniques while fighting with different weapons. The footwork and placement of the hands on the weapons as well as the positioning of the weapons in relationship to the opponent reveal an intention to record certain martial practices as closely as possible. This is also a significant visual difference between jousting and foot combat, firstly in the practice and secondly and most importantly in their representation, which is what a large part of what modern research concerns itself with. Whereas foot combat did not offer the impressive spectacle of mounted combat and the breaking of lances, it had variety of motion and tools to perform it with. The visual representation of this aspect of foot combat is visible throughout relevant iconography, but it is perfectly encapsulated and exploited in Maximilian's books. Not only is the emperor's martial prowess demonstrated, but the combat also looks aesthetically pleasing and is presented with remarkable variety. Similar illustrations of jousting, even from the same books, often rely simply on the variety and magnificence of colour and heraldic devices.

The plethora of weapons used by Maximilian in foot combats in *Freydal* is not supported by other specific accounts. Usually it is possible to trace when and where he competed against the opponents who are mentioned by name in the work but not precisely with which weapons. It is likely that all these weapons could have been used in Maximilian's foot combat tournaments at some point as the emperor toyed with ideas of using different forms and formats of competition varying the technical equipment used. The different forms of jousting Maximilian hosted in his tournaments and those represented in his

---

[73] Clephan, *The Medieval Tournament*, pp. 124–33.

[74] For editions of the three books see: *Theuerdank*, ed. Simon Laschitzer (Vienna, 1888); *Freydal*, ed. Quirin von Leitner; *Der Weisskunig: Nach den Dictaten und eigenhändigen Aufzeichnungen Kaiser Maximilians I.*, ed. Alwin Schultz (Vienna, 1888).

literary works vary, and indeed at times present important visual differences in the equipment used. However, variety and versatility were easier to demonstrate with the various weapons he employed for foot combat, from single-handed and two-handed swords to the pike, halberd, glaive, *ahlspiess*, axe and dagger. Another plausible explanation for this variety lies in the self-image that Maximilian wanted to create through this work, which was one of a master of arms who always overcomes his opponents and demonstrates expertise with all equipment.

Maximilian was arguably the most influential figure in the development and popularisation of foot combat. The unprecedentedly detailed portrayal of various foot combats in *Freydal* attributed a certain dignity to these competitions and linked them as equals to the other components of tournament culture.[75] His practices in the late fifteenth century established, validated and codified foot combat, foreshadowing its increasing popularity in the sixteenth century.

Conclusion

In 1610 a tournament was organised in Whitehall to celebrate the chivalric cult that had developed around Henry Frederick, prince of Wales, eldest son of James VI and I, with an event including intense theatrical elements and allegories.[76] A foot combat competition was specifically organised for the prince because he was too young to participate in the jousting, which is a clear indication of the prevailing ideas on the progression of martial training during this period, as well as of the physical and training requirements needed for mounted combat. The fifteen-year-old Henry competed with the pike and the sword over a barrier, fighting with six more companions on his side against groups of different challengers for several hours.[77] It is worth noting that the long barrier was placed inside the banqueting hall and the competition lasted through a whole evening and night. One of the last depictions of Henry before

---

[75] William Henry Jackson, 'The Tournament and Chivalry in German Tournament Books of the Sixteenth Century and in the Literary Works of Emperor Maximilian I', in *The Ideals and Practice of Medieval Knighthood: Papers from the First and Second Strawberry Hill Conferences*, ed. Christopher Harper-Bill and Ruth Harvey (Woodbridge, 1986), pp. 49–73 (here p. 60).

[76] Young, *Tudor and Jacobean Tournaments*, p. 178–83.

[77] Charles Cornwallis, *This Life and Death of our Late most Incomparable and Heroique Prince Henry, Prince of Wales: A Prince (for Valour and Vertue) fit to be Imitated in Succeeding Times* (London, 1641), pp. 14–15.

he died two years later is an engraving commemorating this tournament.[78] Henry is presented in his foot combat armour without his helmet, holding and ready to thrust with a pike. This image accented the prince's martial prowess, and highlights the tournament as being commensurate with war in the construction of an individual's martial identity. About a century after Emperor Maximilian I, another member of a royal family, who is associated with chivalric culture, is presented with what clearly is an infantry weapon. In contrast to Maximilian, whose innovations affected the development of warfare and tournaments alike, Henry's portrayal reflects the norms of his time. The pike had become an integral tool of war and then part of martial identity not only of the professional soldier, but, through warfare and tournaments of the sixteenth century, of the martial elite. Even at the twilight of tournaments and their transition to either heavily staged courtly events or public competitions, the continuing link between the battlefield and the event as spectacle could still be found at the barriers.[79]

A detailed illumination from one of the books attributed to Paulus Hector Mair from the 1540s shows a judicial duel in the Augsburg wine market in 1409.[80] The two combatants are fighting with sword and shield in a square fenced enclosure. Nobles, city guards and citizens are outside the fence watching the fight. This simple illustration addresses two key characteristics of duels in relation to foot combat competitions. First, duels could also have an audience and be regarded as a spectacle, second, by the middle of the sixteenth century, when foot combats were a common event in tournaments, past duels were reimagined as foot combats. The splendour achieved through colour, detail and plasticity of motion in this illumination clearly draws inspiration from foot combat depictions of previous decades.

The different elements of the foot combat presented here, the space in which the combat was fought, the equipment that was used, and the particular examples of rules and regulations that fragmentarily survive, together make up a larger image. Foot combat, like jousting, showed considerable variety in its conduct and changed throughout the sixteenth century, which can be considered its pinnacle, into a fully developed combat sport. The lack of research, partly due to the fixation on jousting, makes foot combat a rich field for future study, particularly when the scope is narrowed geographically or chronologically.

[78] Simon van de Passe, Engraving of Prince Henry, 1612.
[79] For the decline of the tournament and its changing form in the seventeenth century, see Barber and Barker, *Tournaments*, pp. 209–11.
[80] Munich, Bayerische Staatsbibliothek, MS Cod.icon. 393, fols. 162v–163r.

9 Power and Pageantry: The Tournament at the Court of Maximilian I

Natalie Anderson

We should then talk of another pursuit at which many men-at-arms aim to make their reputation: that is at deeds of arms at tournaments. And indeed, they earn men praise and esteem for they require a great deal of wealth, equipment and expenditure, physical hardship, crushing and wounding, and sometimes danger of death. For this kind of practice of arms, there are some whose physical strength, skill, and agility enable them to perform so well that they achieve in this activity such great renown for their fine exploits; and because they often engage in it, their renown and their fame increases in their own territory and that of their neighbours; thus they want to continue this kind of pursuit of arms because of the success God has granted them in it. They content themselves with this particular practice of arms because of the acclaim they have already won and still expect to win from it. Indeed they are worthy of praise; nevertheless he who does more is of greater worth.[1]

The medieval tournament and the mental images it inspires are central to the modern conception of the Middle Ages. It is a cultural touchstone, familiar to both its original audiences and its contemporary mythologisers,

---

[1] Geoffroi de Charny, *The Book of Chivalry of Geoffroi de Charny: Text, Context, and Translation*, ed. Richard Kaeuper and Elspeth Kennedy (Philadelphia, 1996), pp. 86–87: *Dont de l'autre nous estuet parler, auquel tout plain de gens d'armes entendent a faire leurs corps: ce sont les faiz d'armes des tournoiements. Et veraiement il font bien a loer et priser; car il convient grans mises, grans estofes et grans despens, travail de corps, froisseures et bleceures, et peril de mort aucune foiz. Et pour cesti fait d'armes en y a aucuns que bon corps qu'ilz ont fort et appert et deliver le font sit res bien qu'il on ten ce mestier grant renommee pour leur bienfait, et don't pour ce qu'il le font souvent, et bien leur en croist leur renomee et leut cognoissance et en leurs marches et entour leurs voisins; et ainsi veulent continuer de poursuivre en celi fait d'armes pour les graces que Dieu leur en a faictes. Et de cesti mestier d'armes se tiennent pour contens pour les grans los qu'il en ont entendent a avoir. Et vraiement il font bien a loer, combien que: qui plus fait, miex vault.*

and it encapsulates the often contradictory combination of lofty chivalric ideals and martial violence that helped to define the era. One figure who bridged the gap between the medieval and modern ideal of the tournament was Maximilian I, king of the Romans and Holy Roman Emperor (1459–1519). Maximilian's reputation, in his own lifetime and beyond, was in large part built around the tournament.

In the above passage, the French knight and noted author on chivalry Geoffroi de Charny (c. 1300–56) articulated both the risk and the appeal of the tournament. Competitors had the chance to win fame and renown, as well as financial rewards, while also immersing themselves in the chivalric ethos of the time. The tournament space was an environment in which men could act out the motions of warfare without (usually) the consequences of it.[2] Maximilian found himself at a crossroads of the tournament, and those combats in which he was involved demonstrate this. In many ways, his tournaments embody the most lavish forms of spectacle that could be found in such late medieval events. Yet Maximilian's tournaments managed to do this while retaining some of the intensity and violence of the competitions of earlier centuries. What is undeniable is that, with regard to the words of Charny, Maximilian could safely be called 'he who does more'.

Tournament Forms in the Time of Maximilian

By the time of Maximilian's birth in 1459, the tournament had long been a popular pastime in princely courts across Europe, enjoying rises and falls in popularity (thanks in part to frequent censure by the Church), changes in form and function, and a growing geographical diversity. During Maximilian's lifetime, and thanks in no small part to his influence, the German tournament was to become a unique entity with its own distinctive characteristics. For, while it was already set apart from its other European counterparts in many ways, it is the German tournament as preserved through the efforts of Maximilian that modern scholars are most familiar with and that has served as the foundation on which studies of the subject have been built.

In Maximilian's Holy Roman Empire, the joust as a showcase of skill between two individuals had risen in prominence and popularity, as it had across much of Europe. The mêlée-style competition, in which two groups

---

[2] Josef Fleckenstein, 'Das Turnier als höfisches Fest im hochmittelalterlichen Deutschland', in *Das ritterliche Turnier im Mittelalter: Beiträge zu einer vergleichenden Formen- und Verhaltensgeschichte des Rittertums*, ed. Josef Fleckenstein (Göttingen, 1986), pp. 229–56.

of competitors fought against each other in teams, was still popular in several forms, yet this incarnation undeniably lacked the glamour and prestige that came with the joust, which allowed two individual competitors to show off their martial skills in a one-on-one setting rather than getting lost in the crowd of a tourney. In the medieval German-speaking territories, different forms of the joust were given specific names, and each came with its own rules and its own style of armour. The two main forms were known as the *Gestech* and the *Rennen*, two terms that have no direct English translations.[3] Both are nouns formed from German verbs. *Gestech* comes from the verb *stechen*, meaning 'to stab', 'to stick' or even literally 'to lance'. *Rennen* is a direct verb-to-noun transformation of the verb *rennen*, 'to run' or 'to race'.

Already some of the implicit meaning behind these words as nouns is evident through their etymology, and the evolution of both words makes sense given the meaning of their root verbs. Additionally, a direct linguistic connection may be seen in the rules of the respective styles of joust to the English meanings of their root verbs. For example, in the varying forms of the *Gestech* the primary goal of the competition was often to shatter a lance on one's opponent. In the *Rennen*, on the other hand, the objective was most often to unhorse one's opponent. Thus the verb *stechen* as the root of *Gestech* appropriately implies intense or violent impact of some sort, while the verb *rennen* implies speed as the primary focus. The different emphasis of the two verbs is reflected in the conduct of the two forms of joust, which, by the time of Maximilian's death, had become highly specialised.[4]

While much of modern scholarship on tournaments of this time has tended to stop at this basic distinction of *Rennen* and *Gestech*, these are in fact quite broad terms which have a good deal of flexibility within them. They should really be seen as category headings, which may be further divided into a range of different styles of joust. Indeed, this is how they would have been understood in Maximilian's day. It is certainly how he depicted them in the fictional tournaments of the *Triumphzug*, a critical work produced under Maximilian's supervision. A series of woodcuts depicting a triumphal procession of the glories of Maximilian's court, the *Triumphzug* highlights his cultural, artistic

---

[3] For this reason the German designations for the different forms are used throughout this essay. A good discussion of the difficulties of tournament terminology may be found in Noel Fallows, *Jousting in Medieval and Renaissance Iberia* (Woodbridge, 2010), pp. 24–25.

[4] Matthias Pfaffenbichler, 'Maximilian I. und das höfische Turnier', in *Kaiser Maximilian I: Der letzte Ritter und das höfische Turnier*, ed. Sabine Haag, Alfried Wieczorek, Matthias Pfaffenbichler, and Hans-Jürgen Buderer (Regensburg, 2014), pp. 129–39.

and military accomplishments.[5] The different styles of joust to be found in Maximilian's court are specifically labelled, each with an individual name and different forms of equipment and decoration. The *Triumphzug* clearly presents the *Gestech* and the *Rennen* as two separate categories. The *Gestech* is further subdivided into four varieties, while the *Rennen* is more impressively presented in twelve different forms. The *Triumphzug* played a critical role in memorialising German tournament culture by acting as a survey of forms of joust that interested Maximilian and in which each image clearly demonstrates what defines the various forms and the equipment needed.

At the most fundamental level, the difference between the *Gestech* and the *Rennen* may be defined by the former's use of coronel-tipped lances and the latter's of hooked or pointed lances. In the *Gestech* the object was to either unhorse one's opponent or, ideally, to splinter a lance on him, while in the *Rennen* unhorsing was the primary aim. However, along with this basic division come numerous and wide-ranging variations in arms, armour and rules of conduct for these two courses. These many forms represent the tournament as it was practised in Maximilian's court, yet the line between the *Rennen* and *Gestech* was not always clear, but rather was often blurred as the two forms occasionally intermingled and evolved. Unlike the *Gestech*, the *Rennen* always utilised non-rebated lances that were not as thick as those used in the *Gestech*. The *Rennen* could also be far more hazardous than the *Gestech* in its various incarnations, but the frequent examples of its occurrence in Maximilian's court attest to his particular enjoyment of this joust, whose various forms allowed for creative expression within the German tournament.[6]

There are four sub-categories of the *Gestech*, which can be analysed independently. Not as many forms of the *Gestech* exist as do of the *Rennen*, where Maximilian's tournaments fully embraced a creative range of joust forms. The most popular of these was the *Deutschgestech*, as it is labelled in the *Triumphzug*; it is the definitive version of the standard *Gestech* as practised in Maximilian's court. In sources that mention a *Gestech*, it is likely this form of joust to which they are referring. This could be a way of distinguishing this style, featuring blunted lances and large, 'frog-mouth' helms – a common form of joust throughout Europe at this time – as the German version of the standard combat. The lack of a *Deutsch-* prefix for a *Rennen* would seem to

---

[5] *The Triumph of Maximilian: 137 Woodcuts by Hans Burgkmair and Others*, ed. and trans. Stanley Applebaum (New York, 1964).

[6] Stefan Krause, '"They Call It Royal for Good Reason": The Tournaments of the Late Middle Ages and the Renaissance', in *Habsburg Splendour: Masterpieces from Vienna's Imperial Collections at the Kunshistorisches Museum*, ed. Monica Kurzel-Runtscheiner (New Haven, 2015), pp. 4–55.

mark it as such a distinctly German form of joust that it did not need to be specified as such.

The *Welschgestech* (and its corresponding form the *Welschrennen*) is one of the most unique and distinctive forms of joust practised at Maximilian's court. This joust represents one of the most significant evolutions of the tournament to be popularised by Maximilian – the use of the tilt. This was a wooden barrier which separated the competing knights, allowing them to approach each other without colliding.[7] The tilt was revolutionary in the tournament world in that it minimised risk both to the horses and their riders while increasing the likelihood of the knights successfully striking each other with their lances (missing being an all too common result in many jousts).

While the tilt was still a novelty in the German joust, problems could arise from not knowing how to construct and use it properly. Georg Spalatin wrote that at a tournament at which Maximilian was present several unnamed *Walen und Niederländer*, that is speakers of Romance languages (probably Frenchmen) and Netherlanders, ran a *Welschgestech* over a 'barrier' (*Schranken*), or tilt. According to him, they struck each with hard blows and broke many spears. Unfortunately the eyes and ears of several horses were reportedly injured as well, as the barrier was too low.[8] The tilt was meant to be quite a high barrier, customarily coming up to roughly the level of the horse's back while still allowing the knights' lances to clear it comfortably. Images like many of those in other works produced by Maximilian demonstrate the proper use of the tilt.[9]

Two other forms of the *Gestech*, the *Gestech im Beinharnisch* and the *Hohenzeuggestech*, would already have been old-fashioned in Maximilian's time, yet the emperor was still interested in preserving their memory. The *Gestech im Beinharnisch* simply means the *Gestech* 'in leg armour'. This is the only *Gestech* where the knight's legs are fully exposed to the oncoming rider and his lance, with only armour to protect them and no additional element, thus justifying

---

[7] The noun 'tilt' was also subsequently turned into a verb, 'tilting', which became a synonym for jousting itself in English.

[8] *Georg Spalatins historischer Nachlaß und Briefe*, ed. Christian Gotthold Neudecker (Jena, 1851), pp. 230–31: *Haben einander hart troffen und viel Spieß zerbrochen, auch den Pferden Augen aus und Ohren abgestoßen, aus Ursachen daß die Schranken zu niedrig waren.*

[9] *Freydal: Des Kaisers Maximilian I. Turniere und Mummereien*, ed. Quirin von Leitner (Vienna, 1880), plate 2. See also Stefan Krause, 'Das Turnierbuch *Freydal* Kaiser Maximilians I.', in *Kaiser Maximilian I:Der letzte Ritter und das höfische Turnier*, pp. 167–80.

the attention focused in its name upon the *Beinharnisch*.[10] The *Hohenzeuggestech* was named for the unique high saddle (the titular *hohes Zeug*), which forced the rider to stand upright in his stirrups while sitting elevated off the horse's back on a central bar with his legs slipped through two rings on either side to hold him in place. Large wooden panels extending down over the horse's shoulders also protected his lower torso and legs. This would have given the rider very little control over his horse and required great strength and skill.[11] Although textual sources describing Maximilian's tournaments do not specify if the jousts being performed are ever the *Gestech im Beinharnisch* or the *Hohenzeuggestech* – either because it was incidental information or the authors were not knowledgeable of the terminology – it does appear in commemorative forms in the *Triumphzug*.[12] Maximilian clearly had an interest in preserving these forms, perhaps as a representation of the history of distinctively German forms of joust.

Unlike the *Gestech*, the *Rennen* always utilised non-rebated lances (although this did not necessarily mean that the lances were as sharp as those used on the battlefield) and could be far more hazardous than the *Gestech* in its various incarnations. The multitude of forms preserved in the *Triumphzug* and the frequent real-life examples of its occurrence in Maximilian's circle attest to his particular enjoyment of this joust, whose various forms allowed for a creative expression of the many manifestations of the German tournament. The one counterpoint to this appears to be the *Welschrennen*, which is the first style of *Rennen* to appear in the parade of the *Triumphzug*, just as the *Welschgestech* is the first form of *Gestech*.[13] Yet despite the seeming prominence of the *Rennen* over the *Gestech* in general in Maximilian's court, the *Welschrennen* appears to have been less popular than its counterpart the *Welschgestech*.

A far more popular example of the *Rennen* is the *Geschiftrennen*, which is one of several forms of the *Rennen* practised in Maximilian's court to feature mechanical or spring-loaded elements of armour. These represent a trend not seen in the *Gestech*. Two wing-shaped plates were sometimes fastened over the brow of the sallet by pins and were meant to fly off when struck.[14] In yet

---

[10] *The Triumph of Maximilian*, plate 48.

[11] A surviving example of one of these saddles is preserved in the Royal Armouries, Leeds. Although not specifically associated with Maximilian, the saddle is German and dates from around 1500, showing that such objects were still being produced at that date. Royal Armouries, VI.94.

[12] *The Triumph of Maximilian*, plate 47.

[13] *The Triumph of Maximilian*, plate 49.

[14] Claude Blair, *European Armour circa 1066 to circa 1700* (London, 1958), pp. 162–63.

another type the vamplate of the lance, which protected the hand holding it, also could be engineered to fly off if hit. These mechanical *Rennen* were popular with Maximilian, and several surviving suits of armour associated with the emperor feature these attributes. Other *Rennen* featuring 'exploding' armour in the *Triumphzug* are the *Schweif-* or *Scharfrennen* – the most popular form of *Rennen* – the *Scheibenrennen* and the *Bundrennen*.

Some *Rennen* represented in the *Triumphzug*, like the *Gestech im Beinharnisch* and the *Hohenzeuggestech*, were not practised regularly in Maximilian's court. They rather represent idealised forms of joust, or ones of which Maximilian was aware and wished to memorialise and to have associated with his name. Others like these include the *Feldrennen*, the *Wulstrennen* and the *Pfannenrennen*. The latter two are the most unusual *Rennen* to appear in the *Triumphzug*, and the most outlandish in style. *Wulst*, which can be translated as 'puff', 'embossment' or 'bulge', could be in reference to the knights' elaborate and largely exposed clothing, particularly the sleeves, in this joust, at least as illustrated in the *Triumphzug*. The style appears to be a tournament-themed tribute to the Landsknechts, Maximilian's mercenary forces consisting mainly of foot soldiers using pikes and halberds. These men were known for their sumptuous clothing and often wore tunics with enormous puffed sleeves with a multitude of slashes, allowing another rich textile beneath to show through.[15] It is a style uncannily similar to the jousters of the *Wulstrennen*. The *Pfannenrennen* is a particularly enigmatic form of joust. It is named for the pan-like, extremely small shield borne by the competitors, which was virtually their only piece of armour. These had a prominently raised rim to catch the opponent's lance and, presumably, cause it to snap. Hans Burgkmair the Younger, in a 1553 edition of tournament images originally featured in the *Triumphzug*, labelled this joust as *gar besorglich* or 'extremely dangerous'.[16] It is unlikely, given the obvious dangers of the minimal equipment, that styles of joust such as the *Wulstrennen* and *Pfannenrennen* were practised in actuality.

A Courtly Spectacle

Maximilian raised the tournament, which was already a long-standing and popular pastime, to new heights, and his enthusiasm for the sport was deeply interwoven in his court culture. The makeup and defining elements

---

[15] Robert Jones, *Knight: The Warrior and World of Chivalry* (Oxford, 2011), pp. 216–19.

[16] *Hans Burgkmaiers Turnier-Buch*, ed. Jakob Heinrich von Hefner (Frankfurt am Main, 1853), plate 8.

of Maximilian's court had an influence on how tournaments fitted into this environment. Most notably, Maximilian's court was highly mobile. He lacked a central, permanent capital and favoured travelling from place to place at a rapid rate, sometimes only staying in a city for a matter of days before moving on to another. This form of movement allowed him to keep a close eye on his widespread and often unwieldy empire, although he particularly enjoyed spending time in his own hereditary dominions, notably Austria and Tirol. Maximilian's presence in a city served to remind its citizens of his existence and to simultaneously impress them with the splendour of his presence.

The itinerant nature of the court also meant that its members were rarely consistently the same. Instead, nobles would come and go, depending on their proximity to Maximilian's current city of residence and their own governing responsibilities.[17] Maximilian needed his court to be in a location where he could bring citizens of his empire together in an environment that fostered peace and stability while simultaneously inspiring loyalty to their emperor. In accomplishing this, tournaments served a vital role by offering a distinctive outlet for displaying power through the medium of spectacle. Maximilian used these courtly spectacles in a variety of ways to boost his reputation on the European stage.[18]

Beyond the individual occasions and courtly accompaniments, the tournament served as a political tool in several ways. One element in particular that warrants emphasis is Maximilian's own involvement as a participant, something that made him notable among contemporary monarchs. By taking part himself, Maximilian used the tournament to broadcast his strength as a leader. He was not merely a spectator or sponsor of this spectacle but also a participant within it, not only as a young man, but even after he became Holy Roman Emperor. This participation was highly unusual; it was not common for rulers, especially one as powerful as the Holy Roman Emperor, to participate in tournaments with such frequency, due to the high level of risk involved. But this seemed to be a risk Maximilian deemed worth taking. By taking part himself Maximilian was further emphasising his own virility; he was drawing more attention to himself as both a ruler hosting these grand tournaments and as a skilled competitor within them.

It was a tactic in which Maximilian was evidently successful. In January 1502, the Italian diarist Marino Sanuto described a joust between Maximilian

---

[17] Jan-Dirk Müller, 'The Court of Emperor Maximilian I', in *Princes and Princely Culture: 1450–1650*, ed. Martin Gosman et al., 2 vols (Leiden, 2003), 1: 295–311.

[18] Matthias Pfaffenbichler, 'Das Turnier als Instrument der Habsburgischen Politik', *Waffen- und Kostümkunde: Zeitschrift für Waffen- und Kleidungsgeschichte* 34 (1992), 13–36.

and Wolfgang, count of Fürstenberg. The emperor and the count ran against each other only once, in an encounter that Maximilian won spectacularly by unhorsing his opponent and causing him to fly a full lance's length out of the saddle.[19] Clearly court chroniclers' descriptions of Maximilian's great physical strength were not entirely overstated. The next month, in February 1502, while telling of another joust in which Maximilian competed, Sanuto described how Maximilian proved, in essence, his great manliness (*in la quale la cesarea majestà, a dir il vero, se diportò che homo che fosse*).[20] And it was not just his physical prowess that won him words of praise. Two years later, in February 1504, the Venetian ambassador and visitor to Maximilian's court, Alvise Mocenigo, praised Maximilian for his gallant behaviour after watching him compete in a tournament (*E lauda molto il re di valente*), proving that not only was Maximilian reportedly a powerful jouster but an honourable one as well.[21] These were both qualities which would be viewed not only as desirable in a tournament setting but also, critically, for a ruler; Maximilian was thus demonstrating both to the audience. Add to this the artist Hans Burgkmair's image of Maximilian jousting over the tilt at a tournament as late as 1511.[22] Even as he moved beyond the normal age when most men stopped competing in tournaments, Maximilian was still proving his competence in the lists. This too marks him out as unusual among his peers and helped him to maintain an image of enduring power.

Yet it was not just as a competitor that Maximilian could use tournaments to enhance his reputation as a ruler; he often used the setting of the tournament to display his generosity. In a transaction carried out in November 1502 Maximilian requested that his *Raitkammer* (accounting chamber) in Innsbruck pay out the sum of 32 *Gulden Rheinisch* for a *Zeug* (suit of armour), which Maximilian's *Mundkoch* (court chef) had received from the emperor at tournaments held earlier that year in Innsbruck.[23] The implication is that Maximilian allowed members of his household staff to compete in these tournaments in one way or another; perhaps not in the most prestigious noble jousts, but maybe in a competition among their peers, such as in the *Gesellenrennen*, an often comedic form of mêlée. Moreover, he seems to have rewarded

---

[19] Marino Sanuto, *I Diarii di Marino Sanuto*, 58 vols (Venice, 1879–1903), 4: 217–18.
[20] Sanuto, *I Diarii*, 4: 217.
[21] Sanuto, *I Diarii*, 5: 883.
[22] *Hans Burgkmaiers Turnier-Buch*, ed. Jakob Heinrich von Hefner (Frankfurt am Main, 1853), plates 25–26.
[23] J. F. Böhmer, *Regesta Imperii, XIV: Ausgewählte Regesten des Kaiserreiches unter Maximilian I. 1493–1519*, 4 vols (Cologne, 1990–2004), 4: no. 17048a.

those who were successful with armour of their own, paid for from his own royal funds. Such rewards were not limited to material possessions either. In 1498 Maximilian awarded the Hungarian brothers Georg and Wenceslaus Fuchs, for loyal service to him, a coat of arms that they could use henceforth in war or in tournaments on their flags or shields, as well as on gravestones, seals or rings.[24]

As a ruler, Maximilian found numerous reasons to hold a tournament in his court, each of which could serve many purposes. Occasions worthy of note could include celebrations – either focused on an event or around a time of year – political manoeuvrings, or simple recreational amusements. Each of these groupings could often overlap. Across these categories, the tournament demonstrates its numerous and varied uses and its importance to Maximilian, as a host of, a witness to and a participant in these events. Also evident is the varying levels of effort that might go to into such an event, from lavish spectacle to casual competition, and the wide variety of forms that a tournament might take. Yet each in its own way was vital.

Certain times of year were favoured by Maximilian for holding tournaments. The most popular of these was the period of *Fastnacht* (Shrovetide), the festive time leading up to the liturgical season of Lent, which often lasted from late winter into spring. This extended period was traditionally devoted to feasting, festive activities, and general indulgence in anticipation of the more austere weeks of Lent. Tournaments fitted in well with this motif. These *Fastnacht* tournaments were often held in Maximilian's preferred city in which to base his court. Innsbruck was a city well laid out for tournaments, with its expansive and even-surfaced market square. For Maximilian's tournaments were not held out in the open countryside like those of earlier centuries; they were instead held in his current city of residence's central square, in order to attract the most attention. It was both a practical and a political use of space.[25]

The *Fastnacht* festivities and tournaments at the beginning of 1500, which took place in Innsbruck, illustrate Maximilian's penchant for combining tournament pleasure with imperial politics. He received various Italian noblemen, including Duke Ludovico Sforza of Milan, uncle of his second wife Bianca Maria Sforza, as well as ambassadors from Spain and Naples. A tournament was held in the beginning of the New Year, whose primary purpose was to welcome and entertain Maximilian's foreign guests and to gain their favour

---

[24] *Regesta Imperii, XIV*, 2: no. 6310.

[25] For more on city space utilised in tournaments, see Mario Damen, 'The Town as a Stage? Urban Space and Tournaments in Late Medieval Brussels', *Urban History* 43 (2015), 1–25.

through hospitality. At the same time, Duke Ludovico, as he wrote to his kinsman Cardinal Ascanio Sforza, was able to show Maximilian an important letter that he had received from the Milanese envoy while Maximilian was watching the tournament.[26] Thus, even in the midst of diverting entertainment, political manoeuvrings were happening amongst Maximilian and his peers; indeed, the two often went hand in hand. As part of Maximilian's efforts to impress, alongside descriptions of the tournament frequent references were made by Ludovico to the different meals the emperor hosted: when and where they took place and who was being entertained. There was also mention of dancing taking place after dinner – a customary occurrence accompanying the more lavish tournaments.

One of the most obvious reasons for holding a tournament in any medieval or early modern court was as part of a celebratory event, such as weddings, coronations, holidays, or other festive occasions. Tournaments were a long-standing part of courtly celebrations, and Maximilian's court was no different. Weddings at which tournaments took place included one held in Mechelen in September 1494 to celebrate the marriage of one of Maximilian's most prominent tournament competitors, Wolfgang von Polheim, to Johanna, daughter of Count Wolfhart VI of Borsselen. Polheim was such an integral member of his emperor's tournament circle that he was granted the title of *Rennen und Gestech Meister* ('Master of the *Rennen* and *Gestech*'). The event proved to be a tournament on a grand scale, involving many nobles from around the empire, which took place over several days. Indeed, the marriage ceremony itself would only have been a small part of this celebration; the diarist Georg Spalatin, in his description of events, devotes substantial time to accounts of the tournaments.[27]

The beginning of 1502 marked another instance where tournaments accompanied a wedding: the marriage of Balthasar Wolf von Wolfsthal, Maximilian's *Hofkammermeister* (court chamberlain), again in the favoured city of Innsbruck. This occasion also overlapped with the celebrations for *Fastnacht*. The Venetian ambassador Zaccaria Contarini described the prolonged period of *bagordi*, or 'revelries', in his letters beginning 12 January, saying that throughout the *Fastnacht* many jousts were held and that Maximilian himself took part as well. These competitions were also accompanied by banquets and

---

[26] *Regesta Imperii*, XIV, 3: nos. 9722–23. According to Duke Ludovico, this letter related to the willingness for peace of the Swiss and greatly pleased Maximilian. The contents of the letter probably concerned the recently settled Treaty of Basel, which brought an end to the Swabian War, a conflict between the Swiss Confederacy and the Habsburgs over territorial disputes.

[27] Spalatin, *Georg Spalatin's historischer Nachlaß und Briefe*, pp. 230–31.

balls held in the evenings. Again, the tournaments are just one part of celebrations, which would go on for several days.[28]

These weddings held at court were, in many respects, the ideal time for Maximilian to promote the tournament. Maximilian did not always have the time or the money to put on a full display of his imperial power, and weddings would have offered an opportunity for Maximilian to put on a show. Such an event would have drawn nobles from across his realm to his court, and while there a tournament would make an excellent addition to the schedule. It brought other nobles together in friendly competition, while also allowing Maximilian himself a chance to show off his skill in the lists. The tournament played a critical role in the overall structure of a wedding celebration by enhancing the impression of power and prosperity with which Maximilian wished to imbue his court.

Tournaments at Maximilian's court were not only celebratory events, however. They also played a political role in many ways, either as part of larger events or an event in themselves. Aside from the tournament's draw for knights seeking to enhance their reputation, they could also be a setting for diplomatic manoeuvring within the court. When he was not participating, Maximilian often used tournaments as the ideal setting for meeting and discussing politics with envoys and legates from other kingdoms. The tournament offered an occasion to impress visiting dignitaries, particularly when court life was normally much simpler and pointed displays of wealth were not a daily occurrence.

This ethos was aided by the fact that Maximilian was an extremely active ruler and full of energy that was always in search of an outlet. In February 1502, for example, Maximilian travelled from Innsbruck to the nearby town of Hall in Tirol. There he was to meet with ambassadors from France, Burgundy and Spain, and he had also arranged for a tournament to be held, according to the Venetian legate Zaccharia Contarini. On 4 February Contarini wrote that Maximilian was about to depart from Innsbruck and would be gone for three days. It was also described how, while in Hall, Maximilian would be meeting the visiting ambassadors.[29] In this way the emperor could mix business with pleasure.

---

[28] *Regesta Imperii, XIV*, 4: no. 15899. See also Hermann Wiesflecker, *Kaiser Maximilian I.: Das Reich, Österreich und Europa an der Wende zur Neuzeit*, 5 vols (Munich, 1971–86), 5: 389.

[29] *Regesta Imperii, XIV*, 4: no. 16016.

Political Distractions and Simple Pleasures

Tournaments did not, however, always serve to advance Maximilian's political interests. In fact, they sometimes seemed to be a hindrance rather than a help, as the emperor's love of the tournament sometimes won out over his political obligations. In the same year of 1502, Contarini also complained that he was unable to meet Maximilian because the emperor was busy all day with tournaments and stayed all night at parties and dances.[30] While he was seemingly sometimes able to balance his love of tournaments with his political responsibilities, especially when combining the two to their best advantage, there are numerous other instances where Maximilian appears to have shirked his ruling responsibilities for the enjoyment and escapism of athletic competition.

A particularly interesting example of this is Maximilian's interaction with the Italian knight Gaspare de Sanseverino, marshal to the dukes of Milan and colourfully known as *Frachasso* (literally 'Fracas').[31] In 1498 Sanseverino travelled to Innsbruck accompanied by thirty-three knights. He had been expected to arrive on 16 February, yet he had reportedly ridden ahead in haste, leaving behind his wagons and packhorses, in order to arrive in time to watch a tournament that he had heard was scheduled for the day before. Such enthusiasm makes Sanseverino appear an admirable opponent for Maximilian.[32] Yet Sanseverino was not visiting Maximilian's court purely for the pleasure of participating in tournaments. He was also there to represent the political interests of Ludovico Sforza, duke of Milan, who had instructed him to negotiate with Maximilian while visiting him under the pretence of friendly competition.[33] Clearly other rulers of the time were aware of Maximilian's penchant for tournaments and saw ways to take advantage of this interest by also cleverly working in political discussions. Yet this method did not always work, as the papal legate Leonello Chieregati, residing at Maximilian's court, later complained that Sanseverino had brought no new interesting news, only tournament weapons.[34]

---

[30] *Regesta Imperii*, XIV, 4: no. 15961.

[31] Klaus Brandstätter, 'Aspekte der Festkultur unter Maximilian', in *Maximilian I. (1459–1519): Wahrnehmung – Übersetzungen – Gender*, ed. Heinz Noflascher, Michael A. Chisholm, and Bertrand Schnerb (Innsbruck, 2011), pp. 156–70. A surviving suit of Sanseverino's tournament armour for the *Gestech* (c. 1490) may be seen in the Kunsthistorisches Museum, Vienna (Inv.-Nr. S I).

[32] *Regesta Imperii*, XIV, 2: nos. 5881, 5884.

[33] *Regesta Imperii*, XIV, 2: no. 8466.

[34] *Regesta Imperii*, XIV, 2: no. 5934.

The role of tournaments during imperial diets is of particular interest. Maximilian's initiation of recreational pursuits, such as jousting or hunting, at these events might have been a way for him to promote unity amongst his nobles. However, his oft-described penchant for evading his duties in such circumstances also raises the question of whether these games were a form of escape.[35] For example, at the diet of Freiburg in 1497, the Milanese legate Erasmus Brascha reported wishing to meet with Maximilian, yet the emperor was apparently too busy with preparations for tournaments and was not able to meet with him until two days later.[36] Brascha also expressed the belief that Maximilian would not stay long at the diet of Freiburg, as he had little desire to participate and would much rather be hunting and hawking.[37]

The papal legate Leonello Chieregati further complained that nothing new had been achieved since 16 February, since all were so involved in numerous tournaments, which had not yet come to an end and were preventing the journey onward from Innsbruck, where the court was currently based, to Freiburg. Chieregati had to remain in Innsbruck, where he wrote that he was invited by Maximilian to witness his 'glorious war games'.[38] Such a description makes it sound as though Maximilian was desperate to avoid facing his political obligations at the imperial diet. Yet such actions could also represent a subtle power play on his part; by refusing to make himself easily available, Maximilian was asserting his position as the most important figure present (or absent). He refused to work by anyone's schedule but his own.

Amidst the spectacular tournaments featured at court celebrations, and the tournaments that served as a setting for political negotiations or fell alongside the imperial diets, there were also many tournaments in which Maximilian was involved that appear to have been staged on a far more spontaneous and casual basis. This comes back to the emperor's love of taking part in the tournament, not merely witnessing it. References to this sort of recreational tournament in the primary sources tend to be brief, and give the impression that they were not held for the sake of theatre or to make a statement of power. They were not necessarily held to impress anyone but were rather a manifestation of

---

[35] Dietmar Heil, '"Anfengklich sollet ir inen sagen unser gnad und alles gut": Die Reichstagsinstruktionen und Reichstagsordungen Kaiser Maximilians I. (1486/93–1519)', in *Ordnung durch Tinte und Feder? Genese und Wirkung von Instruktionen im zeitlichen Längschnitt vom Mittelalter bis zum 20. Jahrhundert*, ed. Anita Hipfinger et al. (Vienna, 2011), pp. 49–71.

[36] *Regesta Imperii*, XIV, 2: no. 5925.

[37] *Deutsche Reichstagsakten unter Maximilian I.*, 6 vols (Göttingen, 1972–), 5: 544.

[38] *Regesta Imperii*, XIV, 2: no. 5934.

Maximilian's genuine love of the tournament, for he seems to have truly found pleasure throughout his life in taking part in these events.

During a series of tournaments held in January 1504, for example, Hans Ungelter of Esslingen described a tournament centred on foot combats, along with other festivities and masquerade dances (*Mummerei*) which involved the attendees dressing up as farmers and peasants. During this time, when Maximilian was approaching forty-six, he continued to prove that he was still fit to compete in tournaments. As proof, throughout all of this Maximilian is described by Ungelter as being especially cheerful and happy. *Er rent und sticht und tantzt und hat kostlich welsch tentz und bancket*, Ungelter wrote – 'He [Maximilian] jousts [the *Rennen* and the *Gestech*] and dances and has exquisite Italian dances and banquets.' The impression is reinforced that it was tournaments that Maximilian enjoyed perhaps more than any other aspect of noble life. Describing another such event, also in 1504, Ungelter wrote, *man habe gerennt, des Abends getanzt; der römische König sei ganz fröhlich gewesen* – 'One jousted, danced in the evening; the Roman King [Maximilian] was completely happy.'[39] Clearly Maximilian's enjoyment of the tournament, even as he approached his fiftieth year, was unfeigned.

The choice of men whom Maximilian invited to participate in his tournaments, often against himself, was also significant, as their involvement helped to solidify a network of nobles throughout his empire. Maximilian's fellow competitors in these events were knights and noblemen of his court as well as his friends, the leaders of his armies, and part of a tightly interwoven chivalric community that he created. In ruling such a vast and often disconnected empire, fostering this kind of camaraderie while also drawing men to him through his sporting reputation would have been a valuable device for Maximilian.[40] The emperor had a favoured circle of knights with whom he enjoyed competing in a tournament setting and who were drawn to his court repeatedly for this very purpose. Yet keeping these men close by means of tournaments would have had greater benefits than mere recreational enjoyment. Such a practice would have helped maintain fidelity while also allowing Maximilian to keep a close watch on the high-ranking nobles and princes of his empire. Maintaining such a network in the late medieval Holy Roman Empire would have been a difficult task. While traditionally such ties may have been preserved by

---

[39] *Urkunden zur Geschichte des Schwäbischen Bundes (1488–1533)*, ed. Karl A. Klüpfel, 2 vols (Stuttgart, 1846–53), 1: 497–98.

[40] Joachim Bumke, *Courtly Culture: Literature and Society in the High Middle Ages*, trans. Thomas Dunlap (Berkeley, Calif., 1991), pp. 264–71.

arranging marriages or holding imperial diets, Maximilian found a way to use the tournament as a tool for the same ends.[41]

Many of the men most integral to Maximilian's tournaments – who they were and what made them so important – were connected by blood or marriage to Maximilian as well as to each other, and the number of intertwining ties between them all is dizzying. Additionally, in the early years of his reign, those who were most frequently found competing alongside Maximilian tended to be close to his own age. These courtly tournaments represented a noble fraternity in which the competitors were the young and vital men of the empire. There are two especially interesting individuals who emerge from this crowd: Wolfgang von Polheim (1458–1512) and Anthony von Yfan (died c. 1510).

It was Polheim whose marriage to Johanna von Borsselen in Mechelen was the occasion of a great tournament. Polheim came from one of the oldest and noblest families of Upper Austria, and held the title of *Oberster Hauptmann* (a military commander) in Lower Austria. He was a companion of Maximilian's from childhood and his trusted friend and counsellor. He was closely involved in Maximilian's diplomatic affairs, and in 1500 he became a knight of the chivalric order of the Golden Fleece. In addition to his numerous appearances both in sources relating to Maximilian's tournaments, both real and fictional, Polheim holds a special place of prominence when he features as *Rennen und Gestech Meister* in Maximilian's *Triumphzug*. There he bears a banner in which reads: 'Always promoting new advances / In jousting with hooked or pointed lances, / Thanks to His Highness [Maximilian], I [von Polheim] unfurled / Skills never seen in all the world.'[42]

Maximilian's tournament network was not made up entirely of German-speaking noblemen either. Anthony von Yfan, as he is commonly named in German sources, was, in fact, the Italian nobleman Antonio de Caldonazo, lord of Ivano, in the north of Italy. At the court of Maximilian Yfan played a central role as a competitor in his tournaments, and Maximilian seems to have particularly enjoyed jousting against him. Images of the two men competing can be found across multiple sources.[43] At Wolfgang von Polheim's wedding,

---

[41] John Gillingham, 'Elective Kingship and the Unity of Medieval Germany', *German History* 9 (1991), 124–35.

[42] *The Triumph of Maximilian*, pp. 7–8, plate 44. Some of Polheim's own armour (manufactured in Innsbruck, c. 1510) may be seen in the Kunsthistorisches Museum, Vienna (Inv.-Nr. A 107).

[43] Munich, Bayerische Staatsbibliothek, MS Cod.icon. 398, plates 19, 26, 31, 37, 53. Yfan appears five times, in three of which he is jousting against Maximilian. *Freydal*, plates 43, 45, 101, 105, 129, 193, 232.

Yfan was considered to have emerged the overall victor in the celebratory tournament.[44] Most significantly, like Polheim, Yfan also appears in Maximilian's *Triumphzug*, where he is described as the *Turniermeister* ('Master of the Tournament') and carries a banner stating, 'Much of his [Maximilian's] time was nobly spent / In the true knightly tournament, / A source of valour and elation; / Therefore upon his instigation, / With knightly spirit and bold heart / I [Yfan] have improved this fighting art'.[45]

Maximilian honoured these two men by immortalising them in one of his own personal literary works. They may now forever be associated specifically with Maximilian's tournaments, and his high regard for their skill in that context is reflected in such a tribute. Who else may have held the positions during Maximilian's reign is unknown. However, the very existence of these two official court positions speaks to the value Maximilian placed on the tournament. He placed two men in charge of upholding his own rules, and the words he put in their mouths in the form of the banners they carry reflect not only the advances made to the tournament by Maximilian but also the important positions of Polheim and Yfan in Maximilian's tournament network.

Building a Legacy

All of this personal engagement in tournaments and displays of both physical strength and largesse were only beneficial to Maximilian in the moment in which they occurred and the immediate aftermath. He might prove himself repeatedly in the lists, gaining the immediate respect of his fellow nobles, but he also realised that such success was fleeting. Memorialising these combats in the tournament books, or *Turnierbücher*, of the time was one way of allowing these feats to live on in perpetuity.[46] Maximilian, however, also went on to

---

[44] *Georg Spalatin's historischer Nachlaß und Briefe*, pp. 230–31.

[45] *The Triumph of Maximilian*, p. 7, plate 41. For further information on Yfan, see *Die Inschriften des Bundeslandes Tirol*, 1: *Die Deutschen Inschriften*, ed. Werner Köfler and Romedio Schmitz-Esser (Vienna, 2003), p. 82.

[46] These *Turnierbücher* were not only produced for Maximilian but also for his peers. These works, and Maximilian's frequent presence within them, served to further highlight men's connection to the emperor, and his appearance as a competitor would grant them even greater prestige. For example, Maximilian may be seen in the *Turnierbuch* of Johann of Saxony: *Der Sächsischen Kurfürsten Turnierbücher*, ed. Erich Haenel (Frankfurt, 1910), plates 111–12; and in *The Tournament Book of Gašper Lamberger / Das Turnierbuch des Caspar von Lamberg, Codex A 2290, Kunsthistorisches Museum, Wien, Hofjagd- und Rüstkammer*, ed. Dušan Kos (Ljubljana, 1997), pp. 150–51.

utilise the power of fictional works commemorating his reign to permanently immortalise his skill in the tournament. In such a way could his success in the tournament also hopefully be seen as a symbol for his overall success as a ruler.

The way Maximilian utilised tournaments in the fictional literary works that he commissioned as emperor sheds light on how he viewed their worth in the construction of his image and interpretation of his reign. In fact, fictional tournaments could often play as important a part in how Maximilian wished to portray his court as those that truly took place there. In the fictional realm, Maximilian could entirely control the outcome of every tournament or frame himself as the hero of every joust without having to trouble himself with historical reality.[47] This idea ties into Jan-Dirk Müller's theory that Maximilian wanted to present his court through this early form of propaganda as he wished or imagined that it was, rather than his often financially strained reality.[48]

Paula Fichtner, among others, rightly questions where Maximilian drew the line between reality and fantasy in the images he presented of himself, a process that speaks of a boundless self-assurance. Yet he would have needed such qualities to succeed in the role into which he had been born. When it comes to Maximilian, there was his authentic self and the self he presented in art and literature.[49] Müller points out that Maximilian's self-representations were not original but fitted into certain long-standing models: student, commander, ruler, artist etc. But this does not mean they were all necessarily true.[50] This desire to present himself as part of a long-standing literary tradition of glorified rulers comes to the fore in the trilogy of *Weisskunig*, *Theuerdank* and *Freydal* – the last of which is focused exclusively on the tournament. The three works strike a balance between allegory and true history that allowed Maximilian to present only the best aspects of himself.

An excellent example of the role of tournaments in Maximilian's literary heritage is *Theuerdank*, the allegorical re-telling of Maximilian's courtship of his beloved first wife, Mary of Burgundy, and a product of what Elaine C.

---

[47] Martin Gosman, 'Princely Culture: Friendship or Patronage?', in *Princes and Princely Culture: 1450–1650*, ed. Martin Gosman and others, 2 vols (Leiden, 2003), I, pp. 1–29.

[48] Jan-Dirk Müller, *Gedechtnus: Literatur und Hofgesellschaft um Maximilian I.* (Munich, 1982), p. 264.

[49] Paula Fichtner, *The Habsburgs: Dynasty, Culture and Politics* (Chicago, 2014), pp. 32–33.

[50] Müller, *Gedechtnus: Literatur und Hofgesellschaft um Maximilian I.*, p. 264.

Tennant has dubbed 'the Maximilian industry'.[51] Given the significance of tournaments in both the Burgundian and imperial courts, it is little surprise that tournaments should hold a prominent place in *Theuerdank*. Yet these individual encounters reflect, in fact, far more the legacy of German tournaments that Maximilian hoped to leave behind at the end of his life rather than the Burgundian-style tournaments that he might have encountered at Mary's court during their marriage.

In *Theuerdank*, in order to win his bride, the young Theuerdank (a thinly disguised Maximilian) must compete in three days of combat with knights at the court of the maiden Ehrenreich (i.e., Mary of Burgundy). Each of these three days of combat in which Theuerdank is involved follows a similar format. There is always a joust, followed by a foot combat, and the day ends with dancing. This is a format similar to that seen in another of Maximilian's allegorical yet autobiographical works, *Freydal*, which is devoted in its entirety to the tournaments Maximilian so loved. Thus the audience can see Maximilian, as the originator of these works, aligning the organisation of his tournaments across the sources representing his reign.

By the end of the third day Theuerdank (perhaps unsurprisingly) has emerged victorious from each of his combats. Afterwards the young queen (Mary) greets him and, taking his hands, says, *Ir habt eur macht wol bewert* ('You have truly proved your power'), and further names him 'the noblest hero on the earth' thanks to his accomplishments. There could be no clearer connection established between Theuerdank, i.e. Maximilian's, reputation as a ruler and the importance he placed on success in tournaments.[52]

Theuerdank was first printed in 1517, many decades after Maximilian's marriage to Mary of Burgundy in 1477 and just two years before his death in 1519. Its mix of text and woodcut engravings is a wonderful example of a late medieval monarch harnessing the new power of printing. Maximilian was cleverly using this new technology as a tool to help craft his future legacy. It is one of the reasons why Maximilian favoured woodcuts: because they were relatively inexpensive and could be multiplied and distributed rapidly, rather

---

[51] Elaine C. Tennant, 'Productive Reception: Theuerdank in the Sixteenth Century', in *Maximilians Ruhmeswerk: Künste und Wissenschaften im Umkreis Kaiser Maximilians I.*, ed. Jan-Dirk Müller and Hans-Joachim Ziegeler (Berlin, 2015), pp. 295–348.

[52] *Die Geferlicheiten und geschichten des löblichen streytbaren unnd hochberiempten Helds und Ritters Teürdancks* (Augsburg, 1537) [Inc. Munich, Bayerische Staatsbibliothek, Rar. 2195, p. 516].

than works of art produced by painters or sculptors. Maximilian also knew that he could make his printed works more popular by adding images.[53]

Theuerdank was Maximilian's way of commemorating his marriage to Mary as one of the most significant events of his life. His ties to Burgundy were, at the end of his life, the ones that he most wanted to honour. Yet he did so in a way that incorporated his own subsequent accomplishments as well, by retroactively inserting the German-style tournaments of his court into a Burgundian setting. One interesting example of the way these two factors combine in the *Theuerdank* tournaments is that the hero is gifted a suit of armour from the 'Burgundian' armouries by Ehrenreich in which to compete. The reader is presented with a highly literal representation of the blending of the two cultures – Theuerdank is undertaking German tournaments in Burgundian armour.[54] The choice of the three varieties of joust depicted is also significant. They represent the two most quintessentially German (and most popular under Maximilian) forms of the *Rennen* and the *Gestech*: the *Scharfrennen* and the *Deutschgestech*. The third, the *Welschgestech*, is representative of one of Maximilian's most favoured and unique forms of joust that he promoted.

As a monarch Maximilian undoubtedly wished to emulate the famous tournaments of Mary's father, Charles the Bold – a man whom he greatly admired – at the court of Burgundy. The impressive tournaments held at the Burgundian court were already famous in Maximilian's day, and he would have been well aware of their reputation. *Theuerdank* may have been Maximilian's way of drawing a parallel between his own tournaments and those of the Burgundian father-in-law whom he idolised, while also emphasising the German forms and innovations of his own competitions and, by extension, building his own legacy on top of that of Burgundy. In its literary re-telling, Maximilian also gets to portray himself as the unequivocal hero, saving the damsel in distress, Mary, just as in real life he saved her inheritance from the perceived threat of France, all brought to life in the true Arthurian model.[55]

---

[53] Glenn Elwood Waas, *The Legendary Character of Kaiser Maximilian* (New York, 1941), pp. 118–19.

[54] *Die Geferlicheiten und geschichten … Teürdancks* (1537), p. 490.

[55] Gerhild S. Williams, 'The Arthurian Model in Emperor Maximilian's Autobiographic Writings *Weisskunig* and *Theuerdank*', *Sixteenth Century Journal* 11 (1980), 3–22; Bianca Häberlein, 'Die Konzeption des Abenteuers im *Wilhelm von Österreich* Johanns von Würzburg und im *Theuerdank* Maximilians I.', in *Maximilians Ruhmeswerk: Künste und Wissenschaften im Umkreis Kaiser Maximilians I.*, ed. Jan-Dirk Müller and Hans-Joachim Ziegeler (Berlin, 2015), pp. 281–94.

Gerhild Williams calls Maximilian his own propaganda minister: someone who carefully constructed his public image in order to achieve his goals. Throughout his reign Maximilian wanted to assert his political power over other rulers, such as those of England and France.[56] When he was unsuccessful in doing this in real life, he could at least do it in literary form. This method has earned him both respect and disdain from modern historians. Paul van Dyke vigorously condemned Maximilian's (admittedly undeniable) vanity. He claimed that the emperor's works lacked any artistic knowledge or literary ability; rather, he saw them simply the result of a tremendous effort to produce an enormous volume of work, with nothing worth praising in terms of form or content.[57] While these works' veracity is certainly worth questioning – *Weisskunig*'s portrayal of Maximilian's thorough and wide-ranging education, for instance, is undoubtedly dubious – their impact on how Maximilian's public image was crafted is undeniable.[58] When such works are still the most easily accessible and widespread primary sources relating to Maximilian's reign, thanks to the power of printing, their mission can only have been successful.

In his court, Maximilian created for himself a unique environment by making use of a type of *Kulturtransfer*; he combined elements of Burgundian, Italian and German courtly culture to create his own 'melting pot'. Some elements were absorbed, and some were in part transformed into something new, a process embodied in his tournaments.[59] Throughout his reign Maximilian's connection to the tournament appears threefold: he consistently demonstrated in the running of his court a combination of true enjoyment of the tournament and, at the same time, an understanding of its important role in his court, as well as a consciousness of its place in his legacy.

First, Maximilian, by all accounts, very much enjoyed taking part in tournaments, both in forms of foot combat and also on horseback, often being described as 'happy' while doing so. This enjoyment of the tournament led him to pursue it well into middle age and to continue to prove himself a fit competitor. This would have been particularly useful during times when Maximilian was viewed as lacking in other dimensions as a leader – in the political arena, for instance. Showing himself off as a an adept tournament competitor allowed Maximilian to display his chivalric prowess, something always sure

---

[56] Williams, 'The Arthurian Model in Emperor Maximilian's Autobiographic Writings *Weisskunig* and *Theuerdank*', p. 6.

[57] Paul van Dyke, 'The Literary Activity of the Emperor Maximilian I', *American Historical Review* 11 (1905), 16–28.

[58] Louise Cuyler, *The Emperor Maximilian I and Music* (London, 1973), pp. 8–9.

[59] Brandstätter, 'Aspekte der Festkultur unter Maximilian', pp. 163–65.

to gain a ruler respect, even when he failed to prove himself in other fields. However, this passionate pursuit of the tournament could sometimes come at the expense of his political success. This was a double-edged sword that Maximilian had to deal with throughout his reign.

For, secondly, Maximilian was clearly aware of the power of the tournament as a focal point of courtly activity. He demonstrated over and over numerous ways in which he incorporated tournaments into courtly festivities – at weddings or other celebrations – and brought them heavily into the revelries of the *Fastnacht* period on an annual basis. Not only did these tournaments provide pleasing entertainment to the ladies of the court and other spectators, but they also provided a space for other princes and high-ranking nobles of Maximilian's empire to come together for friendly competition. They could show off and build their chivalric reputations while gaining respect and appreciation for Maximilian's hospitality, and he, in turn, could keep an eye on them and preserve valuable alliances. The events acted as a unifying force in bringing together nobles across his disparate empire. The tournament possessed a universal appeal that would have brought knights to Maximilian's court for the pleasure of competing, no matter the city in which he was currently based. They were also a way for Maximilian to assert his own power as a skilled competitor and to win the respect of both his own subjects and foreign noblemen.

Thirdly, in Maximilian's eyes his court was not just the social world that he built around himself; it was also, in many instances, a theoretical, idealised space that could be used in crafting his image. This court had the power to exist perpetually, preserved forever in art and literature. The role of memory as it relates to the courtly tournament is a critical one to Maximilian. This may be seen in the commemoration of real-life tournaments in which Maximilian was involved through the medium of the *Turnierbücher*, a genre which he and many of his contemporaries popularised. It may also be seen in the prominent place of fictional tournaments in works like *Theuerdank*. In each of these literary or artistic works tournaments are placed, either subtly or obviously, in a central role.

It is also important to note that Maximilian himself had a hand in producing these works, proving that his passion for the tournament was a central factor he wished to emphasise in his public persona. In each of these works Maximilian casts himself as the central character: a knight of the noblest chivalric standards and, above all, a superb competitor in the tournament. He is intentionally harking back to earlier medieval tales of heroic knights and is attempting both to embody and to carry forward this tradition in his own lifetime and beyond. Both chivalry and honour were integral to the world of tournament, a stage on which the highest ideals of knightly ethics could be played out. Maximilian threw himself into this idea, romanticising 'chivalry' in a tradition of nostalgia that would continue for centuries. And he often set himself in centre stage, both in the actual events and in their literary representations. It is little wonder that the honorific that has followed him into the present day is that of 'the Last Knight'.

The tournament was a central facet around which much of Maximilian's reign revolved. Although it may be seen in a negative sense (as a distraction from imperial duties) or positively (as a form of pleasing entertainment), Maximilian throughout his life showed himself to be a devotee of the tournament far surpassing other rulers of his time. He incorporated it in a variety of ingenious ways into his courtly life – across many locations, times, purposes and even artistic mediums. He also demonstrated an awareness of how it might affect his future reputation. As a vital part of courtly life, the tournament served as a key element of Maximilian's reign.

10 The Field of Cloth of Gold: Arms, Armour and the Sporting Prowess of King Henry VIII and King Francis I

Karen Watts

The Field of Cloth of Gold was a summit meeting held in the summer of 1520 at which Henry VIII, king of England, and Francis I, king of France, jousted, tourneyed and fought on foot against knights of both courts.[1] It was the first time that the two young kings met and it served to demonstrate to each other that they were physically powerful potentates. It is interesting to assess how these two kings reacted to each other. This chapter will uniquely consider the arms and armour of the two kings and their participation in the combats of the Field of Cloth of Gold. Rather than being suspicious of each other and acting as rivals, we can see the two kings revelling in each other's company, in every sense.

The tournament was named after the magnificent and very costly cloth-of-gold pavilions embellishing an otherwise drab setting in the Pale of Calais, a wetland region in northern France captured by Edward III and the only part of mainland France to remain in English control at the end of the Hundred Years' War.[2] It was one of the most extraordinary tournaments of the period. Even today it is a byword for chivalry and extravagance. The scene-setting for the Field of Cloth of Gold was certainly elaborate. The palace, pavilions of

---

[1] The context of the tournament was a political and diplomatic alliance between the two kings. A treaty of 'perpetual friendship' and a marriage alliance between their children, the Dauphin Francis and the Princess Mary, was signed on 4 October 1518 in London (Kew, The National Archives, E 30/817A). The culmination was the Field of Cloth of Gold which concluded with declarations of eternal peace and friendship between France and England.

[2] A useful English naval base, Calais was finally recaptured by the French in 1558. The area of the Pale of Calais comprised many communes, including Calais and Guînes. See Julian Munby, 'The Field of Cloth of Gold: Guînes and the Calais Pale Revisited', *English Heritage Historical Review* 9 (2014), 30–63.

cloth of gold and the tournament lists (arenas) were erected especially for the event and removed afterwards.³ It is remarkable that no physical trace of the tournament remains today.

The political and diplomatic intentions, planning, organisation and implications of the Field of Cloth of Gold have been discussed and put into context by French and English historians.⁴ There are numerous and sometimes contradictory primary sources including reports, accounts of revels, letters and chronicles. Sir Richard Wingfield was appointed ambassador at the French court and his letters to Cardinal Wolsey and to King Henry VIII are revealing as he reports candidly on King Francis I during the organisation of the tournament.⁵ The most detailed English source is Edward Hall, whose *Chronicle*, first printed in 1548, is invaluable as it uses an eyewitness account.⁶ A standard French source, the memoir of Guillaume du Bellay, together with various pamphlet commemorations, offers information about the sequence of events.⁷

This essay, however, will consider a unique eyewitness source: the Maréchal de Fleuranges.⁸

Robert III de La Marck, lord of Fleuranges, duke of Bouillon and lord of Sedan (c. 1491–c. 1536) referred to himself as the *Jeune Adventureux* (Young Adventurer) in his memoir recounting events from 1499 to 1521.⁹ He wrote

---

3   Cloth of gold is a textile woven with a weft of gold and a warp of silk.
4   Glenn Richardson, *The Field of Cloth of Gold* (New Haven, 2014); J. G. Russell, *Field of Cloth of Gold: Men and Manners in 1520* (London, 1969); Charles Giry-Deloison, *1520, Le Camp du Drap d'Or: La rencontre d'Henri VIII et de François I* (Paris, 2012); *François Ier et Henri VIII: Deux princes de la Renaissance (1515–1547)*, ed. Roger Mettam and Charles Giry-Deloison (Lille, 1995).
5   *Letters and Papers, Foreign and Domestic, of the Reign of Henry VIII*, vol. 3, ed. J. S. Brewer, (London, 1867), March–June 1520, *passim*.
6   *Hall's Chronicle: Containing the History of England, during the Reign of Henry the Fourth and the Succeeding Monarchs, to the End of the Reign of Henry the Eighth, Carefully Collated with the Editions of 1548 and 1550* (London, 1809), 600–20.
7   *Mémoires de Martin et Guillaume du Bellay*, ed. Victor-Louis Bourrilly and F. Vindry, 4 vols (Paris, 1908–19), 1: 101–2. An example of a French pamphlet is: 'La description et ordre du camp, festins et joustes', in *Letters and Papers, Foreign and Domestic: Henry VIII*, vol. 3, pp. 303–14.
8   'Histoire des choses mémorables advenues du reigne de Louis XII et François Ier', in *Choix de Chroniques et Mémoires sur l'histoire de France*, ed. J. A. C. Buchon (Paris, 1836), pp. 216–95.
9   Fleuranges was sent by his father to the court of Louis XII; he was a childhood companion of Francis I and remained a close friend of the French king at the time of the tournament in 1520. He had a good military career, fighting in the Italian

it in 1525–26, while in prison after the battle of Pavia, a disastrous defeat for Francis I who was himself captured after falling from his horse.[10] Fleuranges wrote a very personal and first-hand account of the Field of Cloth of Gold with lively and credible descriptions of Francis I and Henry VIII at moments of privacy away from public presentations. Fleuranges himself took part in the jousts and tourneys and his presence is attested in English sources, such as Hall and state papers, amongst those who would accompany the French king when he was to meet Henry. Interestingly, he is listed separately amongst the military guard of four hundred archers and one hundred Swiss guards and the only one to be named as 'de Florenges, captain', indicating his military role.[11]

The primary iconographic source for the tournament is a painting in the Royal Collection that was probably commissioned by Henry VIII (Figure 1).[12] Joseph Ayloffe and Sydney Anglo both considered and studied this painting as a valid historical document.[13] It is a synthesis of the whole tournament with multiple events presented as an engaging whole. There is also an interesting and contemporary French source, worthy of study – a series of five bas-reliefs on the Hôtel de Bourgtheroulde in Rouen. These panels represent the elaborate first meeting of the two kings: the English procession leaving Guînes; Cardinal Wolsey and his retinue; the meeting of Henry VIII and Francis I on horseback, wearing their orders of chivalry, saluting each other with their hats and with a military retinue; Adrian Gouffier de Boissy, the French cardinal, and his retinue; and the French procession leaving Ardres.

Wars in 1509–16, and also had a trusted ambassadorial role as witness to the imperial elections in 1519. 'Histoire des choses mémorables advenues du reigne de Louis XII et François Ier', pp. xvi, 217–80.

[10] The memoir was not published in his lifetime and it is uncertain whether it was intended for public circulation. Fleuranges' memoir was first published in 1753 by the Abbé Lambert, who claimed to have received the manuscript from a descendant and to have collated it with three other copies: *Memoires de Martin et Guillaume du Bellai-Langei … auxquels on a joint les memoires du Marechal de Fleuranges …* ed. Abbé Lambert (Paris, 1753). Some errors of chronology are acknowledged, especially regarding the battle of Marignano in 1515. M. Petitot, *Collection complète des mémoires relatifs à l'histoire de France* (Paris, 1826), p. 417.

[11] *Hall's Chronicle*, 617; *Letters and Papers, Foreign and Domestic: Henry VIII*, vol. 3, p. 236.

[12] *The Field of the Cloth of Gold*, British School, 1542–45, London, Royal Collection Trust, RCIN 405794.

[13] Sidney Anglo, 'The Hampton Court Painting of the Field of Cloth of Gold Considered as an Historical Document', *Antiquaries Journal* 46 (1966), 287–307.

The arms and armour of the two kings played both a practical defensive role and a symbolic one. Although no armours for this tournament of Francis I remain, two of Henry VIII are extant in the collection of the Royal Armouries. This chapter will consider the physical engagement and ability of both kings at this tournament.

Physical Description of the Kings: Francis I (1494–1547) and Henry VIII (1491–1547)

At birth, neither king was expected to rule.[14] However, Francis I became king at the age of twenty, in 1515, and Henry VIII at the age of seventeen in 1509. In 1520, both kings were young, fit, strong and tall.

Francis I

The best account of the young Francis I comes from Fleuranges, who described his physical exercises with his close companions: Anne de Montmorency, Marin de Montchenu, Philippe de Brion, Pierre Terrail, the Chevalier Bayard and Guillaume Gouffier, lord of Bonnivet.[15] His notable physical characteristics were a large, prominent nose and thin legs. His height is known from his only surviving armour, although the measurements were taken in spring 1539 and his girth may have changed since 1520. His height was a little under 1.98 metres, on the basis of the height of the armour.[16] One of the earliest portraits of Francis I was painted in 1515 while the other is the renowned and

---

[14] Francis of Angoulême was the third cousin to the young Charles VIII, who died childless, whilst his father's cousin, the duke of Orléans (later Louis XII), had no male heir. Henry Tudor was the third child and second son of Henry VII.

[15] 'Histoire des choses mémorables advenues du reigne de Louis XII et François Ier', p. 217. The boys were about seven to ten years old. The activities included various Italian bat and ball games, archery, hunting with net barriers for deer and other wild animals, shooting arrows from miniature cannons, and attacking and defending miniature fortresses in armour and with swords. When they were 'a little older' they were armed and practised jousts and tournament combats of all types against various practice targets: *commencèrent eulx armer et faire joustes et tournois de toutes les sortes qu'on se pouvoit adviser; et ne feust qu'à jouster au vent, à la selle dessainglée ou à la nappe.*

[16] Armour of Francis I by Jörg Seusenhofer, 1539–40 (Paris, Musée de l'Armée, G.117). Parts of this armour are also in the Hofjagd- und Rüstkammer, Vienna (B 147) and in the Deutsches Historisches Museum, Berlin (W 1016). See Juliette Allix, 'L'Armure de François Ier: Histoires d'un présent diplomatique', *Cahiers de l'École du Louvre* 6 (2015), 15–26; *D'Azincourt à Marignan, chevaliers et bombardes*

much reproduced portrait, painted in 1527–30.[17] There is no physical facial difference between the two portraits, although the earlier shows the incipient beard that may have influenced Henry to grow one. Francis was especially fond of hunting and during the preparations for the Field of Cloth of Gold, he was frequently out hunting when the English ambassador sought information concerning the arrangements for the tournament.

Edward Hall's eyewitness, seeing the French king for the first time, as Henry VIII did, described him: 'Verily of his person the same Frances, the French king, a goodly Prince, stately of countenance, merry of cheer, brown-coloured, great eyes, high nosed, big lipped, fair breasted and shoulders, small legs and long feet'.[18]

Henry VIII

When he came to the throne at the age of seventeen in 1509, Henry VIII was a man of seemingly unlimited energy, purportedly capable of dancing the rest of the court off their feet and of tiring as many as eight or nine horses in a single day's hunting. Nearly 1.88 metres in height, and of strong, athletic build, he excelled as a sportsman. He was not only a fine tennis player, a skilful longbow archer and an accomplished wrestler, but also played football.[19] Henry VIII was also an outstanding jouster, perhaps the best in the land.

Sebastian Giustinian, the Venetian ambassador extraordinary at King Henry's court, wrote descriptions of the king in two letters. They reveal his physique and his jousting prowess. They are among the most famous descriptions of Henry VIII.

> His Majesty is the handsomest potentate I ever set eyes on; above the usual height, with an extremely fine calf to his leg, his complexion very fair and bright, with auburn hair combed straight and short, in the French fashion, his throat being rather long and thick. He was born on the 28th of June 1491, so he will enter his twenty-fifth year the month after next. He speaks French, English, and Latin, and a little Italian, plays well on the lute and harpsichord, sings from book at sight, draws the bow with greater strength

1415–1515, ed. Antoine Leduc, Sylvie Leluc and Olivier Renaudeau (Paris, 2015), p. 238.

[17] Jean Clouet, French, 1515 (Chantilly, Musée Condé, 4690) and Jean Clouet, French, 1527–30 (Paris, Musée du Louvre, 3256).

[18] *Hall's Chronicle*, p. 610.

[19] Maria Hayward, 'Dress and the Court of King Henry VIII', in *Henry VIII: Arms and the Man*, ed. Graeme Rimer, Thom Richardson and John P. D. Cooper (Leeds, 2009), p. 113.

than any man in England, and jousts marvellously. Believe me, he is in every respect a most accomplished Prince; and I, who have now seen all the sovereigns in Christendom, and last of all these two of France and England in such great state, might well rest content.[20]

Henry VIII was particularly curious about the physicality of Francis I and took the opportunity to question the Venetian ambassador, who had just been to the French court and seen the king:

His Majesty came into our arbor, and addressing me in French, said: 'Talk with me awhile! The King of France, is he as tall as I am?' I told him there was but little difference. He continued, 'Is he as stout?' I said he was not; and he then inquired, 'What sort of legs has he?' I replied 'Spare'. Whereupon he opened the front of his doublet, and placing his hand on his thigh, said 'Look here! and I have also a good calf to my leg'.[21]

An early portrait of Henry VIII that can be dated to 1520 is curiously similar in stance, dress and attitude to that of Francis I.[22]

Types of Tournaments

Tilting was the predominant type of combat favoured by the Tudor court (called the Joust Royal). This was a joust of peace (*joute à plaisance*) fought over a barrier called a tilt (from the French word *toile*, this being the cloth that originally separated the combatants). This form of joust used hollow, rebated lances with the purpose of shattering them, points being awarded for striking different parts of the upper body and head. Other tournament combat forms included massed tourneys on horseback and on foot as well as jousts of war (*joute à outrance*) and single foot combat with a variety of weapons, including two-handed swords and various staff weapons. The classic form of tourney was a two-part event, first with lances and then with swords. At the Field of Cloth

---

[20] 30 April 1515. *Letters and Papers, Foreign and Domestic, of the Reign of Henry VIII*, ed. J. S. Brewer, vol. 2 (London, 1864), pp. 116–17.

[21] 3 May 1515. *Letters and Papers, Foreign and Domestic*, vol. 2, p. 120. Giustinian is a good independent witness to the skill of Henry VIII as a jouster in the same letter: *After dinner, his Majesty and many others armed themselves cap-a-pie, and he chose us to see him joust, running upwards of thirty courses, in one of which he capsized his opponent (who is the finest jouster in the whole kingdom), horse and all. He then took off his helmet, and came under the windows where we were, and talked and laughed with us to our very great honour, and to the surprise of all beholders.*

[22] *King Henry VIII*, by unknown Anglo-Netherlandish artist, about 1520 (London, National Portrait Gallery, 4690). Henry is shown with a beard, a French fashion. This portrait may have been influenced by the Chantilly portrait of Francis I.

of Gold, the tourney was only with swords. The tourney course was a combat where pairs of combatants fought each other. This was also seen at the Field of Cloth of Gold.

Armour for the Joust Royal evolved during the reign of Henry VIII. Until the 1520s, jousters wore a great helm with projecting prow-like visor to deflect blows, popularly known as a frog-mouthed helm. The later form was a close helmet worn with pieces of exchange, reinforcing plates over the left side of the body: grandguard (chest-defence), pasguard (upper-arm defence) and manifer (hand-defence).

These royal tournaments, even with allegorical settings, were dangerous. The jousts were hard fought, and Henry complained if he did not get good enough opponents. One of his favourite jousting companions was Charles Brandon, duke of Suffolk. In 1524 Henry, wearing a new armour of his own design, nearly died when jousting against Brandon. The combat form was a Joust Royal. He forgot to close his visor and 'what sorrow it was to the people when they saw the splinters of the duke's spear strike on the king's headpiece. The duke struck the king on the brow right under the defence of the headpiece, on the very skull … [it] broke all the shivers … all the king's headpiece was full of splinters'.[23] With typical bravura, Henry ran six more courses, but it is likely that may have sustained a cerebral injury that affected him thereafter and certainly seemed to manifest itself in severe headaches.

In the Royal Armouries collection of historic royal Tudor lances is one that has long been known as the 'Brandon Lance' in honour of Charles Brandon. It has been made in sections, is 4360mm long and is painted. It weighs 9.1kg. The iron elements, never kept on a lance when in storage, would have been a coronel-tip and a hand-guard called a vamplate.[24]

Planning and Organisation of the Field of Cloth of Gold

There was considerable detail in the planning of this tournament between the chief negotiators and ambassadors of England and France. For England they were principally Cardinal Wolsey aided by Wingfield at the French court. For France it was Guillaume Gouffier, Admiral Bonnivet, a trusted childhood friend of Francis I, who came to England for the planning and preparation.

---

[23] *Hall's Chronicle*, p. 674.

[24] The 'Brandon Lance', English, early sixteenth century (Leeds, Royal Armouries, VII. 550) from the Old Tower Collection. It was first associated with Charles Brandon in 1598. See *Henry VIII: Arms and the Man*, p. 137.

Hall records the actual tournament proclamation of Thomas Wolsey on 12 March 1520 but this is mainly preoccupied with the management, security measures and protocol, defining, for example, the planning of the various meetings between the two monarchs.[25] Wolsey refers to the entire event as an 'interview'. He does state that both kings

> be like in force, corporall beauty and gift of nature, right expert and having knowledge in the art militant, right chivalrous in arms and in the flower and vigour of youth, whereby seemed to us a right assembly that for to décore and illustre the same assembly and to show their forces in armes they shall take counsel and dispose themselves to do some faire feat of arms as well on foot as on horseback against all comers.

It is interesting to note that the kings had agreed and announced that they would do feats of arms on foot as well as on horseback. Foot combat, since it was valued and endorsed by the Holy Roman Emperor Maximilian I from about 1500, was now considered a noble sport. The kings were joint 'challengers' with a mixed team of French and English knights who declared the form and weapons for each type of combat, accepted by the 'answerers', a similarly mixed team. The carefully planned rules of the tournament had agreed that the two kings would fight as brothers-in-arms. As such, they would not actually fight one another and so would avoid the embarrassment of a defeat.

The tournament was elaborately staged. There was an impressive degree of theatricalisation. Both kings revelled in the opportunity for self-dramatisation to promote themselves.[26] The impersonation of allegorical roles was a major feature of the Tudor tournament. The costumes were also often linked to the allegorical framework within which many jousts were set, presenting the jousters as the knights-errant of medieval romantic fiction and the tournament as the response to an heroic challenge.[27] The combatants at the Field of Cloth

---

[25] *Hall's Chronicle*, p. 601. See also *Letters and Papers, Foreign and Domestic: Henry VIII*, vol. 3, p. 224, 13 March 1520.

[26] Lesley Mickel, 'Theatricalisation at the Field of Cloth of Gold, 1520', in *Theatralisierung*, ed. Sabine Coelsch-Foisner, Timo Heimerdinger and Christopher Herzog (Heidelberg, 2016), pp. 69–85.

[27] For example, the Westminster Tournament on 12–13 February 1511 to celebrate the birth of a short-lived son (Henry, duke of Cornwall) to Henry VIII and Katherine of Aragon. The event was recorded for posterity in the vast illuminated vellum roll preserved at the College of Arms. The manuscript only shows the second day of the tournament: 13 February. It shows tilting. The four main jousters at this tournament all adopted allegorical roles and chivalric names. These were Henry VIII: *Noble Cueur Loyal*; Lord Devon (Courtenay): *Bon Vouloir*; Sir Thomas Knyvet (Master of the Horse): *Vaillant Desyr*; Edward Nevill: *Joyeulx Penser*. This habit of

of Gold, whilst ostensibly competing as themselves, adopted allegorical roles during the masquerades. The processions at the start of each day of the tournament had allegorical frameworks, seen in the kings' dress and in the caparisons of their horses.[28] There was also great concern for protocol, for hierarchy, for the formal and carefully timed processional entrances. For example, trumpets sounded for simultaneous departure times by the French and English kings for their first formal encounter.

A defining characteristic of a tournament is that it should be announced by heralds and this was duly done at the Field of Cloth of Gold. The French King of Arms, Orléans, came to the English court and 'made a proclamation that the king of England and the French king in a camp between Ardres and Guînes with eighteen aides in June next ensuing, should abide all comers being gentlemen at the tilt and tourney and at the barriers'. The same proclamation was made by the English King of Arms, Clarencieux, at the court of France.[29]

The Symbolism of the Sword for Foot Combat

The two kings enthusiastically exchanged and shared their love of arms and armour within this chivalric tournament setting. There are two revealing letters sent on the same day (16 March 1520) by Sir Richard Wingfield from the court of Francis I, one addressed to Henry VIII and the other to Wolsey.[30] In the letter to Henry, Sir Richard Wingfield describes the formal presentation of a sword to Francis, a personal gift from the English king.

This element of sword presentation as a symbol of a tournament challenge may well have been influenced by the fifteenth-century tournament manual of René of Anjou, *Traicte de la Forme de Devis d'un Tournoi*, which explains how a tournament should be held. Written about 1460–70, it survives in several copies, including what is considered to be the original in the Bibliothèque nationale de France,[31] which bears the ex-libris of Mary of Luxembourg,

---

externalising qualities and making them visible was important to court society. See Sydney Anglo, *The Great Tournament Roll of Westminster: A Collotype Reproduction of the Manuscripts* (Oxford, 1968).

[28] See the Calendar following this article for examples of the allegorical framework.

[29] *Hall's Chronicle*, p. 600.

[30] Letters from Sir Richard Wingfield to Henry VIII and to Wolsey (16 March 1520): *Letters and Papers, Foreign and Domestic: Henry VIII*, vol. 3, p. 227.

[31] Paris, Bibliothèque nationale de France, MS fr. 2695. Illuminated by Barthélémy d'Eyck.

cousin to Louise of Savoy who was the mother of Francis I. It is likely that it was studied by Francis himself. In this book, the duke of Brittany, appellant, gives the sword to the king of arms to go and present it to the duke of Bourbon, defendant, as a symbol of agreement to participate in a tournament.

The sword that Henry gave to Francis clearly astounded the French king. It was extremely heavy (*pesaunt*) and was lifted with some difficulty. Indeed, the king did not believe it could be used in a foot combat and called Admiral Bonnivet over to try it. Wingfield explained that Henry could use it, by means of a special, secret gauntlet.[32] Francis accordingly requested that Wingfield should ask Henry on his behalf for such a gauntlet. This gauntlet is almost certainly a locking gauntlet, an articulated mitten-shaped gauntlet. The hand would seize the grip of the hilt and the finger-tip plate secured to the inner cuff-plate by a turning pin. Once secured in this manner the sword could not be dropped even if the fingers of the hand let go. The sword effectively became an extension of the armoured gauntlet.

The sword presentation is perhaps significant as the articles of the challenge for foot combat were modified by Francis himself that very day, as stated in the second letter from Wingfield to Wolsey. Three types of sword are mentioned: a 'nimble' sword, a 'pesaunt' sword and a two-handed sword. The 'nimble' sword was to be used in an enclosed arena with more agreed strokes than with the heavy 'pesaunt' sword. Francis wished that 'at the barriers the heavy swords shall be much better to be occupied'. Instead of fighting within an enclosure, they were to fight across a barrier that would separate them. The change of weapon required a change of armour.[33] This is highly significant. Instead of a fully enclosing armour with reinforcing plates ('with pieces of avantage') that would protect the body from multiple heavy blows from all sides, a different armour was needed for fewer strokes of alternating attack and defence. It was now specified that it should be a skirted armour (tonlet) with a large rounded helmet secured to the cuirass (great basinet). The two-handed sword was deemed optional as it was considered a dangerous weapon, and few gauntlets would stand the heavy strokes to which they would be exposed. It

---

[32] Letter from Sir Richard Wingfield to Henry VIII (16 March 1520) (note 30, above): *for the nimble handling whereof he hath or knoweth no feat, but thought it not maniable, and called the Admiral to him and caused him to feel the weight thereof; who showed him that he had seen your grace wield one more pesaunt than the same as delyverly as could be devised, but for such promise as he had made your highness he might not disclose the manner how, saving that it was by means of a gauntlet.*

[33] This was altered by Francis I to a tonlet with great basinet. See Appendix 2 below.

was left, however, to the challengers' pleasure to choose the two-handed sword or the heavy sword.[34]

In a reciprocal gift, Francis offered to make a special cuirass for the tournament, if Henry would send him one of his own arming doublets from which measurements could be taken. This cuirass (breastplate and backplate) appears to have had a method of bolting jousting reinforces that took the weight off the shoulders, 'the secret whereof was only for the easy bearing and sustaining of the weight of such pieces as rest upon the cuirass, which most commonly is borne upon the shoulders; and in this sort of cuirasses the shoulders should sustain no burden'. [35]

It is unknown whether Francis used the heavy sword presented by Henry and indeed if he received the necessary locking gauntlet. On 18 April Wingfield wrote to Wolsey from Blois about Francis I, saying that he 'looketh daily to receive from him as well his measure for the making of the cuirass as also to receive the vauntbrasse and gauntlet'.[36]

The Armours of Henry VIII

Although arms and armour had been made in England since the Middle Ages, most of the fine quality armours seem to have been imported directly from Italy (Milan) or via Flanders. Henry VIII was influenced by the renown of the armourers of the Holy Roman Emperor Maximilian I, reinforced by two magnificent gifts of armour.[37] In 1511 Henry VIII founded his own pri-

[34] Letter from Sir Richard Wingfield to Henry VIII (13 May 1520), in *Letters and Papers, Foreign and Domestic: Henry VIII*, vol. 3, p. 283.

[35] Letter from Sir Richard Wingfield to Henry VIII (16 March 1520), in *Letters and Papers, Foreign and Domestic: Henry VIII*, vol. 3, pp. 227, 685.

[36] Letter from Sir Richard Wingfield to Wolsey (18 April 1520), *Letters and Papers, Foreign and Domestic: Henry VIII*, vol. 3, p. 266. On the same day, Wingfield wrote to Henry saying that Francis would like to receive the Order of the Garter as it had been suggested that they exchange their orders of chivalry. This letter also describes Francis boar hunting and hawking (pp. 265–66).

[37] The first gift armour was the 'Burgundian Bard', probably made in 1510 by Guillem Margot, a Flemish armourer (Royal Armouries, VI.6–12). Embossed with Burgundian devices, including the pomegranate for Katherine of Aragon, it could have been used in tournament processions. The second was an embossed parade armour influenced by and decorated with rich textiles, of which the 'Horned Helmet' alone survives (Royal Armouries, IV.22), made by Konrad Seusenhofer in 1514. It may originally have had alternate pieces for different forms of tournament combat. An examination of the six surviving complete armours of Henry VIII shows him to have expanded from slender and athletic to large and stout. The earliest (1515)

vate armoury to produce fine quality armours exclusively for him. A master armourer headed the workshop which was furnished and financed by the crown. The salaried armourers were not free to take private commissions. This armoury, first established in Southwark, is now known as the Greenwich Workshop. It continued to operate until the English Civil War. The use of foreign armourers shifted away from the Milanese (for example, Filippo de Grampis and Giovanni Angelo de Littis in 1512) to Flemings and Germans by 1515.

We know exactly what Henry's physique was in 1520. He was twenty-eight years old, 1.88 metres in height and very athletic. Amazingly, a suit of armour has survived that fitted the king like a second skin. It is part of the original historic collection of the Royal Armouries,[38] and brings Henry VIII back to life better than any portrait (Figure 2). There is no chink in this armour, which completely encloses the body front and rear. It was made for fighting on foot in a tournament, with a variety of lethal staff-weapons against which a full-enclosing armour was a necessity. Even so, the armour is still 'tailored' in the latest fashions. This can be seen in the steel foot-defences called sabatons. Their broad shape around the toes follows the 'bear-paw' shoe that we can see in contemporary portraits. The large codpiece is also a fashion statement, not a boast. For close combat fighting, complete body protection was required, yet Henry still had to be able to able to bend his knees and arms, run and even roll over to avoid a blow. This armour is an amazing feat of engineering. All the parts lock together with internal turning joints. The helmet rotates on the collar which is bolted to the back and front of the cuirass (chest defence). The gauntlets and sabatons fit under and over the cuff- and ankle-defences, respectively. A fully articulated breech-piece encloses the rump. The armpits, the inner elbows and the rear of the knees have narrow lames, each linked to the next without a gap. Due to the subsequent weight of all these extra plates, it was very rare for an armour to completely enclose the body. This armour weights 42.6 kg, which is twice the weight of normal battle armour. Only a fit and strong man such as the young Henry VIII could have worn it.

---

    is a matching ensemble for the seventeen-year-old king and his horse, the 'silvered and engraved' armour having unusually extensive decoration. It was made by the armourers Guillem Margot and Peter Fevers and the decorator Paul van Vrelant, all of them from Flanders and enticed away from their patron, Maximilian I (Royal Armouries, II.5, VI.1–5).

[38] By Martin van Royne, English, Southwark, 1520 (Royal Armouries, II.6). See *Henry VIII: Arms and the Man*, pp. 114–18.

A curious fact is that the armour was not quite finished. The right neck-guard has not been fitted and the armour was described as still being 'black from the hammer' a century later.[39] This puzzle is resolved by an examination of another armour. In the Royal Armouries Museum there are, strangely, two armours made for King Henry VIII that were both made for the king to wear at the Field of Cloth of Gold. Both were made in the Royal Workshops at Greenwich, and both are for foot combat, yet there are differences. One armour, already mentioned, completely encloses the body, front and rear. The other is distinguished by a tonlet (deep skirt) and a great basinet helmet (Figure 3).[40] This armour shows signs of being hastily assembled, using elements from several earlier armours drawn from store. The basinet, for example, bears the marks of the Italian Giovanni Antonio Missaglia of Milan, showing that it was an old helmet that has been re-used to make up this armour. The leg-harness has spur slots at the heel for cavalry use, yet the armour did not need spurs as Henry was fighting on foot. The etched decoration is lovely and includes a representation of the collar of the Order of the Garter and the Garter itself below the left knee. On either side of the helmet and both shoulder-defences are etched St George and the Virgin and Child, respectively, as tutelary guardians. This armour evidently is made up of disparate pieces quickly put together and decorated; why?

Of the two armours made in 1520 for Henry VIII to wear at the Field of Cloth of Gold tournament, it seems that one was unfinished and the other was hurriedly put together. The first, fully enclosing armour was for fighting within an enclosure with a staff weapon. The other was for fighting on foot over a barrier with a heavy (pesaunt) sword or a two-handed sword. Why did Henry VIII have two different armours for foot combat? The answer is due to the change of rules by Francis I. If Henry wished to fight with the heavy sword that he favoured, then the foot combat would now need to be fought over the barrier wearing armour and weapons that kept the combatants at distance. Henry's armourers managed, in only three months, to produce a second armour with lovely etched decoration that was also originally gilt. Henry must have still looked magnificent.

[39] See *Henry VIII: Arms and the Man*, p. 116.
[40] By Martin van Royne, English, Southwark, with Italian and Flemish components, 1520 (Royal Armouries, II.7). See *Henry VIII: Arms and the Man*, pp. 121–27.

The Two Kings Engage in Combat

Although the general plan was adhered to, the course of events could not be controlled. These were not theatrical performances, despite the costumes that were at times allegorical with complexity of literary allusion. The judges and heralds ensured that real scores were kept, and prizes awarded for the best combatants. Despite the efforts of the advisors of each court, no one could control the behaviour of the kings themselves. It will be seen that they were a joyously disruptive influence on the entire elaborate proceedings. For them, the tournament was real sport.

The chronicle accounts of Fleuranges are revealing, as he was with the French royal party. His account begins with the preparations for the tournament and a description of the setting, describing in particular the cloth-of-gold tents. His eyewitness account of the initial meeting of the two kings describes the accompanying retinue including the 300 archers and Swiss Guard led by himself.[41] His lively account describes the two kings embracing each other whilst still on horseback, although Henry's horse tripped at that moment despite being held still by a lackey.[42] Stationed with his guard by the pavilion, Fleuranges gives a sympathetic description of Henry VIII, who starts to read aloud the declaration and articles of the forthcoming tournament that describe himself as king of England and France, then stops and spontaneously declares that, in the presence of Francis, he will not claim the latter title.[43]

Fleuranges is a good source for the actual behaviour of the two kings towards each other and their sense of play and desire to enjoy each other's company despite all the careful protocol. An example of this is Francis laughing loudly (*fort marry*) and getting up early one day and – taking only the first three servants he saw – quickly mounting an unbarded horse, riding right into Guînes and breaking into the king's bedchamber, rousing Henry. This act of camaraderie was warmly received by Henry, who played along, declaring it a good joke and claiming Francis as his prisoner. Still in bed, Henry then

---

[41] 'Histoire des choses mémorables advenues du reigne de Louis XII et François Ier', p. 283: *et y etoient trois cens archers du roy de France et les Suisses que l'Aventureux menoit.*

[42] 'Histoire des choses mémorables advenues du reigne de Louis XII et François Ier', p. 283: *et se vindrent embrasser tout à cheval et se fisrent merveilleusement bon visage; et broncha le cheval du roy d'Angleterre en embrassant le roy de France et chacun avoit son laquais, qui prindrent les chevaulx.*

[43] 'Histoire des choses mémorables advenues du reigne de Louis XII et François Ier', p. 283: '*Je ne le mettray point puisque vous estes ici, car je mentirois*'. Et dict: *Je, Henry, roy d'Angleterre*'.

impulsively undid a necklace he was wearing and presented it to Francis to wear that day as a gage. Francis responded with a reciprocal gift of his bracelet for love of him which he attached to Henry's wrist. Declining breakfast, as he had to prepare for the morning jousts, Francis speedily returned to Ardres. This episode caused more than mild consternation. Indeed, Fleuranges himself rebuked the king on his return, telling him that he was mad to have done this. However, both kings clearly delighted in each other's company even before the official sport of the tournament was to begin. They absolutely trusted each other, which boded well for the tournament at which they were brothers in arms. The next morning, Henry played the same joke on Francis, also with gift exchanges.

Another revealing anecdote told by Fleuranges shows the physicality of the two kings and their private and personal engagement. One day, after the jousts, entertainment was provided. The kings and queens watched wrestling between French and English teams (the English won) followed by an archery contest with the longbow. Fleuranges was surprised that Henry took part himself and that he was an extraordinarily proficient archer – archery was not considered an aristocratic sport.[44] The kings then retired to a pavilion and took refreshments. Suddenly, Henry grasped Francis round the neck and challenged him to an impromptu wrestling match. Francis, an excellent wrestler, readily responded and swiftly threw Henry to the ground. This was against all protocol and clearly worried both courts. Henry wanted to continue, but both kings were stopped, and they all went to dinner.[45]

Fleuranges describes the jousts and tourneys in general terms without giving details of the outcome of combats, although he does mention himself taking part. It is Edward Hall who describes Fleuranges and his team of twelve as answerers taking part in the jousts against the kings' team.[46] The most interesting and significant combat by Fleuranges was during the tourneys with swords on Thursday 21 June, 'all well and warlike horsed and armed' with field armours and wearing armets. The two 'noble kings' were ready and each

---

[44] 'Histoire des choses mémorables advenues du reigne de Louis XII et François Ier', p. 284: *apres allèrent tirer à l'arc et le roy d'Angleterre lui-même, qui est un merveilleusement bon archer et fort; et le faisoit bon veoir.*

[45] 'Histoire des choses mémorables advenues du reigne de Louis XII et François Ier', pp. 284–85: *le roy d'Angleterre prist le roy de France par le collet, e luy dict 'Mon Frere, je veulx luiter avecques vous' et lui donna une attrape ou deux, et le roy de France qui est un fort bon luiteur, lui donna un tour et le jetta par terre et luy donna un merveilleux sault.*

[46] *Hall's Chronicle*, pp. 614–15: *then began the rushing of spears: the king of England this day ran so freshly and so many courses that one of his best coursers was dead that night.*

of them encountered one man of arms: the French king the earl of Devonshire, the king of England 'Monsire Florenges'. The king of England 'bare back Monsire Fleuranges and broke his pauldron and him disarmed'.[47] Henry demonstrated considerable physical force in breaking Fleuranges's shoulder defence, using a high and difficult sword-blow.

There is an armour attributed to Fleuranges in the Musée de l'Armée (Figure 4).[48] It is likely that Henry sent Fleuranges this armour in recompense and memory of his victory over the Frenchman. It is an early product of the royal armour workshop founded by Henry VIII in 1511 and is datable to 1525. As this armoury was founded by the king to make armours exclusively by his own personal command, it was not possible for any other person to order an armour. This armour would therefore be a personal gift from Henry VIII as only he commissioned armours from his workshop. This is the only English Greenwich armour in a French public collection.

A technical feature concerns the unique construction of the English pauldron. The usual articulation of the various lames comprising a pauldron by French, German or Italian armourers is achieved by a combination of sliding rivets and internal leathers. However, the English pauldron is articulated only on internal leathers, a feature not found elsewhere. The intention is to give greater flexibility of movement, particularly to a high-held sword which might have given an advantage to Henry in that famous combat. This unique feature would be an added incentive to give this armour to Fleuranges as a demonstration of English technical ability.

Conclusion

King Francis I of France and King Henry VIII of England met for the first time at the Field of Cloth of Gold. These two young kings were curious about each other and wanted to impress with their strength in an actual physical way. Their court advisors sought to surround them with carefully choreographed ceremonial and allegorical settings, which was somewhat confounded by the behaviour of Henry and Francis, whose informal encounters show a real friendship in those two weeks in June 1520.

---

[47] *Hall's Chronicle*, pp. 617–18.

[48] Paris, Musée de l'Armée, G.46, H.57. See *D'Azincourt à Marignan*, ed. Leduc, Leluc and Renaudeau, p. 237. The height of the armour, which is missing its sabatons, is 178 cm. The provenance is strong as the armour comes from the armoury at the castle of Sedan, the family seat of the dukes of Bouillon. Fleuranges was duke of Bouillon and was born at Sedan.

There are only two surviving armours, both of King Henry VIII, that are known to have been worn at the Field of Cloth of Gold. No other arms and armour of the kings have survived. The gift armour from Henry to Fleuranges has a good provenance. A study of archival sources, however, does allow an interpretation of the royal weapons and armour used at the tournament. The forms of combat undertaken by both kings can be reconstructed. As brothers in arms, they fully took part in every form of the combats: jousts, tourneys and foot combats. All these different combats required strength, agility and stamina. Henry VIII and Francis I had a keen interest in the latest technology of arms and armour. There is a joyous interplay between the two kings who displayed a delight in each other's company and revelled in the sport.

Fig. 1. Engraving of *The Field of the Cloth of Gold*, British, 1771–99. Leeds, Royal Armouries, I.224.

Fig. 2. Armour for the foot combat of Henry VIII, made in the royal workshop by the master armourer Martin van Royne. English, Southwark, 1520. Leeds, Royal Armouries, II.6.

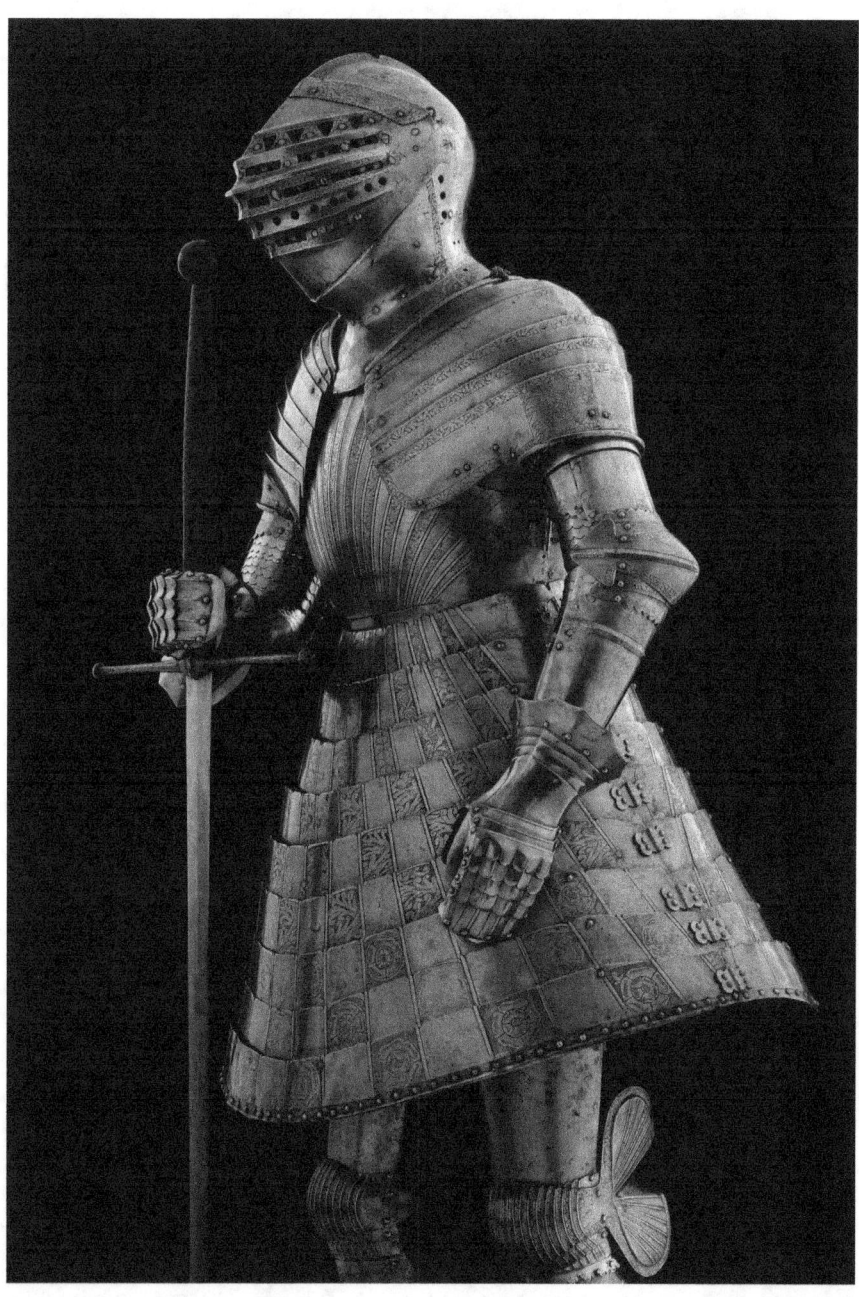

Fig. 3. Armour for the foot combat of Henry VIII, assembled in the royal workshop at Southwark by the master armourer Martin van Royne. English with Italian and Flemish components, 1520. Leeds, Royal Armouries, II.7.

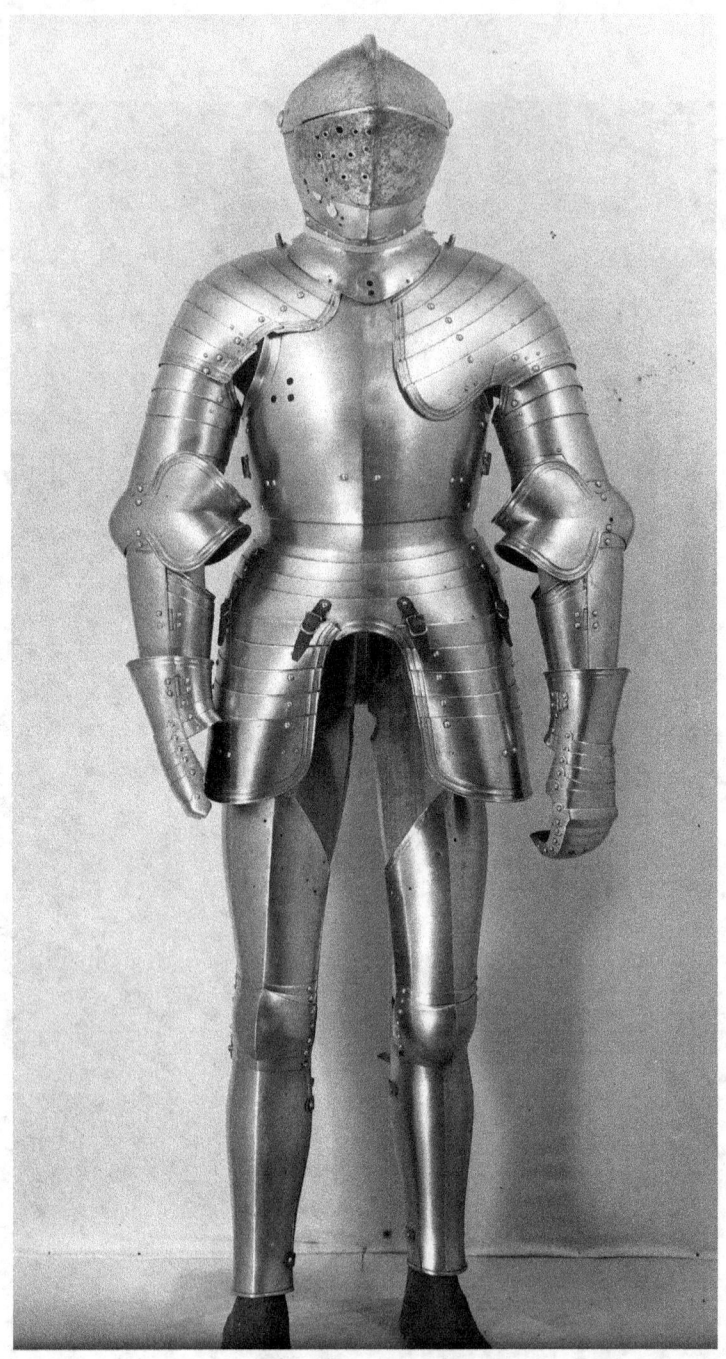

Fig. 4. Armour of Robert III de La Marck, lord of Fleuranges, duke of Bouillon and lord of Sedan, by master armourer Martin van Royne. English, Southwark, 1525 (Paris, Musée de l'Armée, G.46, H.57). The missing armet (H.47) was later identified and reunited with the armour, but it is not the one shown here.

Appendix 1:
Calendar of the Royal Combats at the Field of Cloth of Gold, June 1520[1]

Monday 4 June
Henry VIII arrived in Guînes at a new temporary palace, complete with towered foregate and gilt classical-style fountain and pillar as an admirable frontage. It also included a galleried passage to Guînes Castle for additional lodging for the king and his household. Some of the accompanying nobles were lodged in the palace and others in tents. Meanwhile Francis I had arrived at Ardres, a similarly small town that could not accommodate all, and many were likewise in tents and temporary pavilions. The French king had temporary lodgings erected for himself within the territory of an old castle outside Ardres which comprised a mast-supported pavilion complete with ornamentation of starry heavens and surrounded by yew bushes for a green-garden effect.

Tuesday 5 June
Henry's court went from Guînes to Ardres in an elaborate procession led by Cardinal Wolsey. This event is portrayed on the façade of Hôtel de Bourgtheroulde, Rouen.

Wednesday 6 June
Francis's court went from Ardres to Guînes in a reciprocal visit led by Cardinal Adrian Gouffier de Boissy and his brother Guillaume Gouffier, Admiral Bonnivet. This event is also depicted in the Rouen bas-reliefs.

Thursday 7 June
The two kings met for the first time. Each king, lavishly dressed in cloth of silver and damasked cloth of gold, departed from his own lodgings, timed to meet at the same moment in front of a cloth of gold pavilion that had been set up in the Vale of Andren. They were both accompanied by equally lavishly dressed courtiers and footmen.
 Neither king wore any arms or armour. However, Henry was preceded by Thomas Grey, marquess of Dorset, bearing the king's sword of state, and

---

[1] It is not easy to establish the actual dates and sequence of events at the Field of Cloth of Gold. The primary sources show some confusion and are sometimes contradictory. This appendix is a calendar of the probable sequence of events. The quotations are from Edward Hall (*Hall's Chronicle*, pp. 600–20), with the calendar of events corrected as Hall confused some dates.

Francis was preceded by Charles III, duke of Bourbon, Grand Constable of France (*Grand Connétable de France*), bearing the French sword of state. This was planned, but the way the French sword was carried caused a minor incident. Both should have been carried upwards in their scabbards. However, the French sword was out of the scabbard, with blade visible. 'When it was perceived that the Franch king's sword was borne naked, then the king of England commanded the lorde marques Dorset to drawe out the sword of estate and bear it up naked in presence, which was so done'.[2] This shows the recognised symbolism of the sword, representing the military strength of the monarchy; but a sword carried blade upwards and out of the scabbard was not a recognised gesture of peace in a parade. In the Middle Ages, ceremonial swords called 'bearing swords' were similarly carried in entries to cities.

In a flurry of trumpets, sackbuts and clarions and watched by both courts, the two kings descended to the valley and greeted each other, dismounted and embraced each other. It seems clear that, despite the mistrust of the courtiers, the two young kings immediately engaged with each other with warm friendship: 'After few words, these two noble kings went together into the riche tente of cloth of gold that there was set on the ground for such purpose, thus arm in arm went the French king Frances [*sic*] the first of France and Henry the eight [*sic*] king of England and of France, together passing with communication.' A banquet was served in the tent which was strewn with cushions and Turkish carpets. Each king then departed to his own lodgings.

Friday 8 June
The Tree of Honour was erected at the tournament field, an open area between Ardres and Guînes. The Tree combined and entwined hawthorn for England (*aubespine*) and raspberry (*framboisier*) for France. It was placed on an artificial hill covered with green damask to give the illusion of a mountain. Leaves of green damask, branches, boughs and even withered leaves were made of cloth of gold together with flowers and fruit, all on a timber frame. By this tree were stationed the heralds, all within green damask railings.

The tiltyard was 900 feet long by 320 feet in diameter with a ditch and railings around except at the entrances. Scaffolds with raised seating were set

---

[2] *Hall's Chronicle*, p. 610. The extant French sword of state is called *Joyeuse*, and reputed to be the sword of Charlemagne. *Joyeuse* was the badge of office of the *Grand Connétable de France*. It was altered over its time of use as a coronation sword and is a composite of elements dating from the eleventh to the thirteenth centuries (Paris, Musée du Louvre, inv. no. 84). It is of substantial size. The overall length is 105 cm, of which the blade is 82.8 cm. There is no surviving English sword of state of the early sixteenth century.

around for the noble spectators, with the queen of England on the one side and the queen of France on the other. These were decorated with rich tapestries. Two tents for each king were set up at the entrances. These were so that the kings could be dressed in their armour and rest between combats.

Saturday 9 June
The kings led a procession of knights around the lists preceded by the shields of each king on which were depicted the coat of arms of each king, each within their orders of chivalry, Garter and St Michael. These were hung high and visible, indicating the kings as challengers or joint holders of the tournament. Joining the two kings as challengers were a mixture of French and English nobility. Their coats of arms were hung on the Tree of Honour together with the text of the challenge. These were verified by the chief herald, the King of Arms.

Sunday 10 June
Francis visited the English queen at Guînes, and Henry visited the French queen at Ardres.

Monday 11 June: Jousts
The tournament began with jousting over a barrier (tilting). The queens were seated. The kings in full armour, and their four fellow challengers (three English and one French) arrived on horseback and paraded around the tiltyard. They were all parti-coloured in white on the left and gold and russet on the right as a unifying livery. The parade also included attendants on foot, similarly liveried.

A theatrical element was represented on the horse caparisons. It is particularly interesting in that a literary game was played out over several days. The French king's caparison, or bard, was decorated with a different symbolic image each day that spelled out a phrase elaborated over the duration of the tournament. This was for the amusement of the court spectators. It underpins the fact that this tournament, although public, was a lavish entertainment for educated nobility. For example, on the first day, an image of a curled raven feather (pen) signifying the pain of a raven (called a corbin), which included the word cor for heart. It apparently spelled out the phrase 'a heart fastened in pain endless' (this is similar to the modern amusement of a cryptic crossword).

The first answerer was Charles, duke of Alençon, who faced the French king, his brother-in-law. Francis 'did valiantly and broke many spears mightely'. Although this summary is terse, it would have been clearly understood by a contemporary audience that this was a joust of peace over the barrier (a type of joust called tilting after the tilt barrier that separated them), since the aim was to shatter the lance, unlike the joust of war where the aim was to unhorse, using a solid lance. Francis ran all three designated courses and won all of them.

The second answerer was a Frenchman, 'Monsire Graundeuile', who faced the English king. Henry fought 'with great vigour, so that the spears broke in the king's hand to the vamplate all to shivers'. Henry won the first course, but in a better manner than Francis, as his blow was so powerful that his lance shattered all the way to his vamplate (hand-guard), with the risk of injury to himself with splinters (*shivers*). On his second course, Henry struck Graundeuile successfully on his helm, which headshot carried the highest number of points. The blow was so forceful that the hinge securing Graundeuile's helm to his breastplate was broken. Graundeuile could not complete the third course, to Henry's annoyance.

Other courses were run successively by both challengers and answerers. It should have ended at that point, but the two kings enthusiastically wanted to compete again. 'Then ran again the two noble kings who did so valiantly that the beholders had great joy, after which courses the heralds cried the "disarmez" (disarm yourselves) and the trumpets sounded to lodging.'

Tuesday 12 June: Jousts
Tilting continued without the two kings.

Wednesday 13 June: Jousts
The tilting continued. The two kings appeared in full armour, and 'armed at all pieces, entered into the field right nobly apparelled'. The two kings and ten others comprised one team. Each ran separately against a knight of the opposing team of twelve drawn from both courts. 'The two kinges surmounted all the rest in prowess and valientness'. A second team of twelve faced that of the kings. Many courses were run by both kings. Trumpets sounded the end of the day and the kings departed to Guînes and Ardres.

Thursday 14 June: Jousts
'The people were come to behold the honour and to see the two kings, who all ready armed entered the field to receive and deliver all men of answer of jousts.' Again, the kings' team faced two other teams, one after another: 'They broke both their staves valiantly course after course, the encounter ceased not till they had furnished their five courses. Henry faced a strong gentleman named Raffe Broke and broke his spear and ran course after course till he had finished his courses right noble and like a prince of most valiance.'

In all these accounts, the costumes are described by Hall with their colour, material, design and ornament. There is always reverence to the queens and parading around the lists, sometimes confusingly called 'tilts' where they refer to the barriers and not to the combats of the same name.

Friday 15 June: Jousts

This day seems to have been pre-arranged as a highlight or culmination point, as both kings were dressed especially symbolically. Henry had ciphers of letters in pearls and gold wire spelling 'God my friend, my realm and I may'. Francis completed the puzzle of the phrase elaborated over days with an image of little books that was a play on the Latin words *liber* (book) and *libera me* (free me). The entire phrase was thus interpreted as 'heart fastened in pain endless, when she delivereth me not of bonds'. Curiously, Hall was actually not entirely sure of the interpretation 'whether it were so in all things or not I may not say'. It was possible that sometimes the meanings were so obscurely referenced that they were not understood by those outside of the court.

The first team to face the kings' team was Fleuranges and his team of twelve: 'then began the rushing of spears: the king of England this day ran so freshly and so many courses that one of his best coursers was dead that night'.

Saturday 16 June: no combats

Francis went to the castle of Guînes and met Henry in his privy chamber, 'welcomed in friendly and honourable manner'. Henry then left Francis there and went to Ardres. Each was received by the other's queen and had elaborate banquets and dancing. Henry dressed secretly in 'masker's apparrell' with others.

Sunday 17 June: no combats

Monday 18 June: no combats

The tournament was abandoned due to violent storms.

Tuesday 19 June: Jousting

The kings took part in full armour. The two kings ran against unnamed opponents: 'The king of England was ready and strake his horse with the spurs and so fiercely ran to the counter partie that his grandguard was lost with the great stroke that the king gave him: course after course the king lost none, but evermore his brake his spear and so noble ended his Jousts Royal, for this day ended the king's great challenge and of the king our sovereign lord's doings, all men there that him beheld reported his doings, (so valient were his feats) evermore in honour to be renowned'. Hall acknowledged that the French king 'on his part ran valiantly breaking spears eagerly and so well ended his challenge of jousts, that he ought to be spoken of'.

Wednesday 20 June: Tourneys
The two kings were as usual 'armed at all pieces'. Henry and his team had velvet and cloth of silver caparisons that were embroidered with a picture of an armed knight on a hill being mortally wounded by an arrow from a lady in a cloud with an inscription:'in love whoseo mounteth, passeith in peril'.

This was a tourney with swords only. The French and English kings ran side by side as brothers in arms.

Hall's account is not clear as to the form of the combats. No barriers are mentioned but this combat must have been a tourney course where pairs fought each other, since he does mention 'evermore two for two'. The kings fought well: 'they showed their vigours and strengths and so did nobely that their counter parties had non advantage'. Each fought four 'battles'. Henry then fought one 'battle' with 'Monsire Liskew', who presented him with his horse, 'which the king gentley received and for love incontinent mounted on him and there fought the 5th battle right valiently'.

Thursday 21 June: Tourneys
The combats were tourneys with swords again. The kings were again richly barded. Henry's horse had little mountains and branches of basil with the inscription 'break not these sweet herbes of the rich mount, doute for damage'. This was the combat in which Henry VIII disarmed Fleuranges and broke his pauldron.

Friday 22 June: Foot combats
Foot combats of two types were fought, at the barrier and within enclosed lists: 'The campe was set a barrier for to fight on foot'. There was also a temporary hall, embroidered with a rising sun and the motto *Dieu et mon droit*, for the knights to put on their armour. A line of men fought another team over a central barrier. They each had a 'punchion' spear for the first round and then swords: 'The two valiant kings … fought with such force that the fire sprang out of their armour'. The teams then faced each other over the barrier and threw light spears ('casting darts') at each other. This seems to have been an amusing interlude that was not regulated, as they 'mightily threw their spears the one to the other, ready or not ready'. The presence of the barrier precluded the need for armour for the lower limbs as all the blows were from the waist up. The culmination of the foot combat was with the two-handed sword. The two kings successfully fought the foot combat and 'safe in body and limbs, ended the battle for that day'.

Saturday 23 June: Foot combats

Tents, halls and pavilions were erected and even a chapel with a timber-frame and clad with richly embroidered tapestries and furniture and an altar. High mass was said by Cardinal Wolsey and both kings attended. Then a lavish banquet was held with the kings sitting side by side, each under their cloths of estate with their royal arms in one area and the queens in another.

In the afternoon, the kings 'put themselves in arms with their band and entered the field on foot before the barriers'. They fought the answerer team over the barriers on foot with various weapons. As with the tourney, Hall refers to these as 'battles': 'Thus the said Saturday was fully ended, and all men delivered of articles of jousts and all tourneys and battles on foot by the said two noble kings'.

Sunday 24 June

The tournament concluded with a banquet and masked entertainment, based on the Nine Worthies. Maskers were dressed as classical heroes (Hercules, Hector, Alexander, and Julius Caesar), biblical heroes (David, Joshua and Judas Maccabaeus), and Christian heroes (Charlemagne, Arthur and Godfrey of Bouillon). Each king with his band of maskers departed from Ardres and Guînes at the same time and went to each other's court. After the dinner there was dancing. The two kings met after and 'embrased and amiably together communed ... and for remembrance either to the other gave gifts. The king of England gave to the French king a necklace of jewels of precious stones called Balastes the Sanker furnished with great diamonds and pearls. The French king gave to the king of England a bracelet of precious stones, rich jewels and fayre, and so departe the said two noble kings the said 24th day of June, which was Sunday and Midsomerday.' This was the public presentation of the gifts that were privately exchanged when Francis surprised Henry in his bedchamber.

Appendix 2:
Articles for the Challenge: The Emprise[1]

1. In consequence of the numerous accidents to noblemen, sharp steel not to be used as in times past, but only arms for strength, agility and pastime.

2. The challenge to commence 11 June, and continue for a month, or so long as the two kings shall be together, when the said gentlemen will answer all comers with blunt lances in harness, with pieces of avantage *cramponées ou non cramponées*, without any fastening to the saddle that might prevent mounting or dismounting with ease. Each challenger to have eight courses, with middle-sized lances, or greater, if any of the comers prefer it.

3. The said gentlemen shall ride each one course in the open field with all comers, as many strokes to be given as the comers demand; great lances to be used and single-handed sharp swords, with blunt points, closing not allowed unless the comer desire it.

4. The said gentlemen shall give one encounter to all comers with blunt casting lances, and four strokes with blunted single-handed swords. With the double-handed swords, as many strokes shall be given as the judges think fit, but no closing allowed.

5. Harness with pieces of advantage, means with no head-piece but an armet; neither helm, demi-helm nor bassinet allowed.

6. The challengers shall send round heralds to declare the rules of the combat.

7. On 6 June, a tree shall be chosen, bearing the noble thorn entwined with raspberry, and on it shall be hung the shields of the challengers, and below them three escutcheons, black and grey, gold and tawny, and the last silver. Tablets, guarded by heralds, shall be hung below these for the names of the comers.

---

[1] *Letters and Papers, Foreign and Domestic, Henry VIII, Volume 3, 1519–1523*, ed. J. S. Brewer (London, 1867), 'June 1520', pp. 307–8, translation of *Lordonnance et ordre du tournoy joustes, & combat a pied et a cheval. Le tresdesire & plusque triumpant rencontre entreveue assemblee & visitation des treshaultz & tresexcellens princes les Roys de France & de Angleterre. Et des Roynes leurs compaignes. Et aultres princes et princesses* ... Printed by Jehan Lescaille (Paris, 1520).

Première Emprinse. Those who wish to run in the lists must touch the black and grey shield, and deliver their shield of arms to the herald, who shall write down their names, and how many courses they desire to run, and whether with great lances or middle sized.

Seconde Emprinse. Those who desire to enter for the courses in the field must touch the second shield.

Troisième Emprinse. Those who wish to fight at the barrier must touch the third.

Quatrième Emprinse. Those who desire more than one combat must enter their names in each tablet accordingly. If the judges decide that the challenger is worsted in any combat, he must give a gold token to the lady in whose service the comer fights, and vice versâ. Each gentleman shall fight in the order in which his name has been entered. Any one disarmed so that he cannot complete his courses must be content with what he has done for that day. If any of the challengers are ill or absent by order of their princes, the remainder shall choose a substitute. If the horse of a comer bolts from the lists, and yet runs the course, it shall be counted as a course. Also, if it happens that the horse bolts, it is but fair that the comer shall have a fresh start. If a challenger strikes or kills the horse of his opponent he shall not run again that day, without the ladies' leave. Any who have been once answered what they demanded, shall not make a second demand. Whoever strikes against the saddle of his opponent shall be disallowed two broken lances. All Sundays and feasts of the French and English churches shall be observed, by abstinence from running.

Index of Objects

This index lists armour, weapons, saddles, paintings, tapestries, statues and engravings in the collections of modern museums and art galleries. References to illustrations are in **bold**.

Bayeux, Musée de la Tapisserie
  Bayeux Tapestry   29, 42, 99

Berlin, Deutsches Historisches Museum
  W 1014 (great basinet)   162n
  W 1016 (armour)   211

Chantilly, Musée Condé
  4690 (portrait of Francis I of France)   212

Florence, Uffizi Gallery
  Valois Tapestries   179

Glasgow, Glasgow Museums
  Burrell Collection, 46.80 (tapestry)   **112**
  Burrell Collection, 21.10 (ivory mirror case)   **79**
  Burrell Collection, 45.486.1.b (stained glass panel)   **89**
  Burrell Collection, 2.131.b (vamplate)   **81**
  R. L. Scott Collection, E.1939.65.q.[5] (manifer)   **84**
  R. L. Scott Collection, E.1939.65.q.[6] (polder-mitton)   **87**

Leeds, Royal Armouries
  I.36 (portrait of Robert Radcliffe)   172n, **173**
  I.224 (engraving of Field of Cloth of Gold)   **225**
  II.5 (armour)   219
  II.6 (foot combat armour)   166, 219, **226**
  II.7 (tonlet armour)   162, 165, 220, **227**
  II.173 (armour)   163, **164**
  II.186 (tonlet armour)   166, **167**
  IV.22 (helmet)   218
  VI.1-5 (armour)   219
  VI.6-12 (armour)   218
  VI.94 (high saddle)   109-11, 190n
  VI.95 (low saddle)   113-15
  VII.550 (Brandon Lance)   214
  VII.1509 (pollaxe)   169, **170**
  VII.1510 (bec-de-corbin)   169, **170**
  IX.1217 (tournament sword)   172, **174**

London, National Portrait Gallery,
  4690 (portrait of Henry VIII of England)   213

London, Royal Armouries (Tower of London)
  VI.95 (saddle)   113-14

London, Royal Collection Trust
  RCIN 405794 (painting of Field of Cloth of Gold)   210

New York, Metropolitan Museum of Art
  04.3.274 (foot combat helmet)   162
  14.25.302 (pollaxe)   169
  14.25.465 (bec-de-corbin)   169
  14.25.548 (close helmet)   163
  29.158.37 (helmet for *Kolbenturnier*)   162
  40.135.3 (helmet for *Kolbenturnier*)   162

Nuremberg, Germanisches Nationalmuseum
  Pl. O. 3458 (relief of St George and the Dragon)   107
  W.676 (saddle)   112

Index of Objects

Paris, Musée de l'Armée
   G.117 (armour)   211
   G.178 (foot combat armour)   166
   G.46 (armour of Robert de Fleuranges)   223, **228**
   H.47 (armet)   228
   H.57 (armet)   **228**

Paris, Musée du Louvre
   84 (French sword of state)   230
   3256 (portrait of Francis I of France)   212

Philadelphia, Philadelphia Museum of Art
   1977-167-37 (foot combat armour)   166
   1977-167-128 (close helmet)   163

Verona, Museo Civico di Castelvecchio
   statue of Cangrande I della Scala   103, **104**
   statue of Mastino II della Scala   105–8, **106**

Vienna, Albertina
   DG1926/760 (print of St George and the Dragon)   115n

Vienna, Hofjagd- und Rüstkammer
   B 147 (partial armour)   211

Vienna, Kunsthistorisches Museum
   A 64 (Hungarian saddle)   113n
   A 107 (armour)   200n
   B 33 (tonlet armour)   165
   B 64 (low saddle)   117–18, **117**
   B 71 (foot combat armour)   162, 165
   HJRK A 638 (tonlet armour)   165
   S I (armour for *Gestech*)   197

Washington, D.C., National Gallery of Art
   1966.11 (painting of St George and the Dragon)   115

Index of Manuscripts

References to illustrations are in **bold**.

Berkeley, Berkeley Castle Archives
  Muniment D1/1/30   86

Brussels, KBR (Bibliothèque royale de Belgique/Koninklijke Bibliotheek van België)
  9547   **128, 129**

Cambridge, Gonville & Caius College Library
  424/448   91

Durham, University Library
  Durham Cathedral Muniments   94

Edinburgh, Edinburgh University Library
  83   92

Heidelberg, Universitätsbibliothek
  Pal.germ.848 (Codex Manesse)   41, 101, **102**

Kew, National Archives
  C 66/480/7   95
  C 145/278/37   85
  C 145/296/10   94
  DL 28/1   85, 90, 92, 93, 95, 96
  E 30/817A   208
  E 36/278   83
  E 101/29/38   82, 83, 95
  E 101/338/11   81, 82, 90, 94
  E 101/397/10   82, 85
  E 136/77/4   85, 90, 91, 94, 96
  E 154/1/11B   80, 94, 95
  E 163/6/13   85, 86, 96
  E 361/6/11d   86, 91
  SC 8/268/13392   92

Koblenz, Landeshauptarchiv
  1 C 1 (Codex Balduini Trevirensis)   **79**

Leeds, Royal Armouries Library
  0035 (I.35)   93

Lille, Bibliothèque universitaire
  104   152

London, British Library
  Add.21357   96
  Add.46919   90
  Add.74326 (Sherborne Missal)   **81**
  Cotton Nero D. IX   **88**, 181
  Harley 69   176
  Harley 2358   78
  Harley 4375   168, 179, 180
  Sloane Charter XXXI 2   77, 93

London, College of Arms
  M.6   179, 181

London, Lambeth Palace Library
  Register of Archbishop Arundel, 2   77, 96
  Register of Archbishop Whittlesey, VA6   77

London, London Metropolitan Archives
  Plea & Memoranda Rolls   91, 93
  Letter-Books   91

London, Westminster Abbey
  Muniment 12163   86

Los Angeles, J. Paul Getty Museum
  114 (2016.7)   168, 181

Index of Manuscripts

Mons, Archives de l'État
    Chartrier des archives de la ville 93

Munich, Bayerische Staatsbibliothek
    Cod.icon. 27(1) 177, 180
    Cod.icon. 393 184
    Cod.icon. 398 201
    Rar. 2195 203

New York, Pierpont Morgan Library
    M.638 (Maciejowski Bible) 100
    M.775 86, 179

Nottingham, Nottingham University Library
    Mi I 40 84, 93

Oxford, Bodleian Library
    Ashmole 845 176
    Ashmole III.6 176
    Eng.hist. b.229 84

Paris, Bibliothèque de l'Arsenal
    5208 143

Paris, Bibliothèque nationale de France
    fr.1997 86, 93
    fr.2695 217
    fr.12572 143, **150, 151**
    fr.16830 133, **134**
    latin 16928 94
    portugais 5 101, 107–8, 115

York, Borthwick Institute
    Archbishops' Registers 77

York, York Minster Archives
    L1/17/2 94

General Index

References to illustrations are in **bold**.

ahlspiess *see* pollaxes
Aimon de Varennes, poet 141
Albrecht von Rapperswil **102**
Alonso, bishop of Burgos 97
Anthony von Yfan, lord of Ivano 200–1
Anthony, Great Bastard of Burgundy 59, 141
Antoine de la Sale, author:
   Jehan de Saintré 127–30, **128–29**, 133, 141–42, 148–49
Antonio de Caldonazo *see* Anthony von Yfan
Appellants, Lords 67, 68, 74, 75, 76
Aquitaine 70
Ardres 210, 216, 229–35
armet *see* helmets
armour (harness) 77–97, 162, 165, 166, 218–20, 223, **226, 227**
  breastplate 82–83, 94, 162, 165
  couter (elbow defence) 83
  cuirass 109, 161, 162, 165, 166, 217–18, 219
  gauntlet 83, 86, 177, 217–19
  horse armour 109, 218n, 219n
  legharness 93
  manifer 83–85, **84**
  pauldron 86, 222–23, 234
  piece (metal plate) 80, 90, 94, 217–19, 236
  plates 81–83, 94, 96, 165, 166, 190, 214
  poitrine 82
  polder-mitton 85–88, **87**
  sabatons 219, 223
  storage and upkeep 95
  thigh-defences 118, 166
  tonlet armour 162, 165–66, 217, 220
  vambrace 83, 85–86
armourers 80, 82–83, 91–92, 94, 218–23, 226–28

Arthurian literature 25–26, 50, 148, 204
Arthurian tournaments 43, 148, 204
Arundel, Sir William 75
Augsburg, judicial duel (1409) 184
Austria 25n, 29, 34, 192, 200
axe-hammers *see* pollaxes

Baldwin V, count of Hainaut 59
Bamberg Horseman 100
basinet *see* helmets
Bayeux Tapestry 29, 42, 99–100
Beauchamp Pageant 169, 171, 180n
Beauchamp, Richard, earl of Warwick 169, 171
Beaufort, Thomas, knight 85
bec-de-corbin see pollaxes
behourd see bûhurt
Bergavenny, William Baron 77, 96
Bernhard II, duke of Carinthia 34
bevor *see* helmets
Boucicaut, Jean Le Maingre, marshal of France 46, 61, 148n
Bouillon 135, 209, 223n, 228, 235
Brandon, Charles, duke of Suffolk 214
Brascha, Erasmus 198
Braybrooke, Sir Gerard 75
Bromyard, John, friar 97
Brut Chronicle 66fn, 70fn, 72
bûhurt 30–31, 35
Burgersh, Bartholomew Lord 77
Burgkmair, Hans the Younger, artist 191, 193
Burgundy 47, 49, 60, 70, 165, 196, 218n
  influence on Maximilian I 203–7
  pas d'armes 120–38, 139–54
Burley, Sir Simon 67, 85

Caernarfon, tournament (1284) 65
Calais 208

Cangrande I della Scala   103, **104**
Carinthia   29, 34
caparisons   124–26, 128, 216, 231, 234
Castlemilk   90
Chalon-sur-Saône   146
Châlons-sur-Marne, jousts (1455)   135
chapitres   59, 123–26, 128, 130–35, 147, 152n
Charles, duke of Alençon   231
Charles III, duke of Bourbon   230
Charles the Bold, duke of
 Burgundy   124, 126, 141, 204
Charles VI, king of France   48–49
Charles VII, king of France   135, 211n
Charles, duke of Orléans   133
Charny *see* Geoffrey (Geoffroi) de
 Charny
Chastellain, Georges, author   122n
Chieregati, Leonello   197, 198
Chrétien de Troyes   25, 46, 50, 51–53
Christian I, elector of Saxony   **167**
Claude de Vaudrey   165
Cluj-Napoca   113n
coats of arms *see* crests *and* heraldry
Codex Balduini Trevirensis   **79**
Codex Manesse   40, 101, **102**, 103
Conrad IV, king of Germany   27
Conrad of Hohenstaufen   24
Contarini, Zaccharia   195, 196, 197
Cornwall, Sir John   96
coronels   69, 80–83, 95–96, 109–110, 115,
 168–69, 188, 214
Courtenay, Sir Peter   68
crests   22, 31–32, 57, 126, 135, 149

Dallingridge, Sir Edward   75
dancing   53, 66, 149n, 195, 203, 212, 233,
 235
David II, king of Scotland   65
Della Scala *see* Cangrande I della Scala
 and Mastino II della Scala
Devereux, Sir John   68
Díaz de Gámez, Gutierre   50–51, 55
Diepold, margrave of Vohburg   36, 41
Dietmar von Liechtenstein   41
Dounton, John, keeper of armour   85,
 91–92

Dover Castle   81–82, 83, 95
Duarte, king of Portugal   107, 108n, 115
Dunstable, tournament (1309)   64, 95
dwarves   152n, 153

Edward I, king of England   64–65
Edward II, king of England   63, 64–65
Edward III, king of England   64–66,
 73, 76
 armour   80–81, 82, 94
Edward the Black Prince   83, 90
Elizabeth I, queen of England   180, 182
emprises   120, 126–28, 129, 131, 236–37
Enguerran de Monstrelet   126, 130
entrepreneurs   120–38, 143, 146–47, 149
Ernst von Braunschweig   **118**

Falkirk, tournament (1302)   65
Fastnacht tournaments *see* Shrovetide
 tournaments
Fellbrigg, Sir Simon   75
Ferdinand II, archduke of Tirol   165
Field of Cloth of Gold (1520)   56, 60,
 208–25, **225**, 229–37
 armour   165, 218–20, **226–28**
 archery   222
 calendar of events   229–35
 emprises   236–37
 foot combat   176, 215, 220, 234–35
 jousts   231–33
 planning   214–16
 tourneys   234
 weapons   216–17
 wrestling   222
Fille du comte de Ponthieu, romance   142
Fleuranges, Robert III de La Marck,
 lord of   209–10, 211, 221–23, 228, 233
foot combat   155–84, 215, 234–35
 armour   161–66, **164**, **167**, 218–20, **226,**
 227
 barriers   155, 159, 174, 176–81, 183,
 234–35
 enclosures   178–81
 helmets   161–65, **164**
 judges   180–81
 prizes   177–78

rules 175–78
weapons 166–75, 217–18
Francis I, king of France 56, 208–37
 armour 211n
 physique 211–13
 weapons 217–18
Frederick II, Holy Roman emperor 27
Frederick II, duke of Swabia 24
Freiburg im Breisgau, diet (1497) 198
Friesach, tournament 29, 33, 34–35, 36–40, 41–42
Froben Christoph von Zimmern *see* Zimmern
Froissart, Jean, chronicler 46, 48–49, 59, 68–69, 70, 74
Fuchs, Georg 194
Fuchs, Wenceslaus 194

Garter, Order 65, 66, 68, 70–71, 72–73, 74, 76, 220
Gaspare de Sanseverino 197
Gaston IV, count of Foix 122n, 125, 135, 136,
Gaveston, Piers, earl of Cornwall 64
Geoffrey (Geoffroi) de Charny, author 50, 54, 58, 185–86
George, saint 65, 107, 114, 115, 220
Gerard of Tourney, armourer 80–81, 82, 83–84
Gestech, form of joust 116–17, 187–90, 199
 Deutschgestech 188, 204
 Gestech im Beinharnisch 189–91
 Hohenzeuggestech 112–13, 189–91
 Welschgestech 189, 204
Gheeraerts the Younger, Marcus, artist **173**
Gislebert of Mons, chronicler 23
Giustinian, Sebastian 212–13
Godfrey of Bouillon 135, 235
Golden Fleece, order 147, 200,
Gouffier, Guillaume, lord of Bonnivet 211, 215, 217, 229
Gouffier de Boissy, Adrian, cardinal 210, 229
Gournay/Ressons, tourney (1168) 59

Grey, Thomas, marquess of Dorset 229
Guillaume du Bellay, author 209
Guînes 210, 216, 229–35

Hadamar von Kuenring 38
Hainaut 23, 26–27, 59, 69, 70, 82, 90
Hall in Tirol, tournament (1502) 196
Hall, Edward, chronicler 209, 212, 215, 222
harness *see* armour
Hartmann von Aue, poet 25, 33–34, 42
Heilbronn, tournament (1481) 60
Heinrich I, duke of Anhalt 40
Heinrich IV of Andechs, margrave of Istria 34, 37
Heinrich von Lienz 41
helmets 42, 50, 69, 84–85, **89**, 90–91, 96, 161, 177
 ancient helmets 22
 armet 163, **228**, 236
 basinet 94, 96, 162–65, 217–18, 220
 close helmet 162–65
 conical helmet 42
 frog-mouthed helmet 188, 214
 helmet for *Kolbenturnier* 162n
 padded helmet 156
 reinforces (bevor) 90–91, **91**
 sallet 90, 190
 visors 132, 149, 162–63, 214
Henry III, king of Castile 55
Henry II, king of England 63, 64
Henry III, king of England 63, 64–65
Henry IV, king of England *see* Henry, earl of Derby
Henry V, king of England 113–14
Henry VIII, king of England:
 armours 162, 165, 166, 218–20, 223, **226, 227**
 at Field of Cloth of Gold 56, 176, 208–37
 physique 212–13, 219
 weapons 217–18
Henry I, king of Germany 21
Henry (VII), king of Germany 27
Henry, duke of Cornwall 215n
Henry, archbishop of York 94
Henry, duke of Lancaster 96–97

Henry of Laon, author 50, 55
Henry, earl of Derby (later King Henry IV) 85, 91–92, 95, 96
Henry Frederick, prince of Wales 183
heraldry 27, 31–32, 42–43, 51, 126, 127, 142, 153, 182; *see also* crests
heralds and kings of arms 33n, 51, 120, 126, 129, 131, 136, 144–45, 217, 231, 237
    Charolais Herald 132, **134**
    Clarencieux King of Arms 216
    Gelre Herald 90
    Jerusalem Herald 21–22
    Orléans King of Arms 216
    Toison d'Or King of Arms 131, 147
Histoire de Guillaume le Maréchal 23, 47–48, 54
History of William Marshal see *Histoire de Guillaume le Maréchal*
Holland, John, earl of Huntingdon 58–59, 68
honour 44–61, 72–73, 80, 124, 145, 147–48, 151, 152n, 206, 232–33
horses 30–33, 40, 41–42, 69, 72, 93, 97, 99–104, 108–11, 115, 118, 144, 189–90, 212, 216, 219n, 221, 234, 237
    as booty 42, 47, 51, 54
    injuries 51, 54
    see also caparisons *and* saddles
Hugh III, duke of Burgundy 47
Hungary 113–15

Injuries in tournaments 25n, 30, 35, 39–40, 50, 70, 80, 145, 163, 172n, 214, 232
Innsbruck 193–98
    armourers 200n
    tournament (1498) 197
    tournament (1500) 194–95
    tournaments (1502) 193, 195–96
Isabel of Bavaria, queen of France 48–49
Jacquemart de Hesdin, artist 105, 107
Jacques de Lalaing, author 130–31, 133, 135–37, 139–41, 143–47, 149, 152
James VI and I, king of Scotland and England 183

Jean d'Avanchier 144
Jean de Boniface 144, 149
Jean de Wavrin 143n
Jehan d'Avennes 142–54, **150–51**
Jeu de la Hache, manual 161
Jews 42
John, king of England 27, 63, 64, 65
John II, king of France 54, 65
John of Gaunt, duke of Lancaster 70
joust 46, 50–51, 55, 56, 69–70, **79, 88, 102**, 120, 186–81, 199, 213–14, 231–33
    armour 77–98
    Joust Royal 213–14, 233
    lances 80–82
    origins 33–34
    prizes 66, 70
    saddle 92–93, 104–19
    see also Gestech and *Rennen*

Kassel, tournament (1596) 177, 180
Katzelsdorf, tournament 29, 36–37, 38
kings of arms *see* heralds and kings of arms
Klosterneuburg, tournament 29
Kolbenturnier see tourney
Konrad von Winterstetten, imperial butler 27
Konrad von Würzburg, poet 27

Lancelot-Grail Cycle 45
lances:
    Brandon Lance 214
    grapper or grate 80–83
    jousting lance 46, 51, 58, 69, 78–82, **81**, 85–86, 97, 111, 163, 187–91, 214, 231–32
    lancehead 95–96
    lance-rest 86
    rebated (blunted) lance 46
    storage 214
    tourney lance 30–31, 34, 35–39, 41, 99–101, 103, 105, 108, 115
    transport 31
    vamplate 80, **81**, 82–83, 85, 95, 191, 214, 232
    see also coronels
La Marche *see* Olivier de La Marche

Le Bel, Jean, chronicler 97
Le Fèvre de Saint-Rémy, Jean,
    herald 130, 131, 132, 137
Leopold V, duke of Austria 25n
Leopold VI, duke of Austria 34, 36–37, 41
Libro di giusto 88
Lisbon, tournament (1428) 60
livery 66, 72, 76
Llull, Ramon, author 101n
London:
    armourers 91–92
    citizens 71
    Greenwich (Southwark)
        workshop 219, 220, 223, 226–28
    Tower of London 66, 82, 84–85, 95
    treaty (1520) 208n
    visit of Sigismund of Luxembourg
        (1416) 114
    Whitehall tournament (1610) 183
    see also Smithfield *and* Westminster
Lothar III, Holy Roman Emperor 24
Louis XII, king of France 175, 211n
Louis of Savoy 217

Mair, Paulus Hector, author 184
Malines *see* Mechelen
Malory, Thomas, author 56
Manesse Codex *see* Codex Manesse
manifer *see* armour
Margaret of York, duchess of
    Burgundy 141
Margot, Guillem, armourer 218n, 219n
Martin van Royne, armourer 219n,
    220n, 226, 227, 228,
Mary of Burgundy, wife of Maximilian
    I 203–4
Mary of Luxembourg 217
Masquerades 199, 235
Mastino II della Scala 105–7, **106**
Mathieu d'Escouchy, author 125, 130, 135
Matilda the Empress, queen of
    England 63
Maximilian I, Holy Roman
    Emperor 185–207

armours 162, 165, 218
    court 191–96, 201–7
    foot combat 181–83, 215
    Freydal 112n, 166, 175, 182–83
    jousting 193–94, 199
    saddles 116–18
    Theuerdank, 182, 203–4
    tournament books 201–2
    Triumph(zug) 112–13, 118, 187–88, 190–91, 201
    weapons 171, 175
    Weisskunig 182
Mechelen, tournament (1494) 195
Meinhard, count of Görz 41
mêlée 23n, 39–41, 107n, 186–87, 193
Michael de la Pole 66, 67
Milan:
    armourers 165, 218–19, 220
    church of San Giovanni in
        Conca 108n
    statue of Bernabò Visconti 108
    see also Sforza
Missaglia, Giovanni Antonio,
    armourer 220
Mocenigo, Alvise 193
Mons, castle 93, 95
Montagu, William, earl of Salisbury 97
Monte, Pietro, author 103n
Moors 153
Mortimer, Roger, earl of March 80, 95
Mummerei see masquerades

Nancy, jousts (1455) 135
Nefyn, tournament (1284) 65
Nine Worthies 235
Northampton, tournament (1248) 64
Nottingham 67
Nuremberg 24

Olivier de La Marche, author 123–27, 130–33, 135–37, 152n
Otto of Freising, chronicler 23–24

Paris:
    jousts (1405) 51
    tournament (1389) 48

246

tournament (1415) 60
tournament (1514) 175
Parliament (English) 64, 65fn, 66–67, 68, 73, 74, 75, 76
   Merciless Parliament (1388) 67, 73–74
   Wonderful Parliament (1386) 66–67
Pas d'armes 120–38, 139–54, 158
Pas de l'Arbre Charlemagne (1443) 125–26, 130–31, 132–33
Pas de l'Arbre d'or (1468) 141
Pas de la Belle Pèlerine (1449) 130–31, 132, 137
Pas de la Dame Inconnue (1463) 135
Pas de la Dame Sauvage (1470) 123–24, 137
Pas de la Fontaine des Pleurs (1449) 130–31, 133, **134**, 136–37, 139, 141
Pas de la Joyeuse Garde (1446) 124–26, 129, 138
Pas de Sandricourt (1493) 135–36
Pas du Chevalier Aventureux (1447) 136
Pas du Géant à la Blanche Dame du Pavillon (1446) 136
Pas du Perron Fée (1463) 143–44, 147–48, 149, 152n, 153
Paso de la Fuerte Ventura (1428) 137
Paso de Madrid (1460) 135
Paso de Valladolid (1440) 135
Passo Honroso (1434) 126, 130–31, 133–35
pauldron *see* armour
Peasants' Revolt (1381) 66
Peffenhauser, Anton, armourer 166, **167**
Pero Niño, count of Buelna 50–51
Philip the Bold, duke of Burgundy 70
Philip the Good, duke of Burgundy 143–44
Philip, count of Flanders 47, 59
Philip II, king of Spain 176
Philippa, queen of England 92
Philippe de Lalaing, knight 143–44, 147–48, 149
Pierre de Bauffremont, lord of Charny 131, 132, 133
pikes 174, 183
Pleurs, tournament (1178) 47, 49–50, 52
polder-mitton *see* armour

pollaxes 149, 167–71, **170**
Prague 113n
prizes 35, 46–47, 49–50, 66, 70, **116**, 123, 126, 152, 159, 177–78, 221
   bear 57
   jewellery 176–77
   pike (fish) 47
   shield 123
   sparrowhawk 35
prohibitions on tournaments 64, 65

Radcliffe, Robert, earl of Sussex 172n, **173**
Radcot Bridge 67
René, duke of Anjou 57–58, 60, 103n, 111, 122n, 124, 126, 131, 135, 138, 216–17
Rennen (form of joust) 116–18, 190–91
   Bundrennen 191
   Feldrennen 191
   Geschiftrennen 190–91
   Gesellenrennen 193
   Pfannenrennen 191
   Scharfrennen (*Schweifrennen*) 191, 204
   Scheibenrennen 191
   Welschrennen 190
   Wulstrennen 191
Richard, earl of Arundel 85, 86, 94, 96
Richard, earl of Cornwall 27
Richard I the Lionheart, king of England 25n, 63
Richard II, king of England 62–76, 91–92
Robert III de La Marck *see* Fleuranges
Robert de Vere, earl of Oxford 67
Roger fitz Walter 57
Roger de Jouy 54
Roger of Wendover, chronicler 57
Rogier van der Weyden, artist 115
Roman de Florimont see Aimon de Florennes
Roman de Ponthus et Sidoine 141
Roncolo *see* Runkelstein
Rouen, Hôtel de Bourgtheroulde 210, 229
Rudolf von Ems, poet 26–27, 35, 37, 40

Rudolf von Ras 41
Runkelstein castle 109, 111
Rüxner, Georg, herald 21–22

saddles **98**, 99–119
  high saddle 69, 92–93, 95, 104–113, **105, 110, 112**, 190
  knee protection 103n
  low saddle 113–18, **117**
  Mongolian saddle 113
  thigh protection 101–3, 118
  tourney saddle 93
  war saddle 99–101
Saint-Inglevert, jousting (1390) 58–59, 148
Saint-Laurent-les-Chalons 146
Saladin 142
Sanuto, Marino 192–93
Saracens 142, 149n
Scrope, Henry Lord 95
Sedan 223n
Seusenhofer, Jörg, armourer 211n
Seusenhofer, Konrad, armourer 165n, 211n, 218n
Sforza, Ascanio, cardinal 195
Sforza, Bianca Maria 194
Sforza, Ludovico, duke of Milan 194–95, 197
Sherborne Missal 81, 93
shields 30–31, 32, 40, 51–52, 55, 84, 93, 123, 124, 151, 191, 237
Shrewsbury 67
Shrovetide tournaments 194–96
Sigismund of Luxembourg, Holy Roman Emperor 113–14
Smithfield:
  tournament (1356) 65
  tournament (1390) 46, 66–76, 92–93
spectators 2, 34, 42–43, 62, 124, 127, 130–33, 136–37, 152n, 178n, 180–81, 206, 231
Stanford, tournament (1215) 57
Star, order 54
Stephen atte Fryth, armourer 91, 92, 94
Stephen, king of England 63, 91–92
Stirling, siege (1304) 91

stirrups 31, 41, 97, 99, 107–9, 114, 118, 190
Sturmy, Sir William 75
Suero de Quiñones 126, 127, 130, 131, 133
swords 30–31, 39–40, 49, 103, 105, 108–11, 149, 151–53, 160, 171–72, **174**, 175–78, 183–84, 217–18, 220, 223
  two-handed sword 165–66, 171–72, 175–77, 217–18, 220, 234
  presentation as challenge 216–17
  rapier 172
  swords of state 229–30

Terminology of tournaments:
  English 93–94
  French 24–25, 45–61, 93–94, 113
  German 24–43, 113, 187–91
  Latin 24–25
Thomas, duke of Clarence 86
Thomas, duke of Gloucester 90, 96
Tirol 165, 192
  see also Hall in Tirol *and* Innsbruck
tilt (barrier) 189, 193, 213, 216, 231
To Cry a Joust, tournament text 66, 69, 70n
tourney 21–43, 103, 105, 109–112, 115, 234
  booty 47–48
  captives 42, 53, 55
  division of sides 36–37
  jousting during tourney 37–38
  Kolbenturnier 112, 162
  origins 21–25
  safe areas 41–42
  tactics 29–43
  vesper tournament 34–36
Traunpicz, Hanns 171
tyrocinium 24–25

Ulrich von Liechtenstein:
  tourneys 28–29, 33, 34–35, 36–40, 41–42
  Venus Journey 58
Ungelter, Hans 199

vambrace *see* armour
vamplate *see* lances
Venus, deity 58
Verona 103

Vienna, tournament (1194) 25n
Virgin and Child 220
Visconti, Bernabò 108–9

Warenne, John Earl 77
Wavrin Master, artist 143n
weddings 30, 33, 37–38, 149n, 195–96, 201, 206
Westminster Chronicle 62, 67fn, 70, 71fn, 73fn, 74
Westminster tournament (1511) 215n
White Hart badge 66, 71–73, 76
Wigmore Castle 80
wild men and women 123
William, duke of Guelders 71, 74
William III, count of Hainaut 82, 90
William, count of Ostrevant 70
William Marshal, earl of Pembroke 23, 47–48, 49–50, 52–54
Winchester, siege (1141) 63
Windsor :
  castle 66
  jousts (1358) 83
  tournament (1349) 65, 66, 70
Wingfield, Sir Richard 209, 214, 216–17

Wolfgang, count of Fürstenberg 193
Wolfgang von Polheim 195, 200–1
Wolfger von Gars 41
Wolfhart VI, count of Borsselen 195
Wolfram von Eschenbach, poet:
  Parzival 26, 34, 35–36, 41–42
  Willehalm 37n
Wolfsthal, Balthasar Wolf von, chamberlain 195
Wolsey, Thomas, cardinal 209, 210, 214–15, 216, 217, 218, 229, 235
women 21, 56–59, 60, 61, 66, 72, 127, 147, 152, 237
  as judges 49n, 57, 66
  characters in *pas d'armes* 59, 123–24, 130–37, 141–44
  giving prizes 57
  spectators 51, 62, 137, 206
Wulfing von Stubenberg 38
Würzburg, tournament (1127) 24

Yonne, tournament (c. 1178) 47

Zimmern, Froben Christoph, count of 21–22

www.ingramcontent.com/pod-product-compliance
Lightning Source LLC
Chambersburg PA
CBHW071203240426
43668CB00032B/2029